Non-Verbal Reasoning

for

NTSE, Olympiads & Competitive Exams

Jaya Ghosh

B.Sc. (Maths), MCA, MBA (HR)

Published by:

F-2/16, Ansari road, Daryaganj, New Delhi-110002
☎ 23240026, 23240027 • *Fax:* 011-23240028
Email: info@vspublishers.com • *Website:* www.vspublishers.com

Regional Office : Hyderabad
5-1-707/1, Brij Bhawan (Beside Central Bank of India Lane)
Bank Street, Koti, Hyderabad - 500 095
☎ 040-24737290
E-mail: vspublishershyd@gmail.com

Branch Office : Mumbai
Jaywant Industrial Estate, 1st Floor–108, Tardeo Road
Opposite Sobo Central Mall, Mumbai – 400 034
☎ 022-23510736
E-mail: vspublishersmum@gmail.com

Follow us on:   

Edition 2019

Printed at : Akansha Printers, Darya Ganj, New Delhi–110002

Publisher's Note

With a view to strengthen the career aspirations of student community, V&S Publishers has published this book **NON-VERBAL REASONING for NTSE, Olympiads & Competitive Examinations** under its Gen X Series (Generating Xcellence in Generation X). While the books under Gen X Series are published to propel school students into higher learning orbit, this particular book is intended to boost the success rate of school students appearing or intending to write these research-based and other competitive examinations for higher studies or jobs.

The importance of NTSE and Olympiad examinations lies in the fact that on the basis of its result, a student can win scholarship for five years or more years and succeed in building a bright career. And hence we are giving details of this examination right at the start of the book.

This book covers the Non-Verbal Reasoning part of the MAT (Mental Aptitude Test) question paper, one of the three papers which the students write in each of the Stages-I and II of the National Talent Search Examination (NTSE). Stage-I is conducted by States and Union Territories whereas NCERT conducts Stage-II examination.

This examination is organised to award scholarship to students currently studying at the Class X level. Scholarships are awarded up to Ph.D. in Sciences, Social Sciences, Humanities, Languages, Commerce, Vocational Studies and Fine arts. And up to second degree level for professional courses in medicines, engineering, technology, management and law. NTSE consists of Mental Ability Test (MAT), Language Test (LT) and Scholastic Aptitude Test (SAT) having multiple choice questions. Every year about 1000 scholarships are awarded - Rs.1250/- per month for Class XI & XII and Rs.2000/- at Graduation and Post-graduation level. Scholarship at Ph.D. level is governed by UGC norms.

All students studying in Class X in any recognized school are eligible to appear in Stage-I exam. For Stage-II, there is a quota for each State and Union Territory based on Student enrollment at secondary level. There are 3 papers in both stages–

1. Mental Ability Test (MAT)
2. Language Test (LT) and
3. Scholastic Ability Test (SAT).

Questions are in the form of multiple choices with negative marking deducting 1/3 marks only at the Stage II (National level). The tests are conducted in Asamiya, Bangla, English, Gujarati, Hindi, Kannada, Marathi, Malyalam, Odia, Punjabi, Tamil, Telugu and Urdu. However, language test is available in two languages – English & Hindi.

Test	No. of Questions	Maximum Marks	Time
Mental Ability Test (MAT)	50	50	45 minutes
Language Test	50	50	45 minutes
Scholastic Ability Test (SAT)	100	100	90 minutes

The concepts have been explained through various solved examples and multiple choice questions with answer key besides hints for solving the problems and use of everyday language hopefully enable students to master the subject with relative ease.

V&S Publishers has your welfare in mind, be assured!

Preface

To go through the NTSE examination a student must have a dedicated and serious approach. Students are often misled by the casual approach and the wrong notion that Objective Type Questions are easy to solve but in fact they require an extensive understanding of each prescribed subject or topic. Therefore, only hard work and diligent study can help the candidates crack the exam successfully.

This book provides a brief **Theory** on each topic, **Solved Examples** followed by **Fully Solved Exercises**.

The book contains questions very similar to what have been asked in the previous NTSE examinations of class 10th. I ask students ***Do all the Exercises***, not missing even one of them. Make an attempt to answer the question first, and then read the given answer. I hope, on second reading, students would be able to do that on their own, without looking at the answers. In short, the condidates have to make an honest effort to achieve the goal.

Wish you a grand success in your examination, and a very bright future. I am sure the students will find this book most useful. I will be happy to receive constructive feedback and suggestions.

How to Read This Book

- The book in your hand is a unidirectional effort to guide and prepare students for NTSE/ Olympiad examinations.
- The book covers Non-Verbal Reasoning. It consists of *Key Concepts* followed by *Solved Examples, Multiple Choice Questions* and *Answer Key and Hints and Solution*. The solutions to the MCQ's are provided at the end of each chapter.
- This book will really prove to be an asset for Class 7th, 8th, 9th and 10th students as they hardly find any material which can help them in building a strong foundation.
- The contents of this book have been developed as per the needs of the students *i.e.* the simple approach, conceptual clarity and exhaustive coverage in each section. Questions incorporated in the book conform to the latest pattern of NTSE making this book an exhaustive study material.
- *Previous Years Questions* have been given at the end of each chapter for clear cut understanding of the papers. Hint and Explanations of most of the questions have been provided so that the students could know how the correct answer has been reached at.
- A unique approach has been adopted to explain and illustrate methodology in Mathematics and Logical Reasoning, which is considered to be the key chapter to get an overall good score.
- Last, but not the least, four Mock Test Papers and two Solved Papers have been incorporated for the real exam – time feel.

Happy Reading.......

NTSE : An Introduction

The National Talent Search Examination for students studying in Class X is meant to identify and nurture talent. The examination is conducted every year at two levels: Stage – I (State Level) and Stage – II (National Level). National Talent Search Examination (NTSE) is an annual examination conducted by NCERT at national level. It is one of the most reputed talent search exams in India. It was started in the year 1963 and has grown in prestige and scope ever since. The objective of the exam is to identify students who have potential to excel in Science, Social Science, Engineering, Medicine, Management and Law. The successful students, called NTSE Scholars, receive financial support / scholarships from NCERT till the time they continue to study.

The NTSE not only provides scholarship to the good students but also highlights the students with good aptitude and knowledge.

Scholarships: About One thousand scholarships are awarded for different stages of education as follows:

(a) Scholarship of Rs. 1250/- per month for Class-XI to XII.

(b) Scholarship of Rs. 2000/- per month for Undergraduates and Post-graduates.

(c) Amount of Scholarship for Ph.D. be fixed in accordance with the UGC norms.

Reservation: 15% for students belonging to the SC category, 7.5% for students belonging to the ST category and 3% for Physically Challenged Group of Students.

Selection: Stage-I, selection will be done by States/UTs and those who qualify Stage- I, will be eligible to appear for Stage-II examination, conducted by NCERT.

Qualifying Marks: Qualifying marks for candidates from General category is 40% in each paper and for candidates from SC, ST, PH is 35% in each paper.

Language Test Qualifying in nature and marks obtained for Language Test will not be counted for final merit.

Important Dates: Dates for submission of application form and conduct of examination, are given below:

Stage	Area	Tentative Dates
Stage-I (State)	Last Date for Submission of Application Form	To be notified by the respective State and it may vary from state to state
	Examination in Mizoram, Meghalaya, Nagaland and Andaman and Nicobar Islands	7th November, 2015 (Saturday)
	Examination in All other States and Union Territories	8th November, 2015 (Sunday)
Stage-II (National)	Examination in All States and Union Territories	8th May, 2016 (Sunday)

Eligibility: All students of Class X studying in recognized schools are eligible to appear for the Stage -I examination, conducted by the States/UTs, in which the schools are located. There will be no domicile restriction.

Students registered under Open Distance Learning (ODL) will also be eligible for scholarship, provided the student is below the age of 18 years (as on 1st July of the particular year), the student is not employed and s/he is appearing in class X examination for the first time.

Examination: The pattern of written examination will be as follows:

- Stage I examination at the State/UT level will comprise three parts, namely (a) Mental Ability Test (MAT) (b) Language Test (LT) and (c) Scholastic Aptitude Test (SAT).
- **Qualifying Marks:** Qualifying marks for candidates from General category is 40% in each paper and for candidates from SC, ST, PH is 35% in each paper.
- **Lanuage Test** Qualifying in nature and marks obtained for Language Test will not be counted for final merit.

♦ The pattern of stage I will be as under:

Test		No. of Questions	No. of Marks	Duration (in minutes)
Mental Ability Test (MAT)		50	50	50
Scholastic Test	Language Comprehensive Test	40	40	40
	Aptitude Test	90	90	90
Total		**180**	**180**	**180**

♦ The pattern of stage II will be as under:

Test	No. of Questions	No. of Marks	Duration (in minutes)
(i) Mental Ability Test (MAT)	50	50	45
(ii) Language Test (LT) English/Hindi	50	50	45
(iii) Scholastic Aptitude Test (SAT)	100	100	90

At Stage – II (National Level), there will be negative marking in each paper. For each wrong answer 1/3 marks will be deducted. No marks will be deducted for unattempted questions.

Application Form: You may contact the State/UT Liaison officer for procuring application form.

The completed application form should be signed by the Principal of the school much before the last date of submission. The candidate as well as the Principal of the school must adhere to the last date for submission of the Application Form. **Different states may have different last dates for submission. Please confirm from the liaison officer of your state, the address at which the completed forms are to be submitted.** The State-wise contacts of the liaison officers are given in the CD and are also available on the NCERT website www.ncert.nic.in. **All queries related to application form should be directed to the State Liaison Officers (LOs). No application should be sent to NCERT.**

Fees: States and Union Territories may notify the fee required which will be paid for the Stage-I examination. Therefore, before submitting the application form, you may find out the fees charged for Stage-I Examination and also the mode of payment from the respective State"Liaison Officers (LOs). However, NCERT does not charge any fee for Stage-II examination.

Indian Students Studying Abroad in Class X can appear directly for Stage II NTS Examination under conditions prescribed in the NTS brochure which is available on the NCERT website. Candidates may fill up the Application Form, available on the NCERT website and send to the undersigned along with a photocopy of the mark sheet of previous examination, **latest by February 28th, 2016. Application Form for students study abroad will be uploaded on NCERT website in the month of October, 2015. Announcement for Indian Students Studying Abroad will be announced separately.**

How to Prepare for NTSE

Here are some tips on how to prepare for NTSE :

- **Start your preparation with last year's NTSE papers:** The objective is understood the type of questions asked and your current level. You should take last year's paper or NTSE sample questions and just write the exam once with all seriousness. It does not matter if you have not prepared or never heard of it before. Just sit down and write the test. This will help you gain a knowledge of NTSE and also give you a fair idea of the exam.
- **Analyze your performance:** Make sure to minutely assess what you could do and what you had a hard time with. Is it the knowledge of subject matter that you lacked? Or did you miss out because you made some silly mistakes? Or is it that mental ability questions that took a long time for you to crack? Whatever it is, just analyze your performance very minutely and critically
- **Make a plan:** Once you know your weak points, make a plan. You will definitely need to study and revise the subject matter. That is required not just for NTSE but also for your school. So there is no letting up on that front. You will also need to practice more mental ability questions. But the allocation of time will depend upon your analysis of how weak or strong you are in that particular aspect
- **Practice, practice and practice:** These are the only 3 steps that can lead to success. Get exposed to more questions of mental ability so that you are not shocked on the exam day, solve more papers and then analyze each one in detail. Take help from seniors. As you practice, you can also get confident of your speed, subject knowledge and accuracy.

Tips on How to Write Examination

The written examination (NTSE II stage) comprises two tests namely, MAT (Mental Ability Test) and SAT (Scholastic Ability Test). Each test comprises 100 multiple choice type questions which are attempted in 90 minutes. Thus on an average, the examinee will get around 54 seconds to answer a question. Therefore, both speed and accuracy are essential.

- In the MAT section, questions of the same type are grouped together. Since the instructions for all these questions are the same, read them carefully and answer all the questions.
- Use your time wisely. If you are doubtful at a particular question, omit it and move ahead without wasting much time on it. Do not let yourself get stuck on a tough question and lose time. You can always return to questions that you have omitted before the time is up.
- Do easy questions first because you earn as much credit for correctly answering those questions as you do for correctly answering a difficult question.

Do's for Answering Multiple Choice Questions in NTSE

- If the question is 'conceptual', i.e., if the answer it seeks is a statement, begin by covering the alternatives with a ruler or piece of paper. Then, carefully read and understand the stem of the question before looking at the alternatives.
- Circle or underline key words in the stem, paying special attention to qualifying words such as 'always,' 'major,' 'increase,' etc.
- Use your knowledge of headings from where lecture notes, lab, etc. is drawn. Recall a few salient points about the information. If necessary, jot down any relevant facts you need to process the alternatives. This does not have to take much time but this recall is an essential step.
- Predict an answer, if possible.
- Think over all of the alternatives and check the format of the question. Is only one of the alternatives correct, or can several or all of the alternatives be correct?

- If you know the answer, carefully mark the correct answer on your answer sheet.
- If you do not know the answer, re-check the question. Narrow your choices by eliminating any alternative that you know is incorrect. If two options still look equally appealing, compare each to the stem of the question, making sure that the one you eventually choose answers what is asked.
- If you are unable to make a choice and need to spend more time with the question, put a big question mark beside that question, and move on to the next.
- Don't stick to one question in the exam. It is much better to move on and finish all of those questions that you can answer and then to come back to the problematic questions.
- If the answer that you have calculated, is not one of the given options, check your procedure again, making any necessary changes, and recalculate your answer.
- If you still do not arrive at one of the given options, put a big question mark on that question, and go on to the next. When you get to the end of the exam, go back to any questions that you did not answer the first time.

Don'ts for Answering Multiple-Choice Questions

- Don't guess any choice as the correct answer because there is negative marking.
- Don't select an alternative just because you remember learning the information in the course; it may be a 'true' statement in its own right, but you have to make sure that it is the 'correct' answer to the question.
- Don't pick an answer just because it seems to make sense. You must answer from your knowledge of the course content, not just from your general knowledge and logic.
- Don't dismiss an alternative because it seems too obvious and simple. If you are well prepared for the exam, some of the questions will appear very straight forward to you.

❐

CONTENTS

Non-Verbal Reasoning

UNIT 1

Non-Verbal Classification

In this type of questions, five figures mentioned as a, b, c, d, e are given, four of these five figures have common features/ characteristics and hence are similar in certain way. One of the figures does not share common characteristics and hence does not match with other figures. You have to select the figure which does not belong to that group and the figure is your answer.

Solved Examples

1. Choose the figure which is different from the rest.

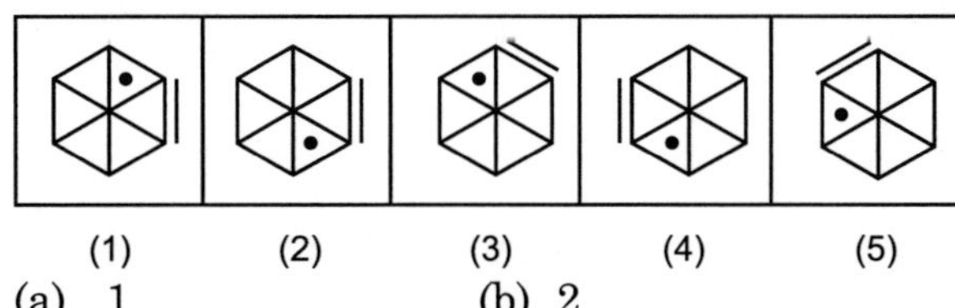

(1) (2) (3) (4) (5)

(a) 1 (b) 2
(c) 3 (d) 4
(e) 5

Solution: Option (b) is correct.

Explanation: In each one of the other figures, the small line segment lies one space ahead of the dot in a CW direction.

2. Choose the figure which is different from the rest.

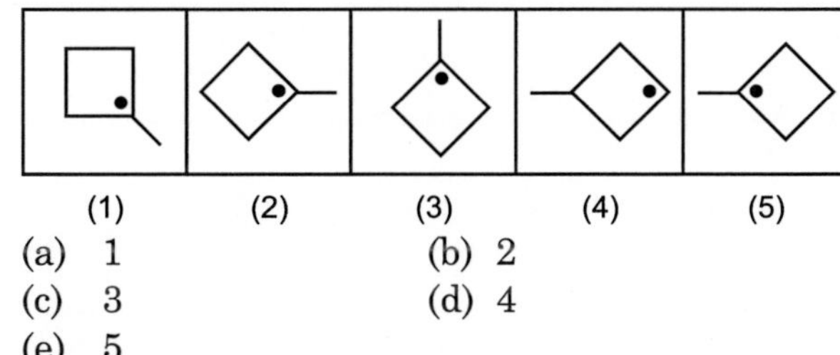

(a) 1 (b) 2
(c) 3 (d) 4
(e) 5

Solution: Option (d) is correct.

Explanation: In all other figures, the dot appears in the same corner of the square as the line outside it.

3. Choose the figure which is different from the rest.

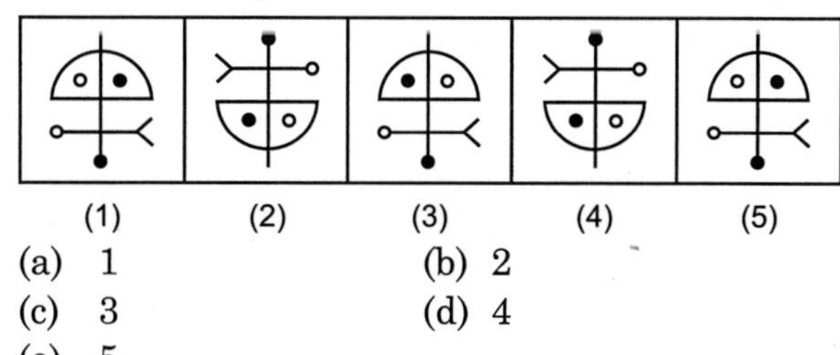

(a) 1 (b) 2
(c) 3 (d) 4
(e) 5

Solution: Option (c) is correct.

Explanation: All other figures can be rotated into each other.

4. Choose the figure which is different from the rest.

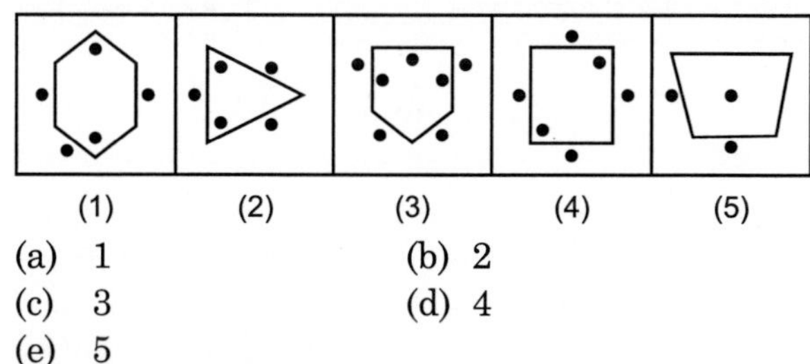

(a) 1 (b) 2
(c) 3 (d) 4
(e) 5

Solution: Option (d) is correct.

Explanation:

In all other figures, the number of dots outside the main figure is one more than the number of dots inside the main figure.

Multiple Choice Questions

1. Choose the figure which is different from the rest.

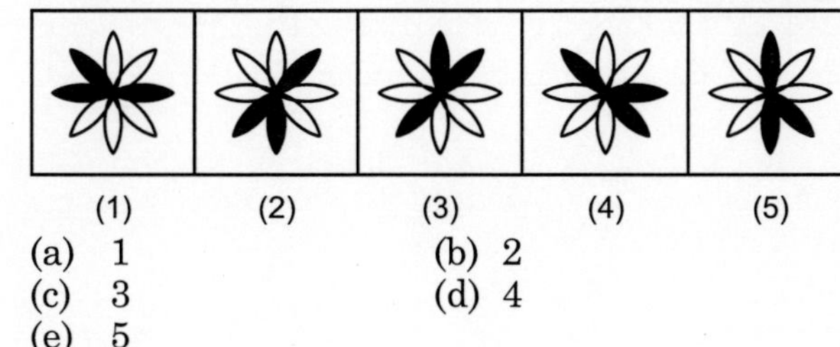

(a) 1 (b) 2
(c) 3 (d) 4
(e) 5

2. Choose the figure which is different from the rest.

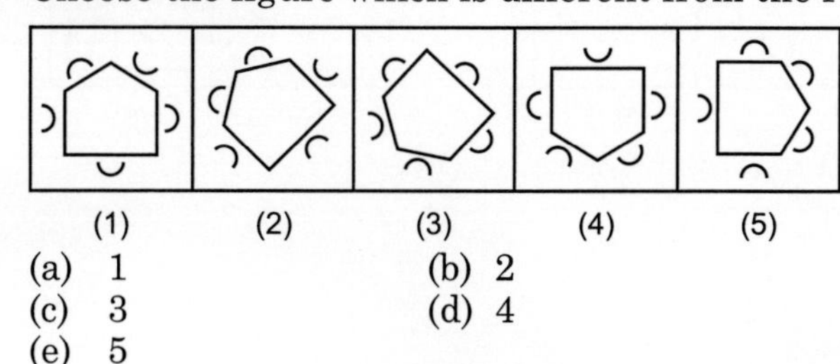

(a) 1 (b) 2
(c) 3 (d) 4
(e) 5

3. Choose the figure which is different from the rest.

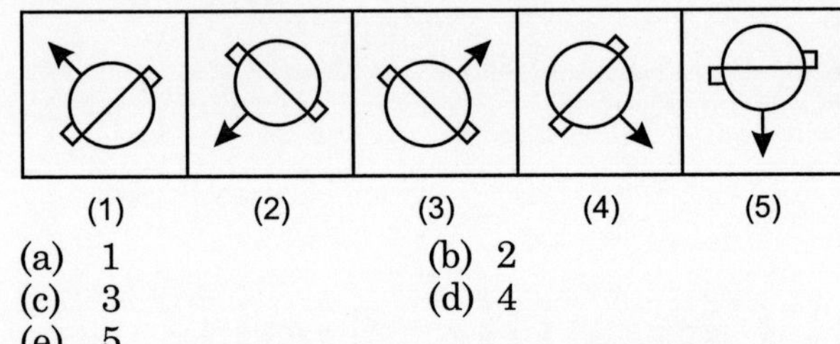

(a) 1 (b) 2
(c) 3 (d) 4
(e) 5

4. Choose the figure which is different from the rest.

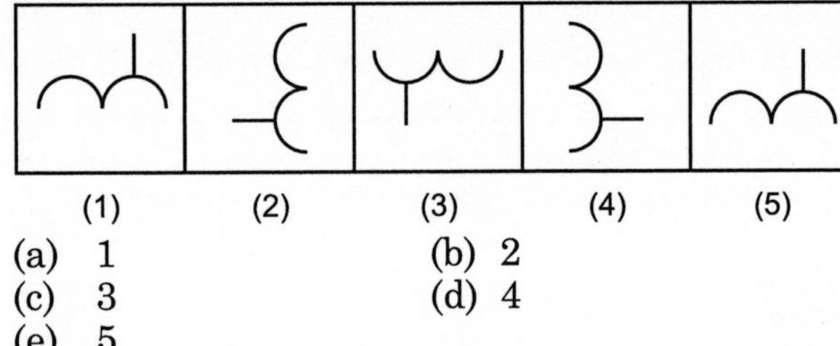

(a) 1 (b) 2
(c) 3 (d) 4
(e) 5

5. Choose the figure which is different from the rest.

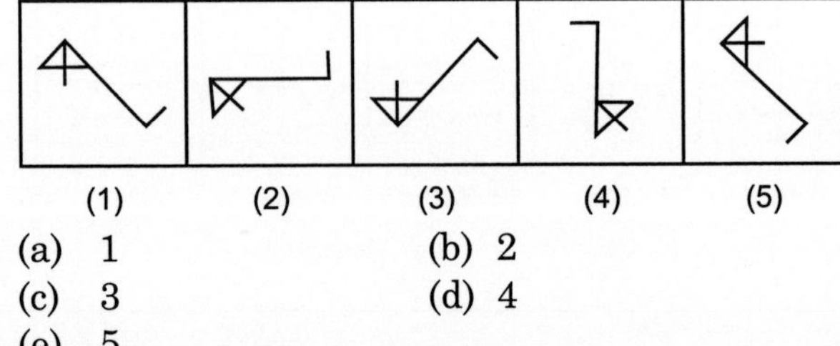

(a) 1 (b) 2
(c) 3 (d) 4
(e) 5

6. Choose the figure which is different from the rest.

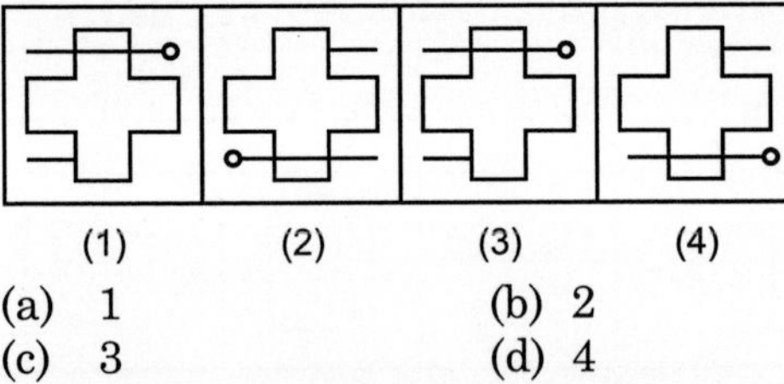

(a) 1 (b) 2
(c) 3 (d) 4

7. Choose the figure which is different from the rest.

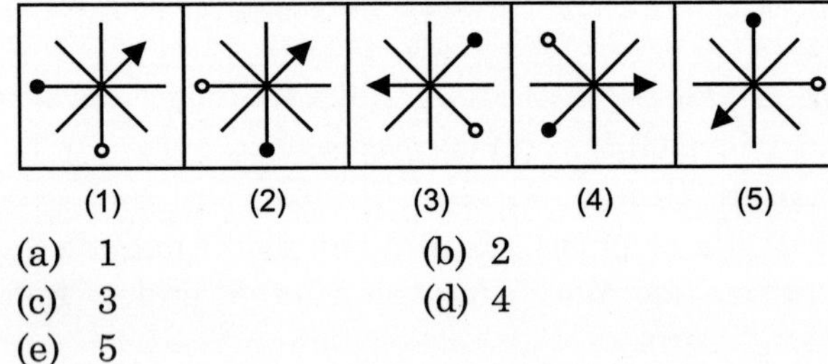

(a) 1 (b) 2
(c) 3 (d) 4
(e) 5

8. Choose the figure which is different from the rest.

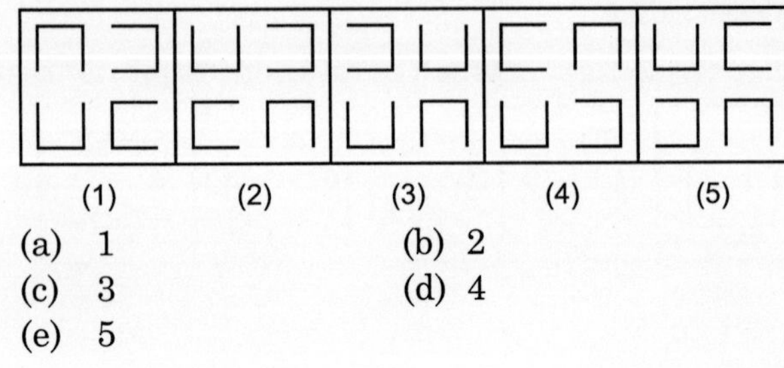

(a) 1 (b) 2
(c) 3 (d) 4
(e) 5

9. Choose the figure which is different from the rest.

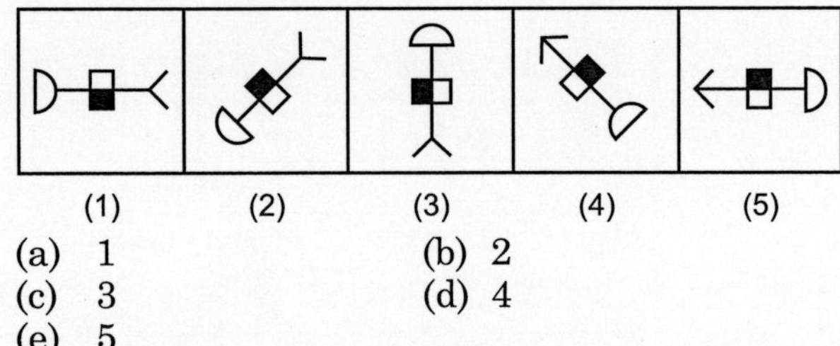

(a) 1 (b) 2
(c) 3 (d) 4
(e) 5

10. Choose the figure which is different from the rest.

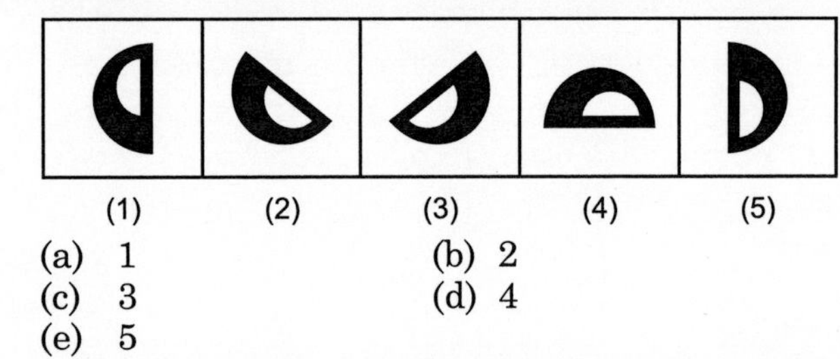

(a) 1 (b) 2
(c) 3 (d) 4
(e) 5

11. Choose the figure which is different from the rest.

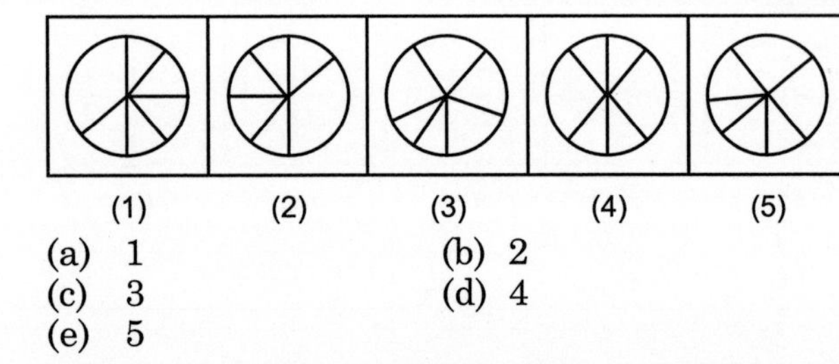

(a) 1 (b) 2
(c) 3 (d) 4
(e) 5

12. Choose the figure which is different from the rest.

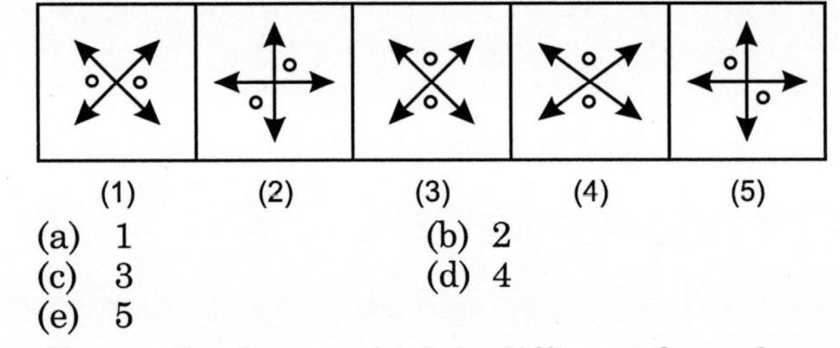

(a) 1 (b) 2
(c) 3 (d) 4
(e) 5

13. Choose the figure which is different from the rest.

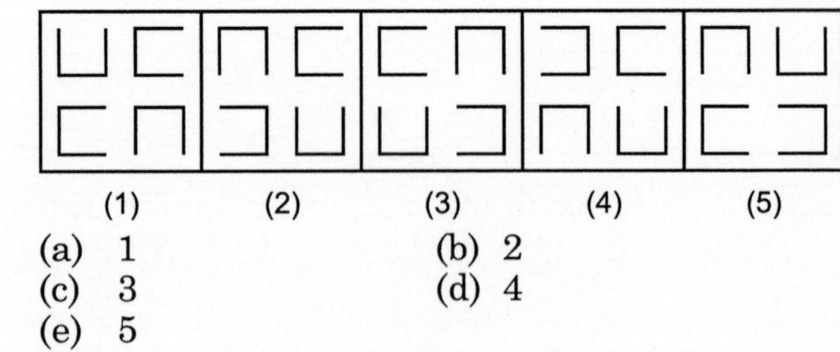

(a) 1 (b) 2
(c) 3 (d) 4
(e) 5

14. Choose the figure which is different from the rest.

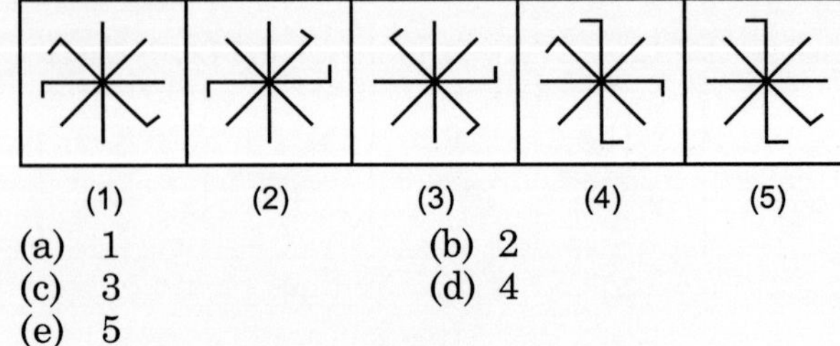

(a) 1 (b) 2
(c) 3 (d) 4
(e) 5

15. Choose the figure which is different from the rest.

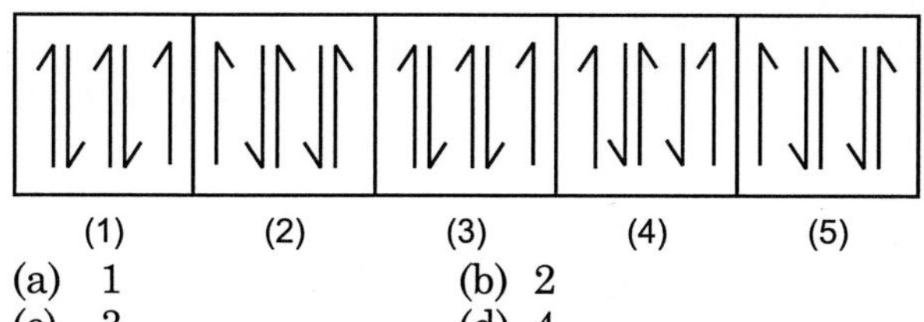

(1) (2) (3) (4) (5)

(a) 1 (b) 2
(c) 3 (d) 4
(e) 5

16. Choose the figure which is different from the rest.

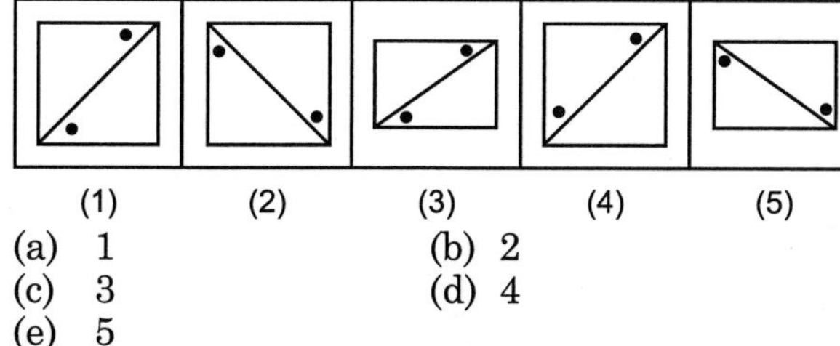

(1) (2) (3) (4) (5)

(a) 1 (b) 2
(c) 3 (d) 4
(e) 5

17. Choose the figure which is different from the rest.

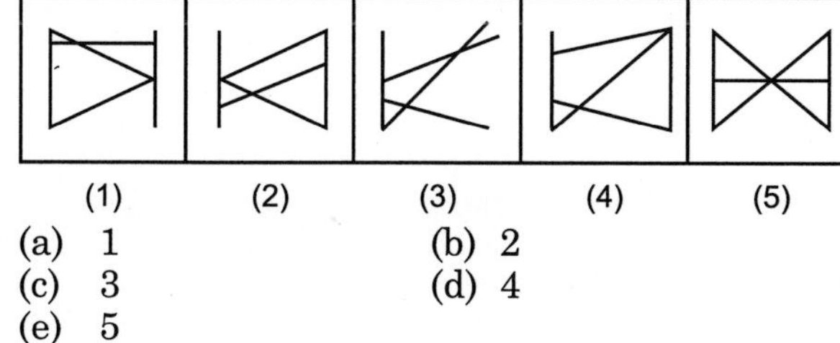

(1) (2) (3) (4) (5)

(a) 1 (b) 2
(c) 3 (d) 4
(e) 5

18. Choose the figure which is different from the rest.

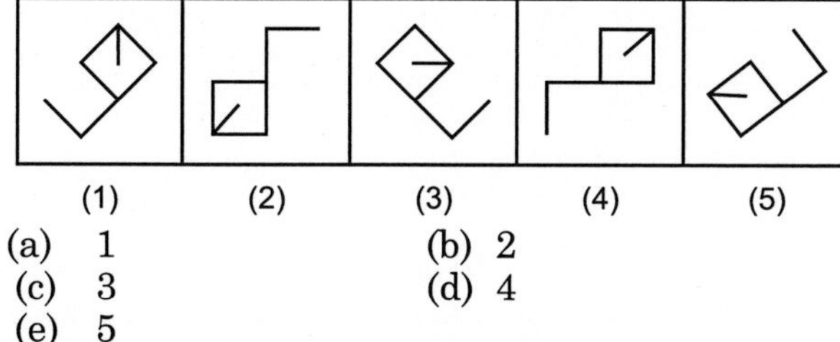

(1) (2) (3) (4) (5)

(a) 1 (b) 2
(c) 3 (d) 4
(e) 5

19. Choose the figure which is different from the rest.

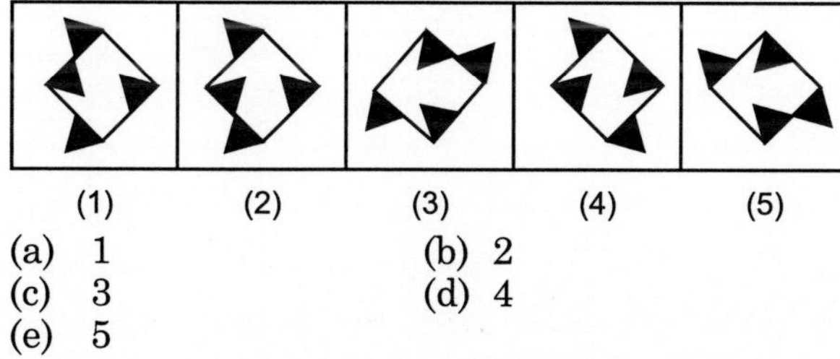

(1) (2) (3) (4) (5)

(a) 1 (b) 2
(c) 3 (d) 4
(e) 5

20. Choose the figure which is different from the rest.

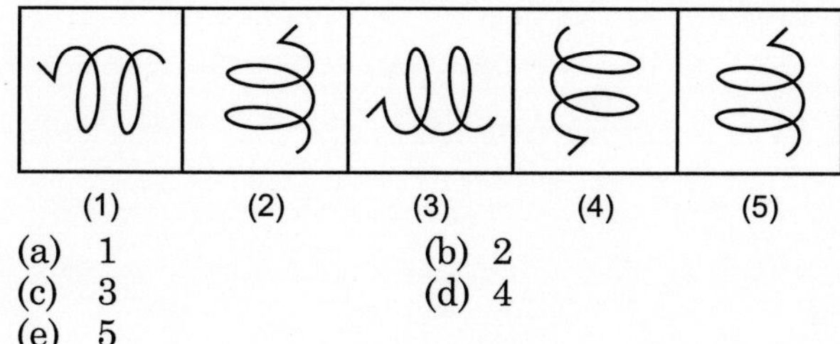

(1) (2) (3) (4) (5)

(a) 1 (b) 2
(c) 3 (d) 4
(e) 5

21. Choose the figure which is different from the rest.

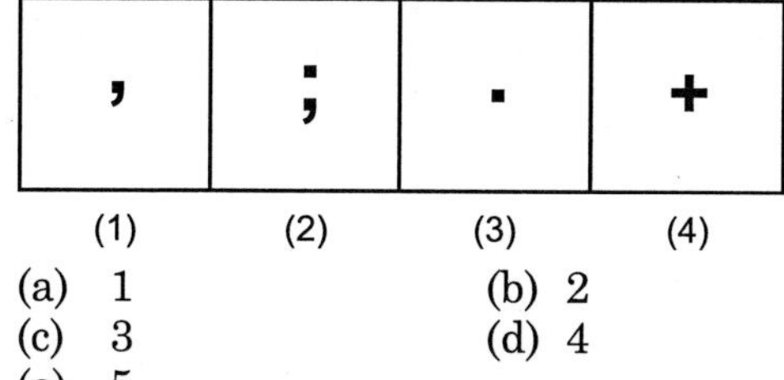

(1) (2) (3) (4)

(a) 1 (b) 2
(c) 3 (d) 4
(e) 5

22. Choose the figure which is different from the rest.

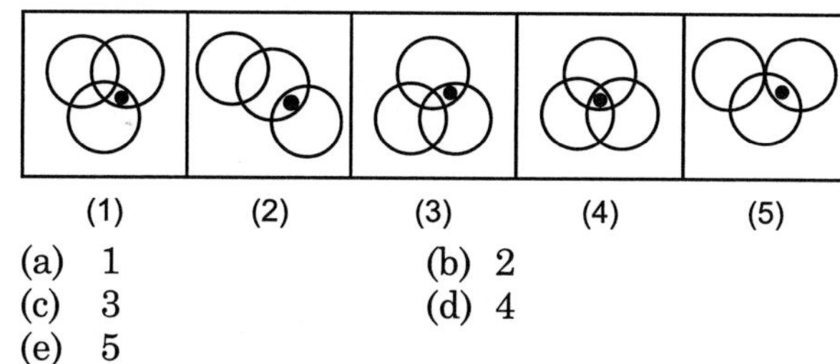

(1) (2) (3) (4) (5)

(a) 1 (b) 2
(c) 3 (d) 4
(e) 5

23. Choose the figure which is different from the rest.

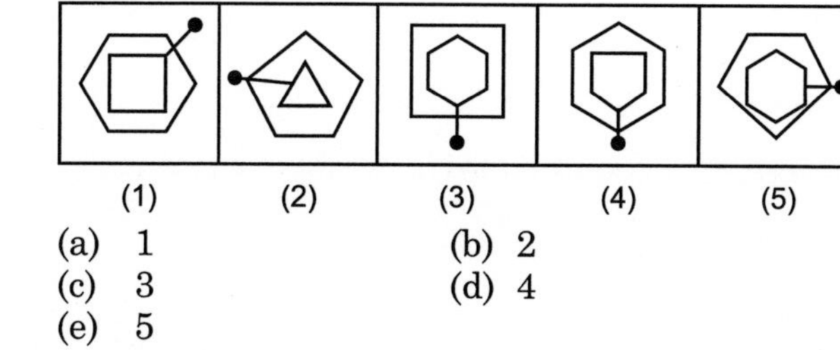

(1) (2) (3) (4) (5)

(a) 1 (b) 2
(c) 3 (d) 4
(e) 5

24. Choose the figure which is different from the rest.

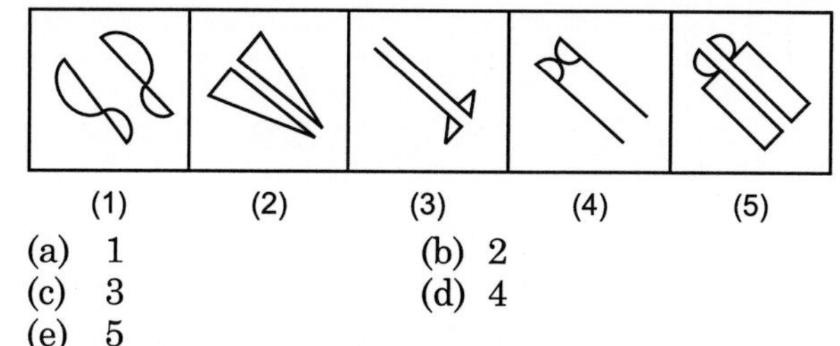

(1) (2) (3) (4) (5)

(a) 1 (b) 2
(c) 3 (d) 4
(e) 5

25. Choose the figure which is different from the rest.

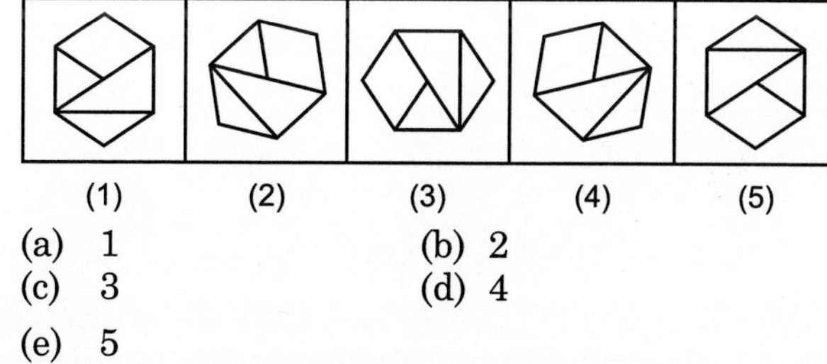

(1) (2) (3) (4) (5)

(a) 1 (b) 2
(c) 3 (d) 4
(e) 5

26. Choose the figure which is different from the rest.

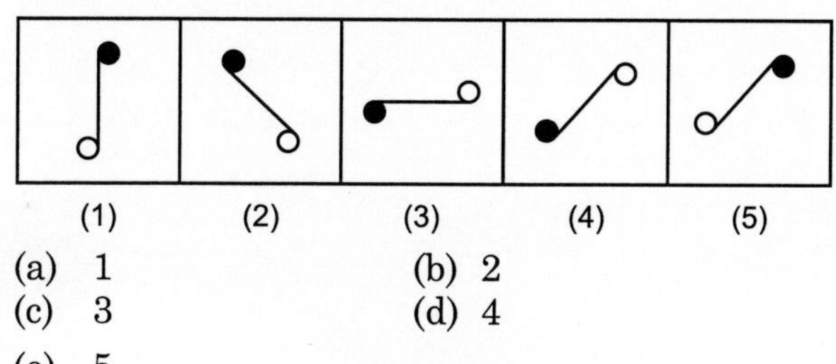

(1) (2) (3) (4) (5)

(a) 1 (b) 2
(c) 3 (d) 4
(e) 5

27. Choose the figure which is different from the rest.

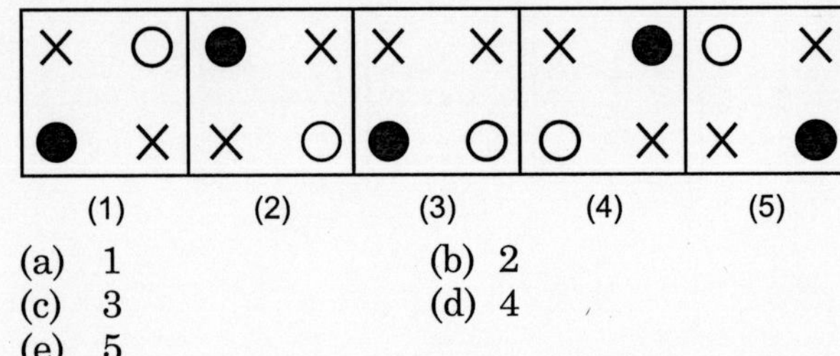

(a) 1 (b) 2
(c) 3 (d) 4
(e) 5

28. Choose the figure which is different from the rest.

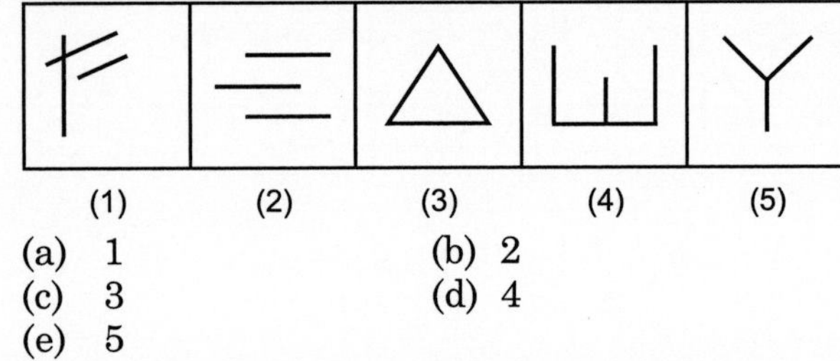

(a) 1 (b) 2
(c) 3 (d) 4
(e) 5

29. Choose the figure which is different from the rest.

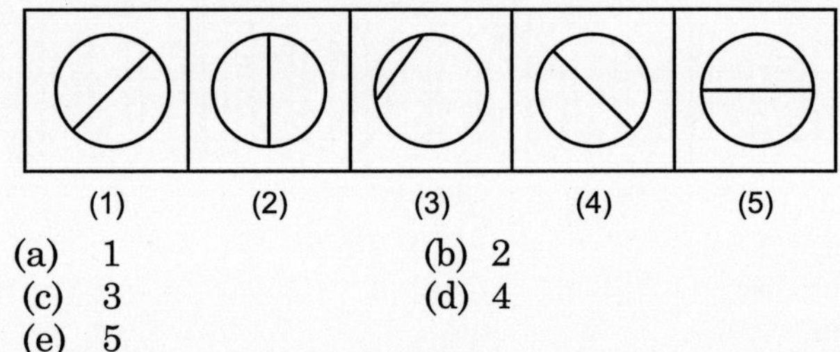

(a) 1 (b) 2
(c) 3 (d) 4
(e) 5

30. Choose the figure which is different from the rest.

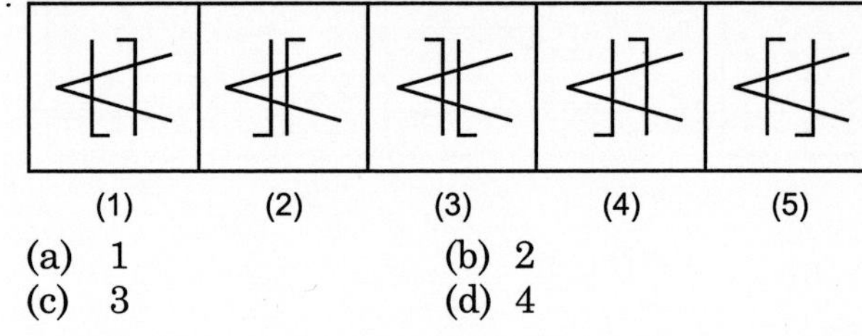

(a) 1 (b) 2
(c) 3 (d) 4

Answer Key

1. (a)	**2.** (b)	**3.** (a)	**4.** (b)	**5.** (d)	**6.** (d)	**7.** (a)	**8.** (c)	**9.** (b)	**10.** (b)
11. (d)	**12.** (d)	**13.** (a)	**14.** (c)	**15.** (d)	**16.** (d)	**17.** (c)	**18.** (c)	**19.** (d)	**20.** (c)
21. (d)	**22.** (d)	**23.** (d)	**24.** (c)	**25.** (d)	**26.** (c)	**27.** (c)	**28.** (d)	**29.** (c)	**30.** (d)

Explanatory Notes

1. (a)
All other figures can be rotated into each other.

2. (b)
In each of the figures except figure (2), three cups open towards the pentagon and two cups open outwards.

3. (a)
All other figures can be rotated into each other.

4. (b)
All other figures can be rotated into each other.

5. (d)
The inclination of the triangle is different in fig. (4).

6. (d)
Only in figure (5), the small line segment lies on the same side (right side) of the main figure as the head of the pin (or all other figures can be rotated into each other).

7. (a)
All other figures can be rotated into each other.

8. (c)
Only in figure (3), two out of the four elements are opening in the same direction.

9. (b)
If all the figures are rotated and the semicircle lies on the top, then the shaded part of the rectangle lies on the LHS.

10. (b)
All other figures can be rotated into each other.

11. (d)
Only figure (4) contains three diameters of the circle.

12. (d)
In all other figures, the two double sided arrows intersect each other at right angles.

13. (a)
Only in figure (1), two of the four elements are oriented in the same direction.

14. (c)
All other figures can be rotated into each other.

15. (d)
In all other figures, each element is obtained by rotating the adjacent element through 180°.

16. (d)
The two dots lie on the same side of the diagonal only in fig. (4).

17. (c)
All other figures contain five line segments while fig. (3) contains four line segments.

18. (c)
The line segment inside the square is attached to the corner which lies opposite to the corner to which the outer L-shaped element is attached.

19. (d)
Only in figure (4), each side of the square has one black triangle attached to it.

20. (c)
All other figures can be rotated into each other.

21. (d)
All others are punctuation marks.

22. (d)
Only in figure (4), the dot appears in the region common to all the three circles.

23. (d)
Only in figure (4), the pin passes through a vertex of each one of the two elements.

24. (c)
All other figures contain a geometrical figure along with its mirror image.

25. (d)
All other figures can be rotated into each other.

26. (c)
All other figures can be rotated into each other.

27. (c)
In each of the figures except figure (3), the two crosses (×) appear in the diagonally opposite corners.

28. (d)
Figure (4) is formed by four line segments while each of the other figures is formed by three line segments.

29. (c)
Only in figure (3), the line segment is not a diameter of the circle.

30. (d)
Only in figure (4), both the parallel lines are bent in the same direction (i.e. towards the left).

❒

Previous Year Questions

1. Choose the figure which is different from the rest.
[NTSE 2006 – Bihar first stage paper]

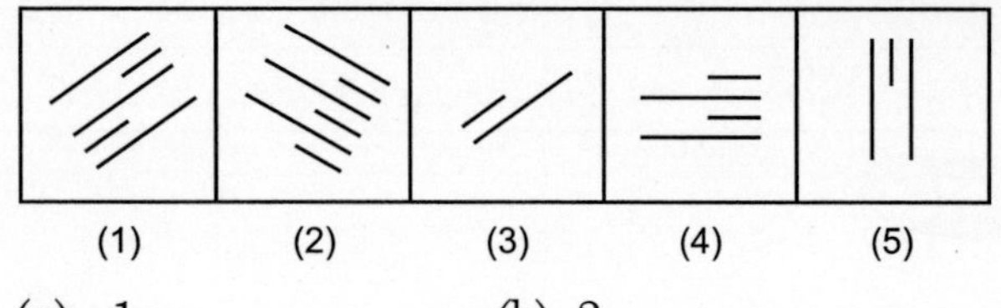

(1) (2) (3) (4) (5)

(a) 1 (b) 2
(c) 3 (d) 4
(e) 5

2. Choose the figure which is different from the rest.
[NTSE 2000 – UP first stage paper]

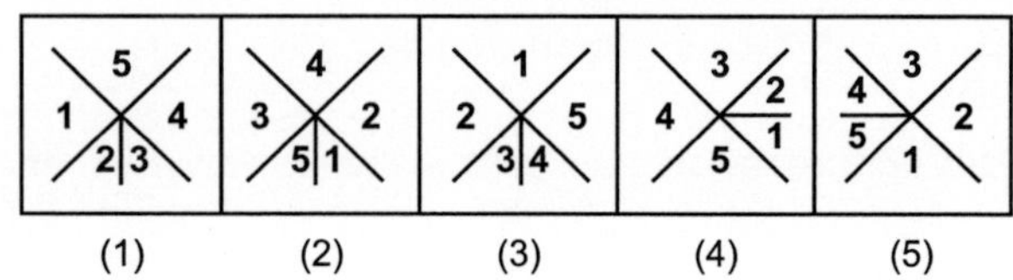

(1) (2) (3) (4) (5)

(a) 1 (b) 2
(c) 3 (d) 4
(e) 5

3. Choose the figure which is different from the rest.
[NTSE 2005 – Delhi second stage paper]

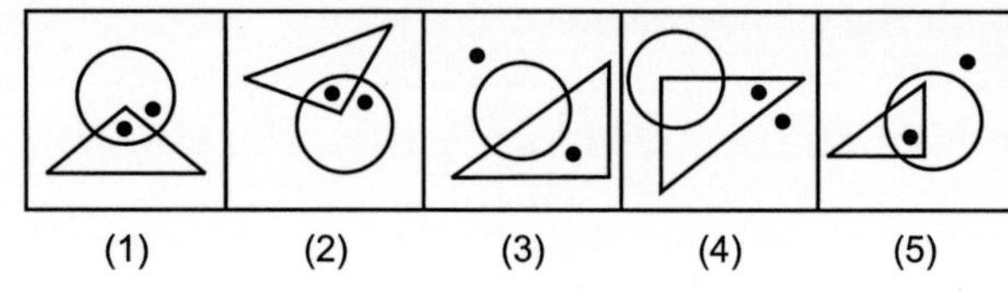

(1) (2) (3) (4) (5)

(a) 1 (b) 2
(c) 3 (d) 4
(e) 5

4. Choose the figure which is different from the rest.
[NTSE 2012 – Karnataka first stage paper]

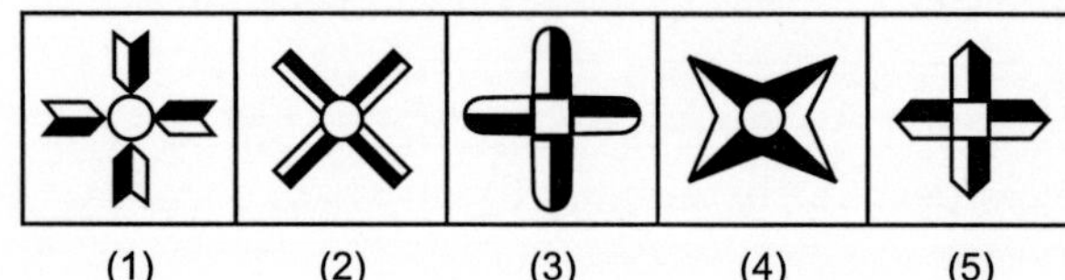

(1) (2) (3) (4) (5)

(a) 1 (b) 2
(c) 3 (d) 4
(e) 5

5. Choose the figure which is different from the rest.
[NTSE 2003 – Maharashtra first stage paper]

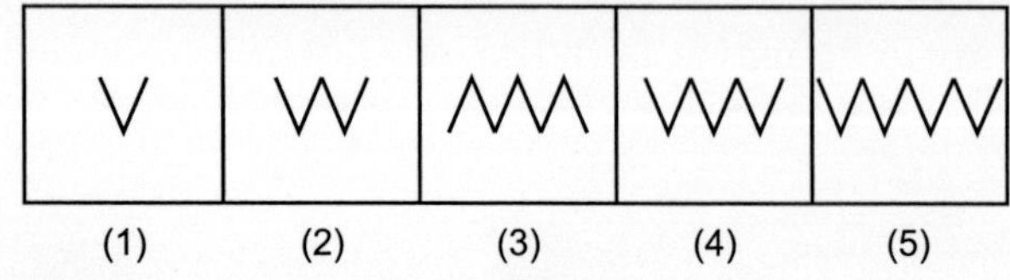

(1) (2) (3) (4) (5)

(a) 1 (b) 2
(c) 3 (d) 4
(e) 5

6. Choose the figure which is different from the rest.
[NTSE 2006 –Delhi first stage paper]

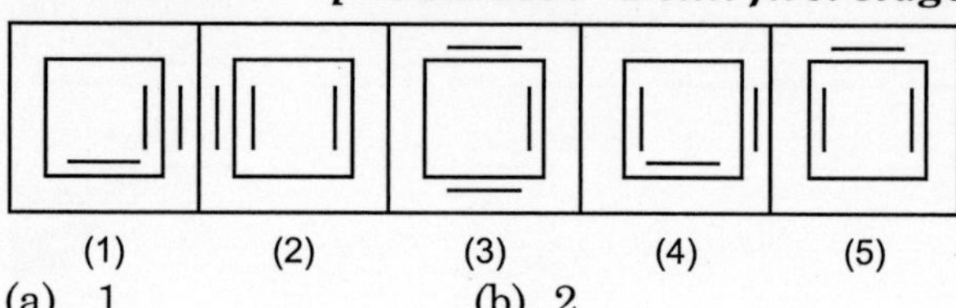

(1) (2) (3) (4) (5)

(a) 1 (b) 2
(c) 3 (d) 4
(e) 5

7. Choose the figure which is different from the rest.
[NTSE 2004 – MP second stage paper]

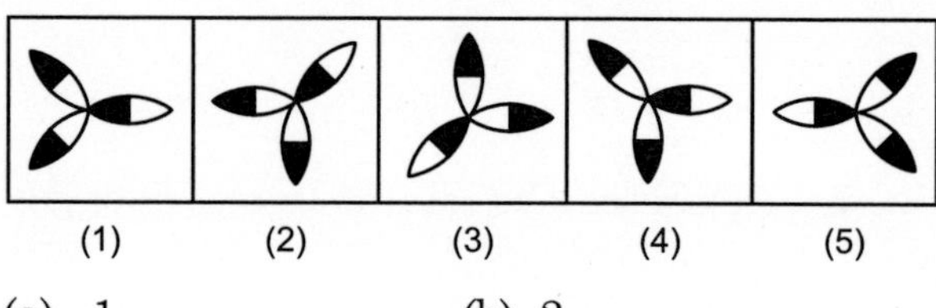

(1) (2) (3) (4) (5)

(a) 1 (b) 2
(c) 3 (d) 4
(e) 5

8. Choose the figure which is different from the rest.
[NTSE 2006 – Punjab first stage paper]

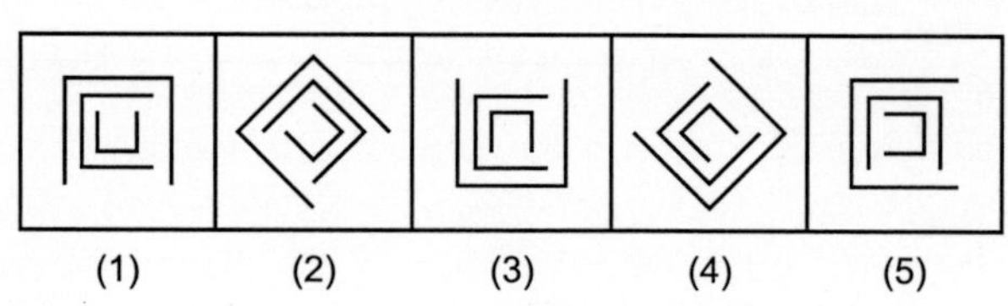

(1) (2) (3) (4) (5)

(a) 1 (b) 2
(c) 3 (d) 4
(e) 5

9. Choose the figure which is different from the rest.
[NTSE 2012 – UP first stage paper]

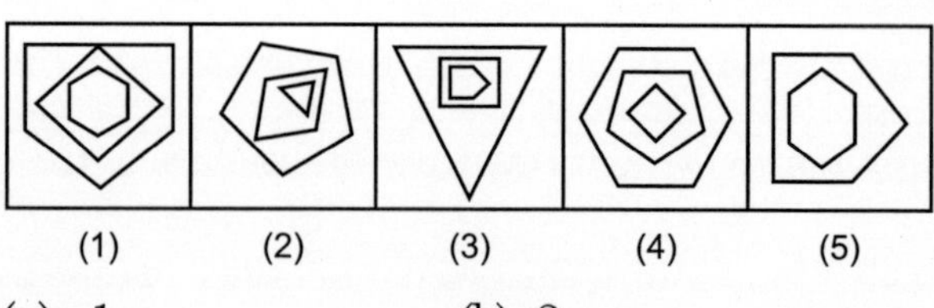

(1) (2) (3) (4) (5)

(a) 1 (b) 2
(c) 3 (d) 4
(e) 5

10. Choose the figure which is different from the rest.
[NTSE 2007 – Delhi second stage paper]

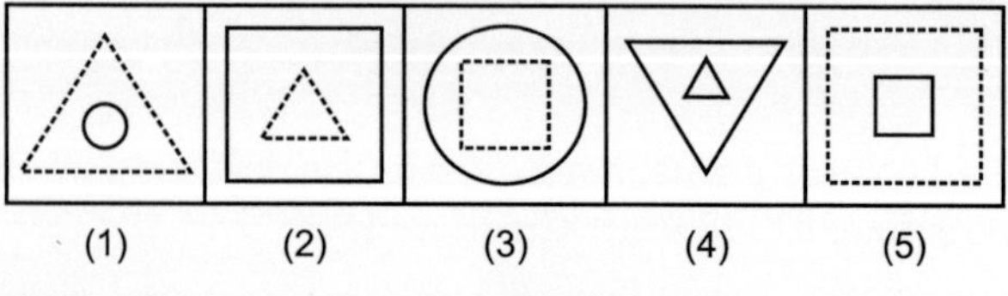

(1) (2) (3) (4) (5)

(a) 1 (b) 2
(c) 3 (d) 4
(e) 5

Answer Key

1. (a)	**2.** (b)	**3.** (a)	**4.** (c)	**5.** (c)	**6.** (c)	**7.** (d)	**8.** (a)	**9.** (d)	**10.** (d)

Explanatory Notes

1. (a)
In all other figures, all the line segments are drawn perpendicular to one base only.

2. (b)
Only in figure (2), while moving in an ACW direction, the numbers do not form a sequence.

3. (a)
In all other figures, one of the dots lies outside the triangle as well as the circle.

4. (c)
All other figures have at least one line of symmetry.

5. (c)
Figure (3) is formed by a combination of A-shaped elements while all other figures are formed by a combination of V-shaped elements.

6. (c)
In all other figures, the square has two line segments inside and one line segment outside.

7. (d)
Only in figure (4), all the leaves have their outer halves shaded.

8. (a)
All other figures can be rotated into each other. (In each figure except figure (1), the middle element is obtained by rotating the outer element through 90°CW and the inner element is obtained by rotating the middle element through 90°CW).

9. (a)
In all other figures, as we move from the innermost to the outermost element, the numbers of sides of the elements either increase or decrease in a sequence.

10. (d)
In each of the other figures, one of the two elements is made of dotted lines.

❒

UNIT 2

Analogy

'Analogy' means 'correspondence'. In the problem on analogy, a pair of related figures is given and a similar relationship is to be found between two other figures by selecting one of them from the set of answer figures. The candidate has to find out which one of the answer figure should be placed in place of the question mark.

Solve Examples

☛ ***Direction to solve (1 to 5) :*** *Each of the following questions consists of two sets of figures. Figures A, B, C and D constitute the Problem Set while figures 1, 2, 3, 4 and 5 constitute the Answer Set. There is a definite relationship between figures A and B. Establish a similar relationship between figures C and D by selecting a suitable figure from the Answer Set, that would replace the question mark (?) in fig.* (D).

1. Select a suitable figure from the Answer Figures that would replace the question mark (?).

Problem Figures : **Answer Figures :**

(A) (B) (C) (D) (1) (2) (3) (4) (5)

(a) 1 (b) 2
(c) 3 (d) 4
(e) 5

Solution : Option (d) is correct

Explanation: The upper and the lower elements interchange places; the element that reaches the upper position gets laterally inverted; the element that reaches the lower position gets laterally inverted and its head also gets laterally inverted; the line segment inside the square (central element) rotates 45°CW.

2. Select a suitable figure from the Answer Figures that would replace the question mark (?).

Problem Figures : **Answer Figures :**

(A) (B) (C) (D) (1) (2) (3) (4) (5)

(a) 1 (b) 2
(c) 3 (d) 4
(e) 5

Solution: Option (*c*) is correct

Explanation : The elements move in the sequence the elements reaching the upper-left and the lower-right positions rotate 90°ACW; the elements reaching the upper-right and lower-left positions rotate 90°CW; the central element rotates 90°ACW and gets laterally inverted.

3. Select a suitable figure from the Answer Figures that would replace the question mark (?).

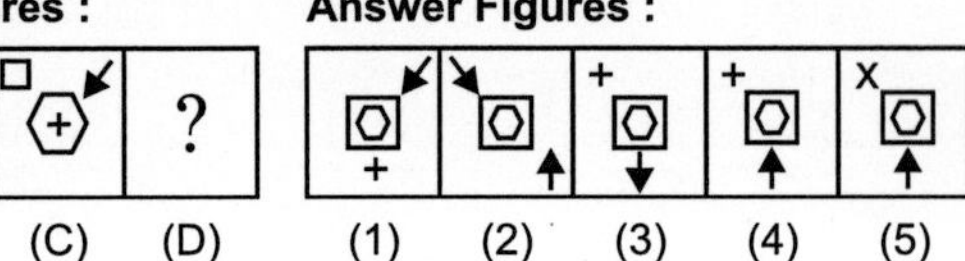

(a) 1 (b) 2
(c) 3 (d) 4
(e) 5

Solution: Option (d) is correct

Explanation: The arrow rotates 135°CW and moves a distance equal to one and a half sides of the square boundary in a CW direction. Out of the two central elements, the outer element diminishes in size and becomes the inner element, the inner element moves to the position of the corner element and the corner element gets enlarged and moves to the central position to become the outer element.

4. Select a suitable figure from the Answer Figures that would replace the question mark (?).

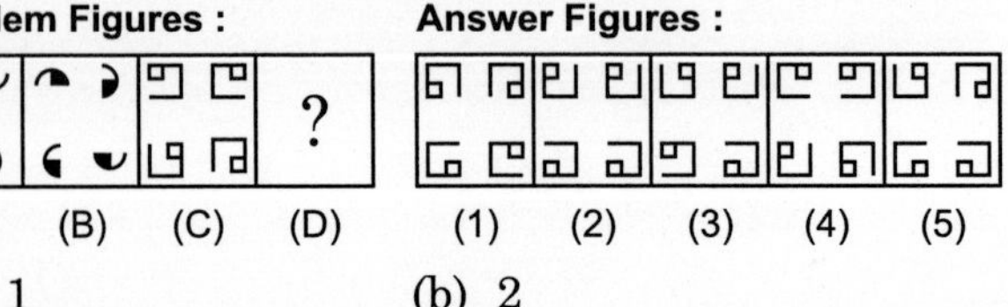

(a) 1 (b) 2
(c) 3 (d) 4
(e) 5

Solution: Option (*c*) is correct

Explanation: The upper-left and the lower-right elements rotate 90°CW while the upper-right and the lower-left elements rotate 90°ACW.

5. Select a suitable figure from the Answer Figures that would replace the question mark (?).

Problem Figures : **Answer Figures :**

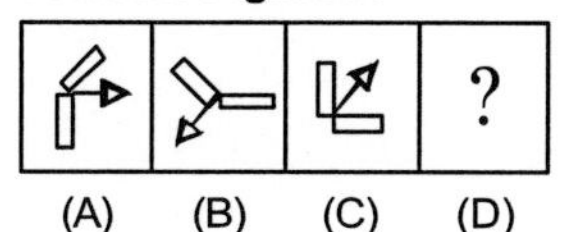
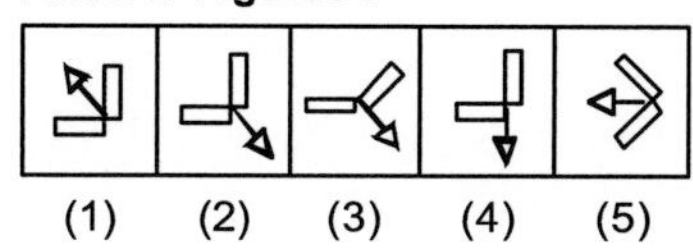

(A) (B) (C) (D) (1) (2) (3) (4) (5)

(a) 1 (b) 2
(c) 3 (d) 4
(e) 5

Solution: Option d) is correct

Explanation: The arrow rotates 135°CW and the remaining part of the figure rotates 90°ACW.

Multiple Choice Questions

1. Select a suitable figure from the Answer Figures that would replace the question mark (?).

Problem Figures : **Answer Figures :**

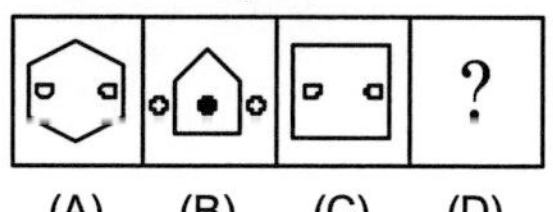

(A) (B) (C) (D) (1) (2) (3) (4) (5)

(a) 1 (b) 2
(c) 3 (d) 4
(e) 5

2. Select a suitable figure from the Answer Figures that would replace the question mark (?).

Problem Figures : **Answer Figures :**

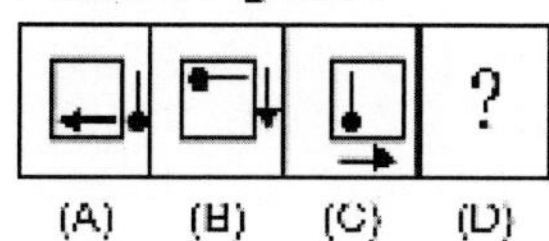
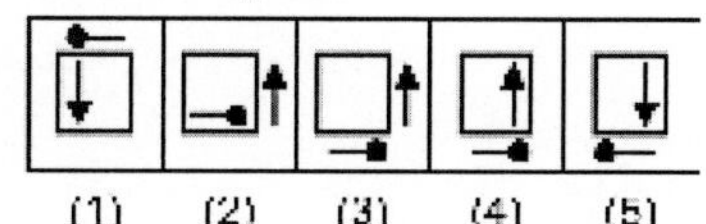

(A) (B) (C) (D) (1) (2) (3) (4) (5)

(a) 1 (b) 2
(c) 3 (d) 4
(e) 5

3. Select a suitable figure from the Answer Figures that would replace the question mark (?).

Problem Figures : **Answer Figures :**

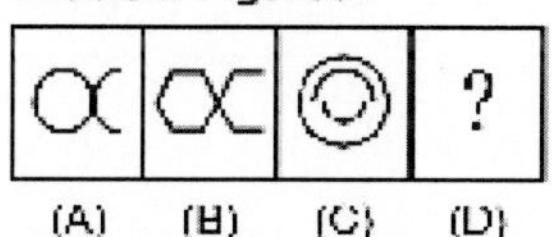
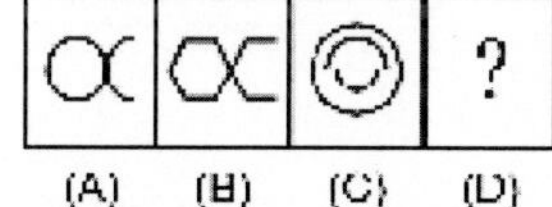

(A) (B) (C) (D) (1) (2) (3) (4) (5)

(a) 1 (b) 2
(c) 3 (d) 4
(e) 5

4. Select a suitable figure from the Answer Figures that would replace the question mark (?).

Problem Figures : **Answer Figures :**

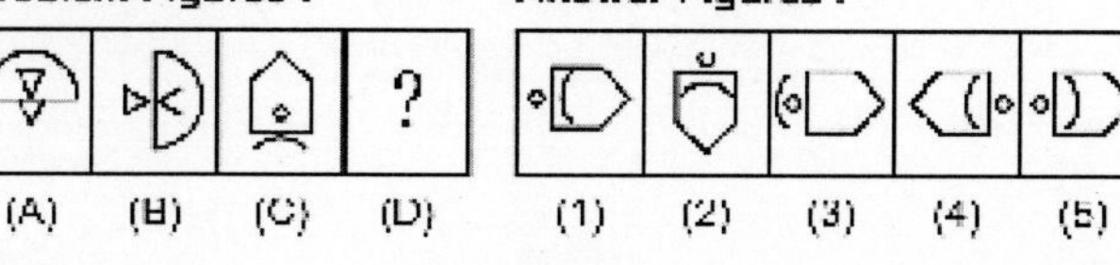

(A) (B) (C) (D) (1) (2) (3) (4) (5)

(a) 1 (b) 2
(c) 3 (d) 4
(e) 5

5. Select a suitable figure from the Answer Figures that would replace the question mark (?).

Problem Figures : **Answer Figures :**

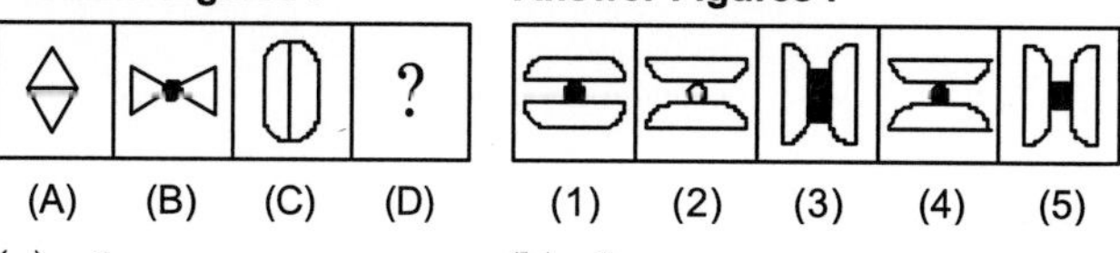

(A) (B) (C) (D) (1) (2) (3) (4) (5)

(a) 1 (b) 2
(c) 3 (d) 4
(e) 5

6. Select a suitable figure from the Answer Figures that would replace the question mark (?).

Problem Figures : **Answer Figures :**

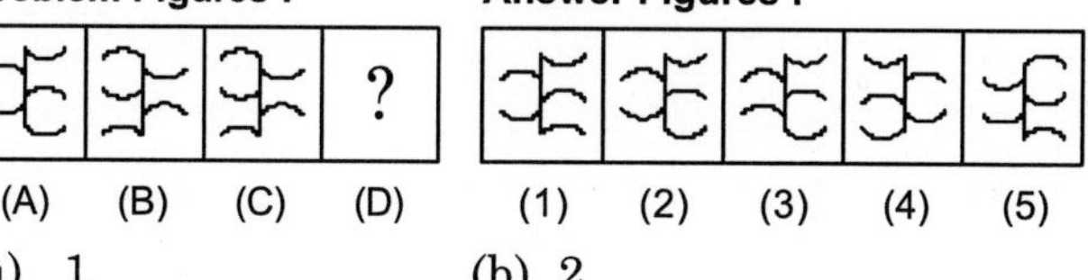

(A) (B) (C) (D) (1) (2) (3) (4) (5)

(a) 1 (b) 2
(c) 3 (d) 4
(e) 5

7. Select a suitable figure from the Answer Figures that would replace the question mark (?).

Problem Figures : **Answer Figures :**

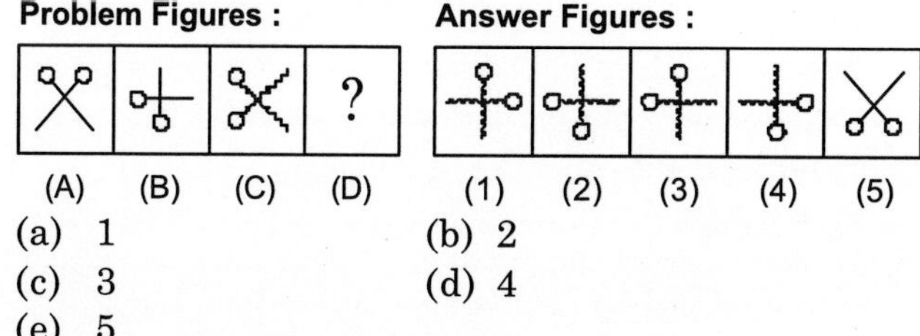

(A) (B) (C) (D) (1) (2) (3) (4) (5)

(a) 1 (b) 2
(c) 3 (d) 4
(e) 5

8. Select a suitable figure from the Answer Figures that would replace the question mark (?).

Problem Figures : **Answer Figures :**

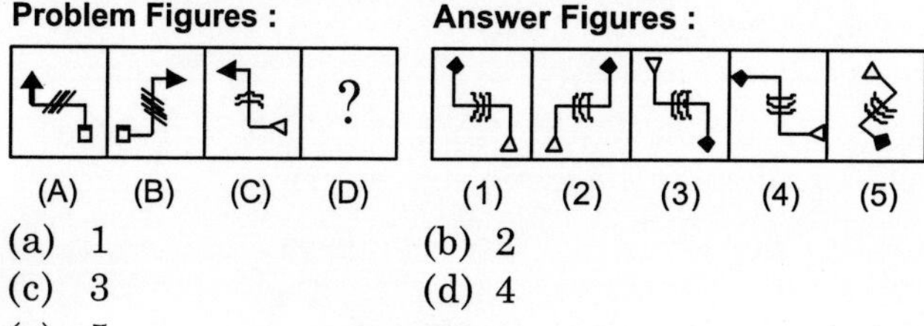

(A) (B) (C) (D) (1) (2) (3) (4) (5)

(a) 1 (b) 2
(c) 3 (d) 4
(e) 5

9. Select a suitable figure from the Answer Figures that would replace the question mark (?).

Problem Figures : **Answer Figures :**

(A) (B) (C) (D) (1) (2) (3) (4) (5)

(a) 1 (b) 2
(c) 3 (d) 4
(e) 5

10. Select a suitable figure from the Answer Figures that would replace the question mark (?).

Problem Figures : **Answer Figures :**

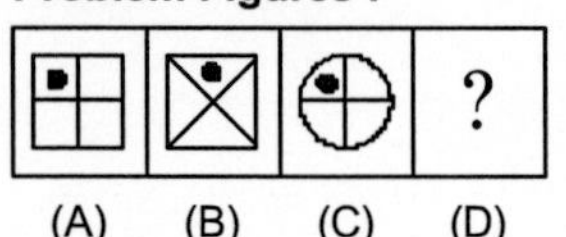
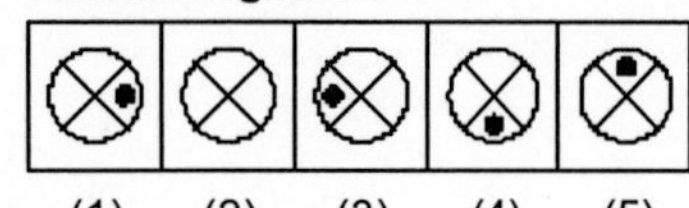

(A) (B) (C) (D) (1) (2) (3) (4) (5)

(a) 1 (b) 2
(c) 3 (d) 4
(e) 5

11. Select a suitable figure from the Answer Figures that would replace the question mark (?).

Problem Figures : **Answer Figures :**

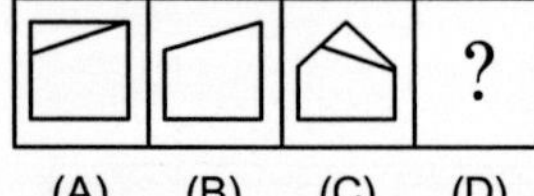
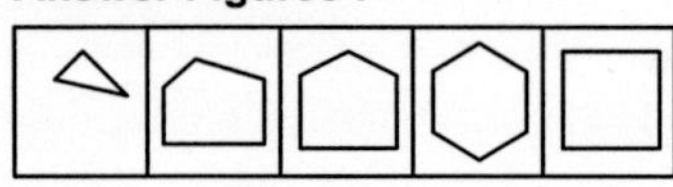

(A) (B) (C) (D) (1) (2) (3) (4) (5)

(a) 1 (b) 2
(c) 3 (d) 4
(e) 5

12. Select a suitable figure from the Answer Figures that would replace the question mark (?).

Problem Figures : **Answer Figures :**

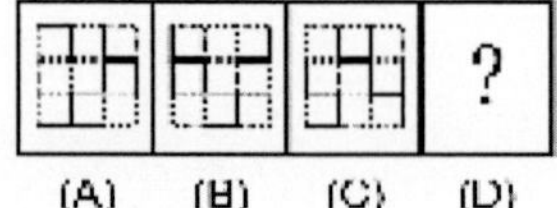
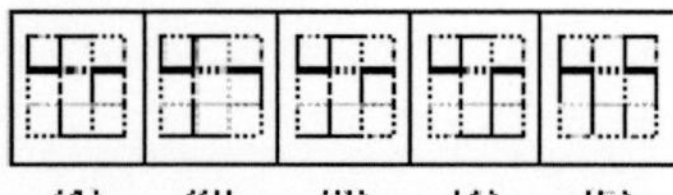

(A) (B) (C) (D) (1) (2) (3) (4) (5)

(a) 1 (b) 2
(c) 3 (d) 4
(e) 5

13. Select a suitable figure from the Answer Figures that would replace the question mark (?).

Problem Figures : **Answer Figures :**

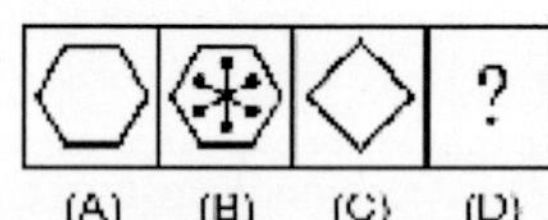

(A) (B) (C) (D) (1) (2) (3) (4) (5)

(a) 1 (b) 2
(c) 3 (d) 4
(e) 5

14. Select a suitable figure from the Answer Figures that would replace the question mark (?).

Problem Figures : **Answer Figures :**

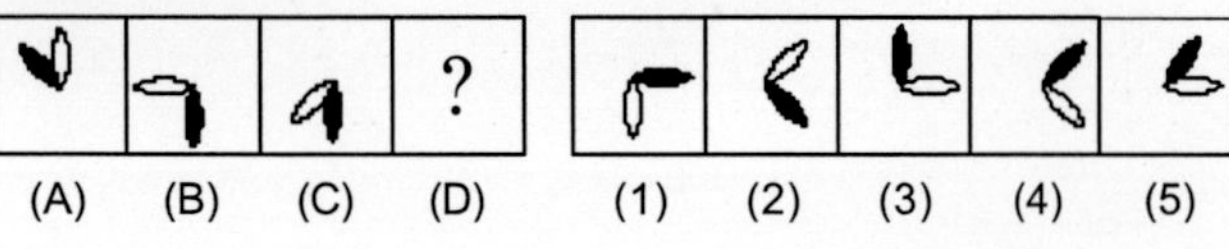

(A) (B) (C) (D) (1) (2) (3) (4) (5)

(a) 1 (b) 2
(c) 3 (d) 4
(e) 5

15. Select a suitable figure from the Answer Figures that would replace the question mark (?).

Problem Figures : **Answer Figures :**

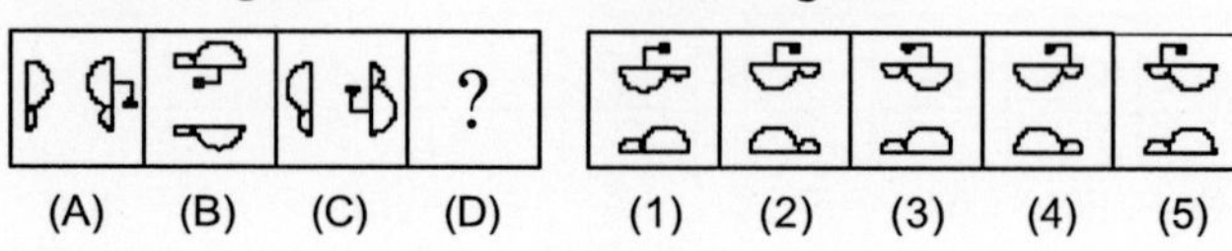

(A) (B) (C) (D) (1) (2) (3) (4) (5)

(a) 1 (b) 2
(c) 3 (d) 4
(e) 5

16. Select a suitable figure from the Answer Figures that would replace the question mark (?).

Problem Figures : **Answer Figures :**

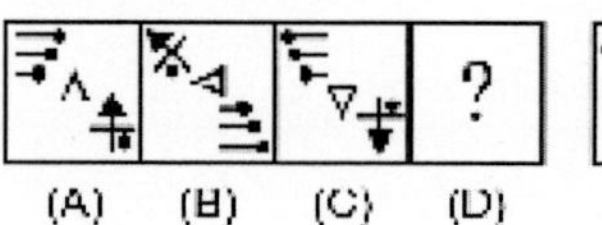
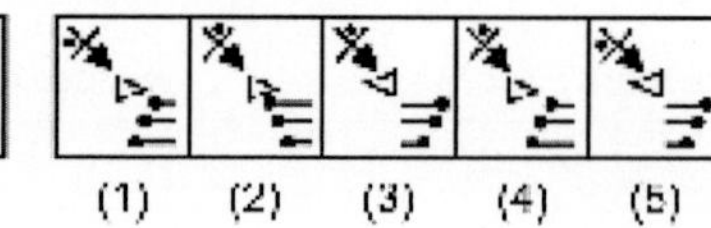

(A) (B) (C) (D) (1) (2) (3) (4) (5)

(a) 1 (b) 2
(c) 3 (d) 4
(e) 5

17. Select a suitable figure from the Answer Figures that would replace the question mark (?).

Problem Figures : **Answer Figures :**

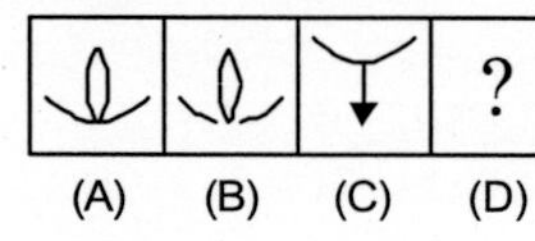
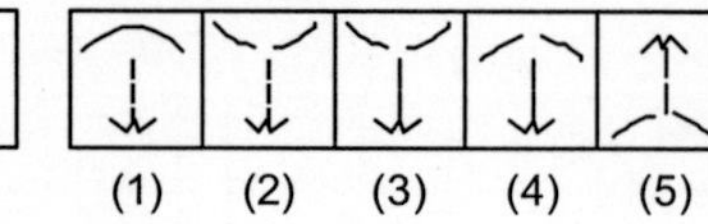

(A) (B) (C) (D) (1) (2) (3) (4) (5)

(a) 1 (b) 2
(c) 3 (d) 4
(e) 5

18. Select a suitable figure from the Answer Figures that would replace the question mark (?).

Problem Figures : **Answer Figures :**

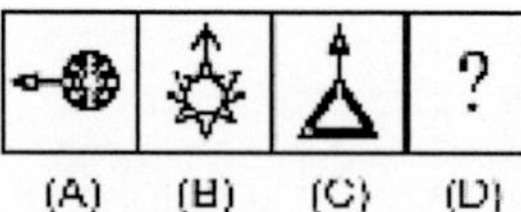
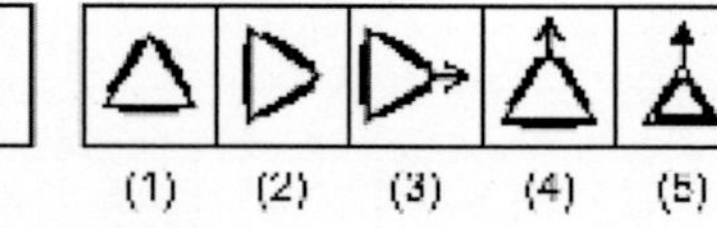

(A) (B) (C) (D) (1) (2) (3) (4) (5)

(a) 1 (b) 2
(c) 3 (d) 4
(e) 5

19. Select a suitable figure from the Answer Figures that would replace the question mark (?).

Problem Figures : **Answer Figures :**

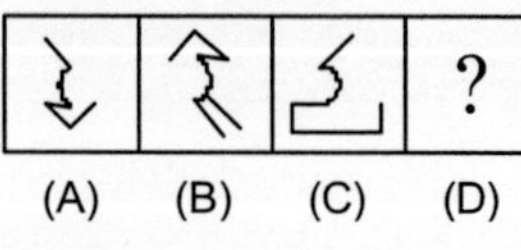
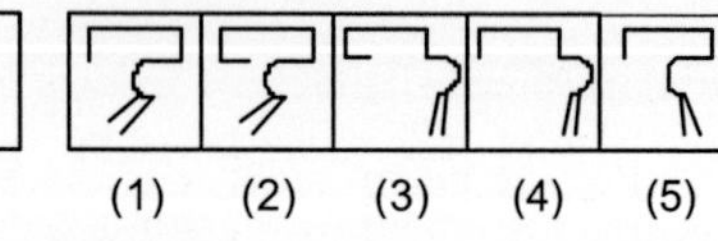

(A) (B) (C) (D) (1) (2) (3) (4) (5)

(a) 1 (b) 2
(c) 3 (d) 4
(e) 5

20. Select a suitable figure from the Answer Figures that would replace the question mark (?).

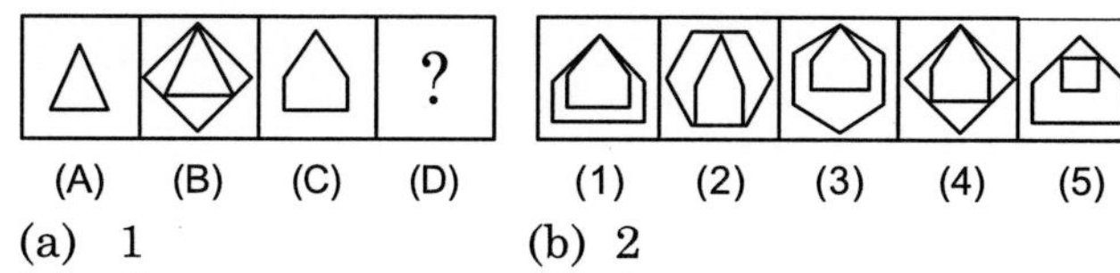

(a) 1 (b) 2
(c) 3 (d) 4
(e) 5

21. Select a suitable figure from the Answer Figures that would replace the question mark (?).

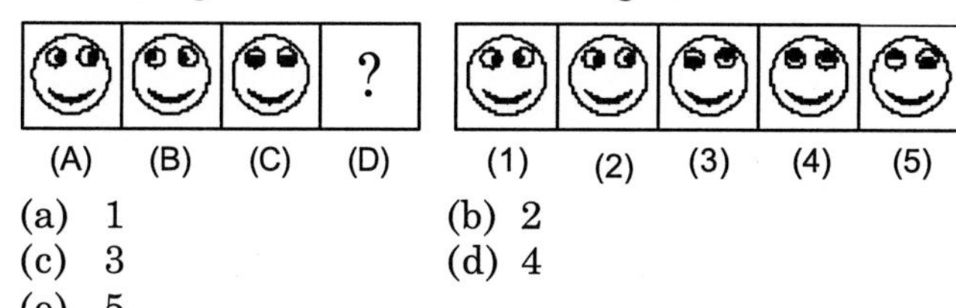

(a) 1 (b) 2
(c) 3 (d) 4
(e) 5

22. Select a suitable figure from the Answer Figures that would replace the question mark (?).

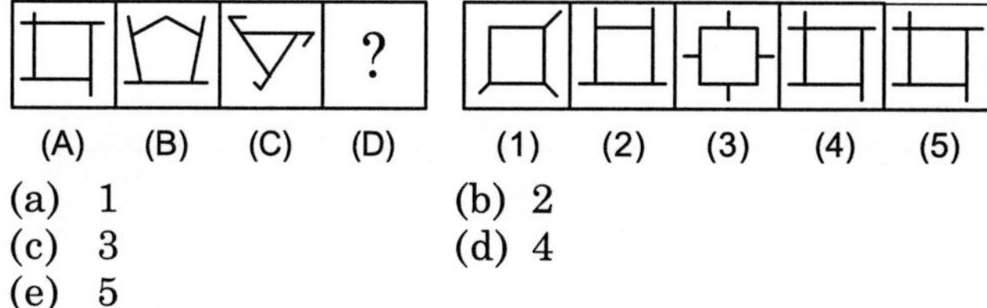

(a) 1 (b) 2
(c) 3 (d) 4
(e) 5

23. Select a suitable figure from the Answer Figures that would replace the question mark (?).

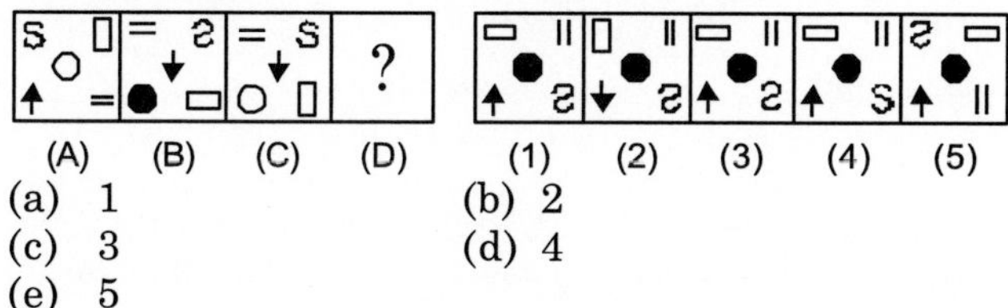

(a) 1 (b) 2
(c) 3 (d) 4
(e) 5

24. Select a suitable figure from the Answer Figures that would replace the question mark (?).

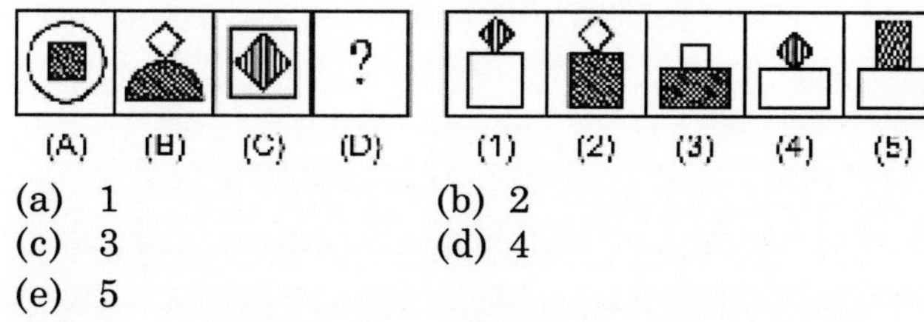

(a) 1 (b) 2
(c) 3 (d) 4
(e) 5

25. Select a suitable figure from the Answer Figures that would replace the question mark (?).

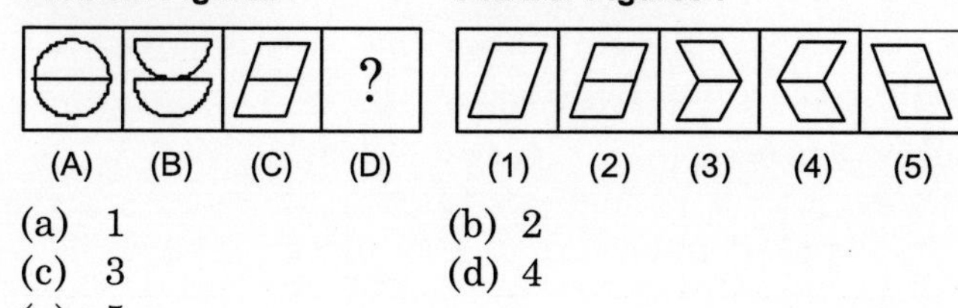

(a) 1 (b) 2
(c) 3 (d) 4
(e) 5

26. Select a suitable figure from the Answer Figures that would replace the question mark (?).

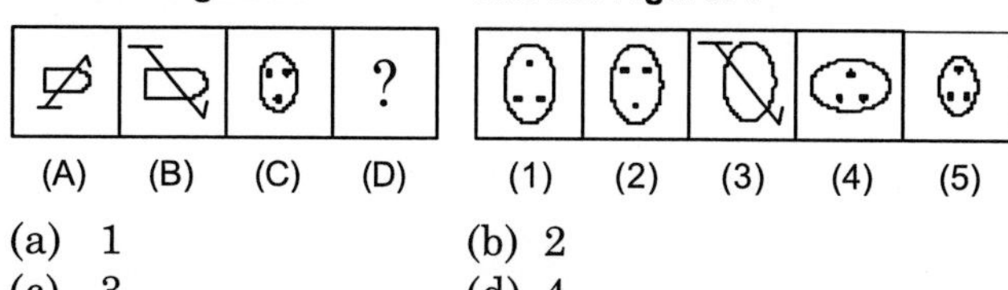

(a) 1 (b) 2
(c) 3 (d) 4
(e) 5

27. Select a suitable figure from the Answer Figures that would replace the question mark (?).

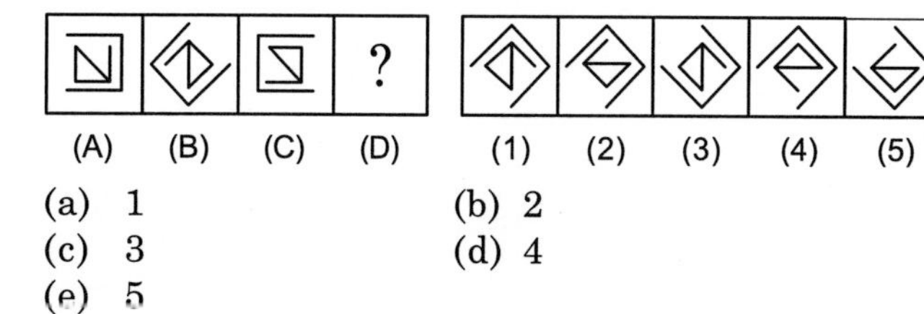

(a) 1 (b) 2
(c) 3 (d) 4
(e) 5

28. Select a suitable figure from the Answer Figures that would replace the question mark (?).

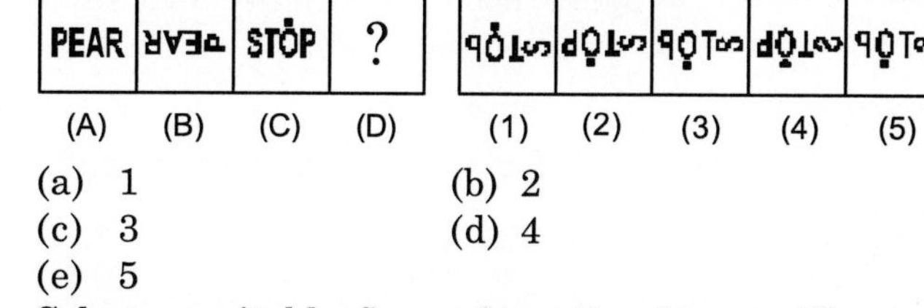

(a) 1 (b) 2
(c) 3 (d) 4
(e) 5

29. Select a suitable figure from the Answer Figures that would replace the question mark (?).

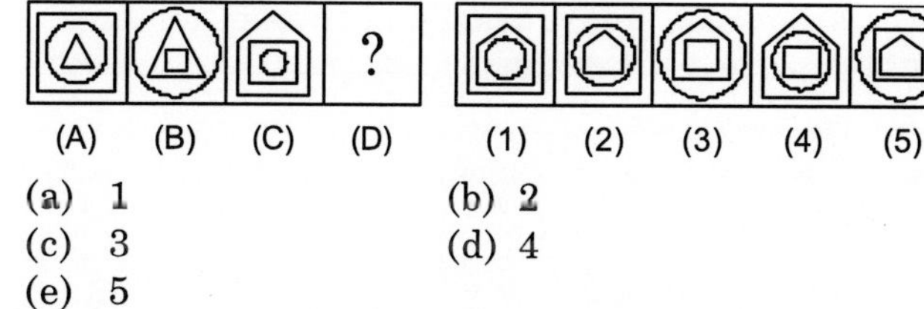

(a) 1 (b) 2
(c) 3 (d) 4
(e) 5

30. Select a suitable figure from the Answer Figures that would replace the question mark (?).

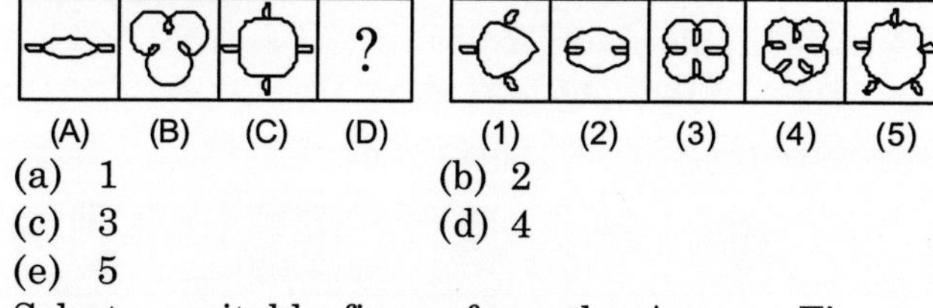

(a) 1 (b) 2
(c) 3 (d) 4
(e) 5

31. Select a suitable figure from the Answer Figures that would replace the question mark (?).

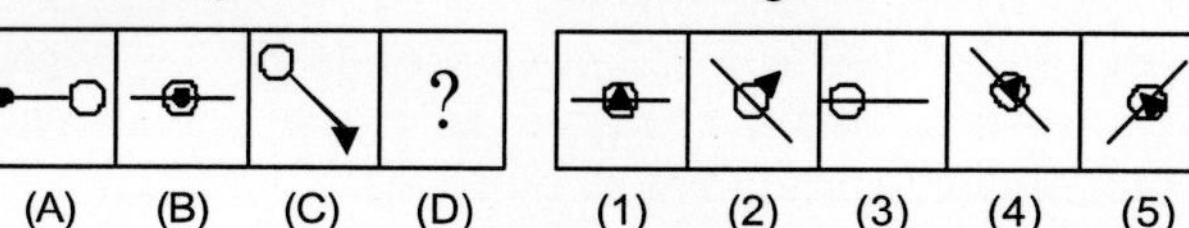

(a) 1 (b) 2
(c) 3 (d) 4
(e) 5

32. Select a suitable figure from the Answer Figures that would replace the question mark (?).

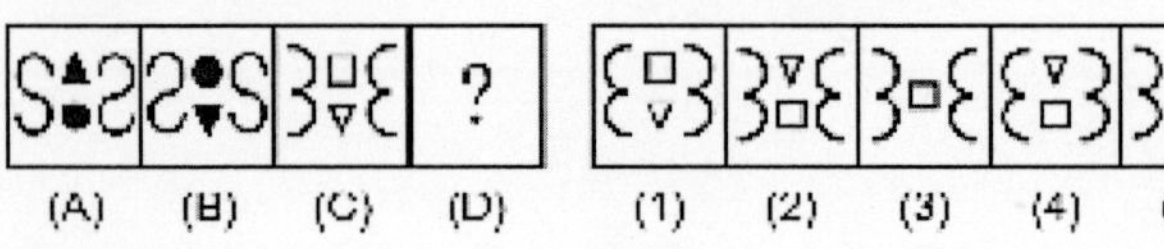

(a) 1 (b) 2
(c) 3 (d) 4
(e) 5

33. Select a suitable figure from the Answer Figures that would replace the question mark (?).

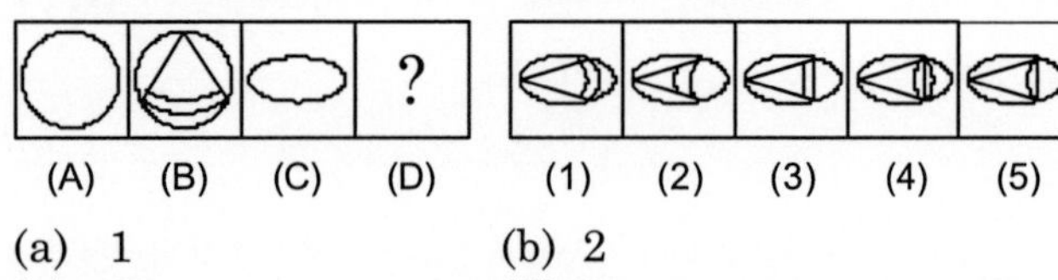

(a) 1 (b) 2
(c) 3 (d) 4
(e) 5

34. Select a suitable figure from the Answer Figures that would replace the question mark (?).

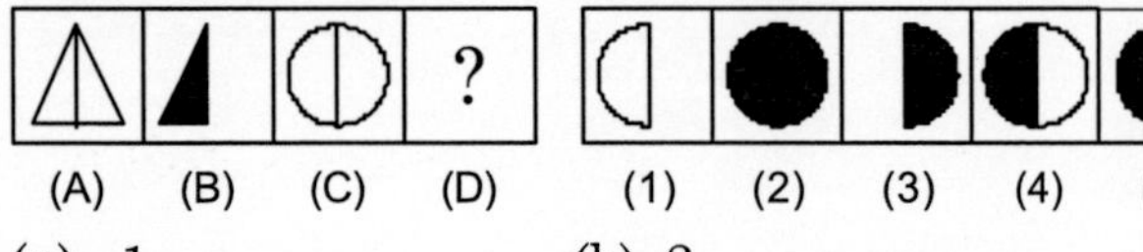

(a) 1 (b) 2
(c) 3 (d) 4
(e) 5

35. Select a suitable figure from the Answer Figures that would replace the question mark (?).

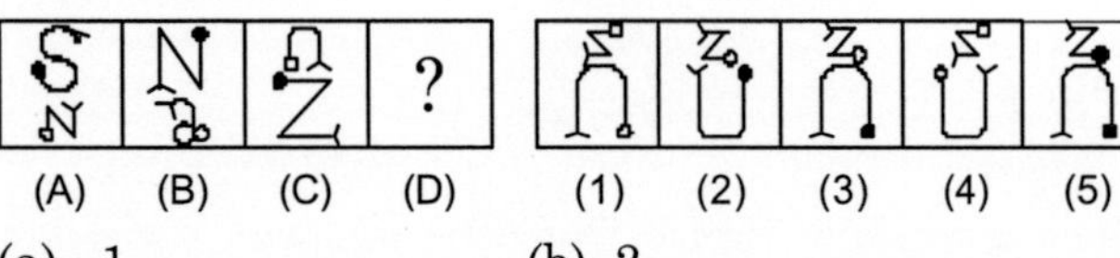

(a) 1 (b) 2
(c) 3 (d) 4
(e) 5

36. Select a suitable figure from the Answer Figures that would replace the question mark (?).

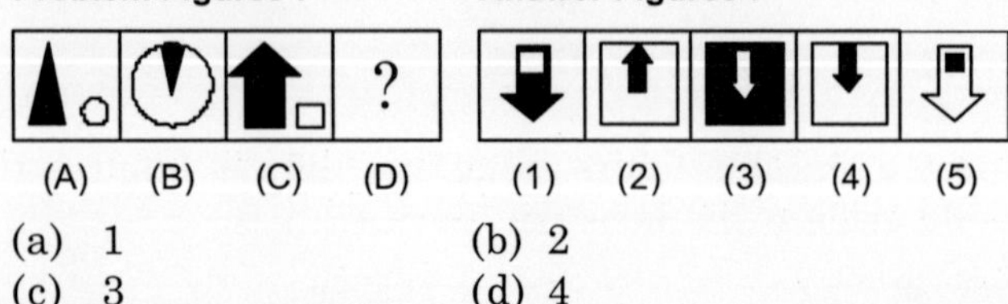

(a) 1 (b) 2
(c) 3 (d) 4
(e) 5

37. Select a suitable figure from the Answer Figures that would replace the question mark (?).

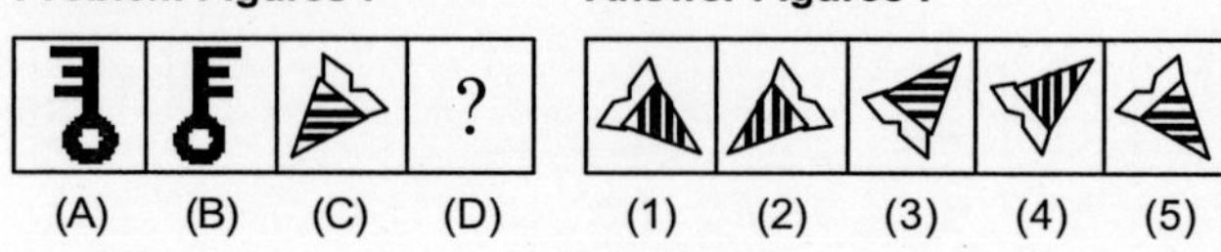

(a) 1 (b) 2
(c) 3 (d) 4
(e) 5

38. Select a suitable figure from the Answer Figures that would replace the question mark (?).

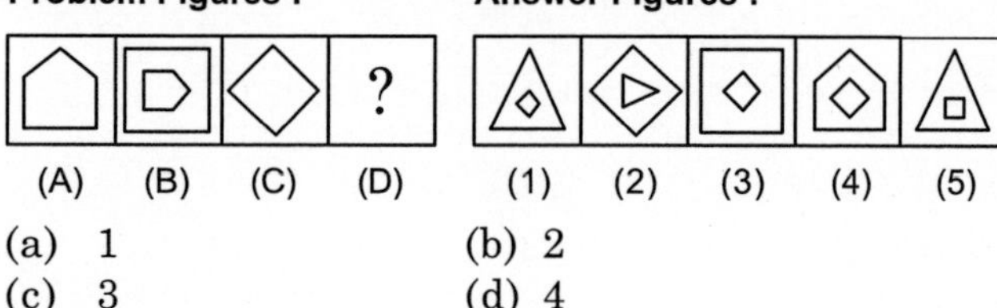

(a) 1 (b) 2
(c) 3 (d) 4
(e) 5

39. Select a suitable figure from the Answer Figures that would replace the question mark (?).

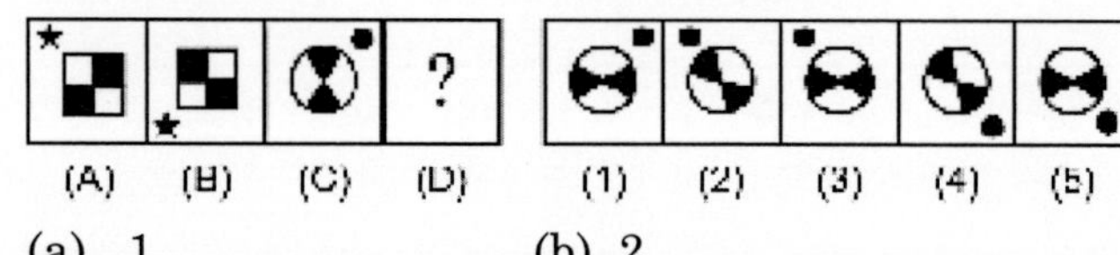

(a) 1 (b) 2
(c) 3 (d) 4
(e) 5

40. Select a suitable figure from the Answer Figures that would replace the question mark (?).

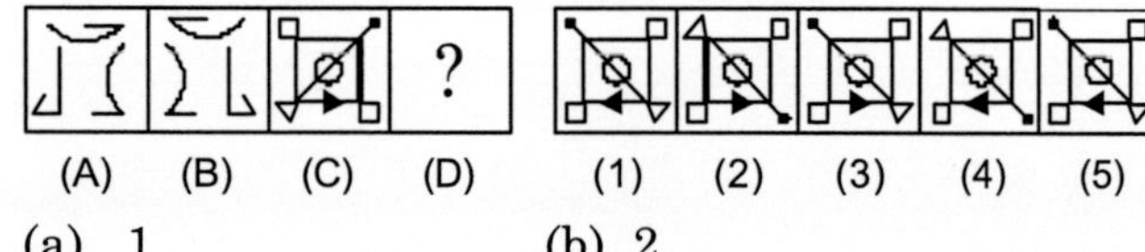

(a) 1 (b) 2
(c) 3 (d) 4
(e) 5

41. Select a suitable figure from the Answer Figures that would replace the question mark (?).

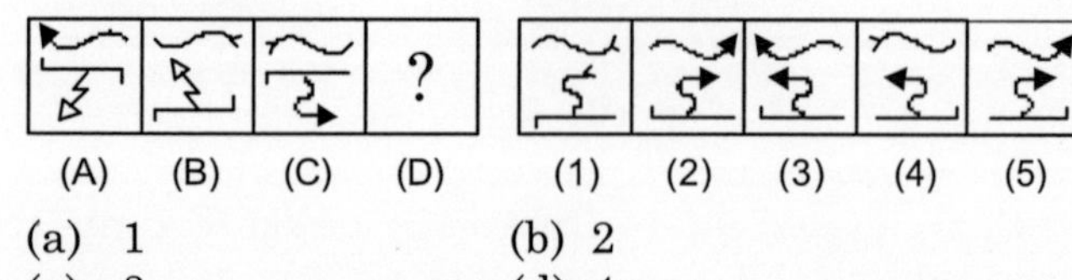

(a) 1 (b) 2
(c) 3 (d) 4
(e) 5

42. Select a suitable figure from the Answer Figures that would replace the question mark (?).

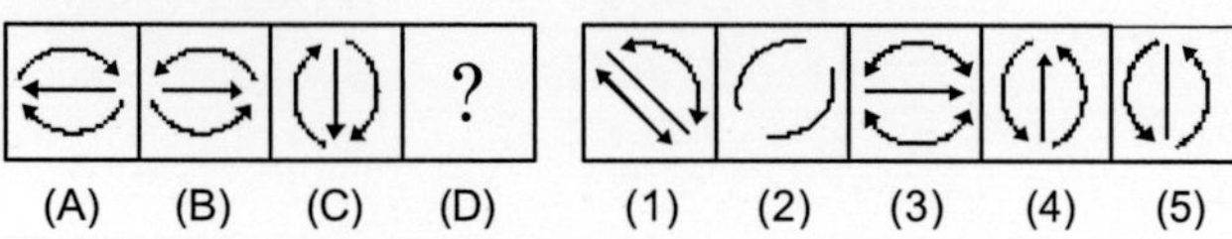

(a) 1 (b) 2
(c) 3 (d) 4
(e) 5

43. Select a suitable figure from the Answer Figures that would replace the question mark (?).

Problem Figures : **Answer Figures :**

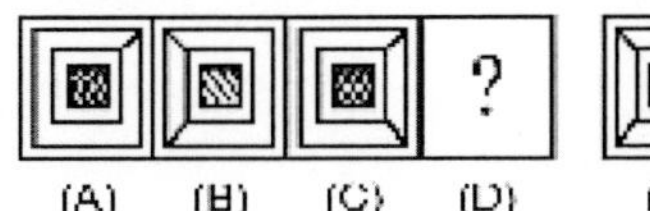
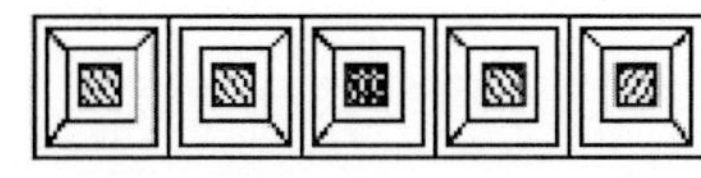

(A) (B) (C) (D) (1) (2) (3) (4) (5)

(a) 1 (b) 2
(c) 3 (d) 4
(e) 5

44. Select a suitable figure from the Answer Figures that would replace the question mark (?).

Problem Figures : **Answer Figures :**

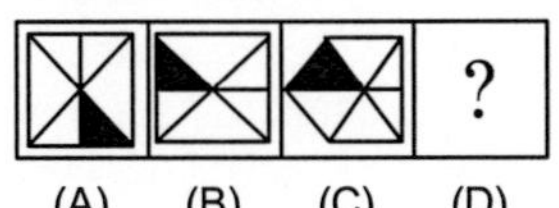
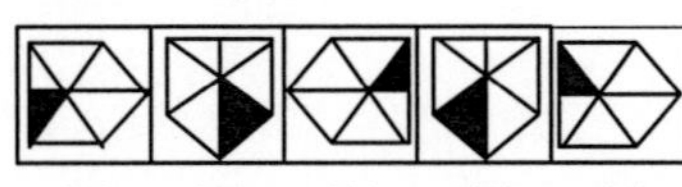

(A) (B) (C) (D) (1) (2) (3) (4) (5)

(a) 1 (b) 2
(c) 3 (d) 4
(e) 5

45. Select a suitable figure from the Answer Figures that would replace the question mark (?).

Problem Figures : **Answer Figures :**

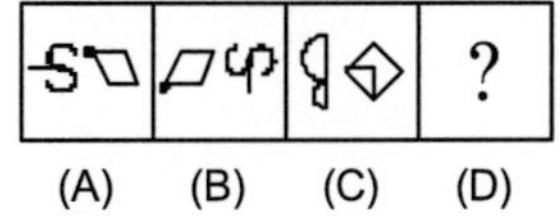
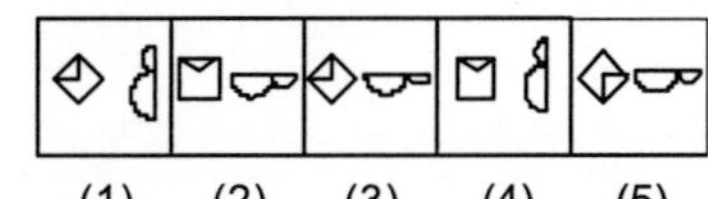

(A) (B) (C) (D) (1) (2) (3) (4) (5)

(a) 1 (b) 2
(c) 3 (d) 4
(e) 5

46. Select a suitable figure from the Answer Figures that would replace the question mark (?).

Problem Figures : **Answer Figures :**

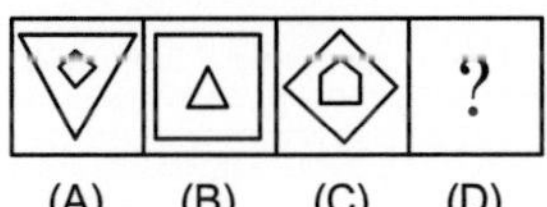
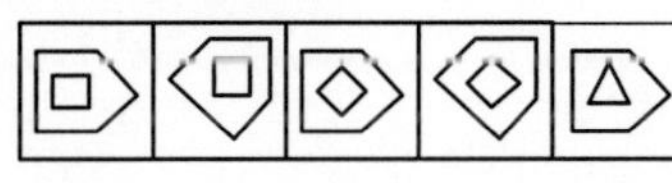

(A) (B) (C) (D) (1) (2) (3) (4) (5)

(a) 1 (b) 2
(c) 3 (d) 4
(e) 5

47. Select a suitable figure from the Answer Figures that would replace the question mark (?).

Problem Figures : **Answer Figures :**

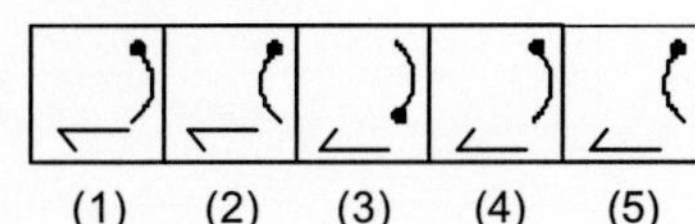

(A) (B) (C) (D) (1) (2) (3) (4) (5)

(a) 1 (b) 2
(c) 3 (d) 4
(e) 5

48. Select a suitable figure from the Answer Figures that would replace the question mark (?).

Problem Figures : **Answer Figures :**

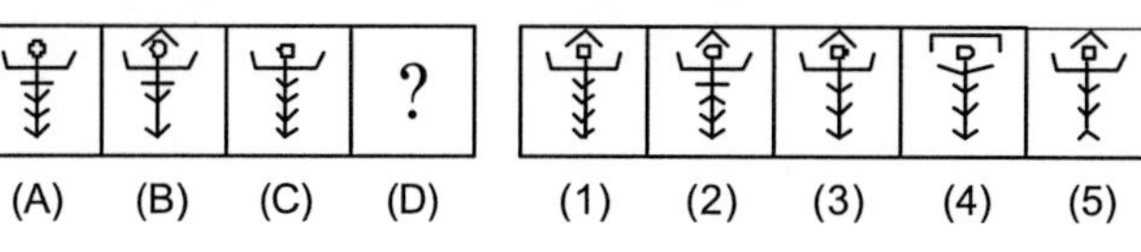

(A) (B) (C) (D) (1) (2) (3) (4) (5)

(a) 1 (b) 2
(c) 3 (d) 4
(e) 5

49. Select a suitable figure from the Answer Figures that would replace the question mark (?).

Problem Figures : **Answer Figures :**

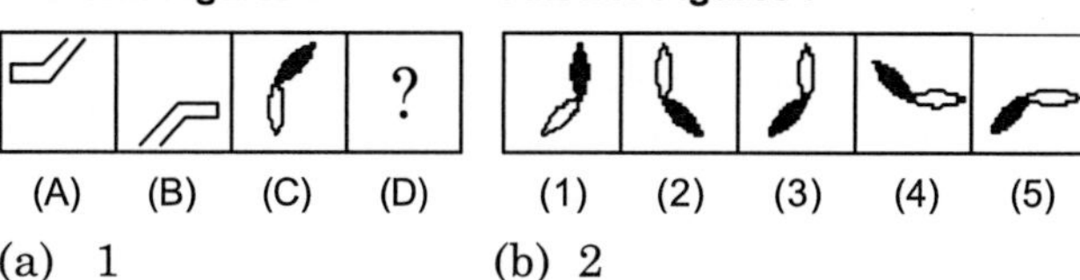

(A) (B) (C) (D) (1) (2) (3) (4) (5)

(a) 1 (b) 2
(c) 3 (d) 4
(e) 5

50. Select a suitable figure from the Answer Figures that would replace the question mark (?).

Problem Figures : **Answer Figures :**

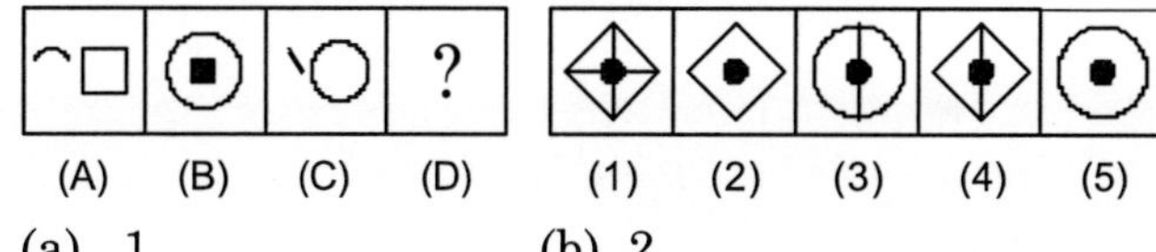

(A) (B) (C) (D) (1) (2) (3) (4) (5)

(a) 1 (b) 2
(c) 3 (d) 4
(e) 5

51. Select a suitable figure from the Answer Figures that would replace the question mark (?).

Problem Figures : **Answer Figures :**

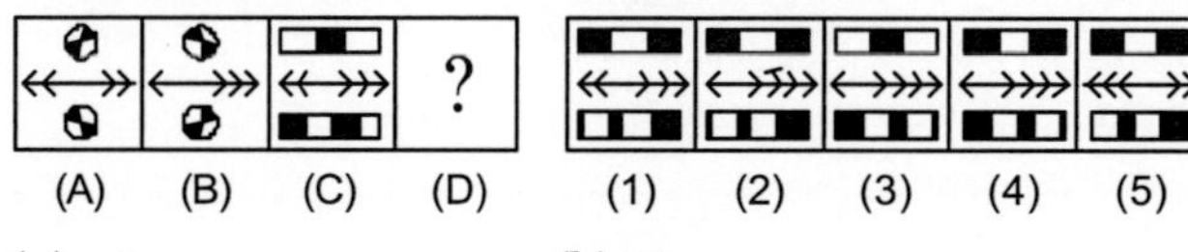

(A) (B) (C) (D) (1) (2) (3) (4) (5)

(a) 1 (b) 2
(c) 3 (d) 4
(e) 5

52. Select a suitable figure from the Answer Figures that would replace the question mark (?).

Problem Figures : **Answer Figures :**

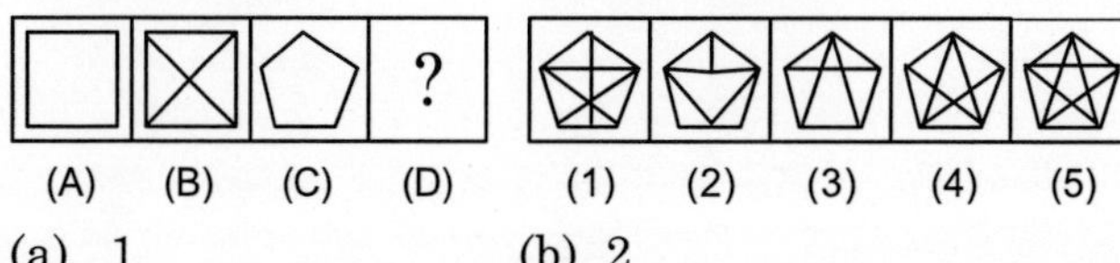

(A) (B) (C) (D) (1) (2) (3) (4) (5)

(a) 1 (b) 2
(c) 3 (d) 4
(e) 5

53. Select a suitable figure from the Answer Figures that would replace the question mark (?).

Problem Figures : **Answer Figures :**

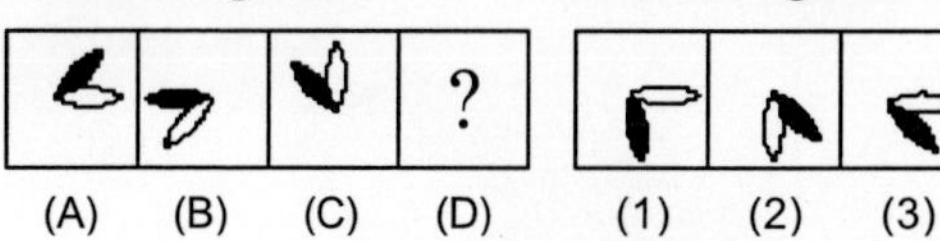

(A) (B) (C) (D) (1) (2) (3) (4) (5)

(a) 1 (b) 2
(c) 3 (d) 4
(e) 5

54. Select a suitable figure from the Answer Figures that would replace the question mark (?).

Problem Figures : **Answer Figures :**

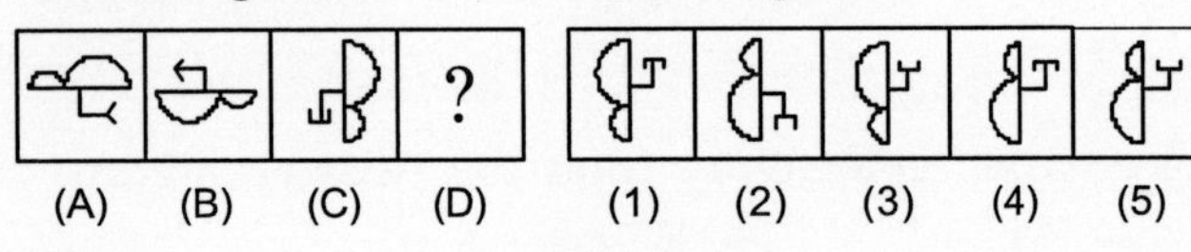

(A) (B) (C) (D) (1) (2) (3) (4) (5)

(a) 1 (b) 2
(c) 3 (d) 4
(e) 5

55. Select a suitable figure from the Answer Figures that would replace the question mark (?).

Problem Figures : **Answer Figures :**

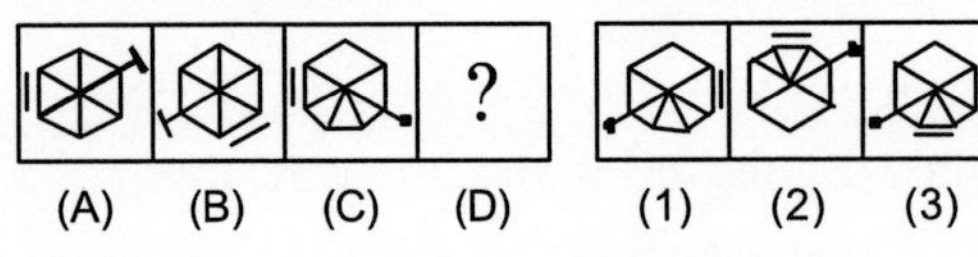

(A) (B) (C) (D) (1) (2) (3) (4) (5)

(a) 1 (b) 2
(c) 3 (d) 4
(e) 5

56. Select a suitable figure from the Answer Figures that would replace the question mark (?).

Problem Figures : **Answer Figures :**

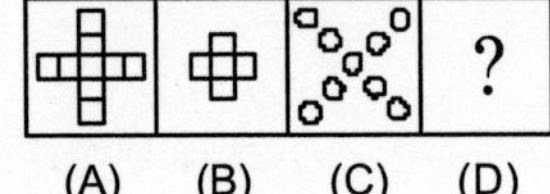

(A) (B) (C) (D) (1) (2) (3) (4) (5)

(a) 1 (b) 2
(c) 3 (d) 4
(e) 5

57. Select a suitable figure from the Answer Figures that would replace the question mark (?).

Problem Figures : **Answer Figures :**

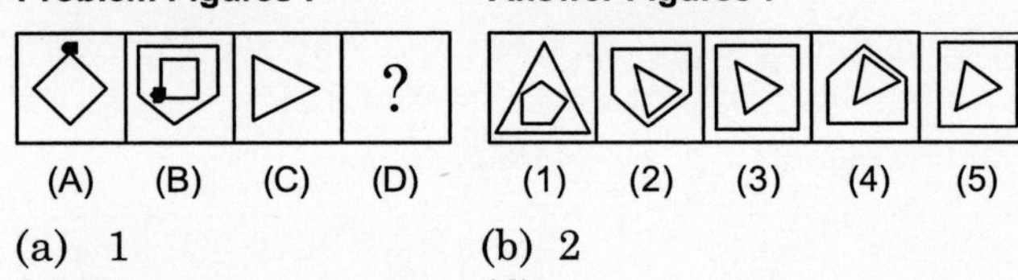

(A) (B) (C) (D) (1) (2) (3) (4) (5)

(a) 1 (b) 2
(c) 3 (d) 4
(e) 5

58. Select a suitable figure from the Answer Figures that would replace the question mark (?).

Problem Figures : **Answer Figures :**

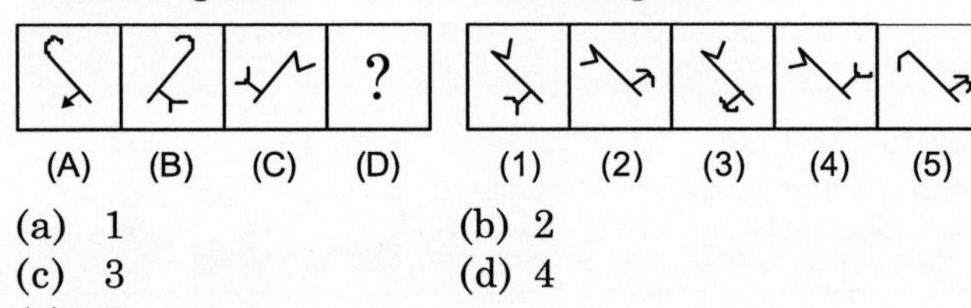

(A) (B) (C) (D) (1) (2) (3) (4) (5)

(a) 1 (b) 2
(c) 3 (d) 4
(e) 5

59. Select a suitable figure from the Answer Figures that would replace the question mark (?).

Problem Figures : **Answer Figures :**

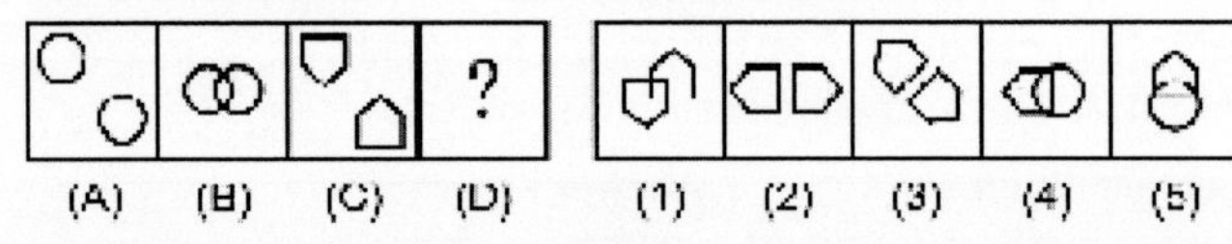

(A) (B) (C) (D) (1) (2) (3) (4) (5)

(a) 1 (b) 2
(c) 3 (d) 4
(e) 5

60. Select a suitable figure from the Answer Figures that would replace the question mark (?).

Problem Figures : **Answer Figures :**

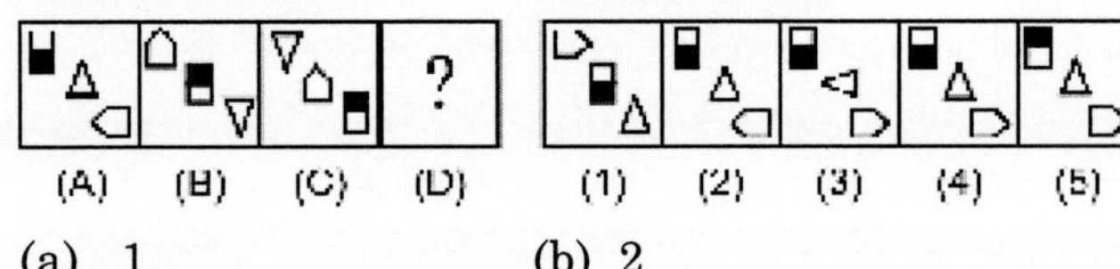

(A) (B) (C) (D) (1) (2) (3) (4) (5)

(a) 1 (b) 2
(c) 3 (d) 4
(e) 5

Answer Key

1. (a)	**2.** (d)	**3.** (e)	**4.** (e)	**5.** (d)	**6.** (b)	**7.** (d)	**8.** (b)	**9.** (c)	**10.** (e)
11. (b)	**12.** (c)	**13.** (b)	**14.** (d)	**15.** (a)	**16.** (d)	**17.** (c)	**18.** (c)	**19.** (a)	**20.** (c)
21. (d)	**22.** (d)	**23.** (a)	**24.** (c)	**25.** (c)	**26.** (a)	**27.** (a)	**28.** (b)	**29.** (b)	**30.** (d)
31. (d)	**32.** (d)	**33.** (a)	**34.** (e)	**35.** (c)	**36.** (d)	**37.** (e)	**38.** (a)	**39.** (c)	**40.** (a)
41. (b)	**42.** (d)	**43.** (a)	**44.** (b)	**45.** (c)	**46.** (d)	**47.** (d)	**48.** (c)	**49.** (c)	**50.** (a)
51. (b)	**52.** (e)	**53.** (e)	**54.** (e)	**55.** (c)	**56.** (b)	**57.** (c)	**58.** (b)	**59.** (a)	**60.** (d)

Explanatory Notes

1. (a)
The number of sides in the main figure reduces by one; the two circles present inside it, move outside and reach the positions on either side of this figure; a new black circle appears inside the figure.

2. (d)
The outer element rotates 90°ACW, moves to the adjacent side of the square in an ACW direction and shifts inside the square. The inner element rotates 90°ACW, moves to the adjacent side of the square in an ACW direction and shifts outside the square.

3. (e)
The circles are converted to hexagons and semicircles are converged to half-hexagons.

4. (e)
The figure rotates 90°CW; the inner element rotates about the main line and turns outwards while the outer element shifts inwards.

5. (d)
The figure rotates through 90°, the two parts get separated along the dividing line; each part gets rotated through 180° and these two parts are joined together by a black circle.

6. (b)
The figure gets laterally inverted and all the arcs get curved in the opposite direction.

7. (d)
The figure rotates through 135°ACW.

8. (b)
The figure rotates 90° CW and the number of straight lines or arcs at the centre increases by one.

9. (c)
The symbols move in the sequence [figure] and the symbol at the encircled position gets replaced by a new one.

10. (e)
The contents of the outer main figure rotate through 45°CW.

11. (b)
The upper part of the figure gets separated along the line and is lost.

12. (c)
The figure rotates 90°CW.

13. (b)
As many pins are introduced inside the figure as the number of sides of the figure. These pins start from the centre of the figure and have their heads pointing towards the sides of the figure.

14. (d)
The black leaf rotates 135°ACW and white leaf rotates 90°ACW.

15. (a)
The RHS element rotates 90°CW and moves to the upper position. The LHS element rotates 90°CW and moves to the lower position.

16. (d)
The set of three pins gets vertically inverted and moves to the lower-right position; the triangle rotates 90°ACW; the third element rotates 45°ACW and moves to the upper-left position. The dot in this element moves to the adjacent portion in a CW direction.

17. (c)
The arc gets divided at one place and the other element gets separated from the arc and gets divided at two places.

18. (c)
The figure is rotated through 90°CW; the triangle is converted to an arrowhead and the zigzag or the lines inside the main figure turn outwards.

19. (a)
The figure is rotated through 180° and a new line segment is added to the figure obtained.

20. (c)
The figure is enclosed in a new figure with one extra number of sides, in such a way that the upper vertex of the two figures coincides.

21. (d)
The two partially shaded circles rotate through 180°.

22. (d)
The number of sides of the central figure increases by one and the number of line segments attached to the central figure decreases by one.

23. (a)
The elements move in the sequence [figure]. The 'S'-shaped element gets laterally inverted; the rectangle rotates through 90°, the '=' symbol rotates through 90°; the arrow gets vertically inverted and the circle gets shaded.

24. (c)
The outer element divides into two equal parts; the lower half is lost; the upper part gets shaded and moves to the lower position. The inner element reduces in size, rotates through 45°, gets unshaded and reaches the upper position.

25. (c)
The upper part of the figure gets vertically inverted.

26. (a)
The figure gets vertically inverted and enlarged.

27. (a)
The outer element rotates 135°CW and the inner element rotates 135°ACW.

28. (b)
The complete figure rotates through 180° and the element that reaches the RHS position rotates further by 90°CW.

29. (b)
The middle and the inner elements get enlarged to become the outer and the middle elements respectively. The outer element gets reduced in size and becomes the inner element.

30. (d)
The number of arcs in the central element increases by one; the number of small ellipses increases by one and these ellipses shift to the inner side of the central element.

31. (d)
The two elements at the ends of the line segment move to the centre of the line segment.

32. (d)
The RHS and the LHS elements interchange positions and the two central elements also interchange positions.

33. (a)
A cone is introduced inside the figure. The arcs in the cone are parts of the main figure.

34. (e)
The right half of the figure is lost and the remaining portion is shaded.

35. (c)
The upper element moves to the lower position, changes its size (reduces in size if initially larger and enlarges if initially smaller), gets laterally inverted and its circular part changes colour (becomes black if initially white and vice-versa). The lower element moves to the upper position, changes its size (reduces in size if initially larger and enlarges if initially smaller), rotates through 180° and its circular part changes colour (becomes black if initially white and vice-versa).

36. (d)
The smaller element gets enlarged. The larger element reduces in size, gets vertically inverted, moves inside the other element and gets attached to its upper end.

37. (e)
The figure gets laterally inverted.

38. (a)
The figure rotates 90°CW, gets reduced in size and also gets enclosed in a figure with one less number of sides.

39. (c)
The figure rotates through 90°ACW.

40. (a)
The figure gets laterally inverted.

41. (b)
The upper element rotates through 180° and its head gets inverted. The lower element gets vertically inverted.

42. (d)
All the arrows reverse their directions.

43. (a)
The existing line segments that join the corners of the squares move to the adjacent corners in an ACW direction and one more line segment appears in the next corner at the ACW end. The shading inside the innermost square changes from dots to slanting lines.

44. (b)
The figure rotates 90°CW and gets laterally inverted.

45. (c)
The two elements interchange positions; the element that reaches the LHS position gets vertically inverted and the element that reaches the RHS position rotates 90°ACW.

46. (d)
The inner element gets enlarged, rotates 45°CW and becomes the outer element. The outer element reduces in size, gets vertically inverted and becomes the inner element.

47. (d)
The half-arrow rotates 90°ACW and gets laterally inverted and moves to the adjacent side of the square boundary in a CW direction. The bent pin rotates 90°ACW and moves to the adjacent side of the square boundary in a CW direction.

48. (c)
One of the arrowheads moves from the lower part to the upper part of the figure above the circle and gets vertically inverted.

49. (c)
The figure rotates through 180°.

50. (a)
The LHS element becomes a closed figure by combining with three similar elements. The RHS element gets reduced in size, turns black and moves to the centre of the other figure.

51. (b)
In the upper and the lower elements, the white part turns black and the black turns white. In the central arrow, one of the arrowheads from the LHS gets laterally inverted and moves to the RHS.

52. (e)
All the diagonals of the figure have been drawn.

53. (e)
The black leaf rotates 135°ACW and the white leaf rotates 135°CW.

54. (e)
The figure rotates through 180° and the head of the arrow attached to the main figure gets inverted.

55. (c)
The line segment along one of the sides of the figure moves two spaces ACW (each space is equal to a side of the figure) and the other element moves three spaces CW.

56. (b)
The four parts at the outer ends of the figure are lost.

57. (c)
The figure rotates through 135°ACW and is placed inside another figure with one more number of sides.

58. (b)
The figure gets laterally inverted and the head of the arrow (the arrowhead may be a 'V' or an arc) gets inverted.

59. (a)
The two elements approach each other and get overlapped.

60. (d)
The elements move downwards along the diagonal and the lowermost element moves to the uppermost position. The triangle and the half shaded rectangle get vertically inverted and the pentagon rotates 90°CW.

❐

Previous Year Questions

1. Select a suitable figure from the Answer Figures that would replace the question mark (?).
[NTSE 2012 - Delhi first stage paper]

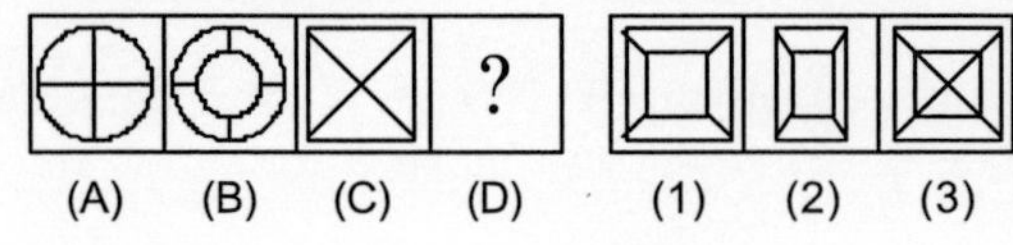

(a) 1 (b) 2
(c) 3 (d) 4
(e) 5

2. Select a suitable figure from the Answer Figures that would replace the question mark (?).
[NTSE 2005 – Karnataka first stage paper]

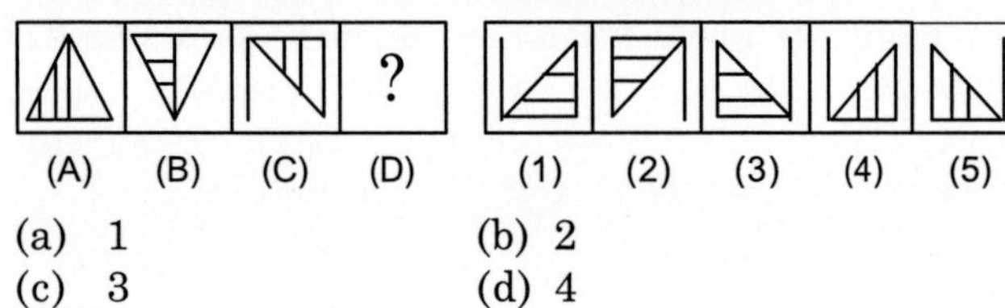

(a) 1 (b) 2
(c) 3 (d) 4
(e) 5

3. Select a suitable figure from the Answer Figures that would replace the question mark (?).
[NTSE 2001 – UP first stage paper]

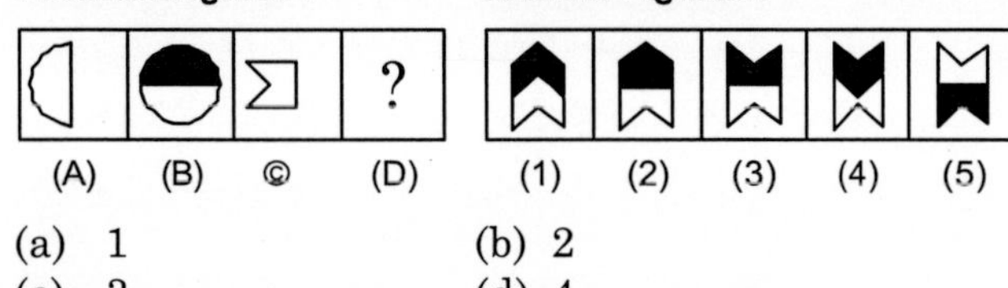

(a) 1 (b) 2
(c) 3 (d) 4
(e) 5

4. Select a suitable figure from the Answer Figures that would replace the question mark (?).
[NTSE 2003– Punjab first stage paper]

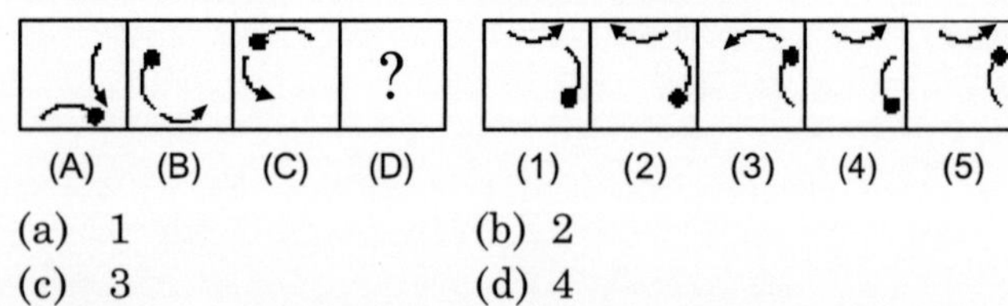

(a) 1 (b) 2
(c) 3 (d) 4
(e) 5

5. Select a suitable figure from the Answer Figures that would replace the question mark (?).
[NTSE 2012 – Punjab second stage paper]

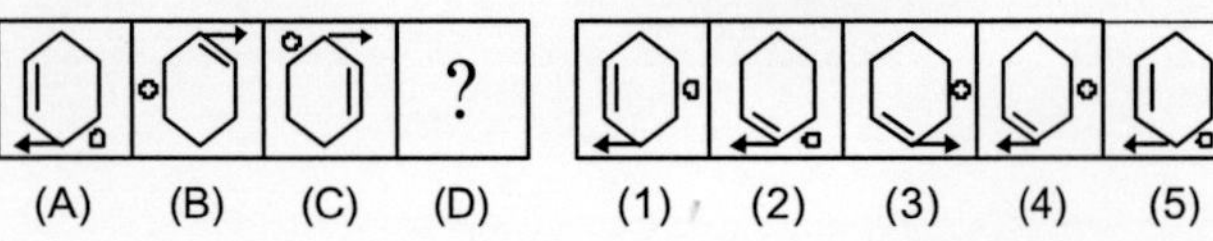

(a) 1 (b) 2
(c) 3 (d) 4
(e) 5

6. Select a suitable figure from the Answer Figures that would replace the question mark (?).
[NTSE 2007 – Andhra Pradesh first stage paper]

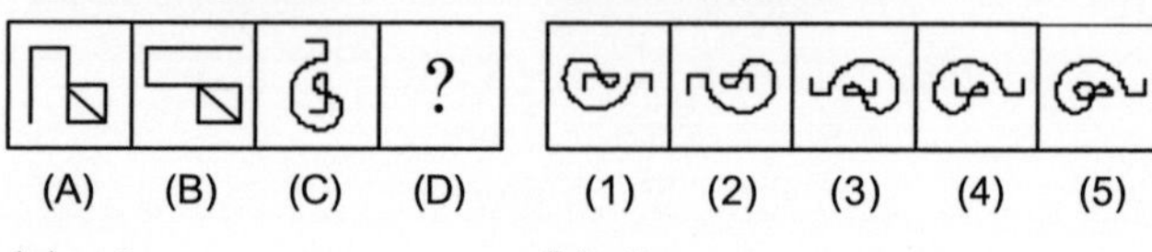

(a) 1 (b) 2
(c) 3 (d) 4
(e) 5

7. Select a suitable figure from the Answer Figures that would replace the question mark (?).
[NTSE 2007 – Bihar second stage paper]

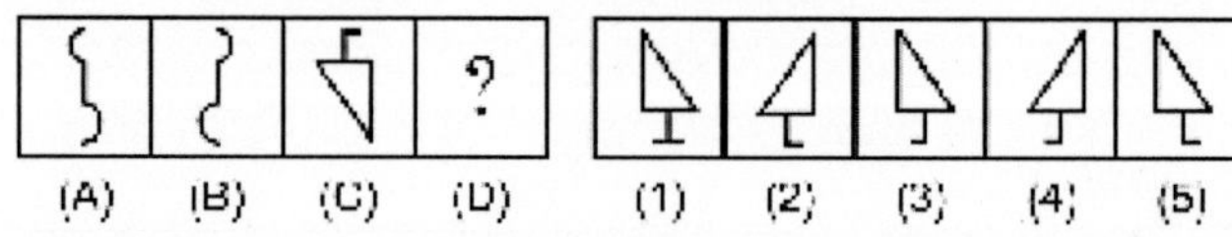

(a) 1 (b) 2
(c) 3 (d) 4
(e) 5

8. Select a suitable figure from the Answer Figures that would replace the question mark (?).
[NTSE 2012– Tamilnadu second stage paper]

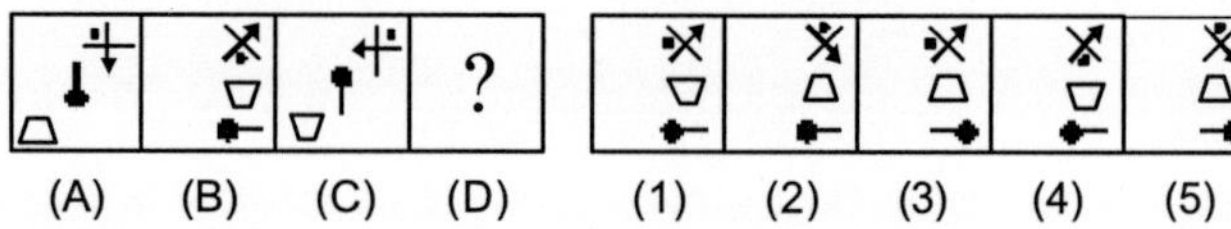

(a) 1 (b) 2
(c) 3 (d) 4
(e) 5

9. Select a suitable figure from the Answer Figures that would replace the question mark (?).
[NTSE 2002 – Bihar second stage paper]

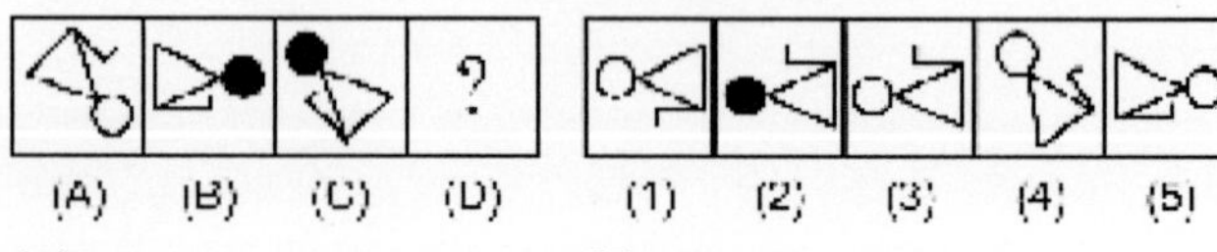

(a) 1 (b) 2
(c) 3 (d) 4
(e) 5

10. Select a suitable figure from the Answer Figures that would replace the question mark (?).
[NTSE 2006 – Haryana second stage paper]

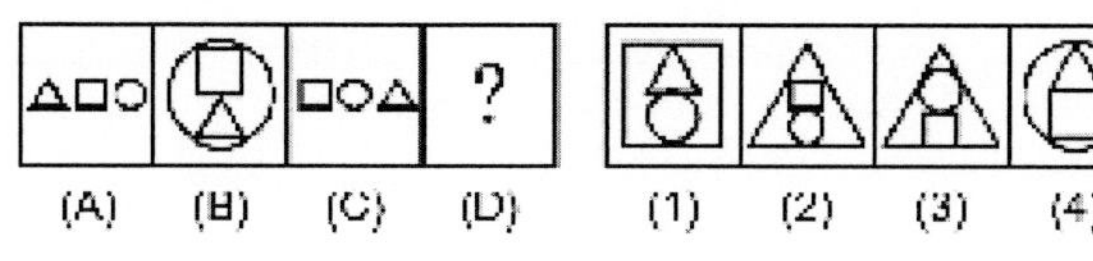

(a) 1 (b) 2
(c) 3 (d) 4
(e) 5

11. Select a suitable figure from the Answer Figures that would replace the question mark (?).
[NTSE 2007 – MP first stage paper]

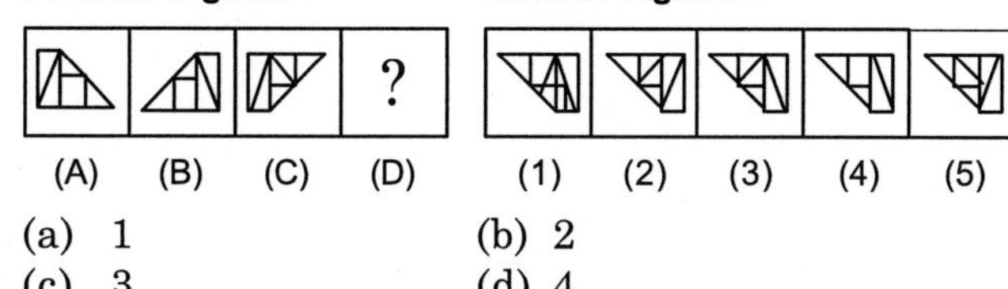

(a) 1 (b) 2
(c) 3 (d) 4
(e) 5

12. Select a suitable figure from the Answer Figures that would replace the question mark (?).
[NTSE 2000 – Delhi second stage paper]

Problem Figures : **Answer Figures :**

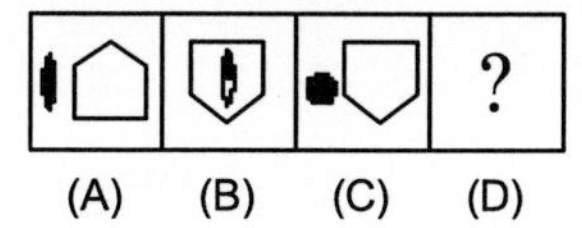

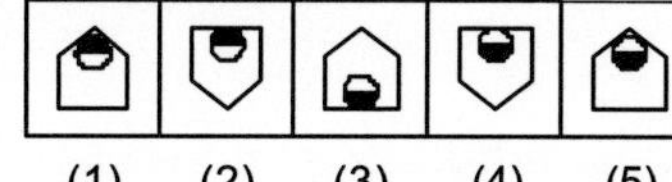

(a) 1 (b) 2
(c) 3 (d) 4
(e) 5

13. Select a suitable figure from the Answer Figures that would replace the question mark (?).
[NTSE 2003 – Uttrakhand second stage paper]

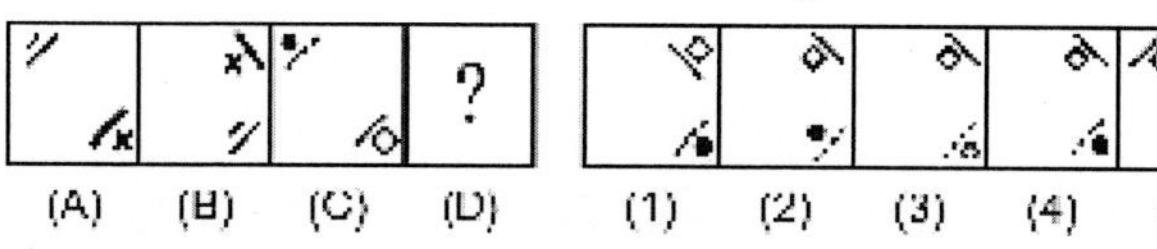

(a) 1 (b) 2
(c) 3 (d) 4
(e) 5

14. Select a suitable figure from the Answer Figures that would replace the question mark (?).
[NTSE 2000– Bihar first stage paper]

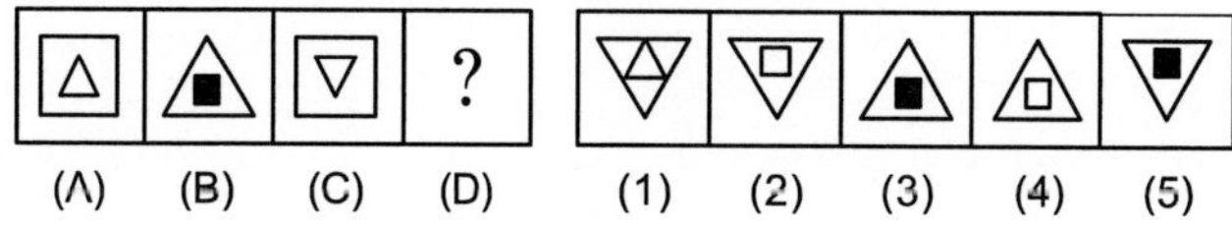

(a) 1 (b) 2
(c) 3 (d) 4
(e) 5

15. Select a suitable figure from the Answer Figures that would replace the question mark (?).
[NTSE 2005 – UP second stage paper]

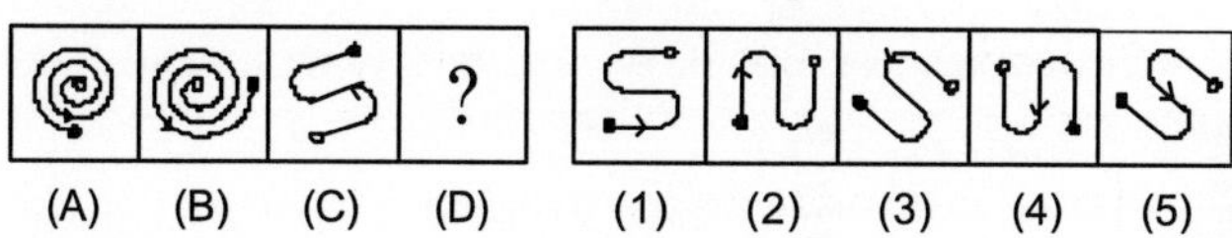

(a) 1 (b) 2
(c) 3 (d) 4
(e) 5

Answer Key

1. (a)	**2.** (a)	**3.** (c)	**4.** (d)	**5.** (d)	**6.** (d)	**7.** (b)	**8.** (c)	**9.** (c)	**10.** (c)	**11.** (c)
12. (a)	**13.** (b)	**14.** (e)	**15.** (e)							

Explanatory Notes

1. (a)
An element similar to but smaller than the outer element appears as the inner element and it hides the parts of the line segments that come under it.

2. (a)
The figure gets vertically inverted and the two vertical lines inside the figure get rotated through 90°.

3. (c)
The figure rotates 90°ACW and its black inverted image is placed over it.

4. (d)
The curved pin rotates 90°ACW and moves to the adjacent side (of the square boundary) in a CW direction. The curved arrow rotates 90° ACW and moves to the adjacent side in a CW direction.

5. (d)
The arrow moves four spaces (each space is equal to a side of the hexagon) in a CW direction while the line segment and the circle move two spaces in a CW direction.

6. (c)
The figure rotates 90°ACW and gets vertically inverted.

7. (b)
The figure gets vertically inverted.

8. (c)
The trapezium gets vertically inverted and move to the middle right position; the pin rotates 90°CW and moves to the lower-right position; the third element rotates 135°ACW.

9. (c)
The figure rotates 45°ACW; the circle changes colour (turns black if initially white and vice-versa). The 'L'-shaped element shifts to the other side of the main figure.

10. (c)
The rightmost element enlarges to become the outer element; the leftmost element becomes the inner-lower element and the middle element becomes the inner-upper element.

11. (c)
The figure gets laterally inverted.

12. (a)
The pentagon gets vertically inverted. The lower half of the black element becomes white and this element moves inside the pentagon and gets attached to its upper end.

13. (b)
The combination of two symbols placed at the lower-right corner, rotates 90°CW and moves to the Upper-right corner. Also, the combination of two symbols placed at the upper-left corner, moves to the lower-right corner.

14. (e)
The inner element enlarges to become the outer element while the outer element reduces in size, turns black and becomes the inner element.

15. (e)
The figure rotates through 90°ACW and the arrowhead shifts closer to the black circle.

❒

UNIT 3

SERIES COMPLETION (Sequence/Order)

In this type of non-verbal reasoning test, two sets of figures are given. The sets are named as:

- Problem figure set
- Answer figure set

The problem figure set consists of four or five figures numberd A, B, C, D, E followed by the answer figure set which contains five figures numbered as 1, 2 , 3, 4 and 5. The four or five figures in the problem figure set follow a sequence and hence, form a series. In other words, the figures in the problem figure set follow a systematic change from left to right. The aspirant has to find the nature of the change and then decide the next figure(from the figures in the answer figure set) subject to the same change. These changes can be of different nature.

Solve Examples

1. Select a figure from amongst the Answer Figures, which will continue the same series as established by the five Problem Figures.

Problem Figures : **Answer Figures :**

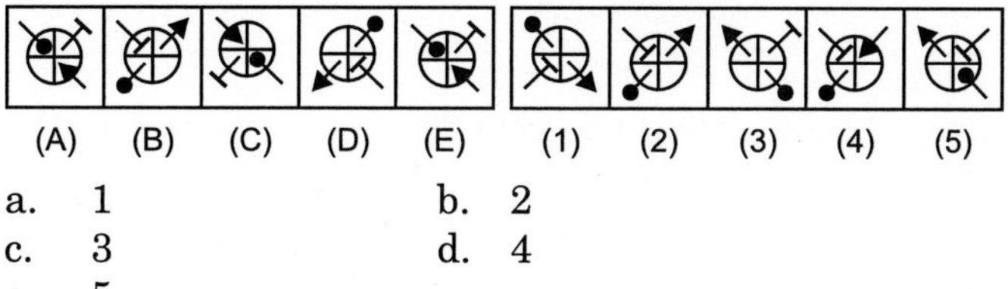

(A) (B) (C) (D) (E) (1) (2) (3) (4) (5)

a. 1 b. 2
c. 3 d. 4
e. 5

Solution: Option (b) is correct.

Explanation:

All the elements move one space ACW (each space is equal to a quadrant of the circle) and get inverted in each step.

2. Select a figure from amongst the Answer Figures , which will continue the same series as established by the five Problem Figures.

Problem Figures : **Answer Figures :**

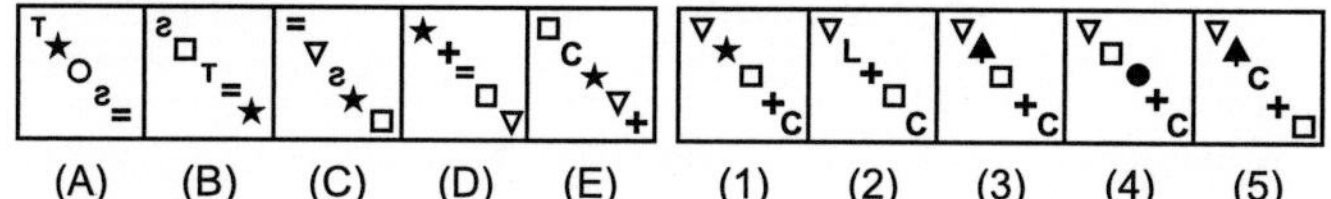

(A) (B) (C) (D) (E) (1) (2) (3) (4) (5)

Solution: Option (c) is correct.

Explanation:

In each step, the symbols move in the sequence  and the symbol that reaches the encircled position gets replaced by a new one.

Multiple Choice Questions

1. Select a figure from amongst the Answer Figures, which will continue the same series as established by the five Problem Figures.

Problem Figures : **Answer Figures :**

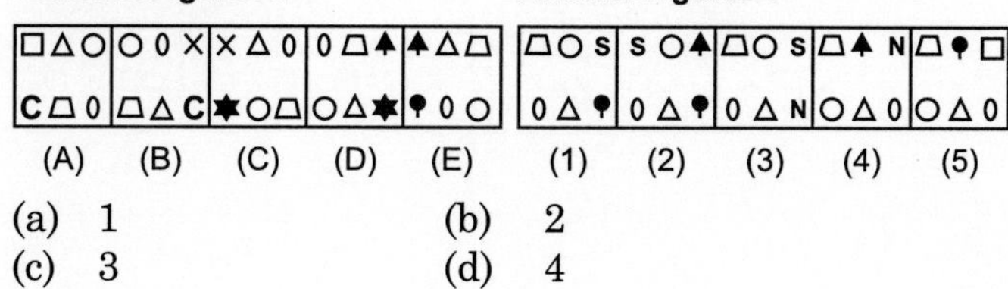

(A) (B) (C) (D) (E) (1) (2) (3) (4) (5)

(a) 1 (b) 2
(c) 3 (d) 4
(e) 5

2. Select a figure from amongst the Answer Figures, which will continue the same series as established by the five Problem Figures.

Problem Figures : **Answer Figures :**

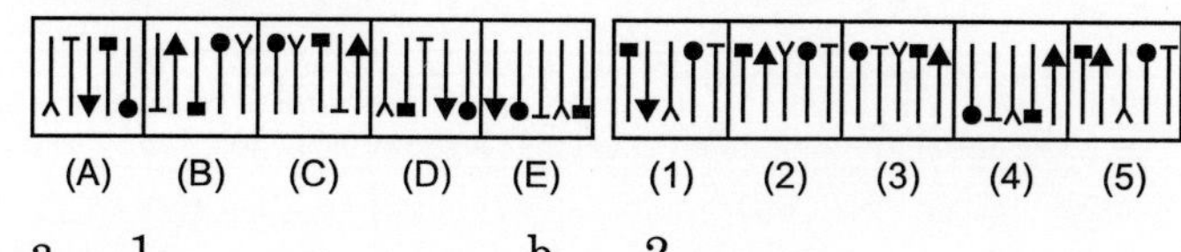

(A) (B) (C) (D) (E) (1) (2) (3) (4) (5)

a. 1 b. 2
c. 3 d. 4
e. 5

3. Select a figure from amongst the Answer Figures, which will continue the same series as established by the five Problem Figures.

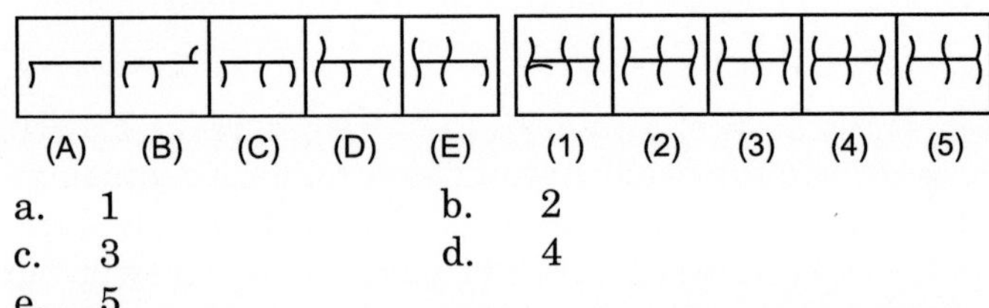

a. 1 b. 2
c. 3 d. 4
e. 5

4. Select a figure from amongst the Answer Figures, which will continue the same series as established by the five Problem Figures.

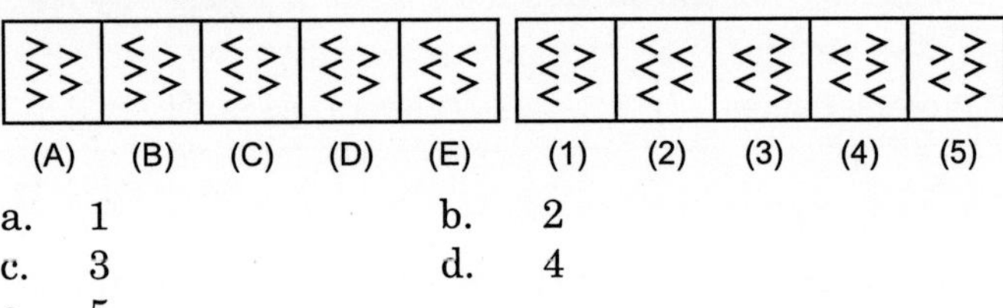

a. 1 b. 2
c. 3 d. 4
e. 5

5. Select a figure from amongst the Answer Figures, which will continue the same series as established by the five Problem Figures.

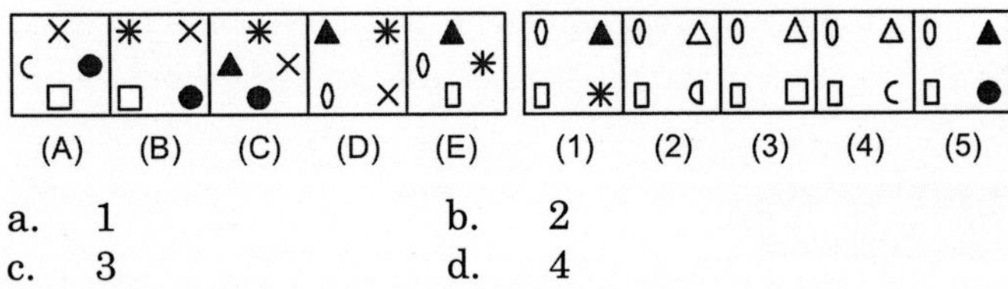

a. 1 b. 2
c. 3 d. 4
e. 5

6. Select a figure from amongst the Answer Figures, which will continue the same series as established by the five Problem Figures.

Problem Figures : Answer Figures :

(A) (B) (C) (D) (E) (1) (2) (3) (4) (5)

a. 1 b. 2
c. 3 d. 4
e. 5

7. Select a figure from amongst the Answer Figures, which will continue the same series as established by the five Problem Figures.

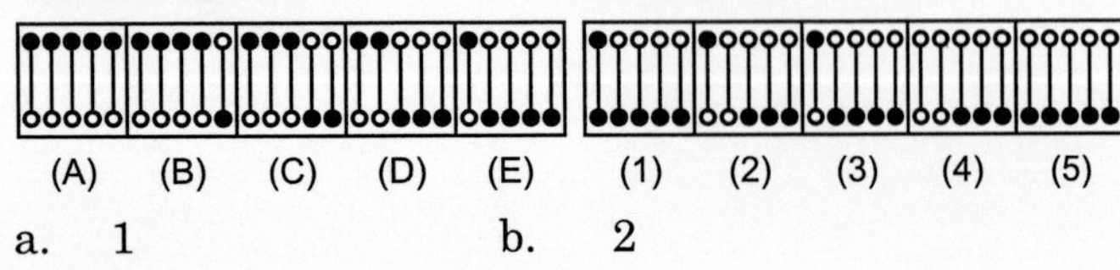

a. 1 b. 2
c. 3 d. 4
e. 5

8. Select a figure from amongst the Answer Figures, which will continue the same series as established by the five Problem Figures.

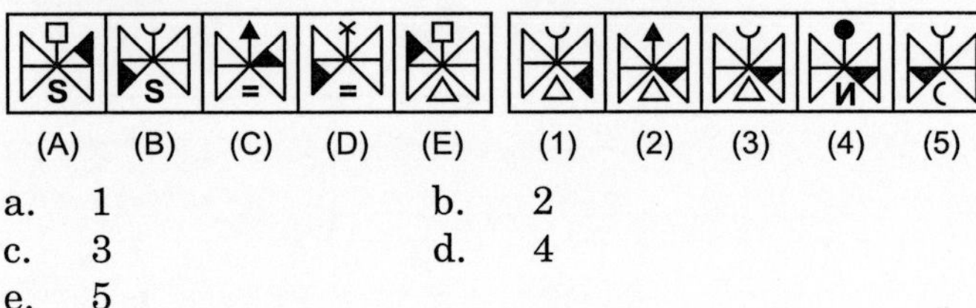

a. 1 b. 2
c. 3 d. 4
e. 5

9. Select a figure from amongst the Answer Figures, which will continue the same series as established by the five Problem Figures.

Problem Figures : Answer Figures :

(A) (B) (C) (D) (E) (1) (2) (3) (4) (5)

a. 1 b. 2
c. 3 d. 4
e. 5

10. Select a figure from amongst the Answer Figures, which will continue the same series as established by the five Problem Figures.

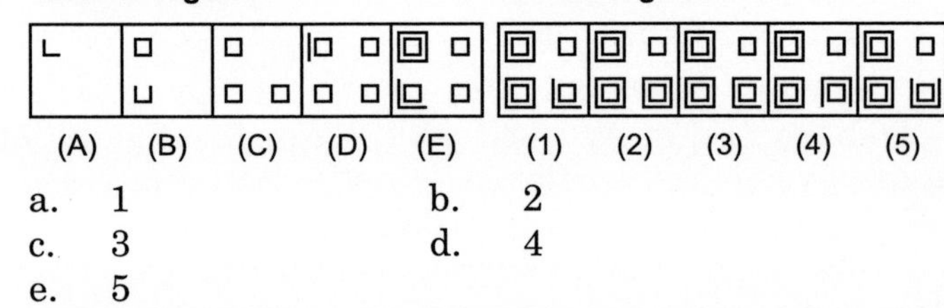

a. 1 b. 2
c. 3 d. 4
e. 5

11. Select a figure from amongst the Answer Figures, which will continue the same series as established by the five Problem Figures.

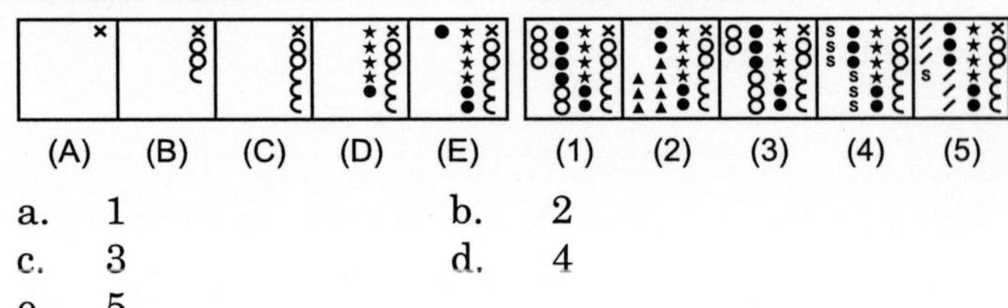

a. 1 b. 2
c. 3 d. 4
e. 5

12. Select a figure from amongst the Answer Figures, which will continue the same series as established by the five Problem Figures.

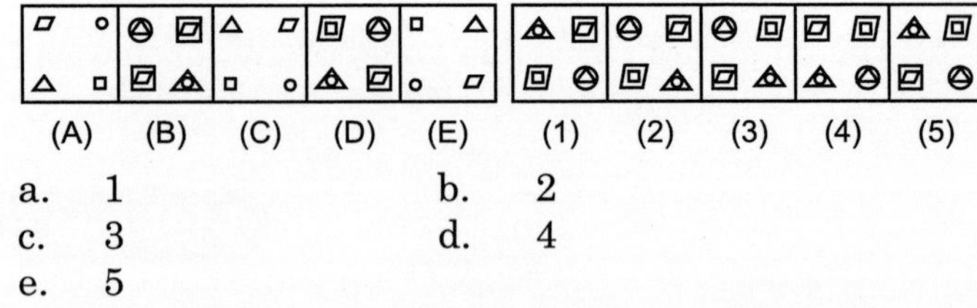

a. 1 b. 2
c. 3 d. 4
e. 5

13. Select a figure from amongst the Answer Figures, which will continue the same series as established by the five Problem Figures.

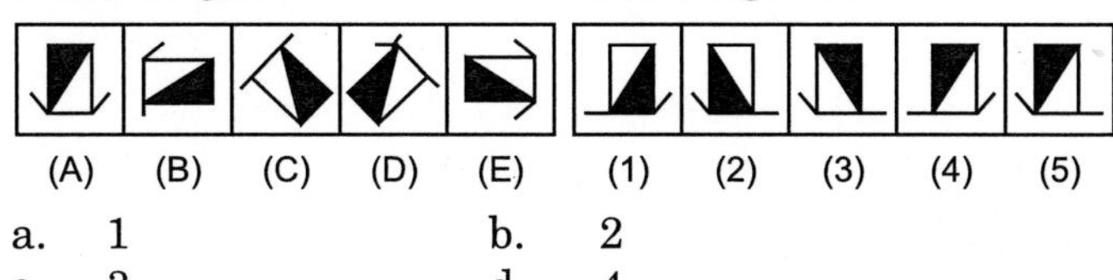

a. 1 b. 2
c. 3 d. 4
e. 5

14. Select a figure from amongst the Answer Figures, which will continue the same series as established by the five Problem Figures.

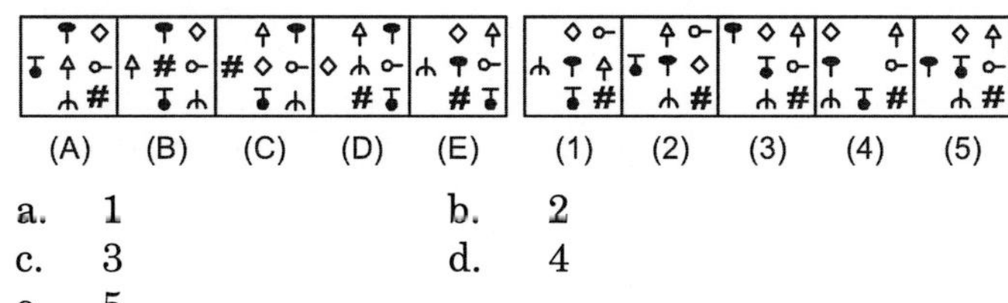

a. 1 b. 2
c. 3 d. 4
e. 5

15. Select a figure from amongst the Answer Figures, which will continue the same series as established by the five Problem Figures.

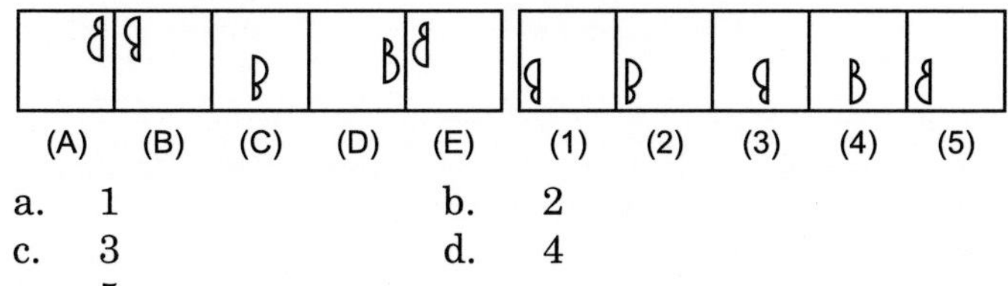

a. 1 b. 2
c. 3 d. 4
e. 5

16. Select a figure from amongst the Answer Figures, which will continue the same series as established by the five Problem Figures.

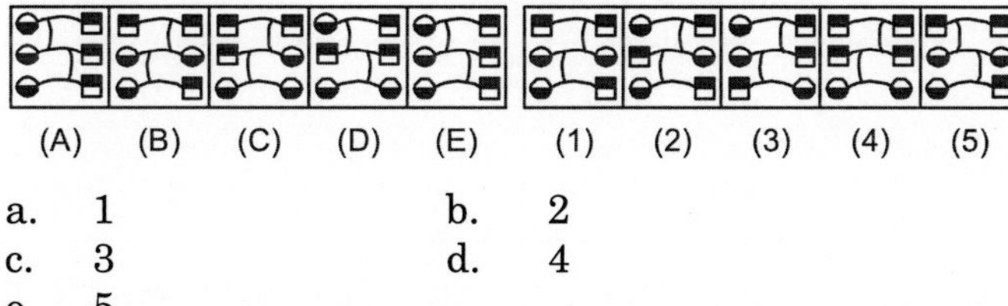

a. 1 b. 2
c. 3 d. 4
e. 5

17. Select a figure from amongst the Answer Figures, which will continue the same series as established by the five Problem Figures.

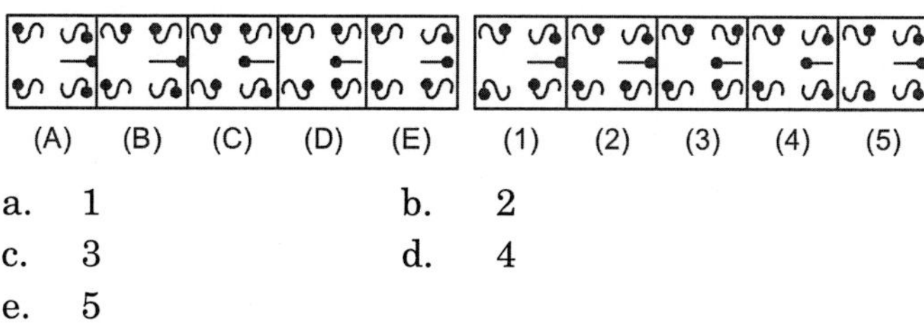

a. 1 b. 2
c. 3 d. 4
e. 5

18. Select a figure from amongst the Answer Figures, which will continue the same series as established by the five Problem Figures.

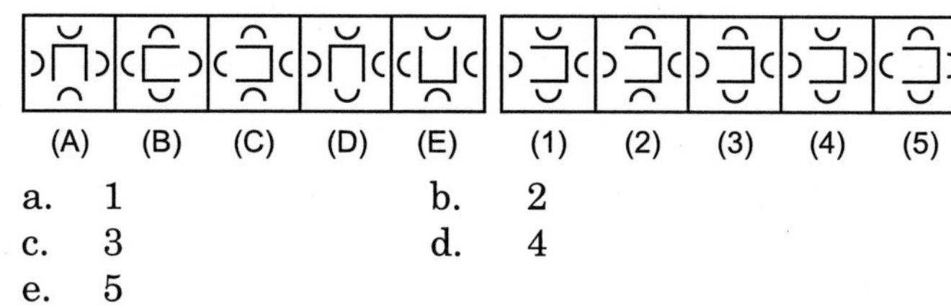

a. 1 b. 2
c. 3 d. 4
e. 5

19. Select a figure from amongst the Answer Figures, which will continue the same series as established by the five Problem Figures.

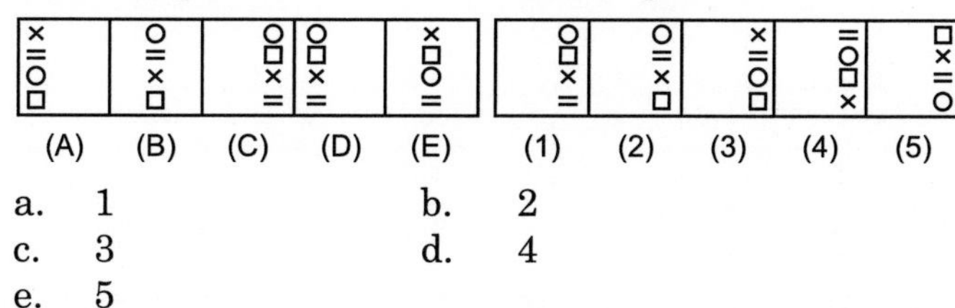

a. 1 b. 2
c. 3 d. 4
e. 5

20. Select a figure from amongst the Answer Figures, which will continue the same series as established by the five Problem Figures.

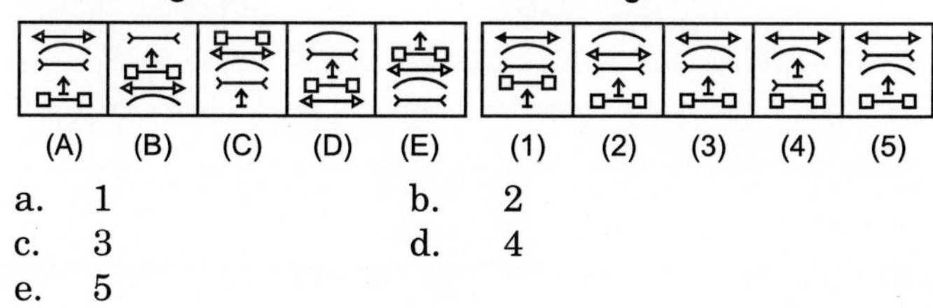

a. 1 b. 2
c. 3 d. 4
e. 5

Answer Key

1. (a)	2. (c)	3. (a)	4. (c)	5. (b)	6. (b)	7. (e)	8. (c)	9. (e)	10. (c)
11. (e)	12. (e)	13. (c)	14. (e)	15. (a)	16. (a)	17. (d)	18. (e)	19. (c)	20. (c)

Explanatory Notes

1. (a)
The elements move in the sequences 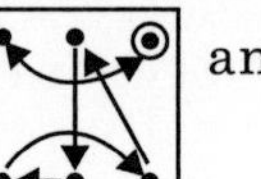 and alternately. Also, in each step, the symbol that reaches the encircled position, gets replaced by a new symbol.

2. (c)
In one step, all the elements get vertically inverted and interchange positions in the sequence . In the next step, the elements interchange their positions in the sequence 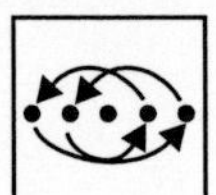 and the third element gets vertically inverted.

3. (a)
Three elements (encircled in the figures below) rotate through 90°CW in each step. This rotation takes place in the following sequence:

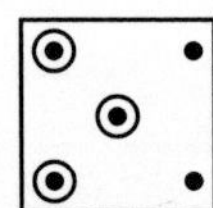
In 1st step

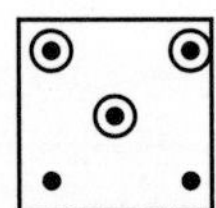
In IInd step

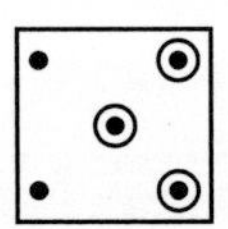
In IIIrd step

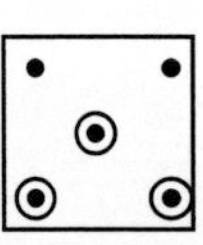
In IVth step

This sequence is repeated to continue the series.

4. (c)
In each step, all the existing arcs get laterally inverted and a new arc is added, which is oriented in a direction opposite to that of the last added arc. The arcs are added at various positions in the following sequences:

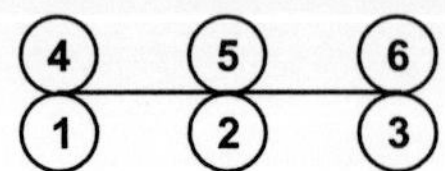

5. (b)
In each step, one of the elements gets laterally inverted.

6. (b)
All the symbols move CW, half the side of the square in each step. The symbols are replaced by new ones sequentially in an ACW direction.

7. (e)
One of the pins gets inverted in each step. The pins get inverted sequentially from right to left.

8. (c)
The shading moves in the sequence as shown in the figure:

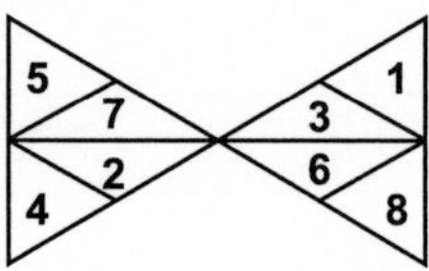

The similar upper element appears in every fourth step. The lower element is replaced by a new element in every second step.

9. (e)
Five line segments are added in each step to complete the squares in an ACW direction.

10. (c)
The number of symbols added sequentially is 3, 2, 5, 2, 7, 2, ... These symbols are added to form a sequence of 1, 2, 3, 4, 5, 6 identical symbols.

11. (e)
Similar figure appears alternately and each time a figure reappears, all the elements move one step CW.

12. (e)
One extra line is added in each step in a set order.

13. (c)
Similar figure reappears in every fourth step and each time a figure reappears, it rotates through 90°ACW.

14. (e)
In one step, the elements move in the sequence 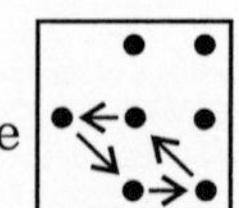 and in the next step, the elements move in the sequence 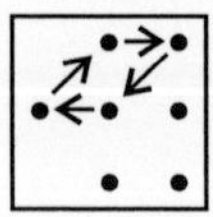 The two steps are repeated alternately.

15. (a)
The symbol gets vertically inverted and laterally inverted alternately. It also moves in ACW direction through distances equal to two half-sides (of square boundary) and three half-sides alternately.

16. (a)
The elements interchange their positions in the orders 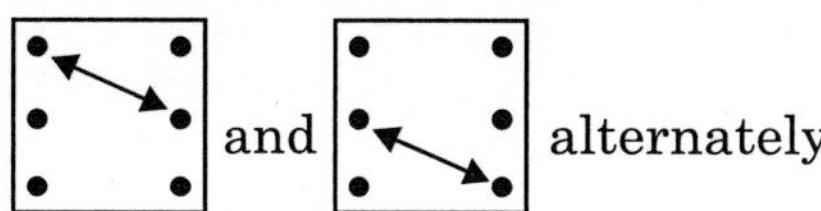 alternately.

17. (d)
The upper-left element gets laterally inverted in first, third, fifth. .... steps; the upper-right element gets rotated through 180° in first, fourth, seventh,.... steps; the lower-left element gets laterally inverted in second, fourth, sixth, ... steps; the lower-right element gets rotated through 180° in third, sixth,... steps and the pin at the middle-right position gets laterally inverted in every second step.

18. (e)
Three and two arcs are inverted alternately. The central element rotates 90°ACW and 180° alternately.

19. (c)
All the elements together move one space to the right in each step and once they reach the rightmost position, then in the next step, they move to the leftmost position. Also, in the first step, the first (uppermost) and the third elements interchange their positions; in the second step, the second and the fourth elements interchange their positions and in the third step, none of the elements interchange positions. These three steps are repeated to continue the series.

20. (c)
In each step, the elements move in the order 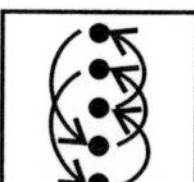.

❒

Previous Year Questions

1. Select a figure from amongst the Answer Figures, which will continue the same series as established by the five Problem Figures.

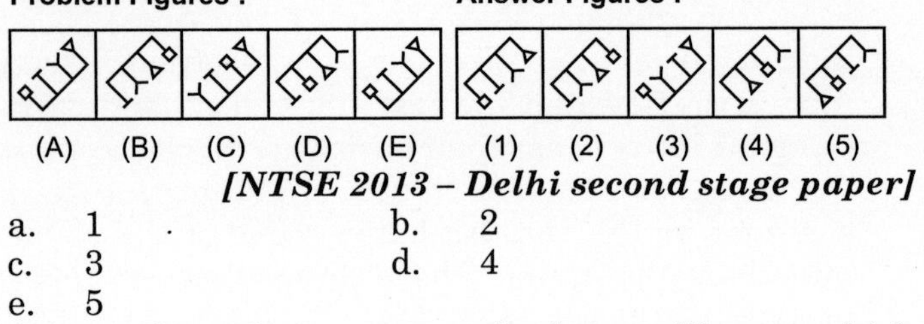

[NTSE 2013 – Delhi second stage paper]

a. 1 b. 2
c. 3 d. 4
e. 5

2. Select a figure from amongst the Answer Figures, which will continue the same series as established by the five Problem Figures.

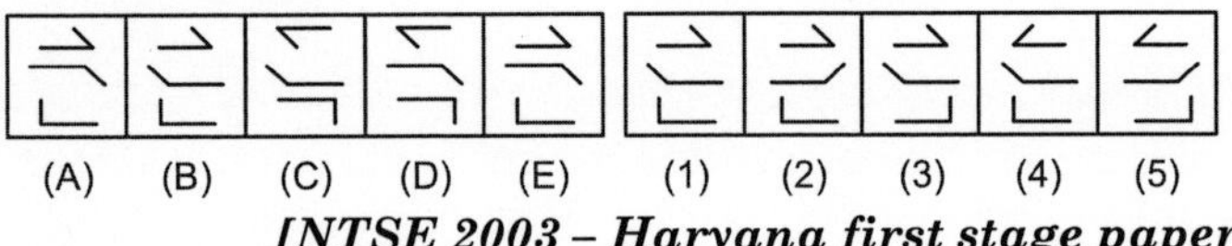

[NTSE 2003 – Haryana first stage paper]

a. 1 b. 2
c. 3 d. 4
e. 5

3. Select a figure from amongst the Answer Figures, which will continue the same series as established by the five Problem Figures.

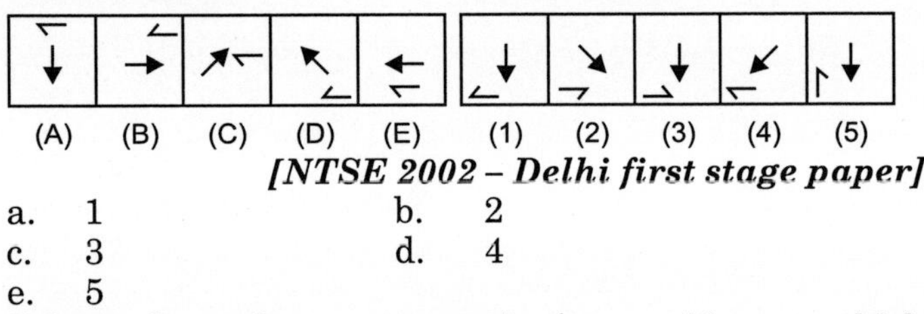

[NTSE 2002 – Delhi first stage paper]

a. 1 b. 2
c. 3 d. 4
e. 5

4. Select a figure from amongst the Answer Figures, which will continue the same series as established by the five Problem Figures.

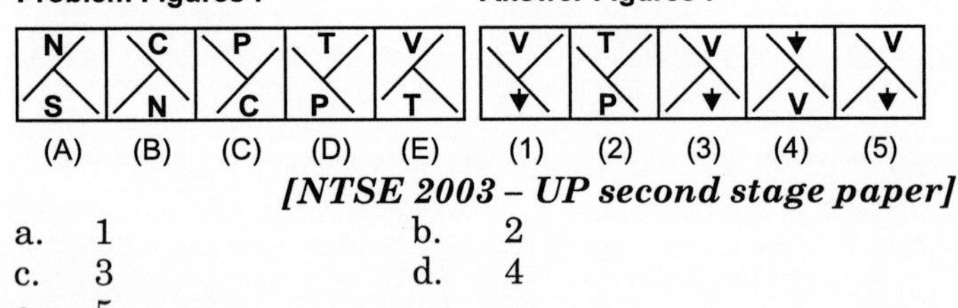

[NTSE 2003 – UP second stage paper]

a. 1 b. 2
c. 3 d. 4
e. 5

5. Select a figure from amongst the Answer Figures, which will continue the same series as established by the five Problem Figures.

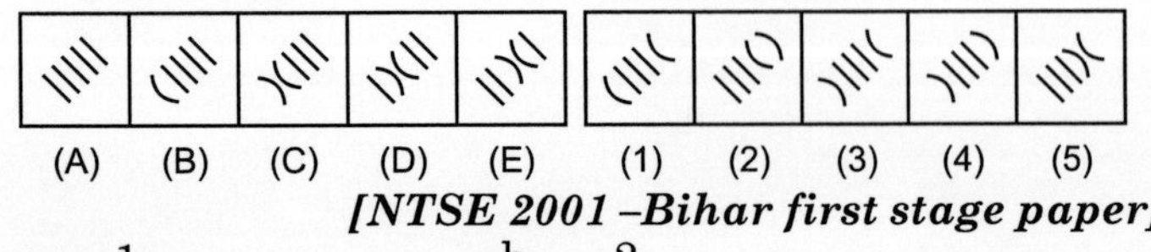

[NTSE 2001 –Bihar first stage paper]

a. 1 b. 2
c. 3 d. 4
e. 5

6. Select a figure from amongst the Answer Figures, which will continue the same series as established by the five Problem Figures.

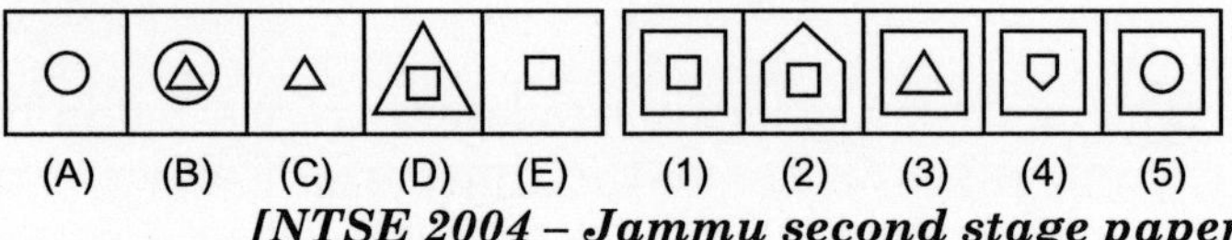

[NTSE 2004 – Jammu second stage paper]

a. 1 b. 2
c. 3 d. 4
e. 5

7. Select a figure from amongst the Answer Figures, which will continue the same series as established by the five Problem Figures.

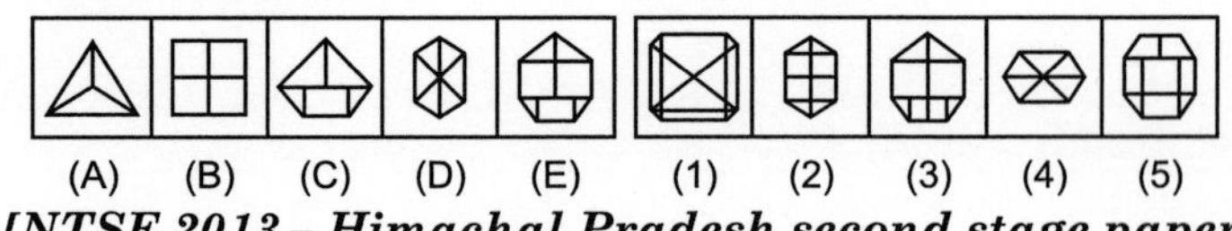

[NTSE 2013 – Himachal Pradesh second stage paper]

a. 1 b. 2
c. 3 d. 4
e. 5

8. Select a figure from amongst the Answer Figures, which will continue the same series as established by the five Problem Figures.

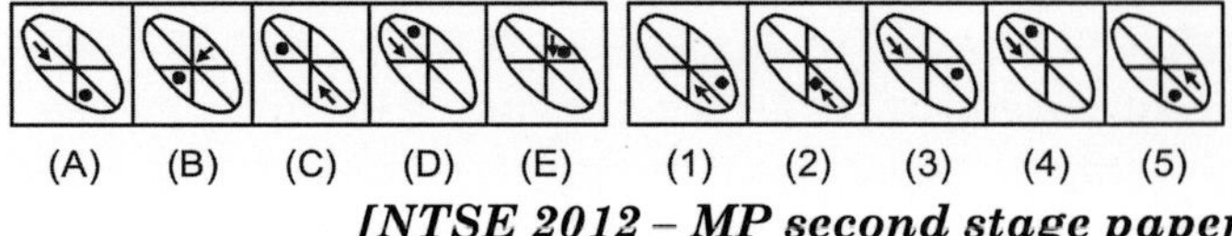

[NTSE 2012 – MP second stage paper]

a. 1 b. 2
c. 3 d. 4
e. 5

9. Select a figure from amongst the Answer Figures, which will continue the same series as established by the five Problem Figures.

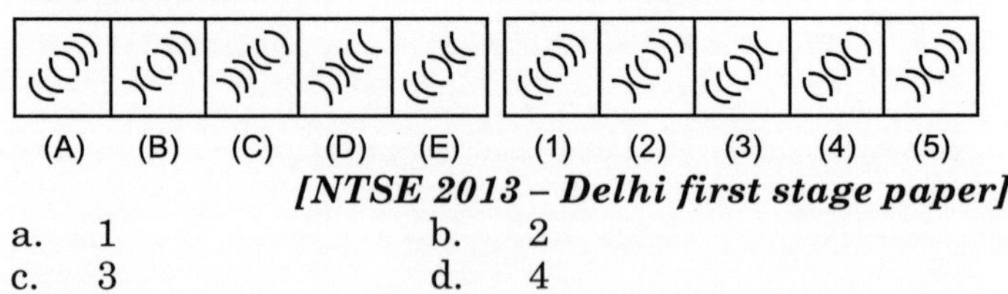

[NTSE 2013 – Delhi first stage paper]

a. 1 b. 2
c. 3 d. 4
e. 5

10. Select a figure from amongst the Answer Figures, which will continue the same series as established by the five Problem Figures.

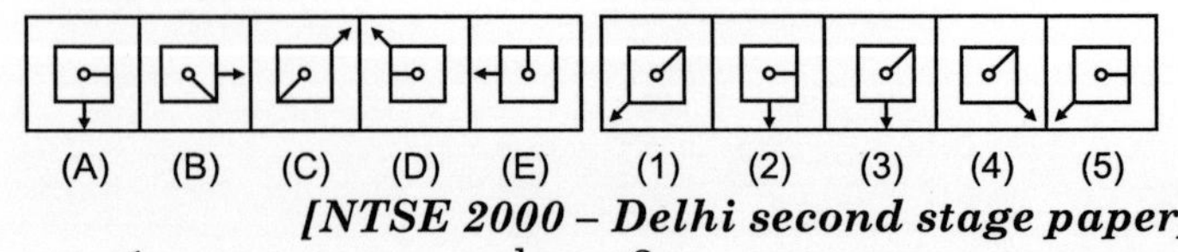

[NTSE 2000 – Delhi second stage paper]

a. 1 b. 2
c. 3 d. 4
e. 5

Answer Key

1. (b)	2. (a)	3. (a)	4. (d)	5. (e)	6. (d)	7. (e)	8. (a)	9. (c)	10. (c)

Explanatory Notes

1. (b)
   Similar figure reappears in every second step. Each time the first figure reappears, the elements interchange their positions in the order : . And, each time the second figure reappears, the elements interchange their positions in the order : .
2. (a)
   In one step, the middle element rotates through 180° and in the next step, the other two elements rotate through 180°. The two steps are repeated alternately.
3. (a)
   The central arrow rotates 90°ACW and 45°CW alternately. The half-arrow moves half-a-side of the square boundary in a CW direction and its head turns to the other side of the line in each step.
4. (d)
   The 'T' shaped large element rotates 90°CW in each step. The two small symbols interchange their positions and the symbol that reaches the upper position gets replaced by a new one.
5. (e)
   In the first step, the lowermost line segment is converted into a curve. In the second step, the second line segment also gets converted into a curve and the existing curve is inverted. In each subsequent step, all the elements (line segments and curves) move in the sequence 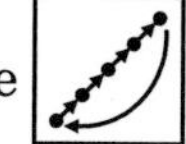.
6. (d)
   In one step, the existing element enlarges and a new element appears inside this element. In the next step, the outer element is lost.
7. (e)
   The number of parts increases by one along with the number of sides in the figure.
8. (a)
   In each step, the dot moves one space CW and the arrow moves two spaces CW.
9. (c)
   One arc and four arcs get inverted alternately.
10. (c)
    The pin rotates 45° CW and 90° CW alternately and moves one space (each space is equal to half-a-side of the square) and two spaces CW alternately. The arrow rotates 90°ACW and 45°ACW alternately and moves two spaces and one space.

UNIT 4

Figure Formation and Analysis

In this chapter, the problems related to the figure formation and their analysis are given. The type of questions asked on the figure formation are as follows :

(a) Formation of a particular figure from the given parts.
(b) Fragmenting the given figure into simple parts.
(c) Analysis of patterns in view of similar figures.
(d) Rotation of identical figures
(e) Analysing various rearrangement of the given patterns or figures. A few examples will clarify the concept.

Solved Examples

1. Find out which of the figures (1), (2), (3) and (4) can be formed from the pieces given in figure (X).

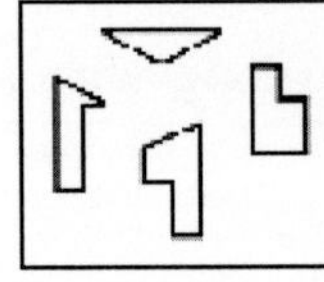
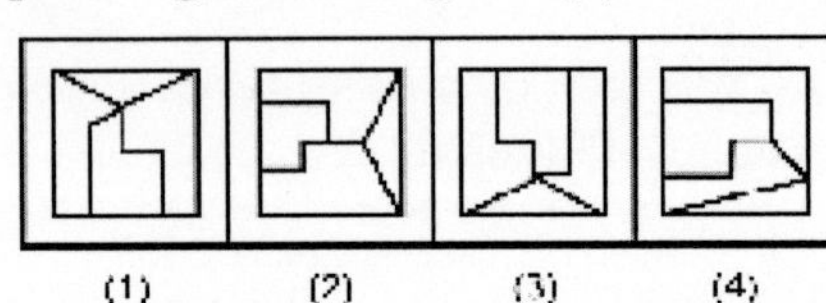

(a) 1 (b) 2
(c) 3 (d) 4

Solution: Option (c) is correct.

2. Find out which of the figures (1), (2), (3) and (4) can be formed from the pieces given in figure (X).

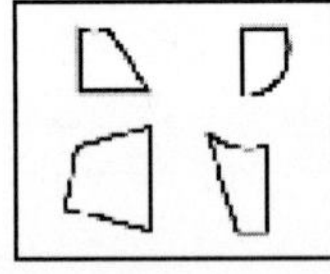
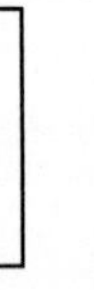
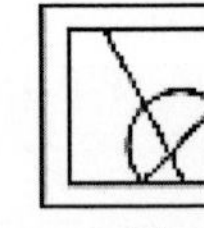
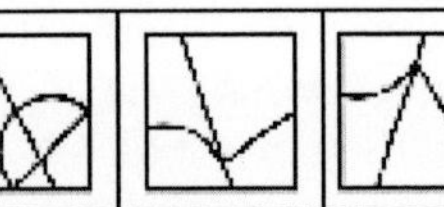
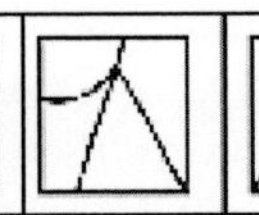
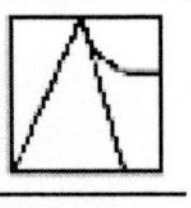

(a) 1 (b) 2
(c) 3 (d) 4

Solution: Option (b) is correct.

3. Select the alternative in which the specified components of the key figure (X) are found.

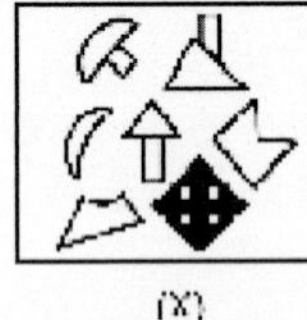
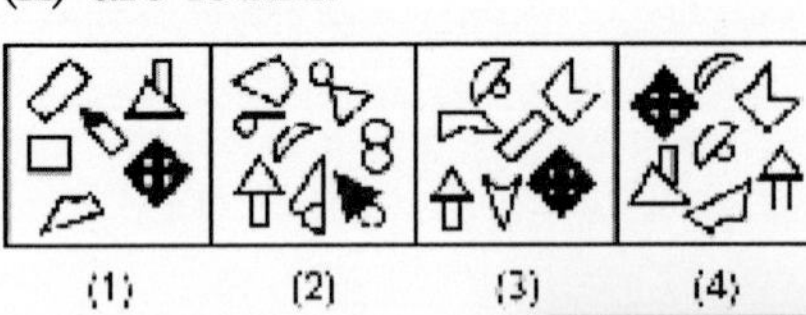

(a) 1 (b) 2
(c) 3 (d) 4

Solution: Option d) is correct.

4. Find out how will the key figure (X) look like after rotation.

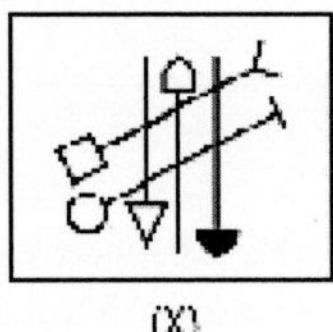
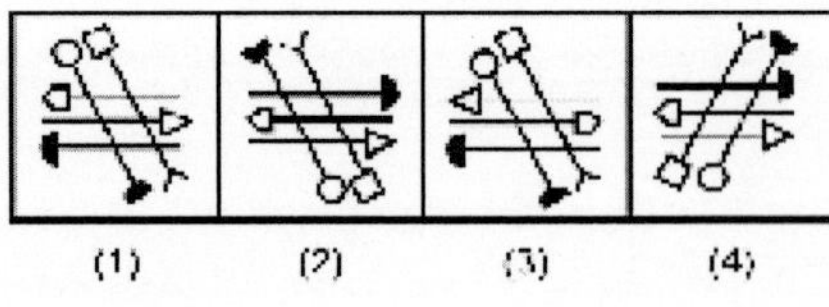

(a) 1 (b) 2
(c) 3 (d) 4

Solution: Option (c) is correct.

5. Find out how will the key figure (X) look like after rotation.

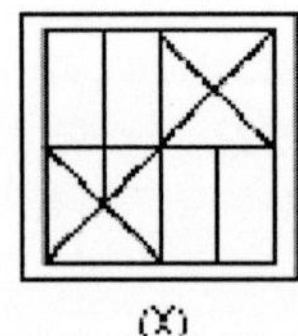
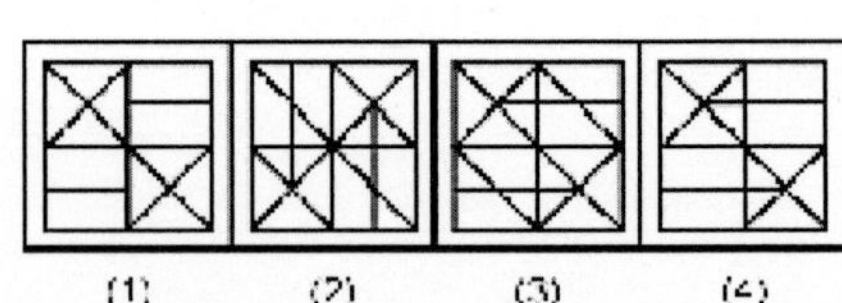

(a) 1 (b) 2
(c) 3 (d) 4

Solution: Option d) is correct.

Multiple Choice Questions

1. Find out which of the figures (1), (2), (3) and (4) can be formed from the pieces given in figure (X).

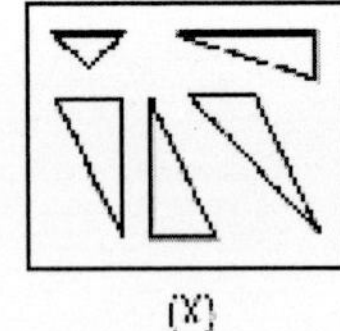
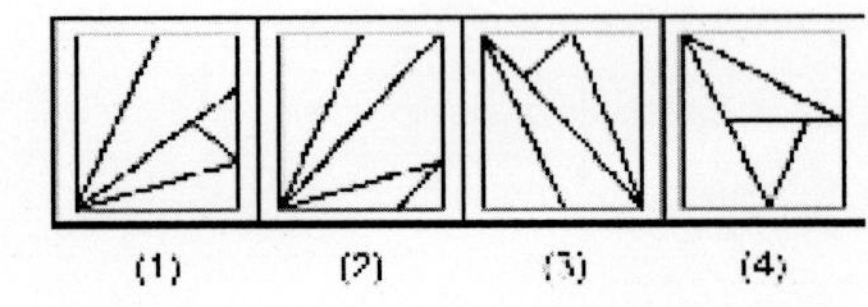

(a) 1 (b) 2
(c) 3 (d) 4

2. Find out which of the figures (1), (2), (3) and (4) can be formed from the pieces given in figure (X).

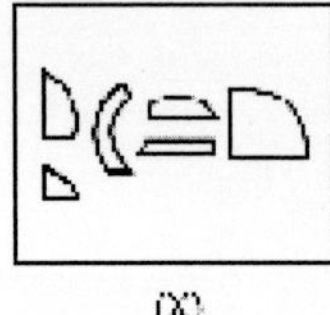
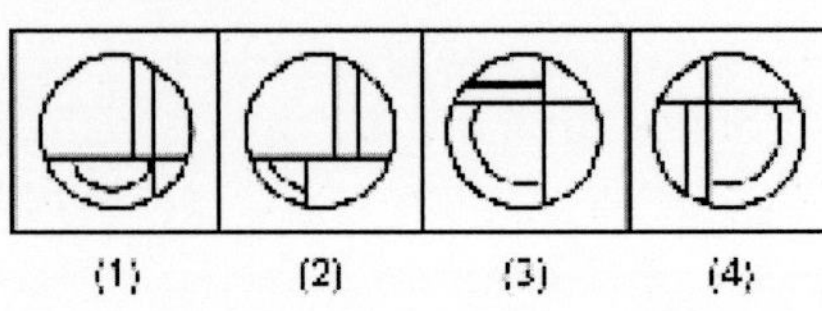

(a) 1 (b) 2
(c) 3 (d) 4

3. Find out which of the figures (1), (2), (3) and (4) can be formed from the pieces given in figure (X).

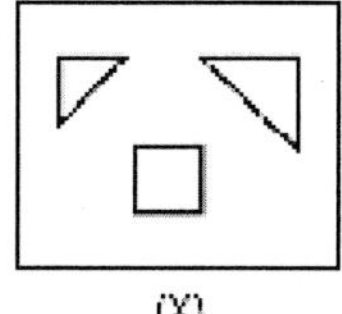
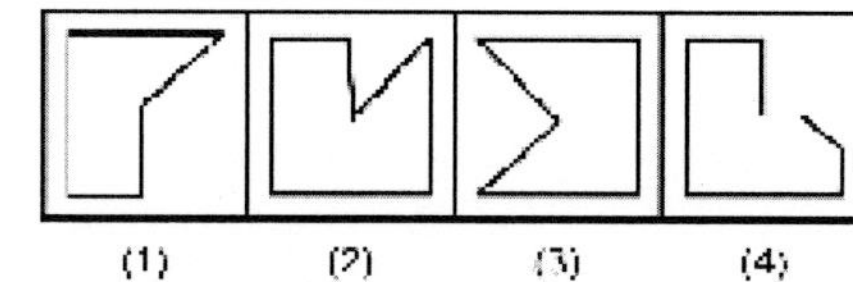

(a) 1 (b) 2
(c) 3 (d) 4

4. Find out which of the figures (1), (2), (3) and (4) can be formed from the pieces given in figure (X).

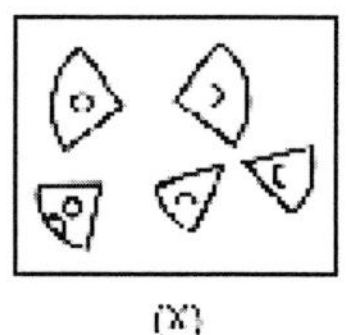
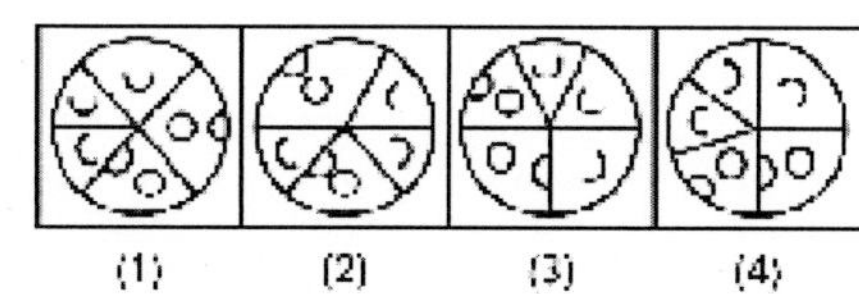

(a) 1 (b) 2
(c) 3 (d) 4

5. Find out which of the figures (1), (2), (3) and (4) can be formed from the pieces given in figure (X).

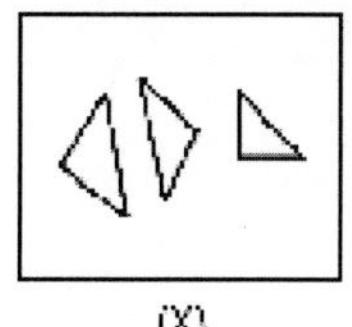
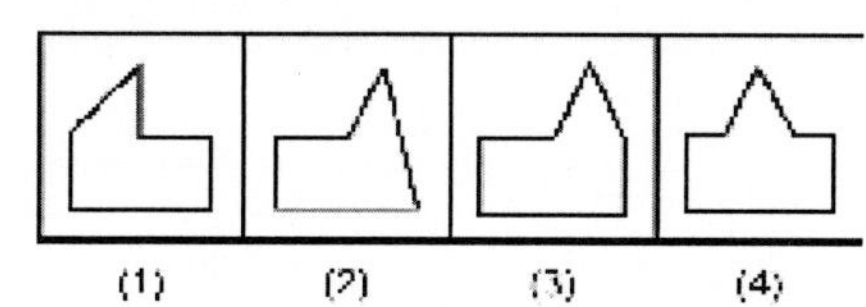

(a) 1 (b) 2
(c) 3 (d) 4

6. Find out which of the figures (1), (2), (3) and (4) can be formed from the pieces given in figure (X).

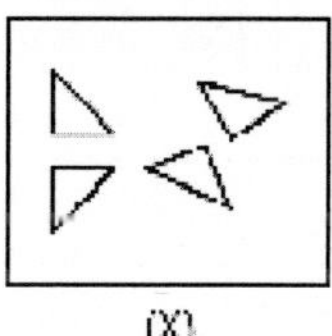
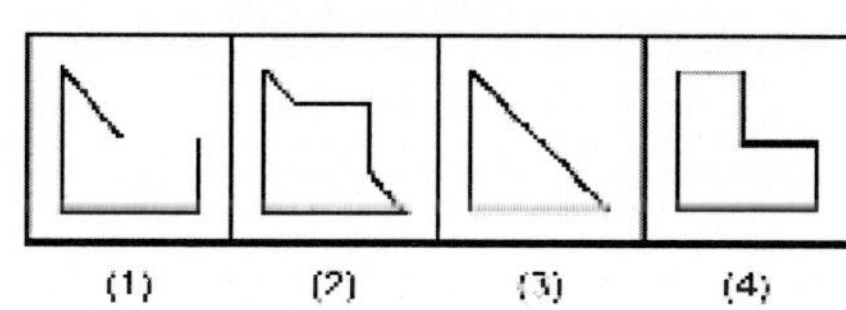

(a) 1 (b) 2
(c) 3 (d) 4

7. Find out which of the figures (1), (2), (3) and (4) can be formed from the pieces given in figure (X).

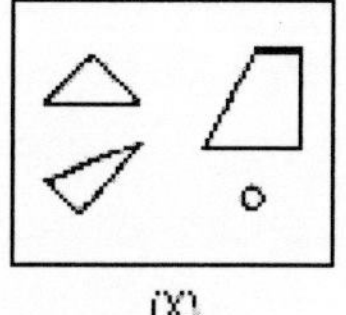
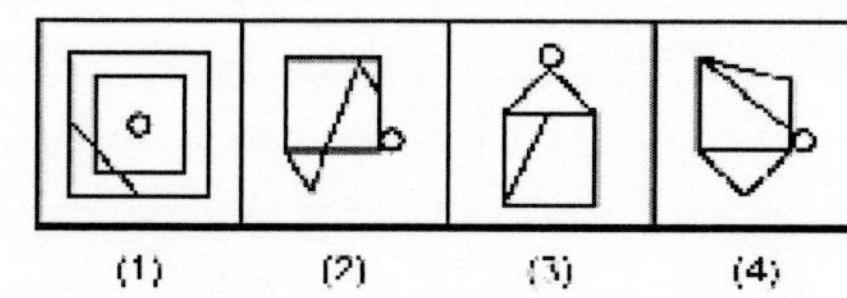

(a) 1 (b) 2
(c) 3 (d) 4

8. Find out which of the figures (1), (2), (3) and (4) can be formed from the pieces given in figure (X).

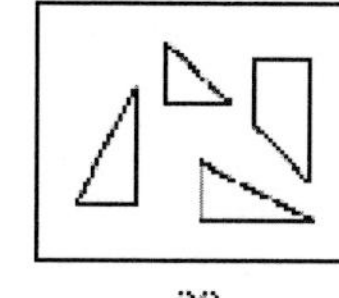
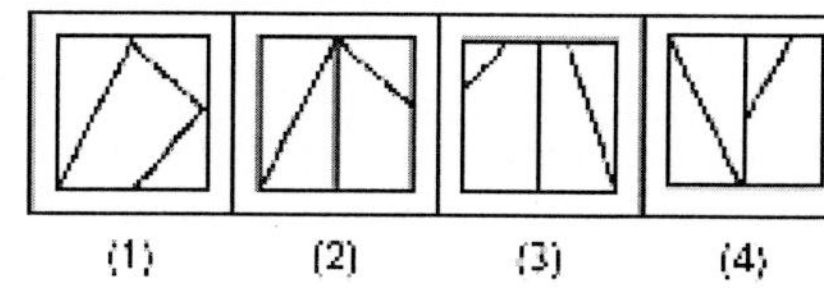

(a) 1 (b) 2
(c) 3 (d) 4

9. Find out which of the figures (1), (2), (3) and (4) can be formed from the pieces given in figure (X).

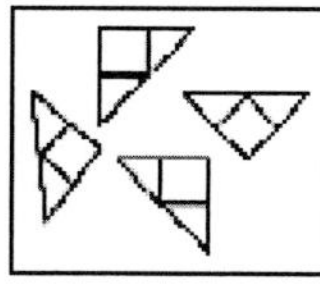
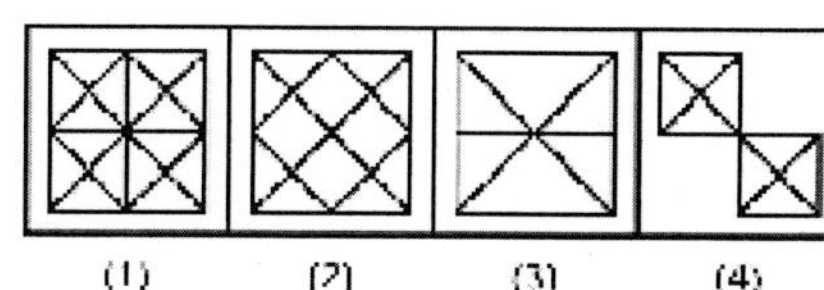

(a) 1 (b) 2
(c) 3 (d) 4

10. Find out which of the figures (1), (2), (3) and (4) can be formed from the pieces given in figure (X).

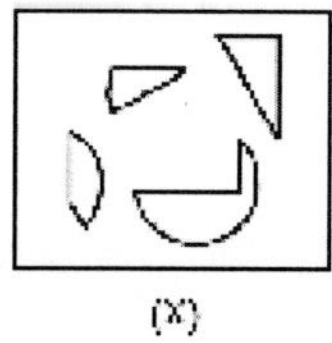
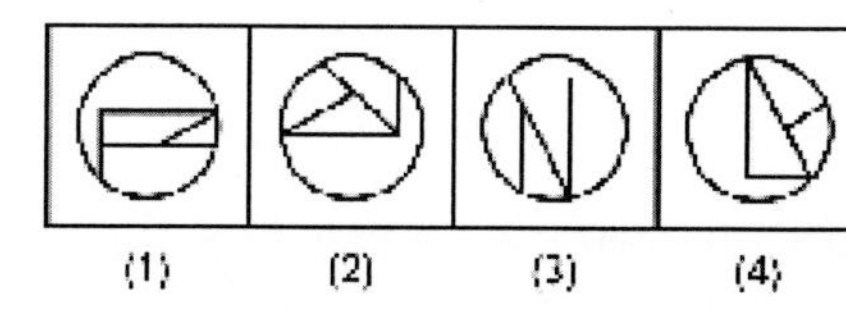

(a) 1 (b) 2
(c) 3 (d) 4

11. Select the alternative in which the specified components of the key figure (X) are found.

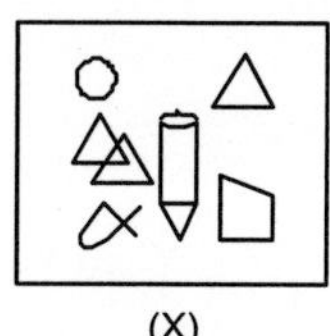
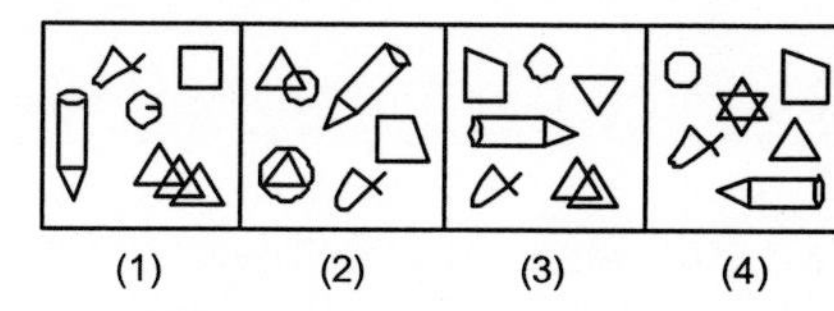

(a) 1 (b) 2
(c) 3 (d) 4

12. Select the alternative in which the specified components of the key figure (X) are found.

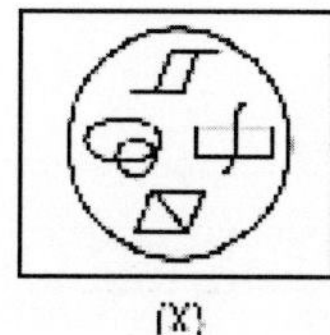
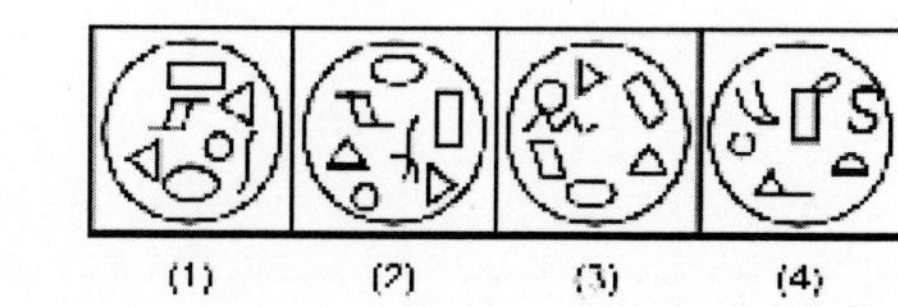

(a) 1 (b) 2
(c) 3 (d) 4

13. Select the alternative in which the specified components of the key figure (X) are found.

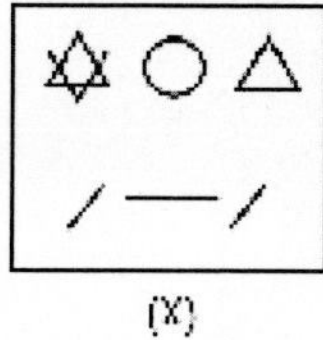
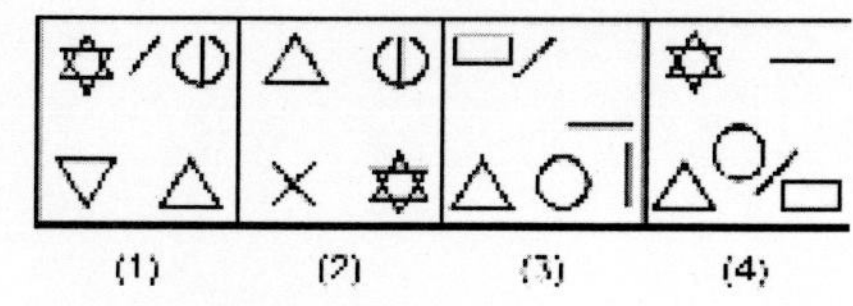

(a) 1 (b) 2
(c) 3 (d) 4

14. Select the alternative in which the specified components of the key figure (X) are found.

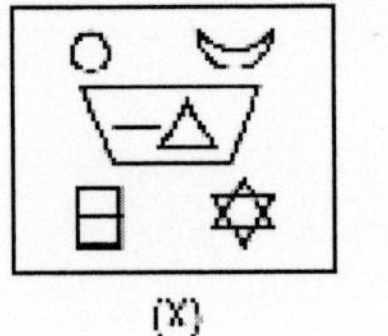

(X)

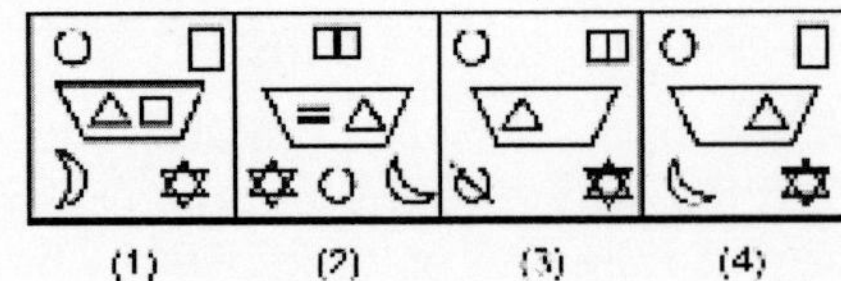

(1) (2) (3) (4)

(a) 1 (b) 2
(c) 3 (d) 4

15. Select the alternative in which the specified components of the key figure (X) are found.

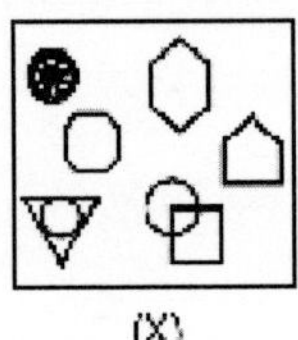

(X)

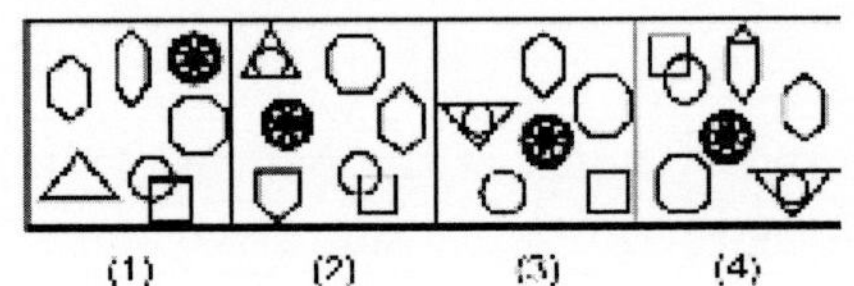

(1) (2) (3) (4)

(a) 1 (b) 2
(c) 3 (d) 4

16. Find out how will the key figure (X) look like after rotation.

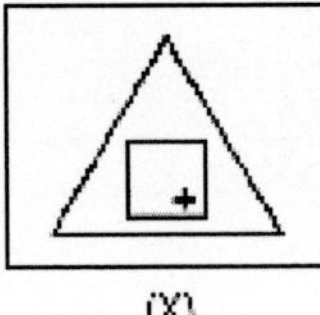

(X)

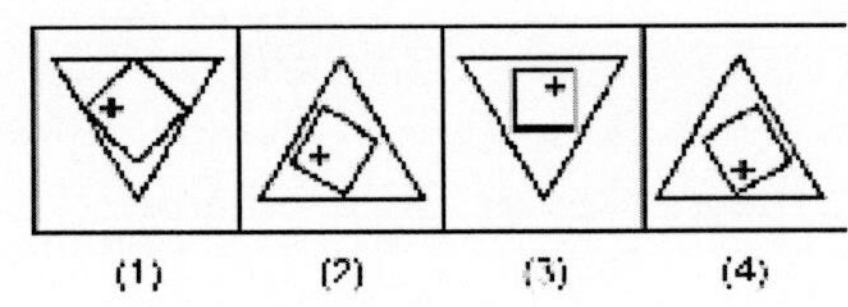

(1) (2) (3) (4)

(a) 1 (b) 2
(c) 3 (d) 4

17. Find out how will the key figure (X) look like after rotation.

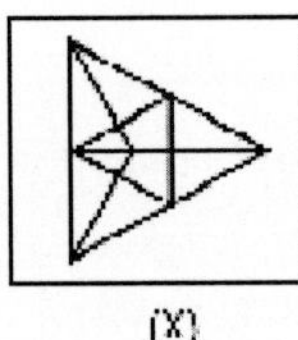

(X)

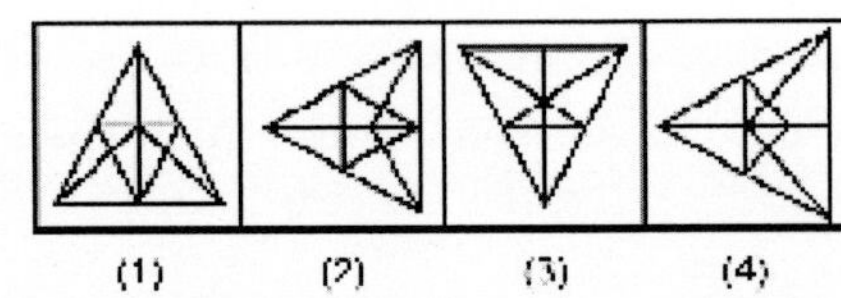

(1) (2) (3) (4)

(a) 1 (b) 2
(c) 3 (d) 4

18. Find out how will the key figure (X) look like after rotation.

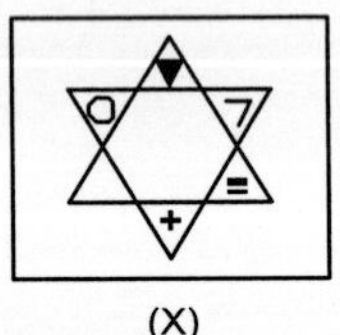

(X)

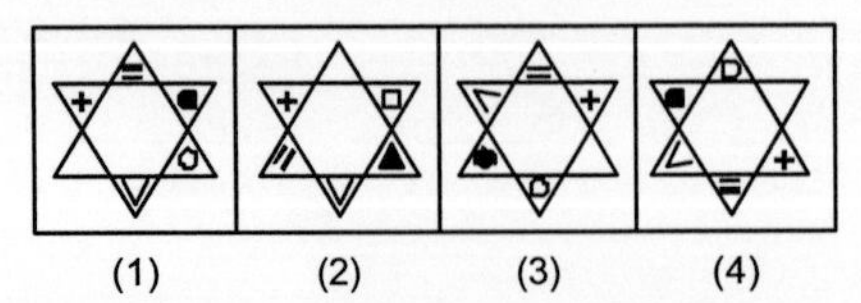

(1) (2) (3) (4)

(a) 1 (b) 2
(c) 3 (d) 4

19. Find out how will the key figure (X) look like after rotation.

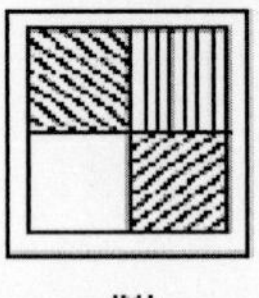

(X)

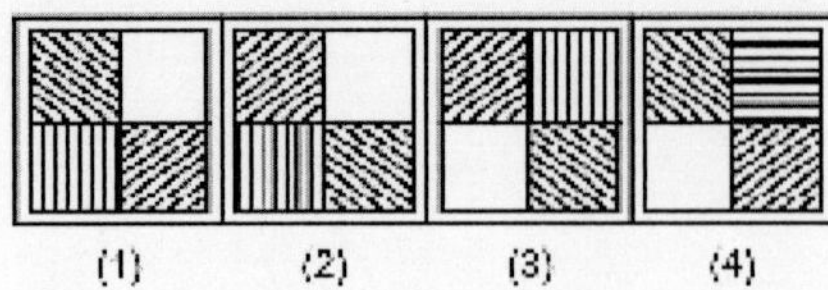

(1) (2) (3) (4)

(a) 1 (b) 2
(c) 3 (d) 4

20. Find out how will the key figure (X) look like after rotation.

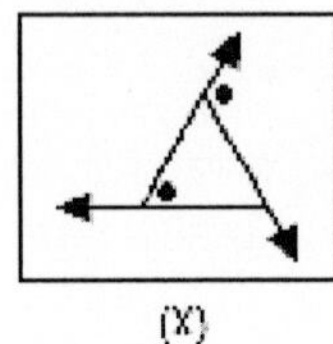

(X)

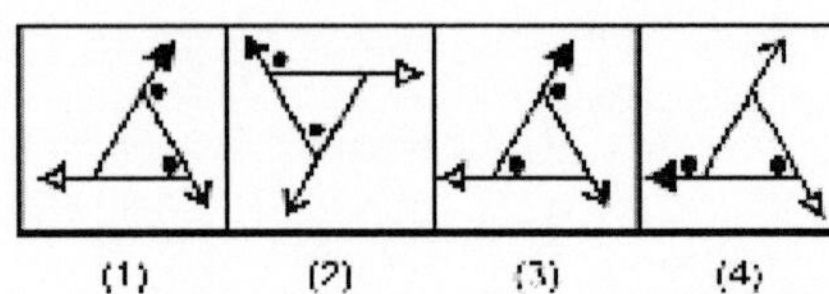

(1) (2) (3) (4)

(a) 1 (b) 2
(c) 3 (d) 4

21. Find out how will the key figure (X) look like after rotation.

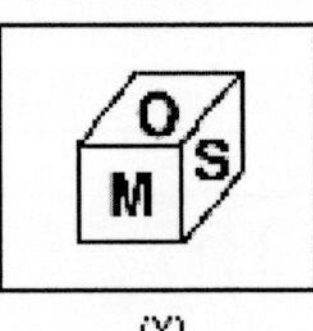

(X)

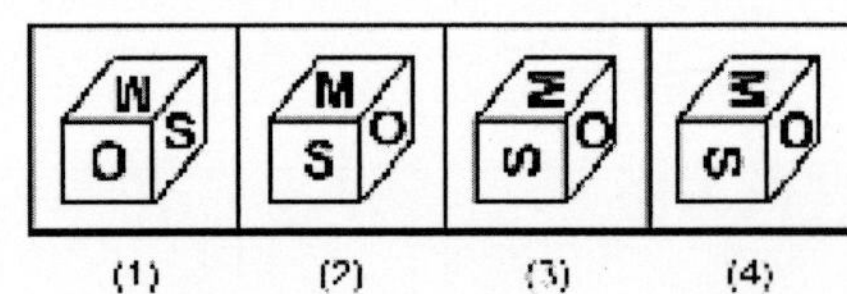

(1) (2) (3) (4)

(a) 1 (b) 2
(c) 3 (d) 4

22. Find out how will the key figure (X) look like after rotation.

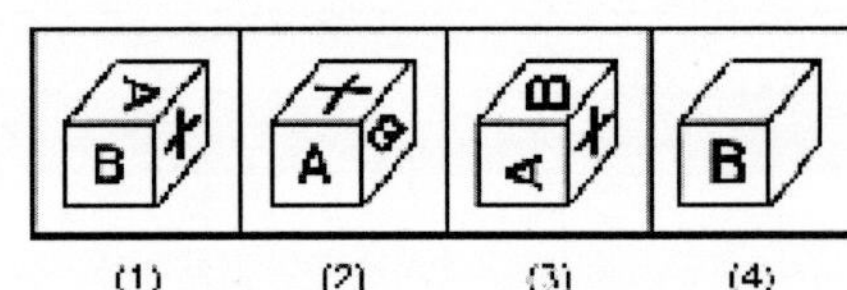

(X) (1) (2) (3) (4)

(a) 1 (b) 2
(c) 3 (d) 4

23. Find out how will the key figure (X) look like after rotation.

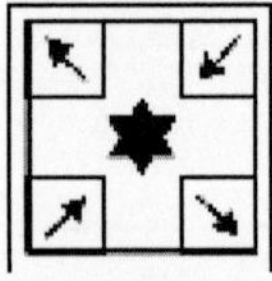

(X)

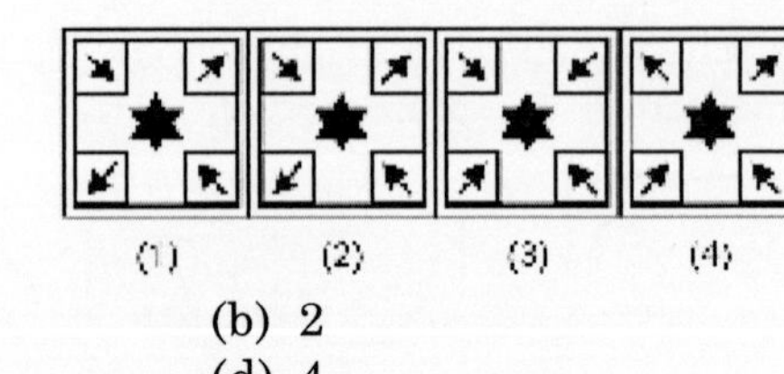

(1) (2) (3) (4)

(a) 1 (b) 2
(c) 3 (d) 4

24. Find out how will the key figure (X) look like after rotation.

(X)

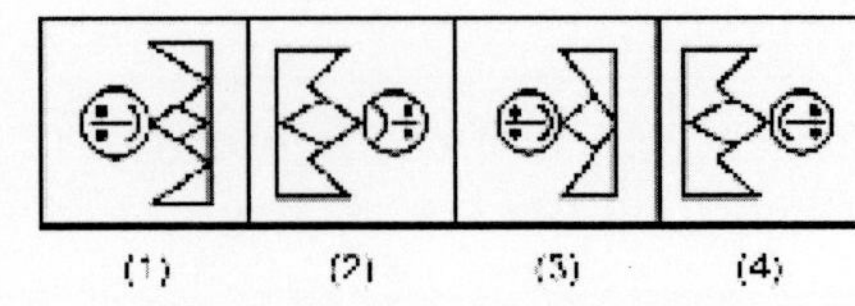

(1) (2) (3) (4)

(a) 1 (b) 2
(c) 3 (d) 4

25. Find out how will the key figure (X) look like after rotation.

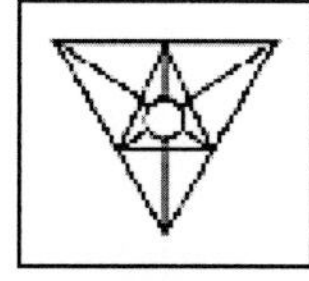
(X)

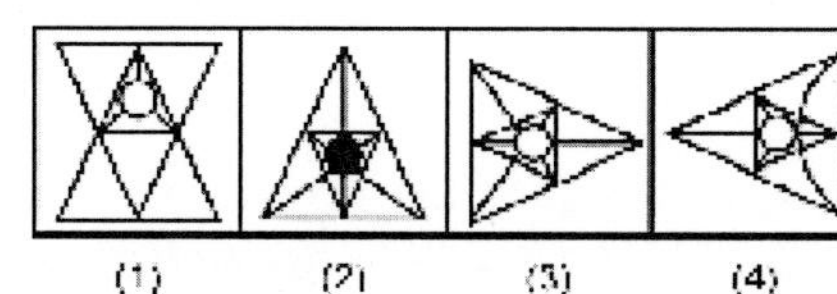
(1) (2) (3) (4)

(a) 1 (b) 2
(c) 3 (d) 4

26. Find out which figure is the rearrangement of the parts of the given figure (X).

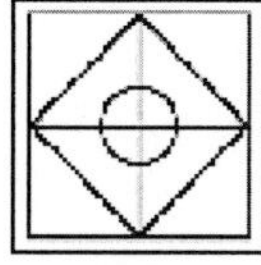
(X)

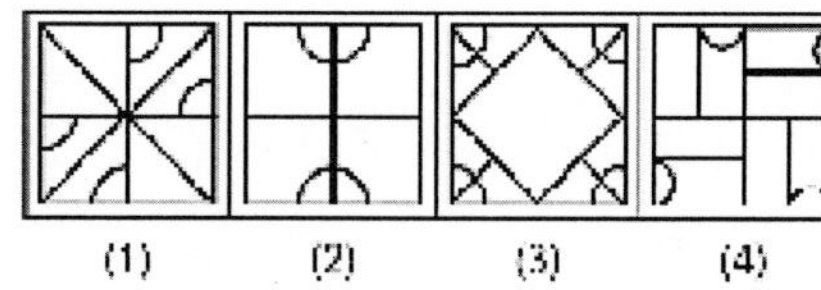
(1) (2) (3) (4)

(a) 1 (b) 2
(c) 3 (d) 4

27. Find out which figure is the rearrangement of the parts of the given figure (X).

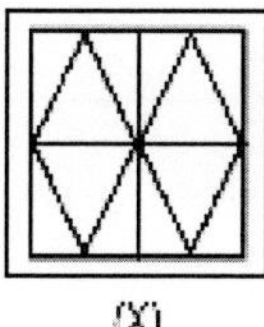
(X)

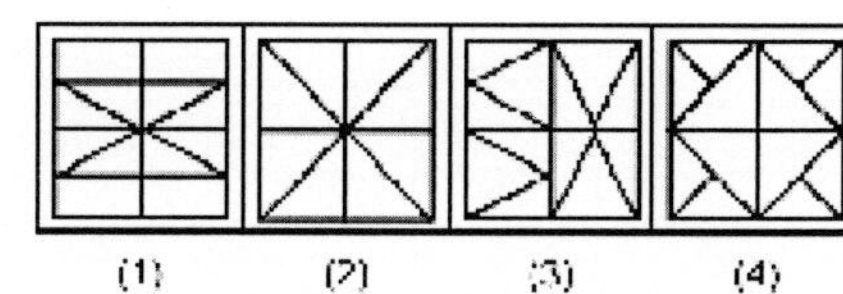
(1) (2) (3) (4)

(a) 1 (b) 2
(c) 3 (d) 4

28. Find out which figure is the rearrangement of the parts of the given figure (X).

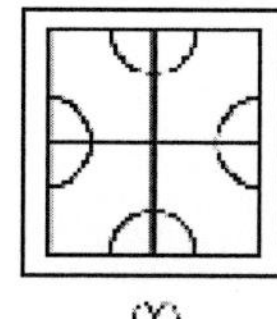
(X)

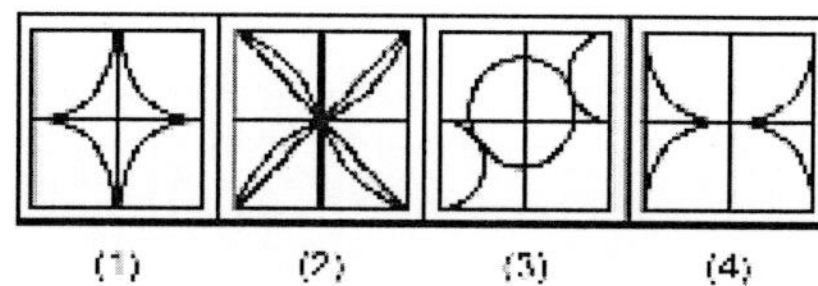
(1) (2) (3) (4)

(a) 1 (b) 2
(c) 3 (d) 4

29. Find out which figure is the rearrangement of the parts of the given figure (X).

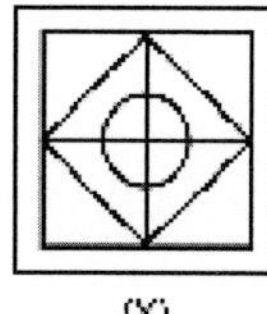
(X)

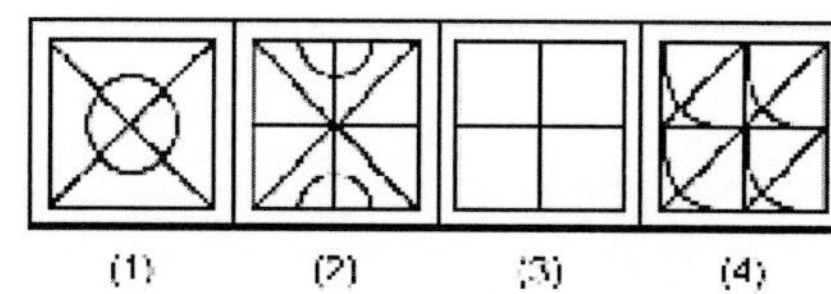
(1) (2) (3) (4)

(a) 1 (b) 2
(c) 3 (d) 4

30. Find out which figure is the rearrangement of the parts of the given figure (X).

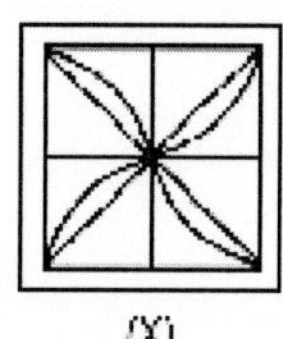
(X)

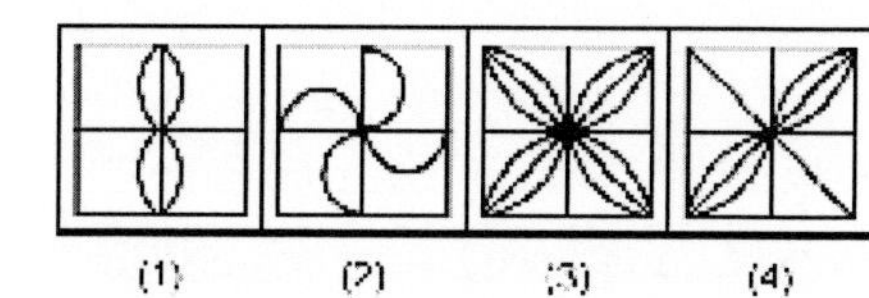
(1) (2) (3) (4)

(a) 1 (b) 2
(c) 3 (d) 4

Answer Key

1. (c)	**2.** (a)	**3.** (a)	**4.** (c)	**5.** (b)	**6.** (c)	**7.** (c)	**8.** (b)	**9.** (b)	**10.** (c)
11. (c)	**12.** (a)	**13.** (b)	**14.** (d)	**15.** (b)	**16.** (b)	**17.** (b)	**18.** (b)	**19.** (b)	**20.** (d)
21. (d)	**22.** (c)	**23.** (b)	**24.** (d)	**25.** (d)	**26.** (a)	**27.** (c)	**28.** (c)	**29.** (b)	**30.** (d)

Previous Year Questions

1. Find out which of the figures (1), (2), (3) and (4) can be formed from the pieces given in figure (X).
[NTSE 2012 – Tamilnadu first stage paper]

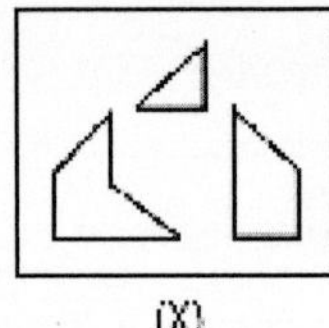
(X)

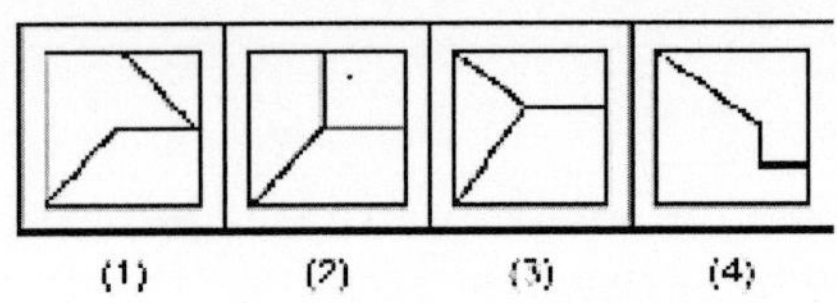
(1) (2) (3) (4)

(a) 1 (b) 2
(c) 3 (d) 4

2. Find out which of the figures (1), (2), (3) and (4) can be formed from the pieces given in figure (X).
[NTSE 2012 – UP second stage paper]

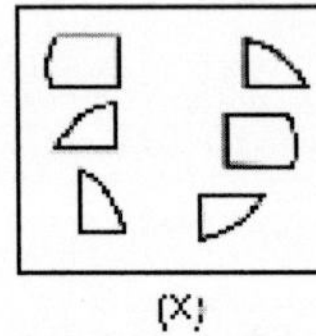
(X)

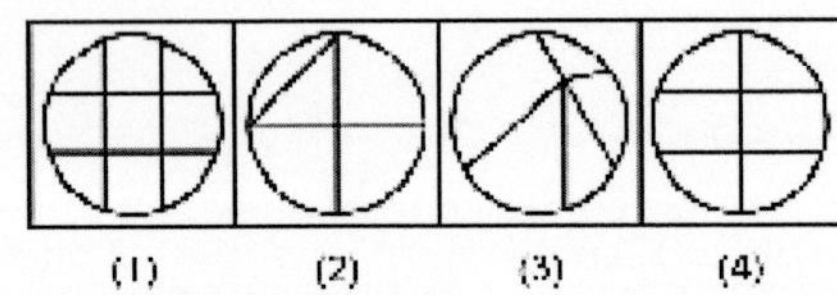
(1) (2) (3) (4)

(a) 1 (b) 2
(c) 3 (d) 4

3. Select the alternative in which the specified components of the key figure (X) are found.
[NTSE 2002 – Delhi first stage paper]

(X)

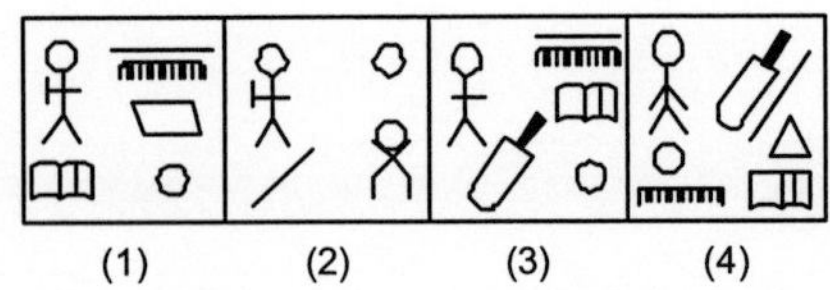
(1) (2) (3) (4)

(a) 1 (b) 2
(c) 3 (d) 4

4. Select the alternative in which the specified components of the key figure (X) are found.
[NTSE 2001 – Karnataka second stage paper]

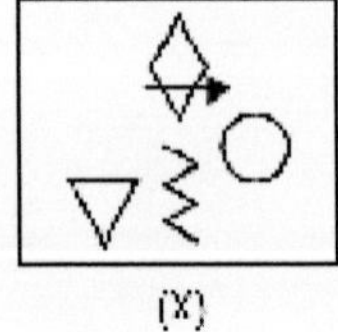
(X)

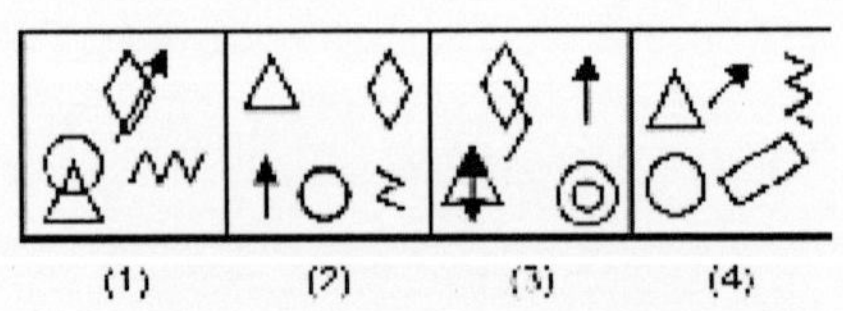
(1) (2) (3) (4)

(a) 1 (b) 2
(c) 3 (d) 4

5. Select the alternative in which the specified components of the key figure (X) are found.
[NTSE 2000– Rajasthan second stage paper]

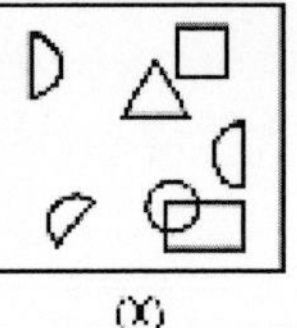
(X)

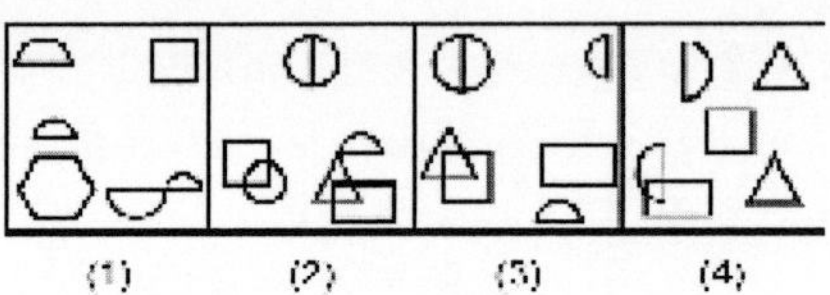
(1) (2) (3) (4)

(a) 1 (b) 2
(c) 3 (d) 4

6. Find out how will the key figure (X) look like after rotation. **[NTSE 2000– Jammu first stage paper]**

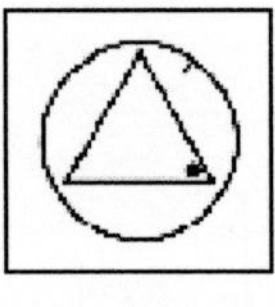
(X)

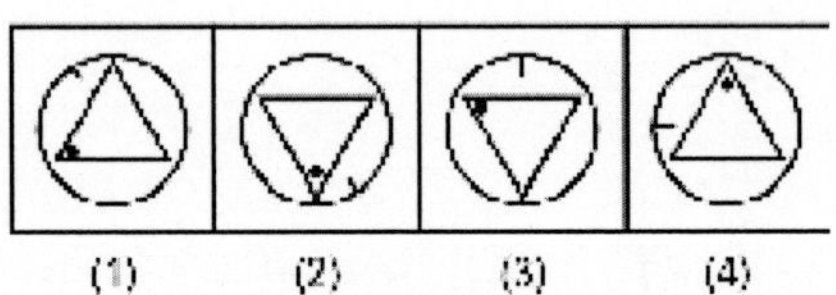
(1) (2) (3) (4)

(a) 1 (b) 2
(c) 3 (d) 4

7. Find out how will the key figure (X) look like after rotation. **[NTSE 2001– MP second stage paper]**

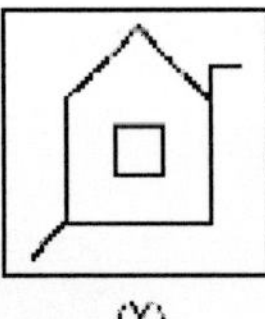
(X)

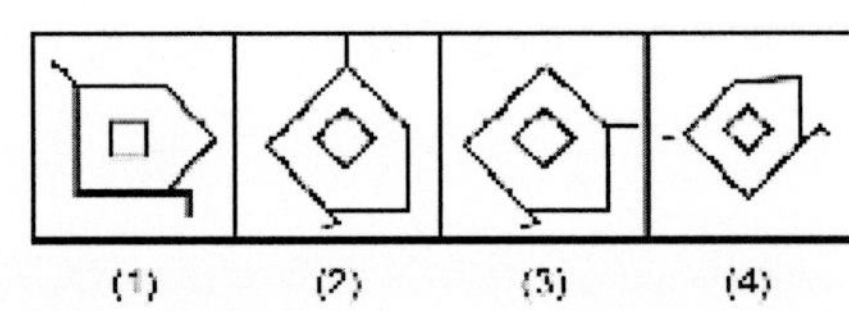
(1) (2) (3) (4)

(a) 1 (b) 2
(c) 3 (d) 4

8. Find out which figure is the rearrangement of the parts of the given figure (X).
[NTSE 2005– Delhi first stage paper]

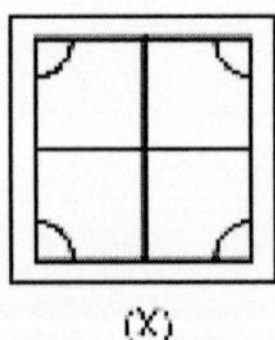
(X)

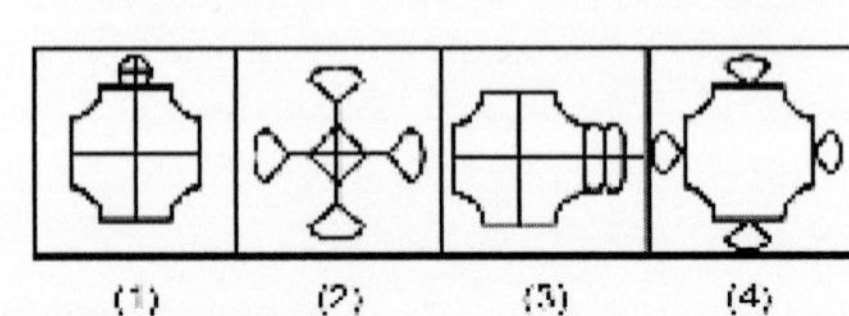
(1) (2) (3) (4)

(a) 1 (b) 2
(c) 3 (d) 4

9. Find out which figure is the rearrangement of the parts of the given figure (X).
[NTSE 2000– Andhra Pradesh second stage paper]

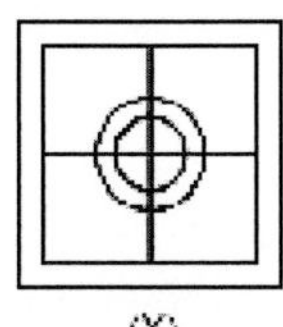

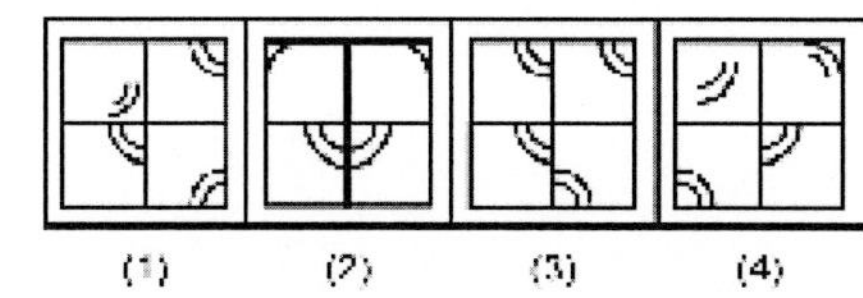

(a) 1 (b) 2
(c) 3 (d) 4

10. Find out which figure is the rearrangement of the parts of the given figure (X).
[NTSE 2012– Uttaranchal first stage paper]

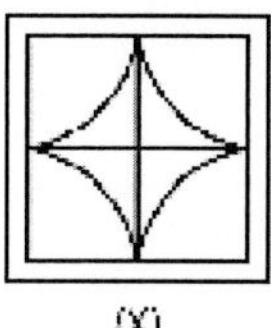

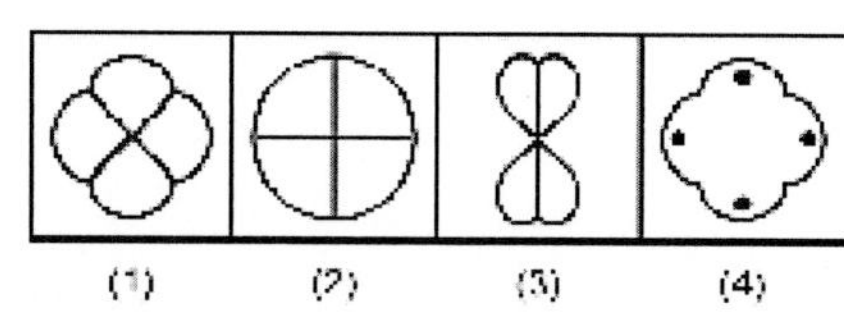

(a) 1 (b) 2
(c) 3 (d) 4

Answer Key

1. (a)	2. (d)	3. (c)	4. (a)	5. (b)	6. (d)	7. (d)	8. (a)	9. (c)	10. (b)

❒

UNIT 5

Figure Matrix

A matric consists of rows and columns. Horizontal line is called row while the vertical line is called column. There is a certain relation between the elements of rows and columns. In this type of questions a matrix is given in which one space is left blank or denoted by a question mark. Four answer figures are followed by the matrix. The candidate has to find out which answer figure will replace the question mark.

Solved Examples

1. Select a suitable figure from the four alternatives that would complete the figure matrix.

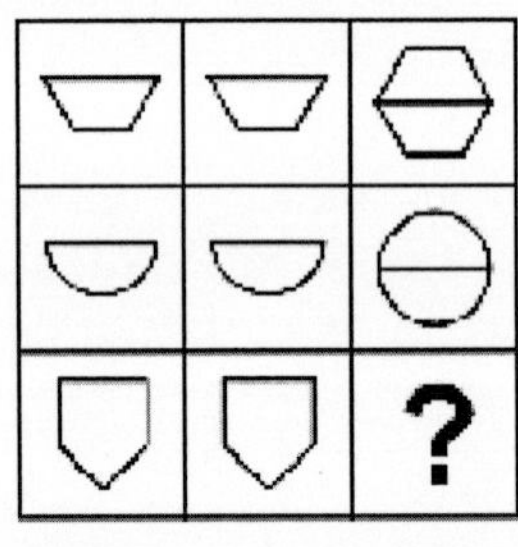

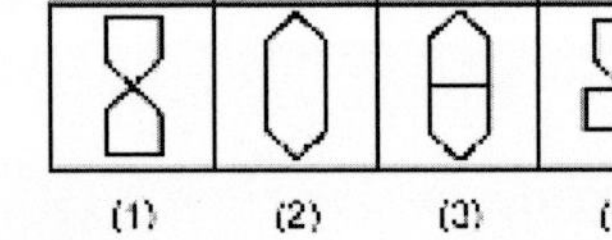

(a) 1 (b) 2
(c) 3 (d) 4

Solution: Option (c) is correct.

2. Select a suitable figure from the four alternatives that would complete the figure matrix.

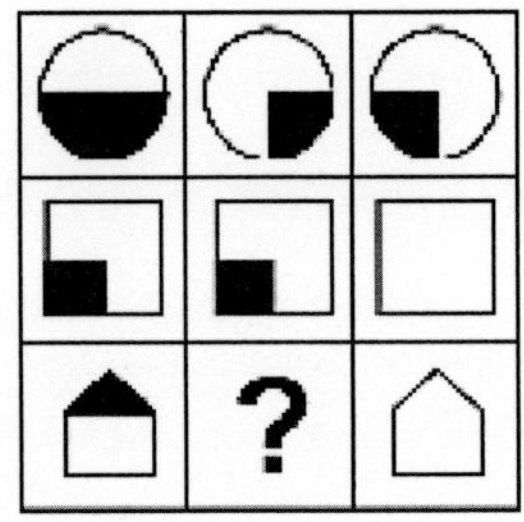

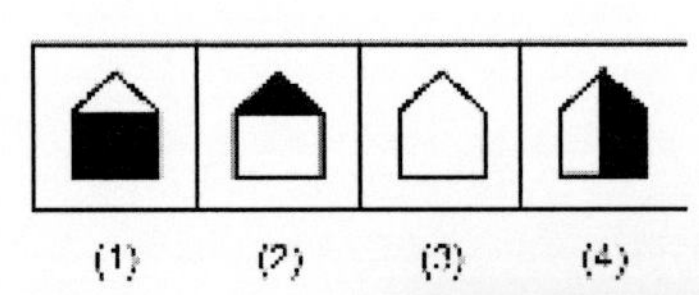

(a) 1 (b) 2
(c) 3 (d) 4

Solution: Option (c) is correct.

3. Select a suitable figure from the four alternatives that would complete the figure matrix.

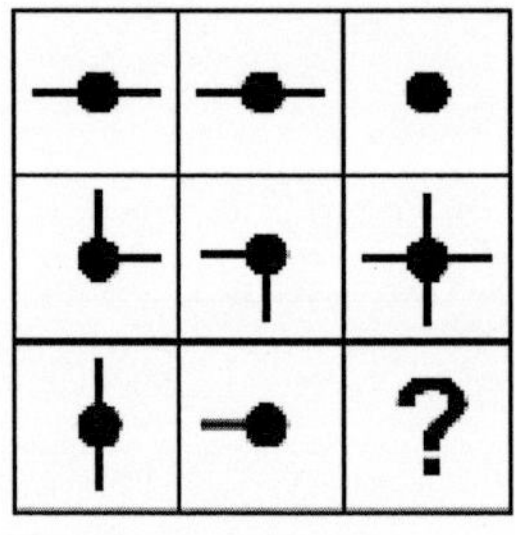

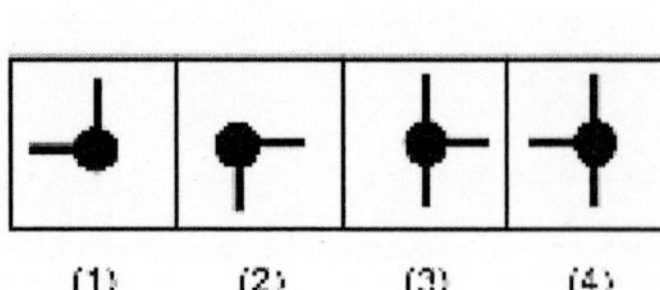

(a) 1 (b) 2
(c) 3 (d) 4

Solution: Option (d) is correct.

Multiple Choice Questions

☛ ***Direction to Solve (1 to 35):*** *In each of the following questions, find out which of the answer figures (1), (2), (3) and (4) completes the figure matrix.*

1. Select a suitable figure from the four alternatives that would complete the figure matrix.

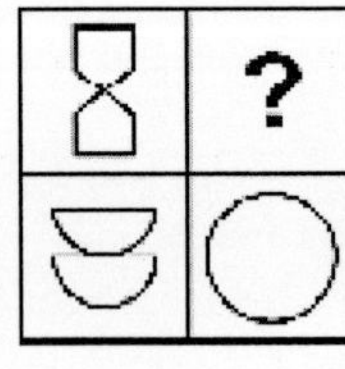

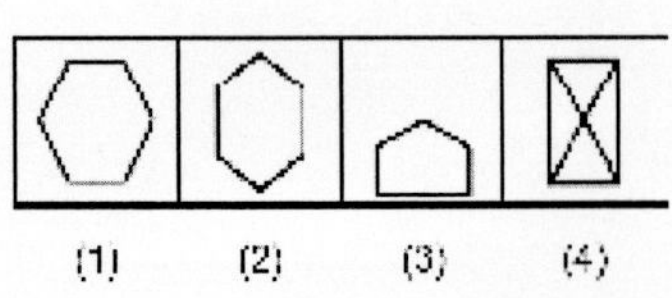

(a) 1 (b) 2
(c) 3 (d) 4

2. Select a suitable figure from the four alternatives that would complete the figure matrix.

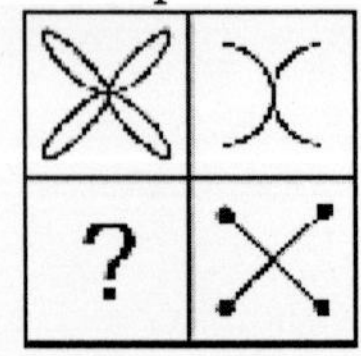

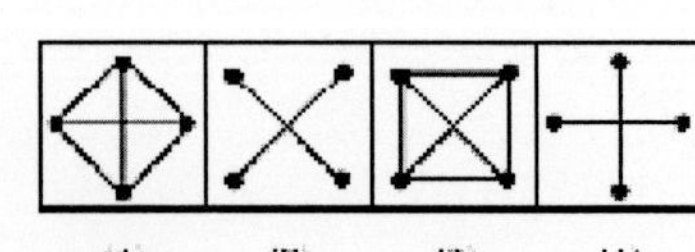

(a) 1 (b) 2
(c) 3 (d) 4

3. Select a suitable figure from the four alternatives that would complete the figure matrix.

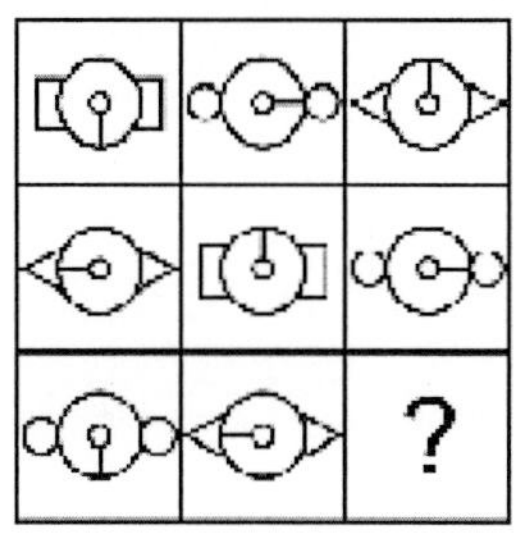

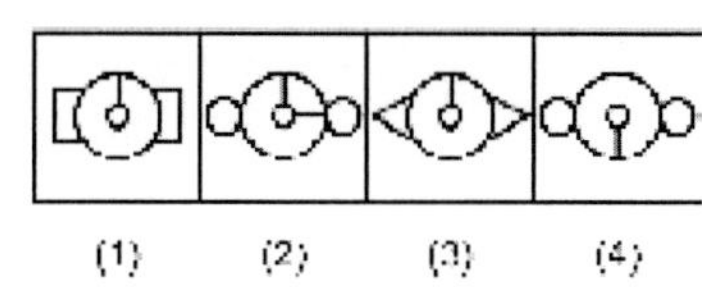

(1) (2) (3) (4)

(a) 1 (b) 2
(c) 3 (d) 4

4. Select a suitable figure from the four alternatives that would complete the figure matrix.

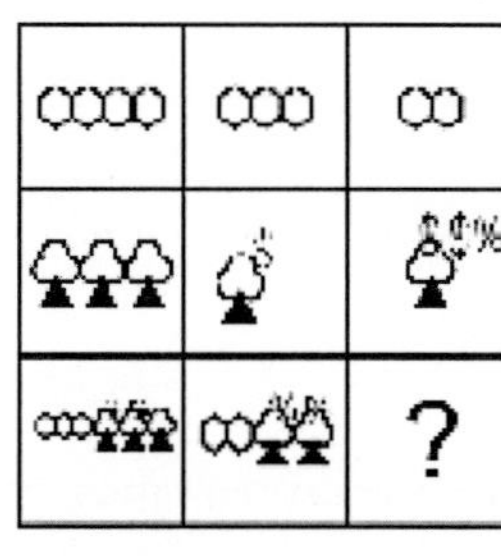

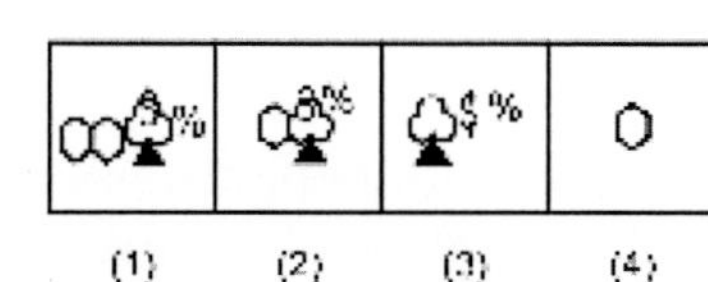

(1) (2) (3) (4)

(a) 1 (b) 2
(c) 3 (d) 4

5. Select a suitable figure from the four alternatives that would complete the figure matrix.

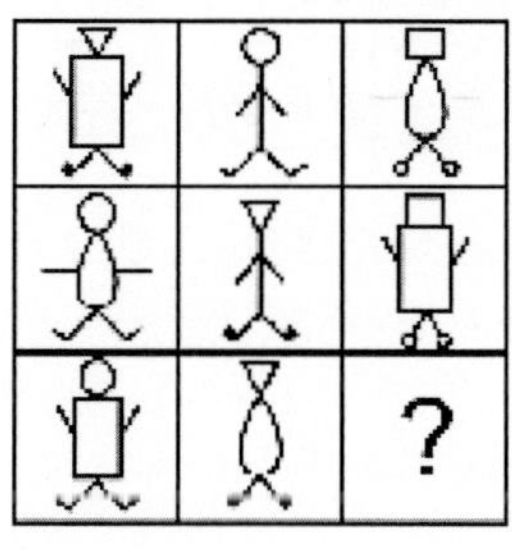

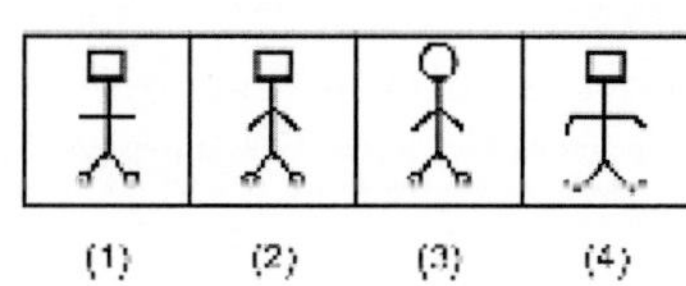

(1) (2) (3) (4)

(a) 1 (b) 2
(c) 3 (d) 4

6. Select a suitable figure from the four alternatives that would complete the figure matrix.

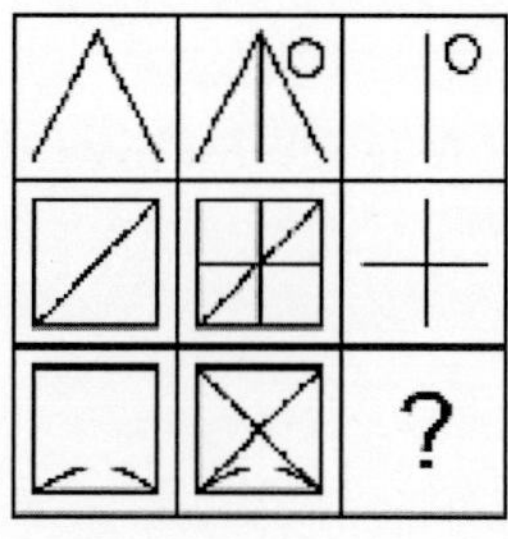

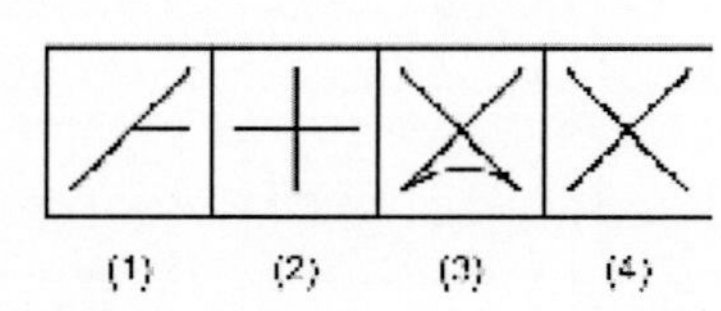

(1) (2) (3) (4)

(a) 1 (b) 2
(c) 3 (d) 4

7. Select a suitable figure from the four alternatives that would complete the figure matrix.

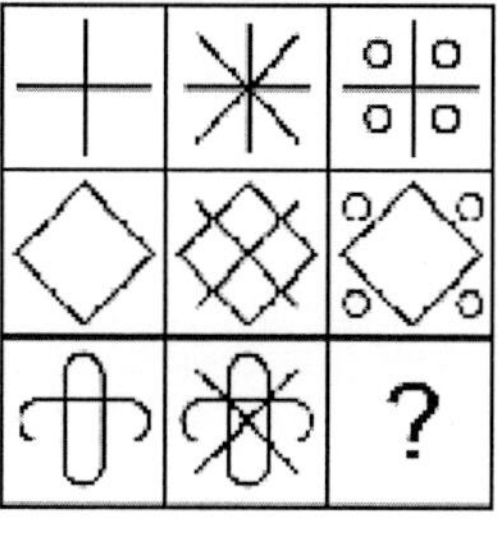

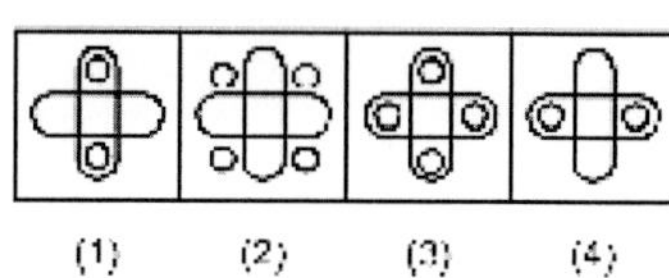

(1) (2) (3) (4)

(a) 1 (b) 2
(c) 3 (d) 4

8. Select a suitable figure from the four alternatives that would complete the figure matrix.

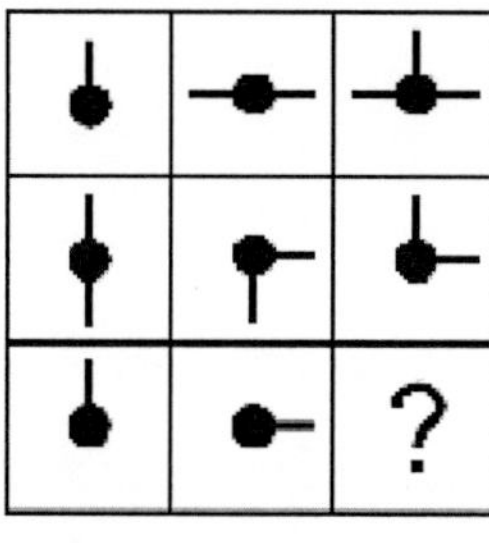

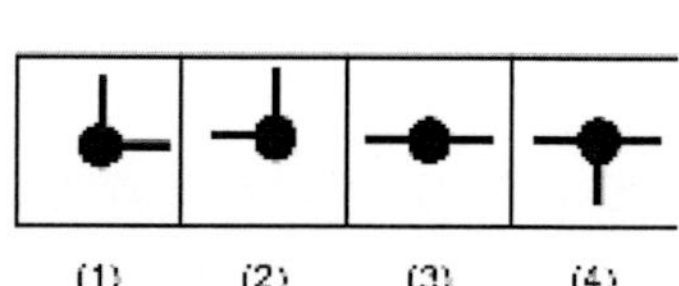

(1) (2) (3) (4)

(a) 1 (b) 2
(c) 3 (d) 4

9. Select a suitable figure from the four alternatives that would complete the figure matrix.

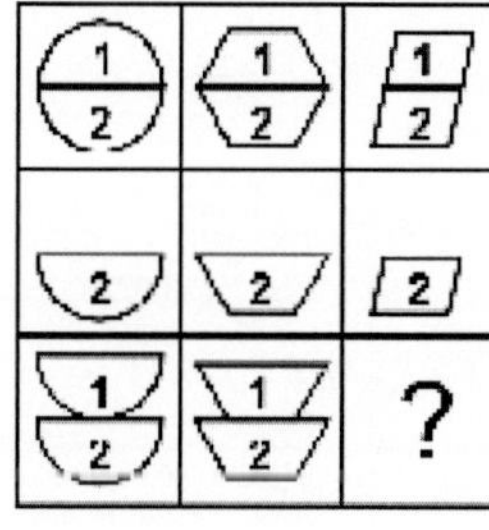

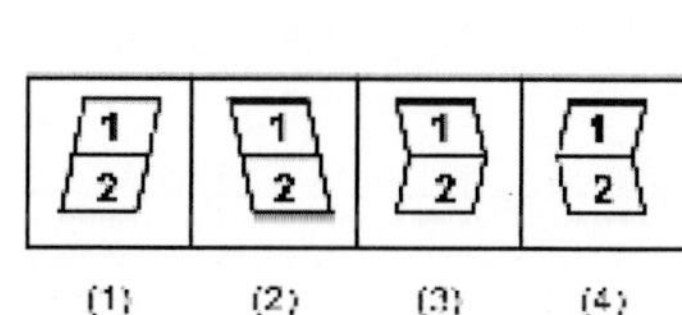

(1) (2) (3) (4)

(a) 1 (b) 2
(c) 3 (d) 4

10. Select a suitable figure from the four alternatives that would complete the figure matrix.

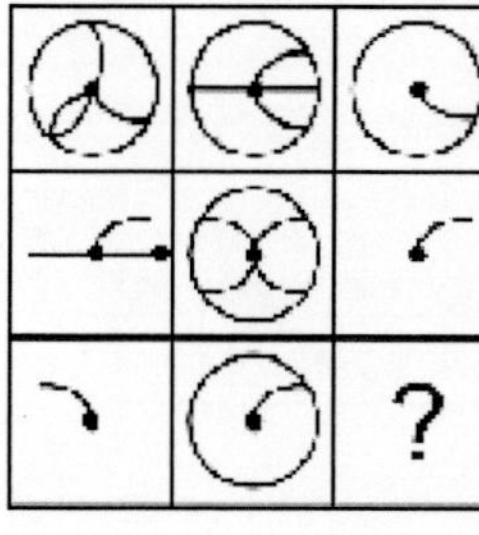

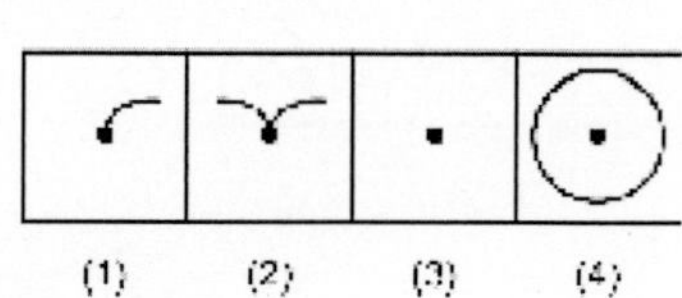

(1) (2) (3) (4)

(a) 1 (b) 2
(c) 3 (d) 4

11. Select a suitable figure from the four alternatives that would complete the figure matrix.

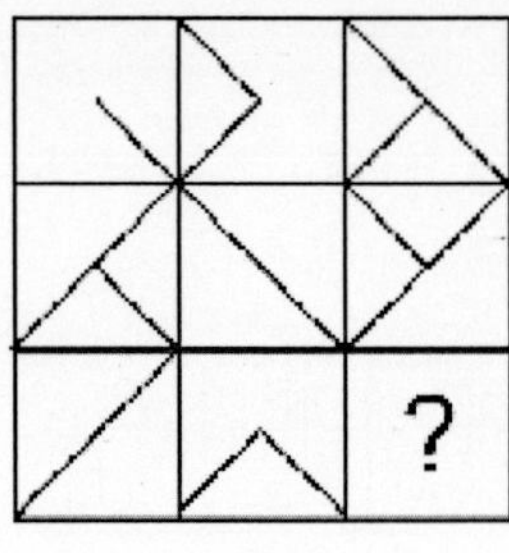

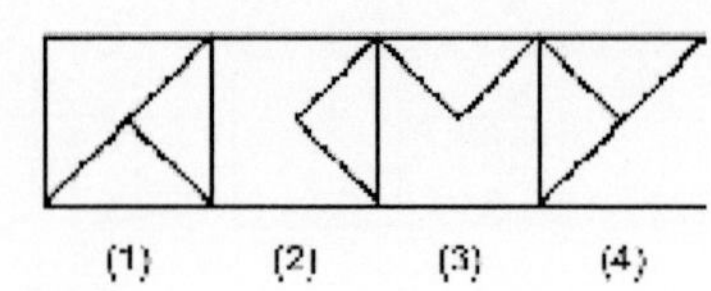

(a) 1 (b) 2
(c) 3 (d) 4

12. Select a suitable figure from the four alternatives that would complete the figure matrix.

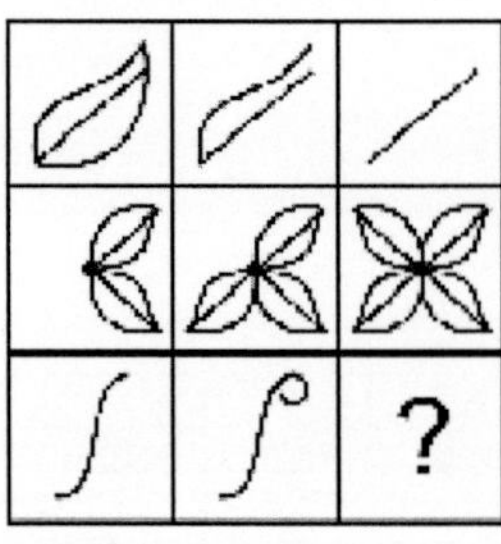

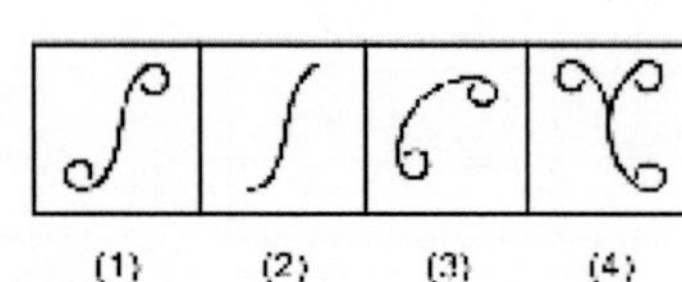

(a) 1 (b) 2
(c) 3 (d) 4

13. Select a suitable figure from the four alternatives that would complete the figure matrix.

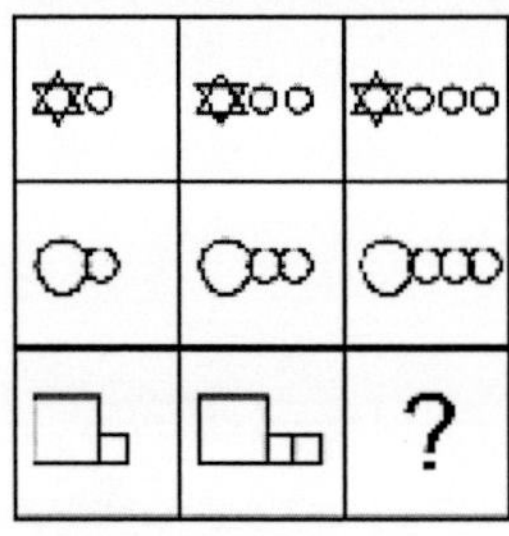

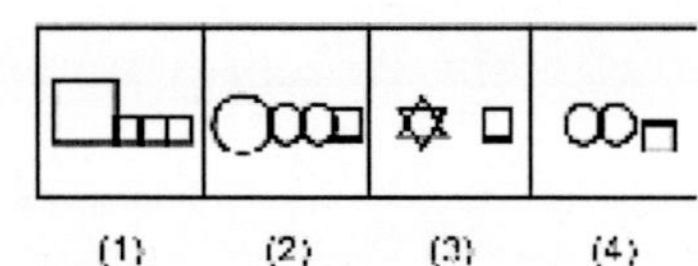

(a) 1 (b) 2
(c) 3 (d) 4

14. Select a suitable figure from the four alternatives that would complete the figure matrix.

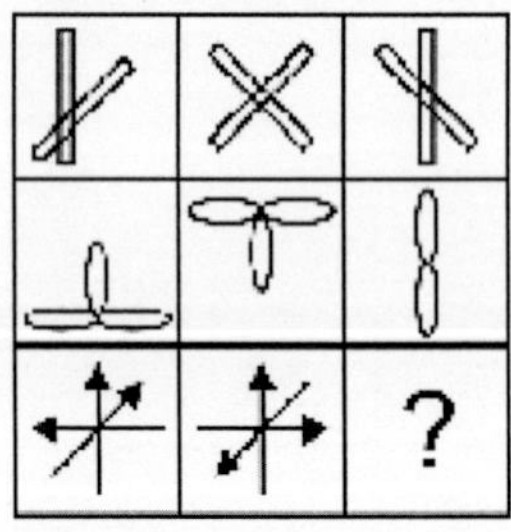

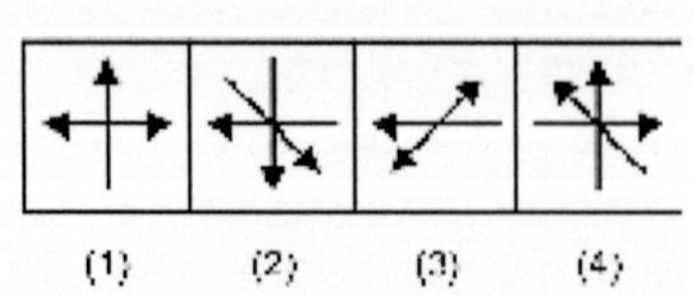

(a) 1 (b) 2
(c) 3 (d) 4

15. Select a suitable figure from the four alternatives that would complete the figure matrix.

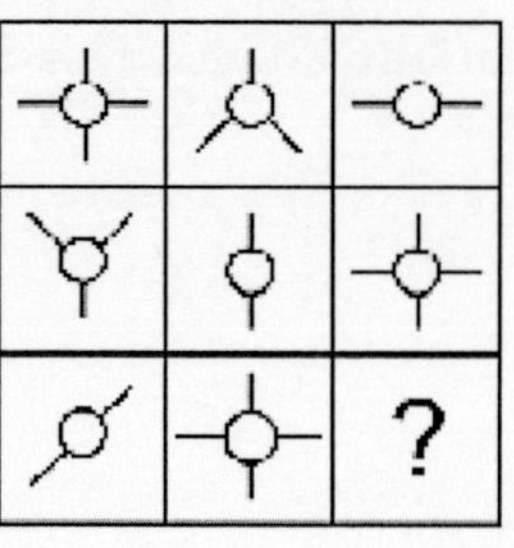

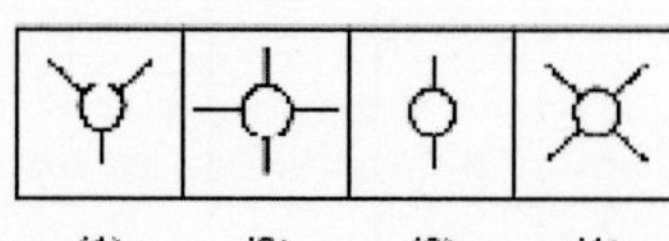

(a) 1 (b) 2
(c) 3 (d) 4

16. Select a suitable figure from the four alternatives that would complete the figure matrix.

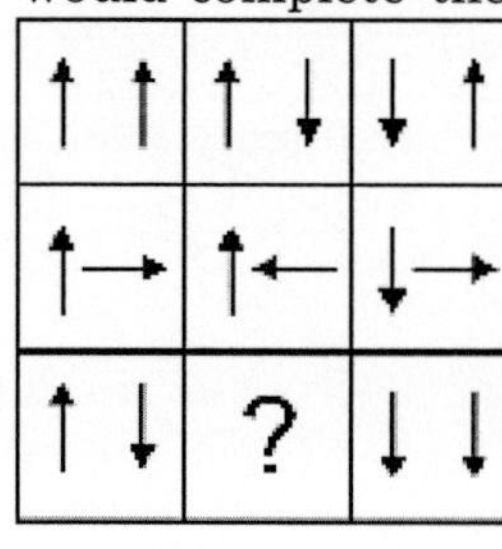

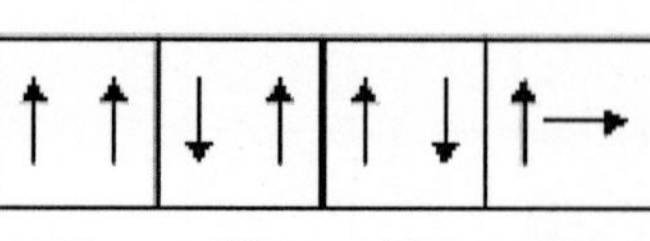

(a) 1 (b) 2
(c) 3 (d) 4

17. Select a suitable figure from the four alternatives that would complete the figure matrix.

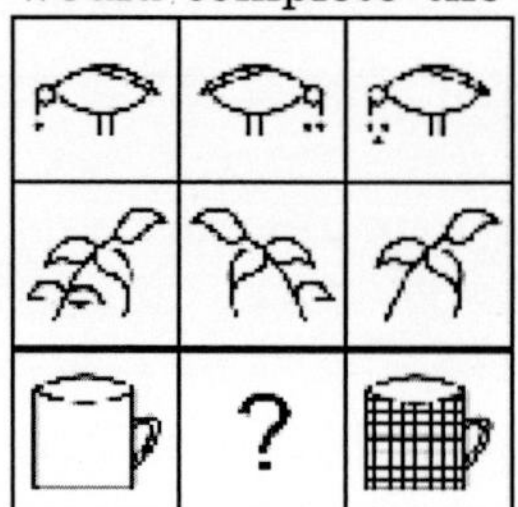

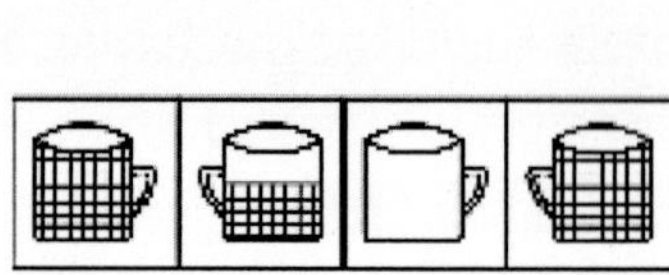

(a) 1 (b) 2
(c) 3 (d) 4

18. Select a suitable figure from the four alternatives that would complete the figure matrix.

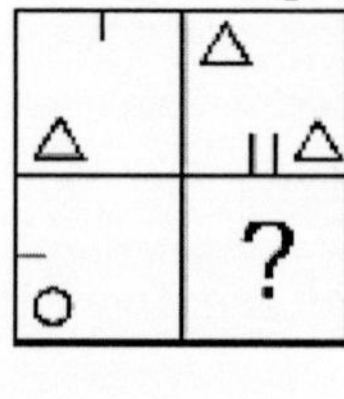

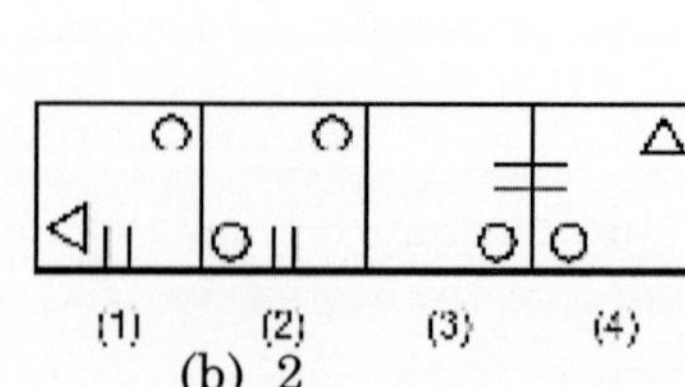

(a) 1 (b) 2
(c) 3 (d) 4

19. Select a suitable figure from the four alternatives that would complete the figure matrix.

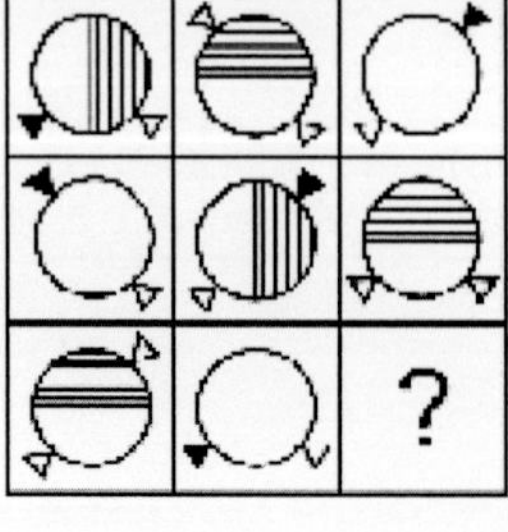

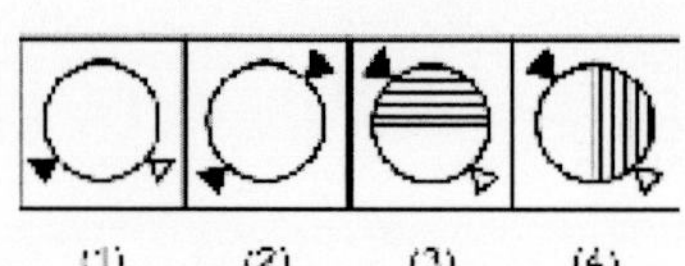

(a) 1 (b) 2
(c) 3 (d) 4

20. Select a suitable figure from the four alternatives that would complete the figure matrix.

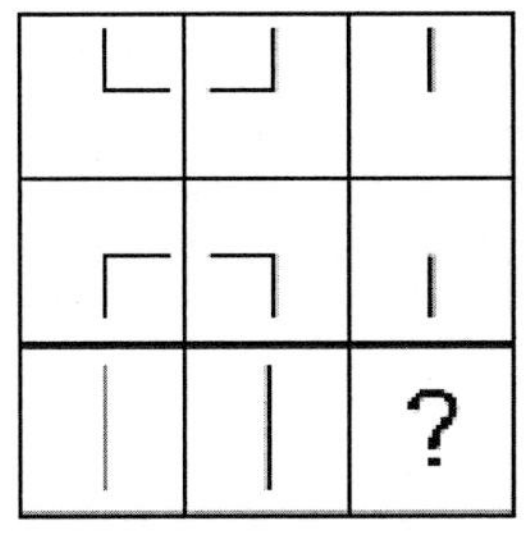

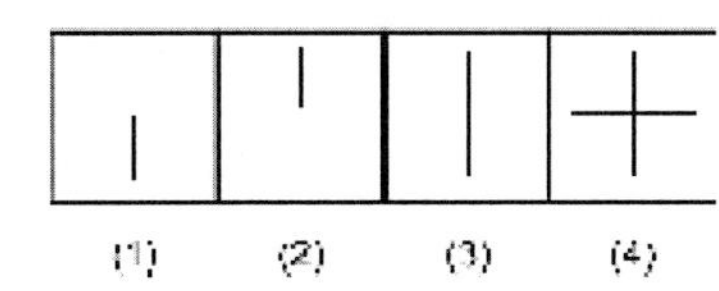

(a) 1 (b) 2
(c) 3 (d) 4

21. Select a suitable figure from the four alternatives that would complete the figure matrix.

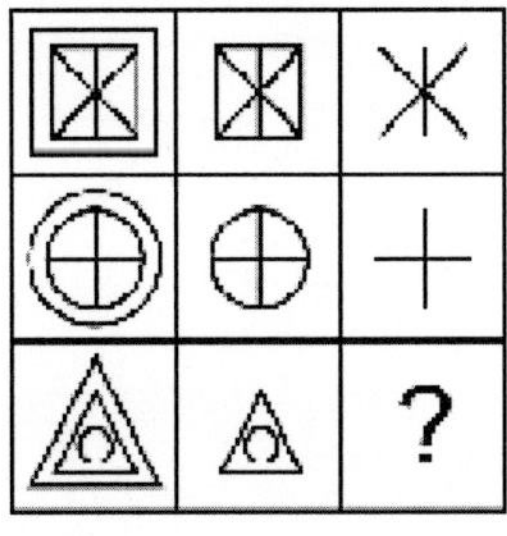

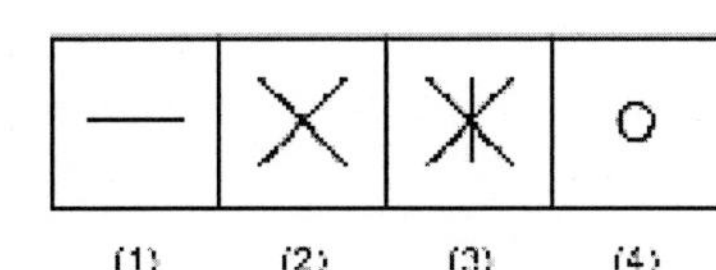

(a) 1 (b) 2
(c) 3 (d) 4

22. Select a suitable figure from the four alternatives that would complete the figure matrix.

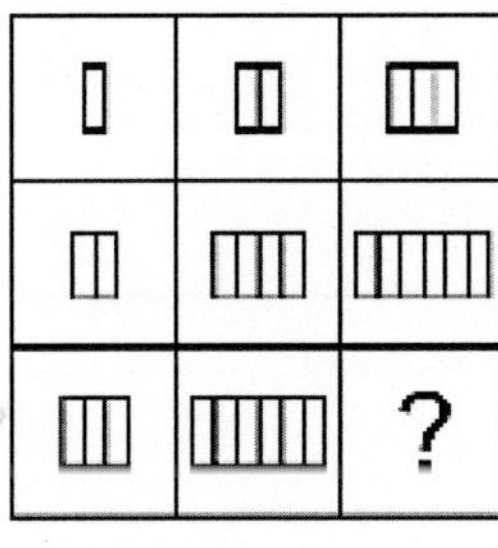

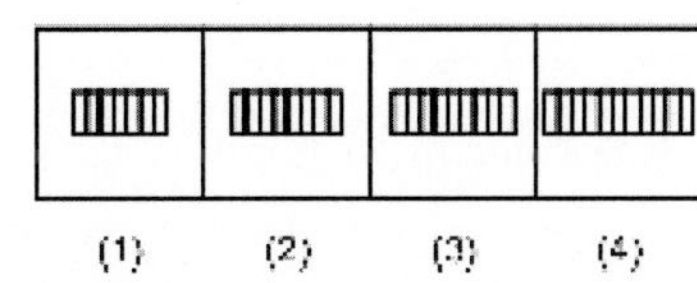

(a) 1 (b) 2
(c) 3 (d) 4

23. Select a suitable figure from the four alternatives that would complete the figure matrix.

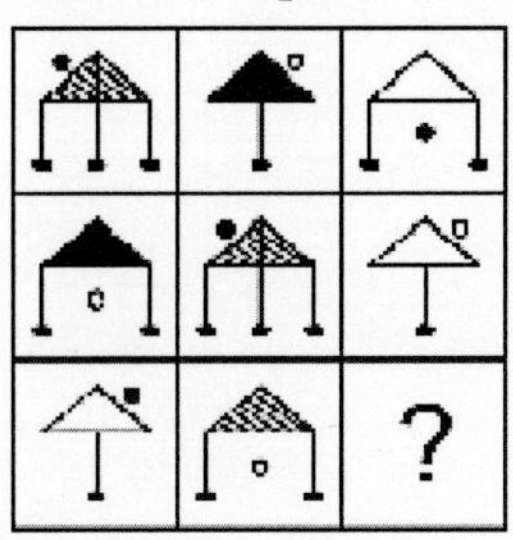

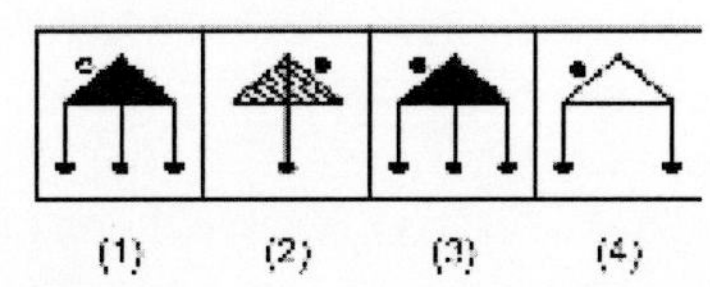

(a) 1 (b) 2
(c) 3 (d) 4

24. Select a suitable figure from the four alternatives that would complete the figure matrix.

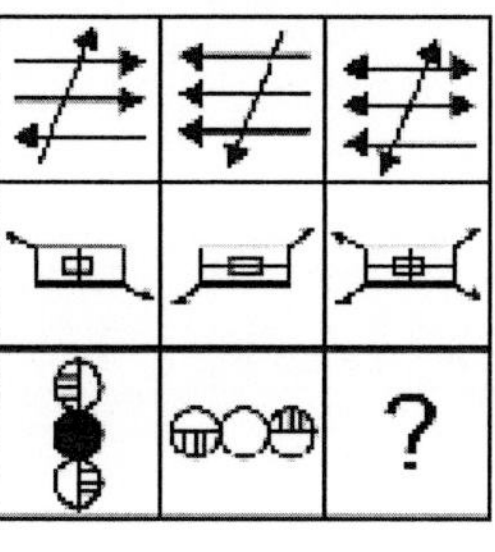

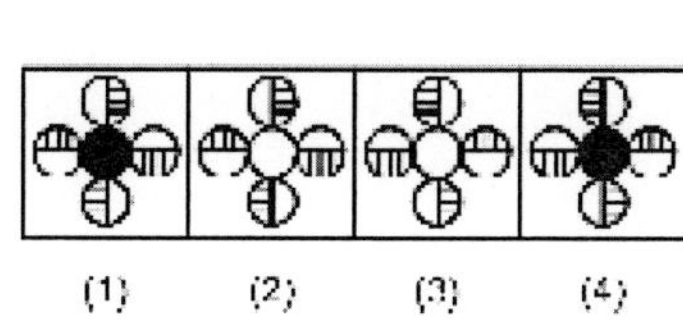

(a) 1 (b) 2
(c) 3 (d) 4

25. Select a suitable figure from the four alternatives that would complete the figure matrix.

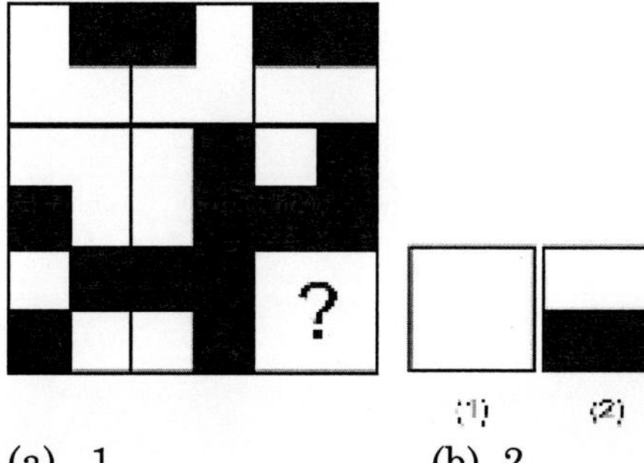

(a) 1 (b) 2
(c) 3 (d) 4

26. Select a suitable figure from the four alternatives that would complete the figure matrix.

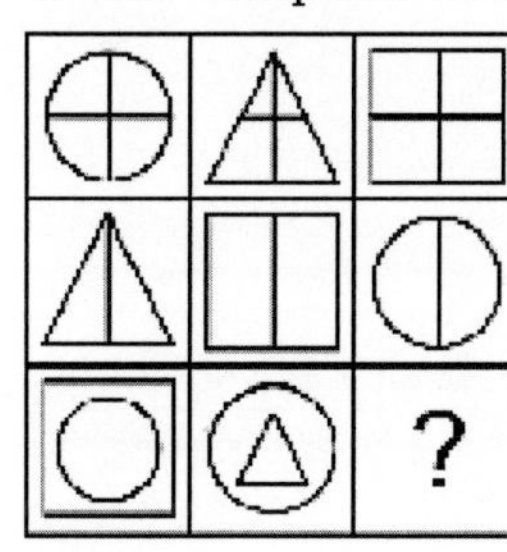

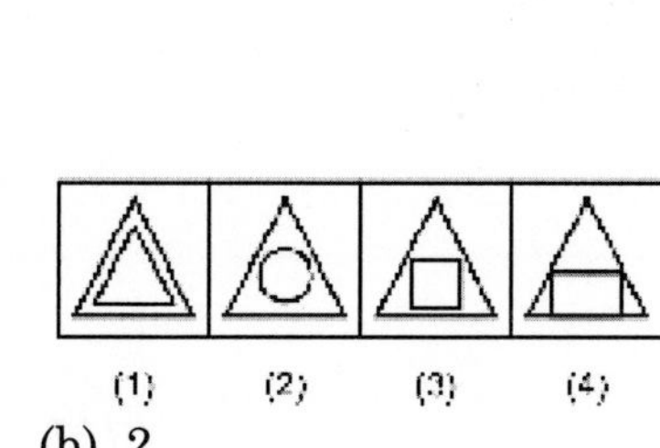

(a) 1 (b) 2
(c) 3 (d) 4

27. Select a suitable figure from the four alternatives that would complete the figure matrix.

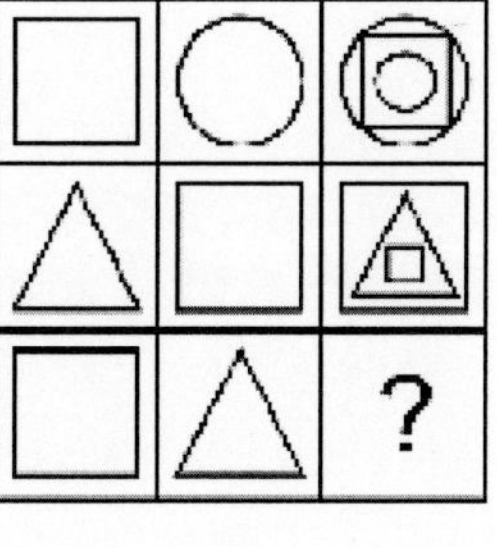

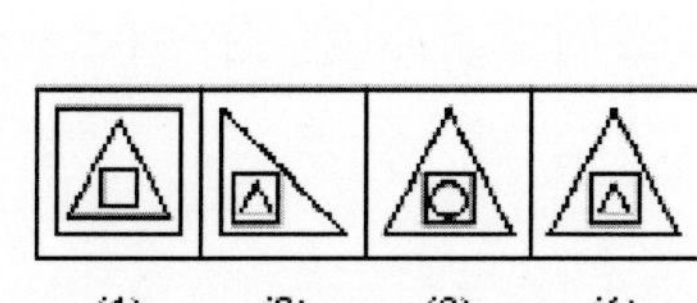

(a) 1 (b) 2
(c) 3 (d) 4

28. Select a suitable figure from the four alternatives that would complete the figure matrix.

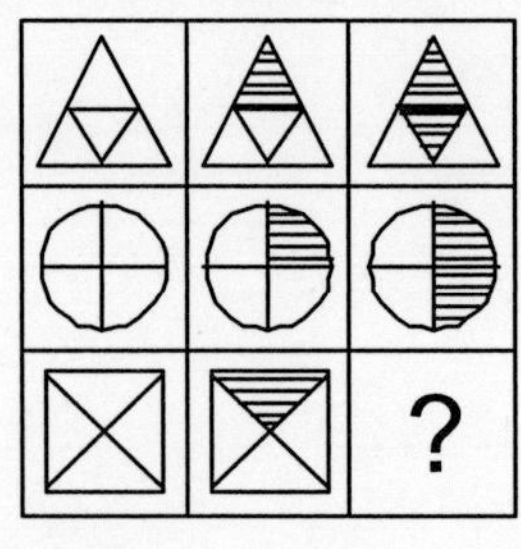

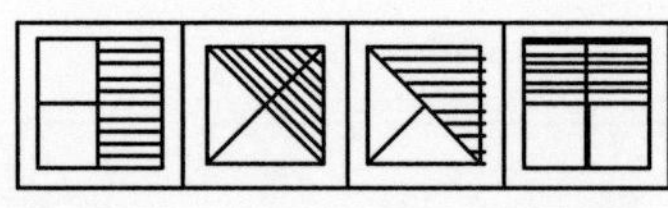

(1) (2) (3) (4)

(a) 1 (b) 2
(c) 3 (d) 4

29. Select a suitable figure from the four alternatives that would complete the figure matrix.

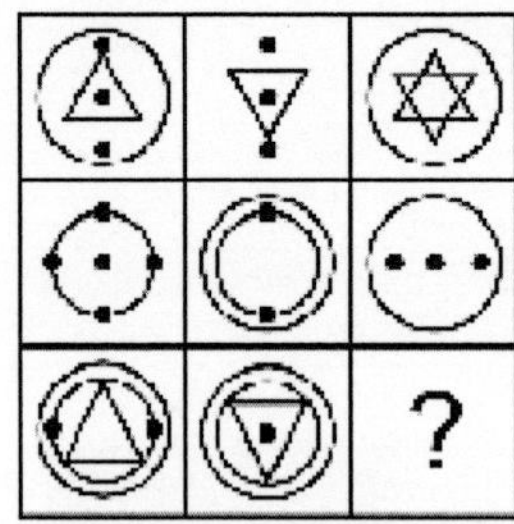

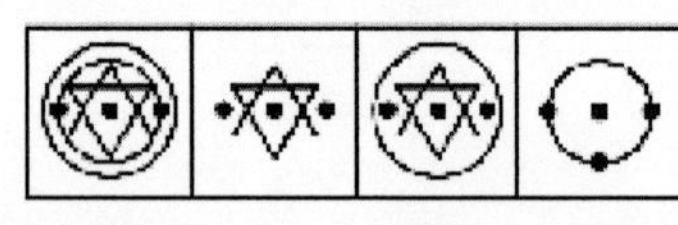

(1) (2) (3) (4)

(a) 1 (b) 2
(c) 3 (d) 4

30. Select a suitable figure from the four alternatives that would complete the figure matrix.

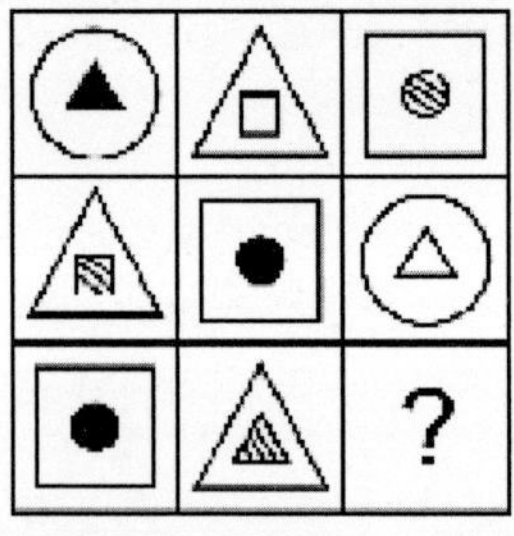

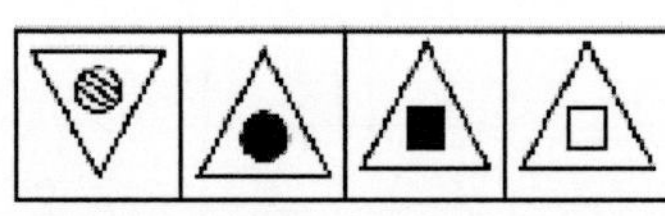

(1) (2) (3) (4)

(a) 1 (b) 2
(c) 3 (d) 4

31. Select a suitable figure from the four alternatives that would complete the figure matrix.

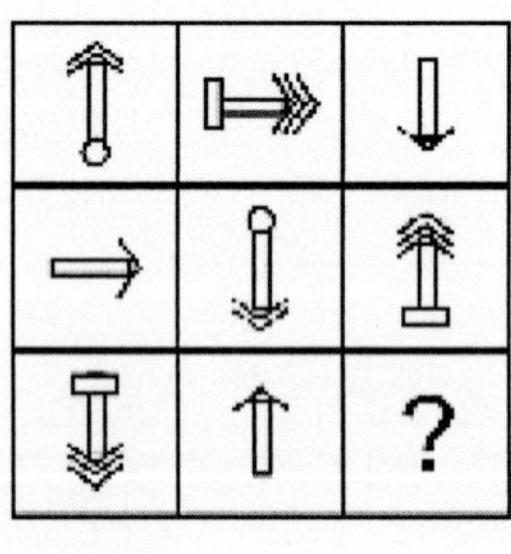

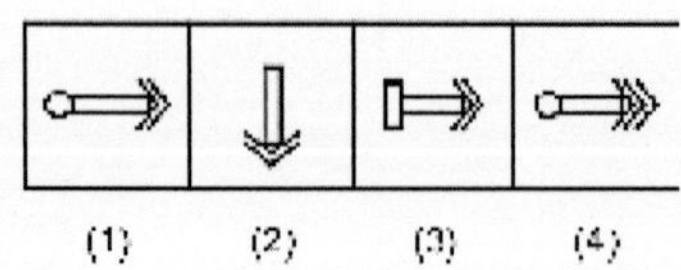

(1) (2) (3) (4)

(a) 1 (b) 2
(c) 3 (d) 4

32. Select a suitable figure from the four alternatives that would complete the figure matrix.

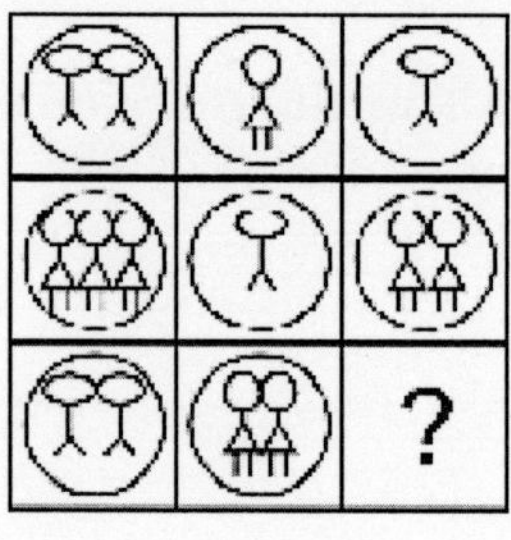

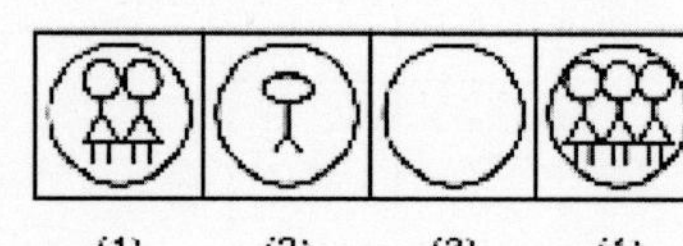

(1) (2) (3) (4)

(a) 1 (b) 2
(c) 3 (d) 4

33. Select a suitable figure from the four alternatives that would complete the figure matrix.

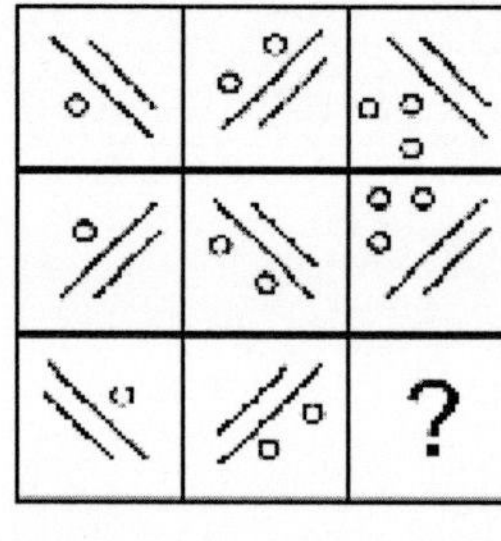

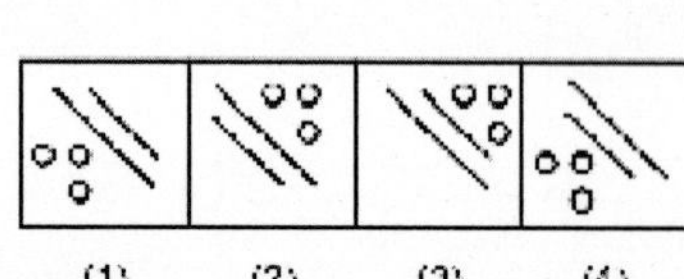

(1) (2) (3) (4)

(a) 1 (b) 2
(c) 3 (d) 4

34. Select a suitable figure from the four alternatives that would complete the figure matrix.

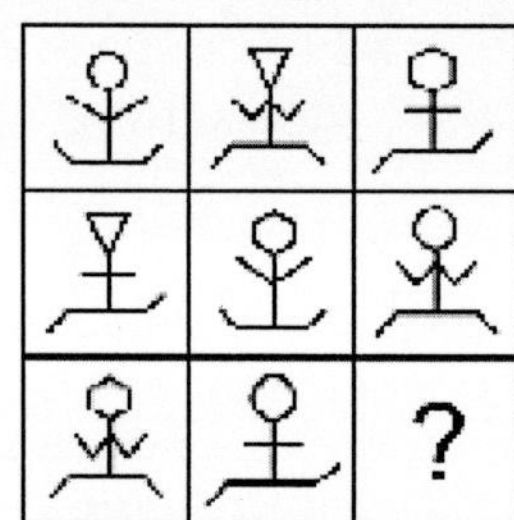

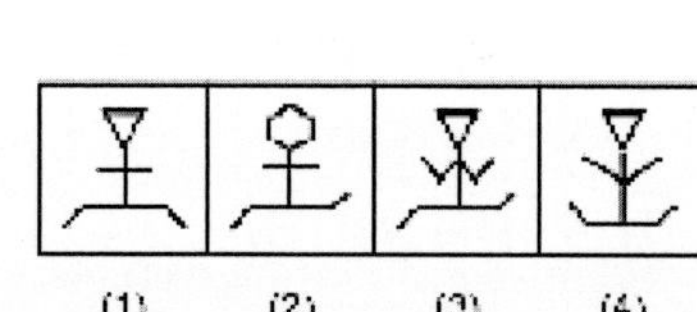

(1) (2) (3) (4)

(a) 1 (b) 2
(c) 3 (d) 4

35. Select a suitable figure from the four alternatives that would complete the figure matrix.

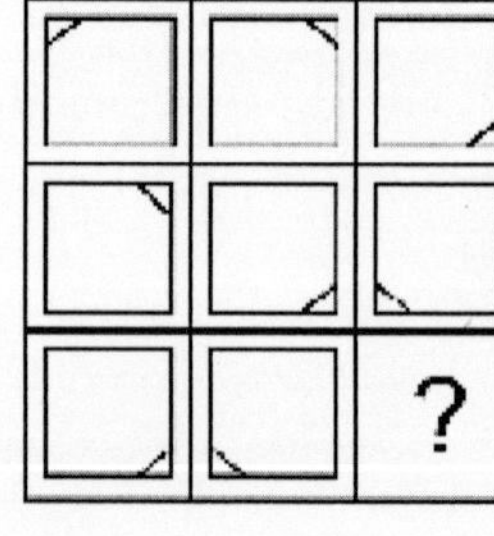

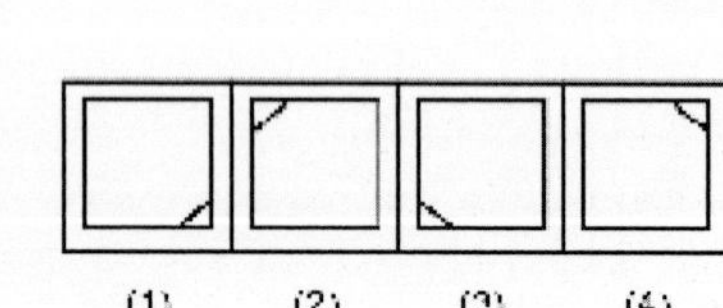

(1) (2) (3) (4)

(a) 1 (b) 2
(c) 3 (d) 4

Answer Key

1. (b)	**2.** (c)	**3.** (a)	**4.** (b)	**5.** (b)	**6.** (d)	**7.** (b)	**8.** (a)	**9.** (c)	**10.** (c)
11. (b)	**12.** (a)	**13.** (a)	**14.** (c)	**15.** (a)	**16.** (a)	**17.** (b)	**18.** (c)	**19.** (d)	**20.** (c)
21. (d)	**22.** (c)	**23.** (c)	**24.** (d)	**25.** (d)	**26.** (c)	**27.** (d)	**28.** (b)	**29.** (b)	**30.** (d)
31. (a)	**32.** (c)	**33.** (b)	**34.** (d)	**35.** (b)					

Explanatory Notes

1. (b)
The two parts of the first figure are rearranged and joined along the longer sides. The common side is then lost to form the second figure.

2. (c)
The second figure is a part of the first figure (but is not exactly the same as the first figure).

3. (a)
In each row, the central part of the first figure rotates either 90° CW or 90° ACW to form the central part of the second figure and the central part of the first figure rotates through 180° to form the central part of the third figure. Also, in each row, there are 3 types of side elements - rectangles, circles and triangles.

4. (b)
In each column, the third figure (lowermost figure) contains one less number of hexagons as the first figure (uppermost figure) and the same number of trees as the second figure (middle figure).

5. (b)
There are 3 types of faces, 3 types of bodies, 3 types of hands and 3 types of legs, each of which is used only once in a single row. So, the features which have not been used in the first two figures of the third row would combine to produce the missing figure.

6. (d)
The third figure in each row comprises the parts which are not common to the first two figures.

7. (b)
In each row, the second figure is obtained from the first figure by adding two mutually perpendicular line segments at the centre and the third figure is obtained from the first figure by adding four circles outside the main figure.

8. (a)
In each row, the third figure comprises a black circle and only those line segments which are not common to the first and the second figures.

9. (c)
In each column, the second figure (middle figure) is obtained by removing the upper part of the first figure (uppermost figure) and the third figure (lowermost figure) is obtained by vertically inverting the upper part of the first figure.

10. (c)
The third figure in each row comprises the parts common to the first two figures.

11. (b)
The third figure in each row comprises the parts which are not common to the first two figures.

12. (a)
The number of components in each row either increases or decreases from left to right. In the third row, it increases.

13. (a)
In each row, the second figure is obtained from the first figure by increasing the number of smaller elements by one and the third figure is obtained from the second figure by increasing the number of smaller elements by one.

14. (c)
The third figure in each row comprises the parts which are not common to the first two figures.

15. (a)
Each row (as well as each column) contains three figures: a figure consisting of a circle and two line segments, a figure consisting of a circle and three line segments and a figure consisting of a circle and four line segments.

16. (a)
In each row, the second figure is obtained from the first figure by reversing the direction of the RHS arrow and the third figure is obtained from the second figure by reversing the direction of both the arrows.

17. (b)
In each row, the figures are getting laterally inverted in each step. The number of components or the quantities are either increasing or decreasing from left to right sequentially.

18. (c)
The second figure is obtained from the first figure by moving the line segment to the opposite side of the square boundary and by replacing it with two similar line segments. Also, the element in the lower-left corner gets replaced by two similar elements - one placed in the upper-left and the other placed in the lower-right corner.

19. (d)
In each row, there are 3 types of shadings of circles - a circle is unshaded, another circle has its right half

shaded with vertical lines and yet another circle has its upper half shaded with horizontal lines. There are three specified positions of the two triangles each of which is used only once in a row. Also, two of the figures in each row have one triangle shaded.

20. (c)
In each row, the third figure is a collection of the common elements (line segments) of the first and the second figures.

21. (d)
In each row, the second figure is obtained by removing the outermost element of the first figure and the third figure is obtained by removing the outermost element of the second figure.

22. (c)
In each row (as well as in each column), the number of rectangles in the second figure is two times the number of rectangles in the first figure and the number of rectangles in the third figure is three times the number of rectangles in the first figure.

23. (c)
There are 3 types of shadings in the triangles, 3 types of legs, 3 positions of circles, each of which is used only once in a single row. The circle is shaded in alternate figures.

24. (d)
In each row, the third figure is a combination of the first and the second figure.

25. (d)
In each row (as well as each column), the third figure is a combination of all the elements of the first and the second figures.

26. (c)
In each row, the triangle follows the circle, the square follows the triangle and the circle follows the square. In case of the third row, the above rule exists for the inner as well as the outer elements.

27. (d)
In each row, the second figure forms the innermost and the outermost elements of the third figure and the first figure forms the middle element of the third figure.

28. (b)
In each row, the second figure is obtained by shading one of the four parts of the first figure and the third figure is obtained by shading two out of the four parts of the first figure.

29. (b)
The third figure in each row comprises the parts which are not common to the first two figures.

30. (d)
In each row, there are three types of outer elements (circle, triangle and square), three types of inner elements (circle, triangle and square) and three types of shadings in the inner elements (black, white and lines).

31. (a)
In each row, there are three types of arrows - an arrow with a single head and without any base, an arrow with double head having a circle at its base, an arrow with triple head having a rectangle at its base. Also, in each row, the arrows point in three directions - upwards, downwards and towards the right.

32. (c)
In each row, the number of elements in the third figure is equal to the difference in the number of elements in the first and second figures. Also, the third figure has the same types of elements (if any) as the elements in the first figure.

33. (b)
In each row, the second figure is obtained by rotating the first figure through 90°CW or 90° ACW and adding a circle to it. Also, the third figure is obtained by adding two circles to the first figure (without rotating the figure).

34. (d)
There are 3 types of faces, 3 types of hands and 3 types of legs. Each type is used once in each row. So, the features not used in the first two figures of the third row would together form the missing figure.

35. (b)
In each row, the first figure is rotated through 90° CW to obtain the second figure and the second figure is rotated through 90° CW to obtain the third figure.

❒

Previous Year Questions

1. Select a suitable figure from the four alternatives that would complete the figure matrix.
[NTSE 2006 – Bihar first stage paper]

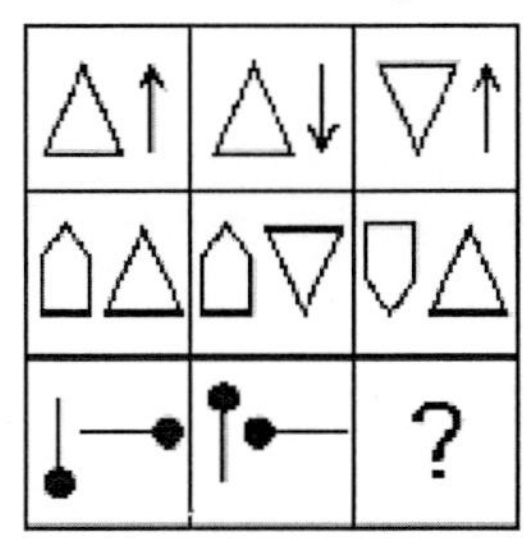

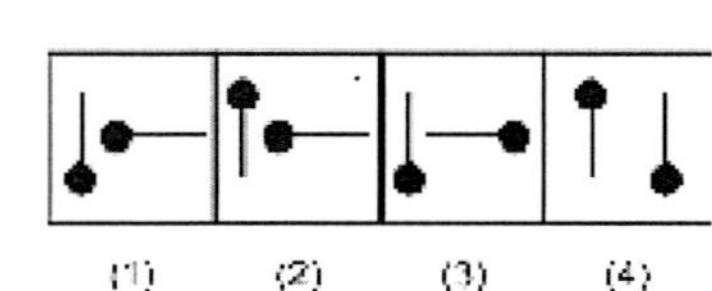

(a) 1 (b) 2
(c) 3 (d) 4

2. Select a suitable figure from the four alternatives that would complete the figure matrix.
[NTSE 2005 – Punjab first stage paper]

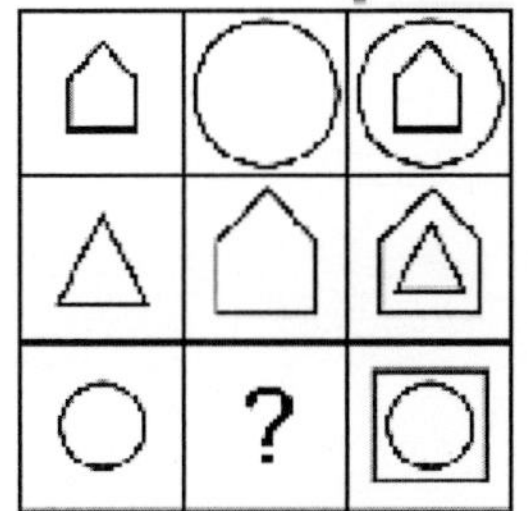

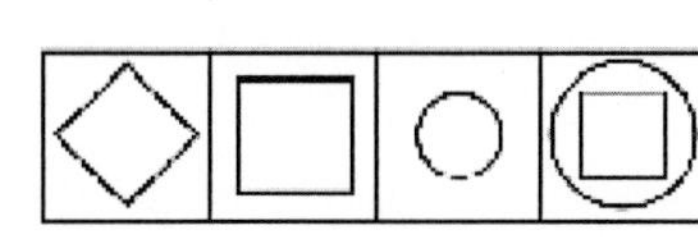

(a) 1 (b) 2
(c) 3 (d) 4

3. Select a suitable figure from the four alternatives that would complete the figure matrix.
[NTSE 2002– Rajasthan first stage paper]

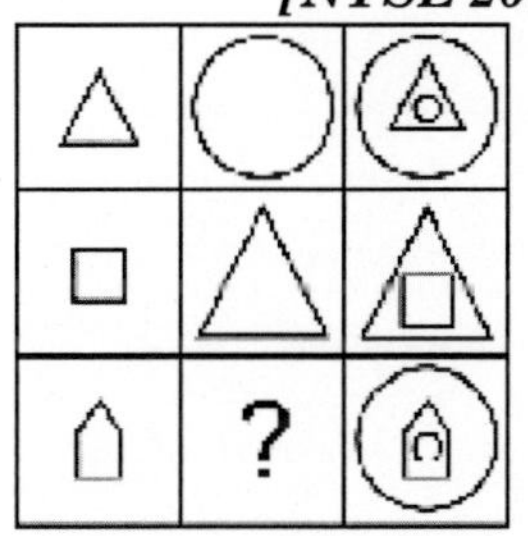

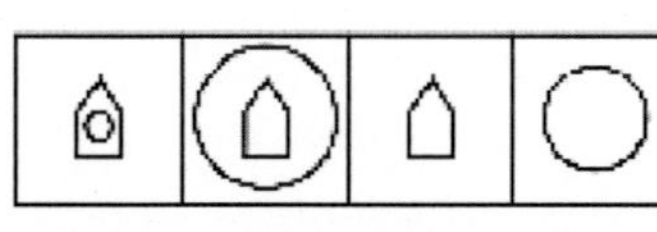

(a) 1 (b) 2
(c) 3 (d) 4

4. Select a suitable figure from the four alternatives that would complete the figure matrix.
[NTSE 2006 – Delhi first stage paper]

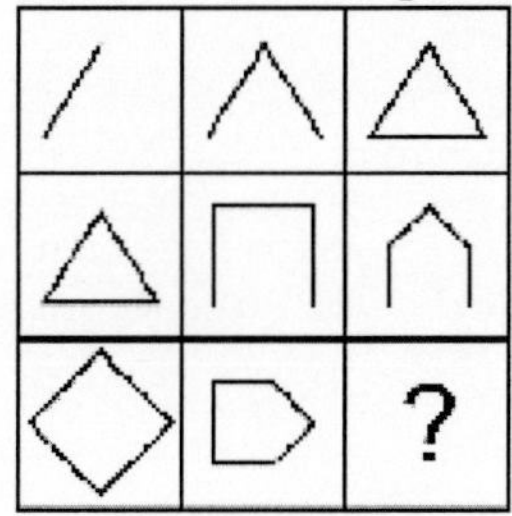

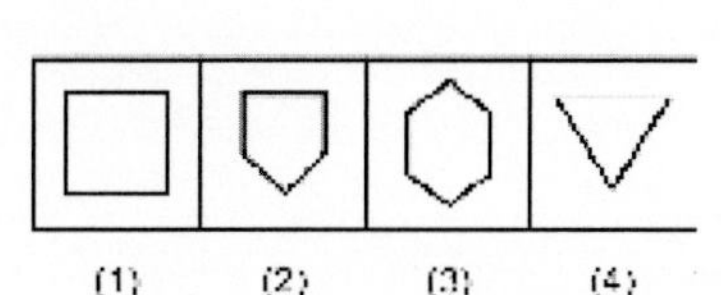

(a) 1 (b) 2
(c) 3 (d) 4

5. Select a suitable figure from the four alternatives that would complete the figure matrix.
[NTSE 2012 – Delhi second stage paper]

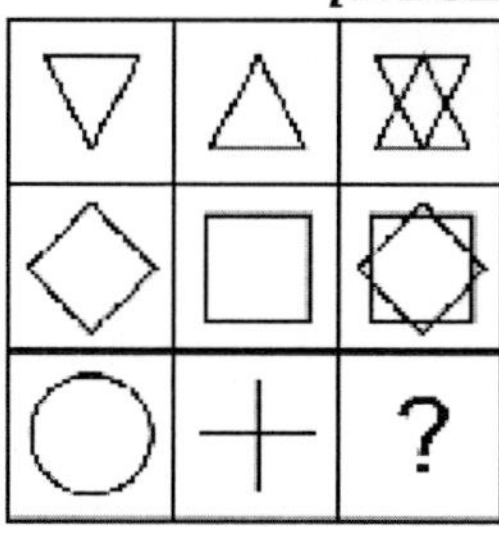

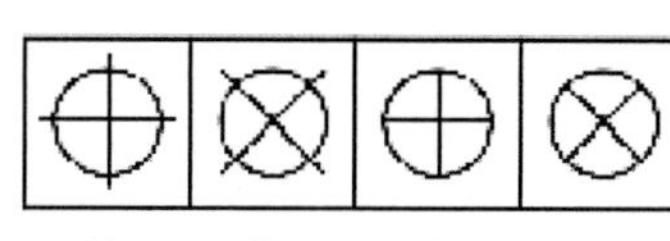

(a) 1 (b) 2
(c) 3 (d) 4

6. Select a suitable figure from the four alternatives that would complete the figure matrix.
[NTSE 2003 – Bihar first stage paper]

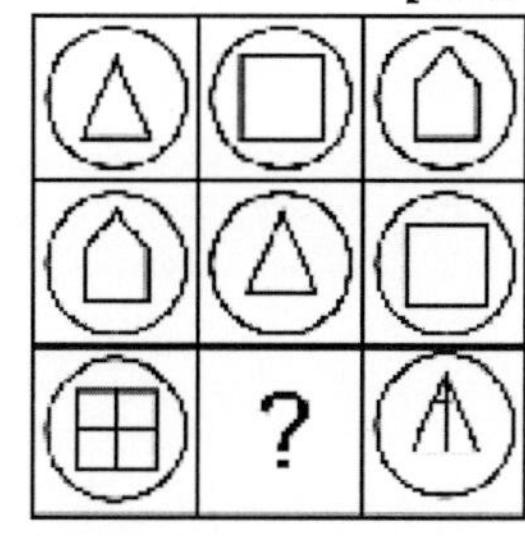

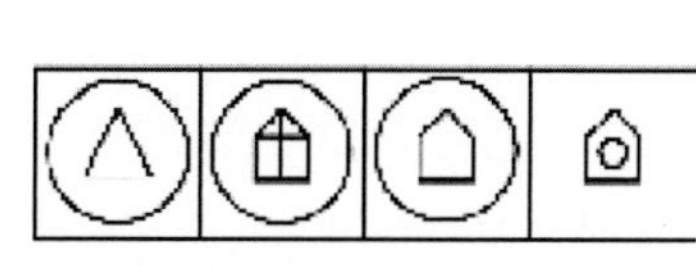

(a) 1 (b) 2
(c) 3 (d) 4

7. Select a suitable figure from the four alternatives that would complete the figure matrix.
[NTSE 2002 – UP first stage paper]

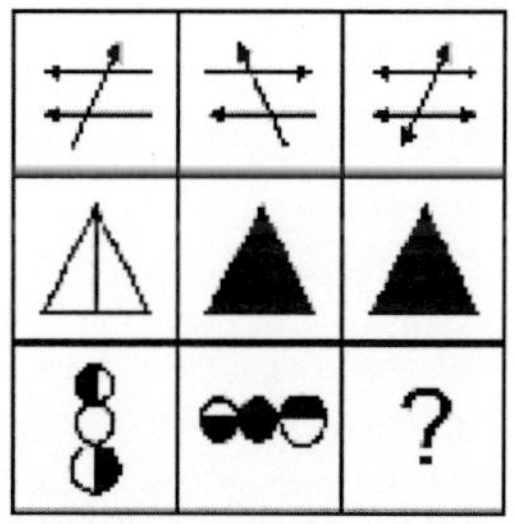

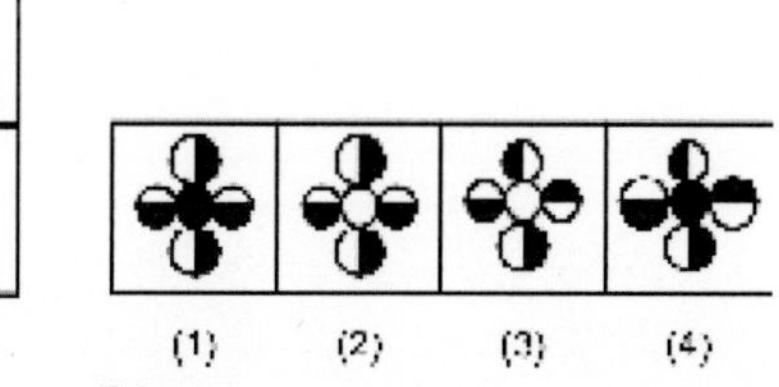

(a) 1 (b) 2
(c) 3 (d) 4

8. Select a suitable figure from the four alternatives that would complete the figure matrix.
[NTSE 2012 – Karnataka first stage paper]

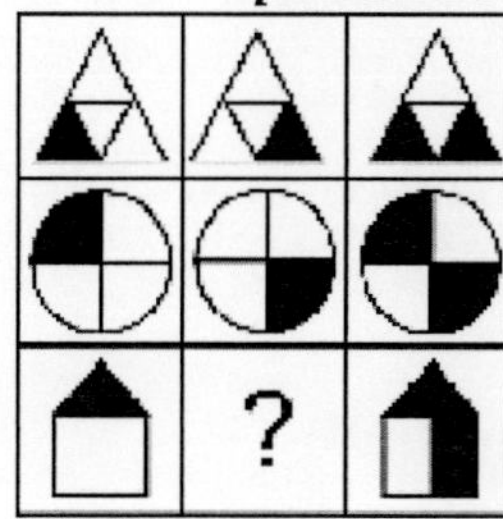

(a) 1 (b) 2
(c) 3 (d) 4

9. Select a suitable figure from the four alternatives that would complete the figure matrix.

[NTSE 2012 – Bihar first stage paper]

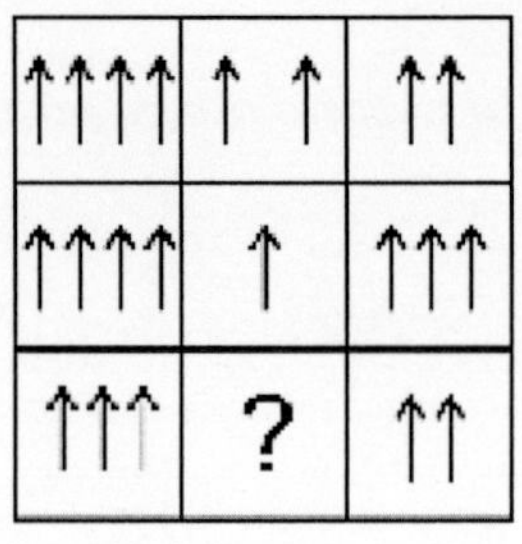

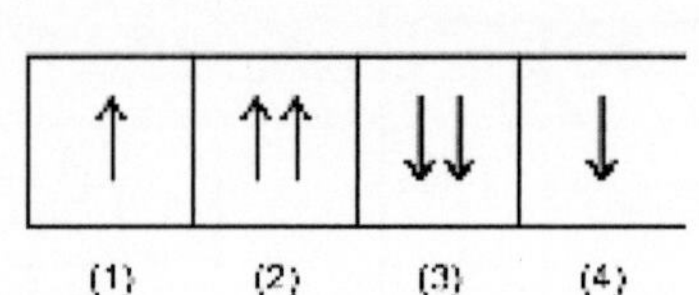

(a) 1 (b) 2
(c) 3 (d) 4

10. Select a suitable figure from the four alternatives that would complete the figure matrix.

[NTSE 2005 – Tamilnadu first stage paper]

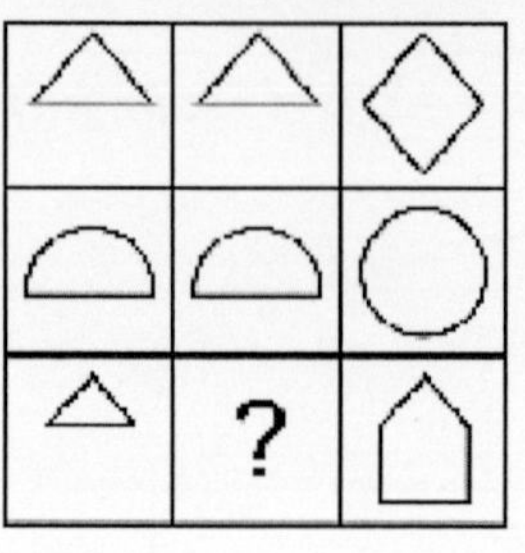

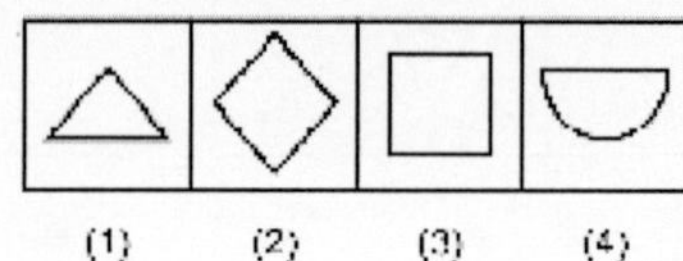

(a) 1 (b) 2
(c) 3 (d) 4

Answer Key

1. (c)	2. (b)	3. (d)	4. (c)	5. (a)	6. (b)	7. (d)	8. (a)	9. (a)	10. (c)

UNIT 6

Transparent Paper Folding

A transparent sheed is used in this type of questions. Some marks are made on the transparent sheet and a dotted line is made on the sheet. Then this sheet is folded along the dotted line. Four answer figures are also given with the problem figure. The candidate has to find out that figure among the answer figures, which resembles the pattern formed when the transparent sheet carrying a design is folded along a dotted line.

Solved Examples

☛ ***Direction to Solve (1 to 4) :*** In each of the following problems, a square transparent sheet (X) with a pattern is given. Figure out from amongst the four alternatives as to how the pattern would appear when the transparent sheet is folded at the dotted line.

1. Find out from amongst the four alternatives as to how the pattern would appear when the transparent sheet is folded at the dotted line.

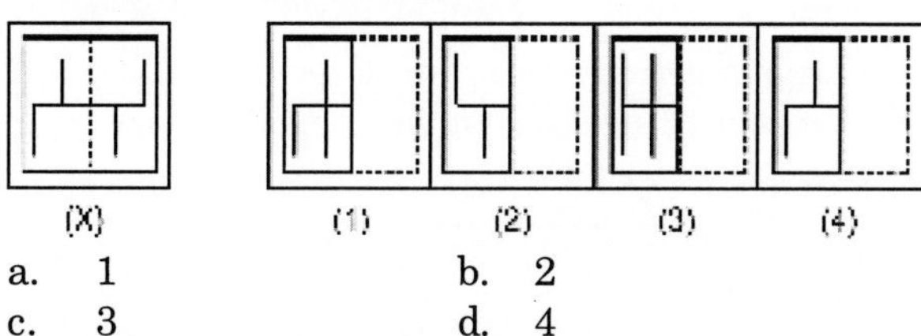

a. 1 b. 2
c. 3 d. 4

Solution: Option (c) is correct.

2. Find out from amongst the four alternatives as to how the pattern would appear when the transparent sheet is folded at the dotted line.

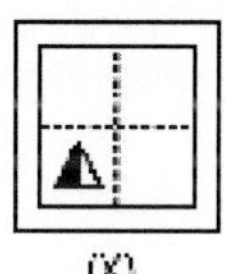

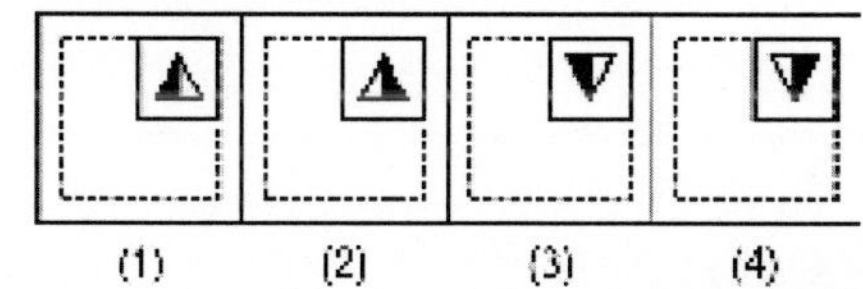

a. 1 b. 2
c. 3 d. 4

Solution: Option (c) is correct.

3. Find out from amongst the four alternatives as to how the pattern would appear when the transparent sheet is folded at the dotted line.

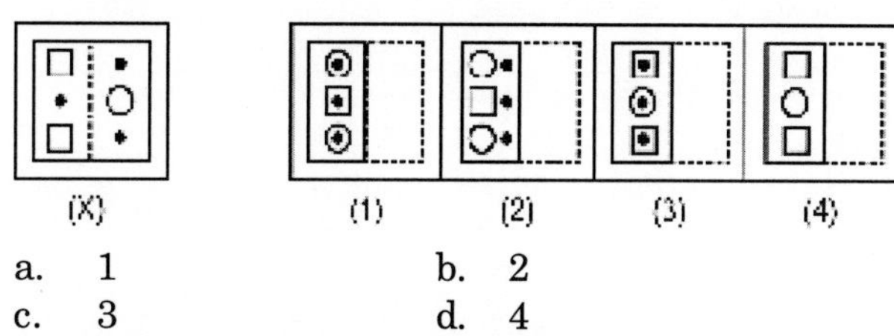

a. 1 b. 2
c. 3 d. 4

Solution: Option (c) is correct.

4. Find out from amongst the four alternatives as to how the pattern would appear when the transparent sheet is folded at the dotted line.

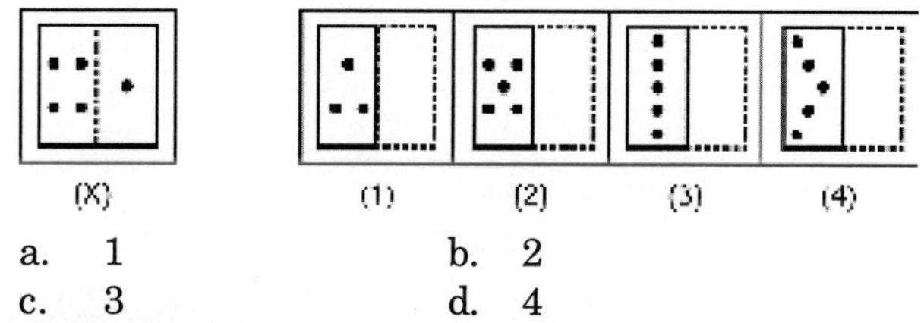

a. 1 b. 2
c. 3 d. 4

Solution: Option (b) is correct.

Multiple Choice Questions

☛ ***Direction to Solve (1 to 30) :*** *In each of the following problems, a square transparent sheet (X) with a pattern is given. Figure out from amongst the four alternatives as to how the patter would appear when the transparent sheet is folded at the dotted line.*

1. Find out from amongst the four alternatives as to how the pattern would appear when the transparent sheet is folded at the dotted line.

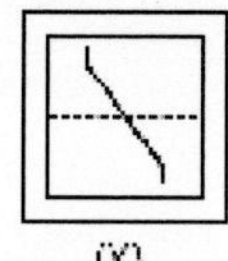

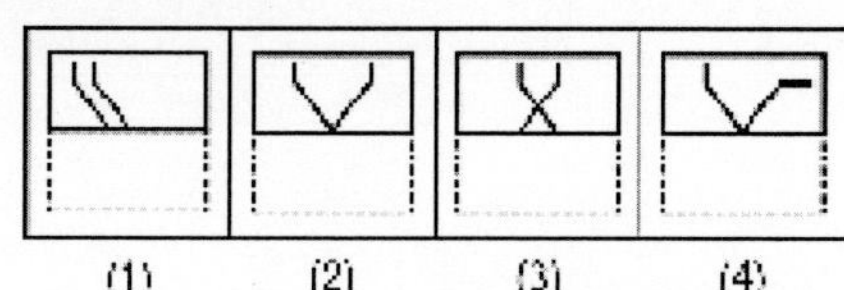

(a) 1 (b) 2
(c) 3 (d) 4

2. Find out from amongst the four alternatives as to how the pattern would appear when the transparent sheet is folded at the dotted line.

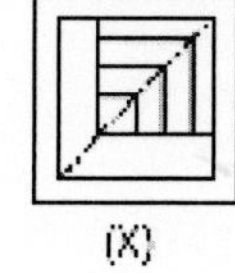

(a) 1 (b) 2
(c) 3 (d) 4

3. Find out from amongst the four alternatives as to how the pattern would appear when the transparent sheet is folded at the dotted line.

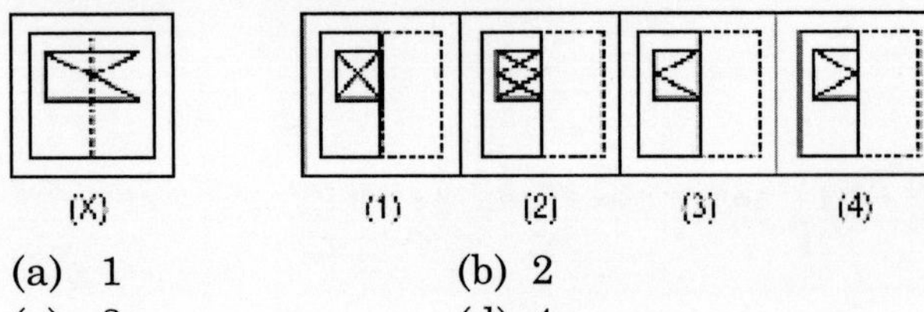

(a) 1 (b) 2
(c) 3 (d) 4

4. Find out from amongst the four alternatives as to how the pattern would appear when the transparent sheet is folded at the dotted line.

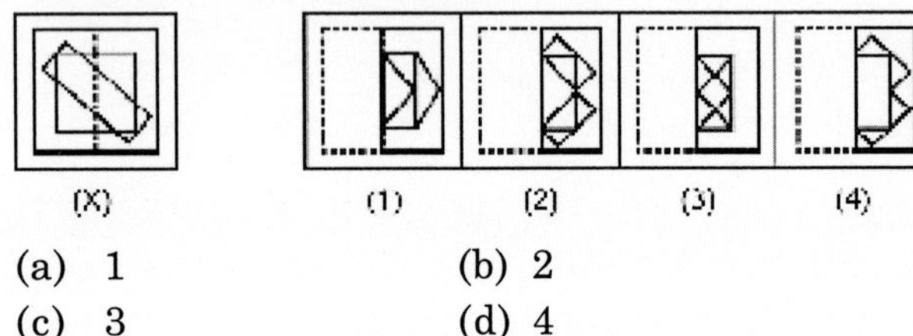

(a) 1 (b) 2
(c) 3 (d) 4

5. Find out from amongst the four alternatives as to how the pattern would appear when the transparent sheet is folded at the dotted line.

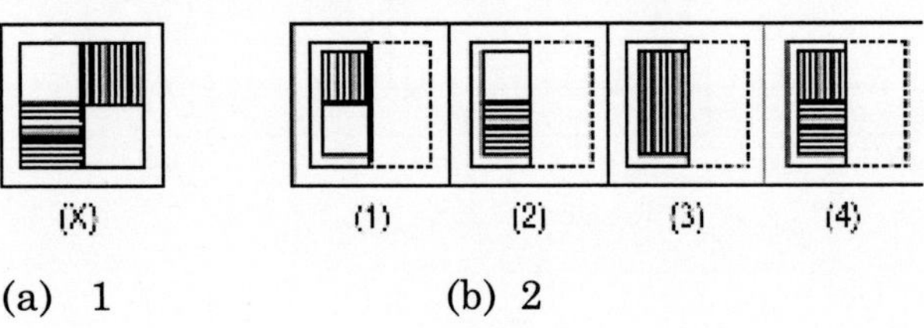

(a) 1 (b) 2
(c) 3 (d) 4

6. Find out from amongst the four alternatives as to how the pattern would appear when the transparent sheet is folded at the dotted line.

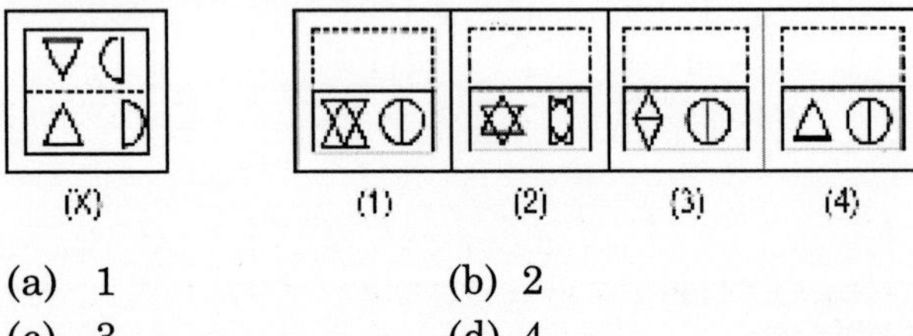

(a) 1 (b) 2
(c) 3 (d) 4

7. Find out from amongst the four alternatives as to how the pattern would appear when the transparent sheet is folded at the dotted line.

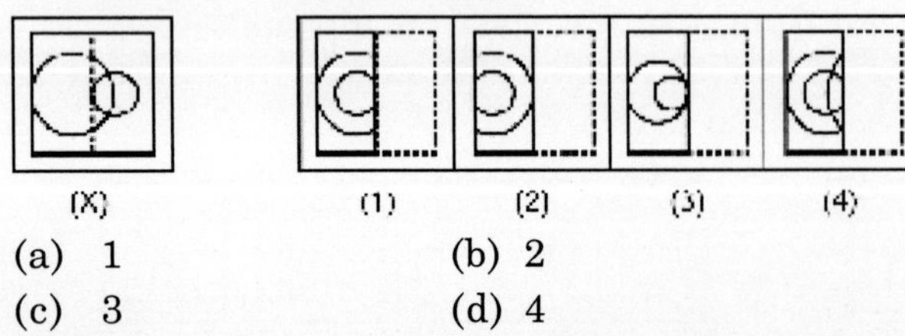

(a) 1 (b) 2
(c) 3 (d) 4

8. Find out from amongst the four alternatives as to how the pattern would appear when the transparent sheet is folded at the dotted line.

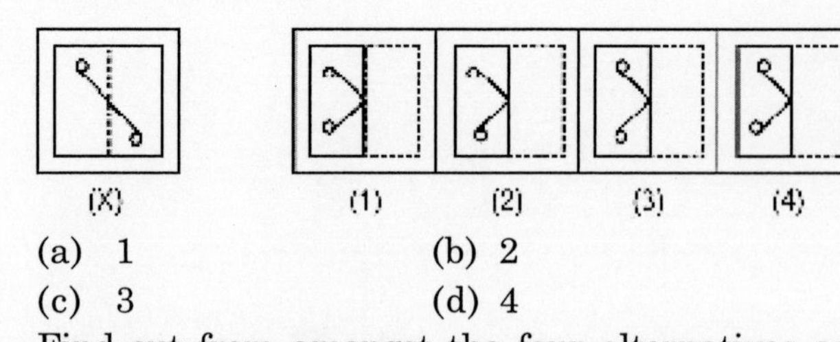

(a) 1 (b) 2
(c) 3 (d) 4

9. Find out from amongst the four alternatives as to how the pattern would appear when the transparent sheet is folded at the dotted line.

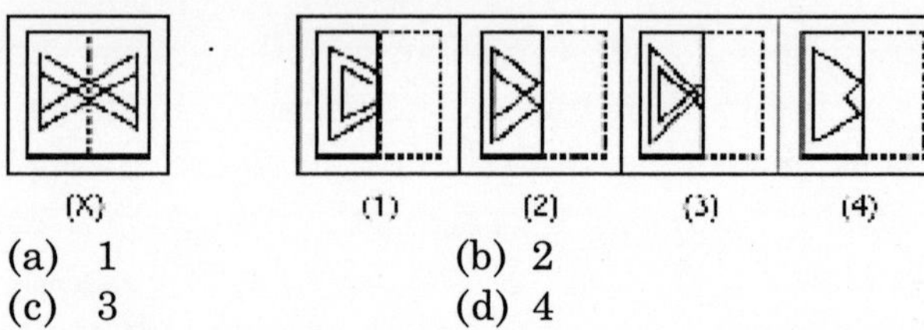

(a) 1 (b) 2
(c) 3 (d) 4

10. Find out from amongst the four alternatives as to how the pattern would appear when the transparent sheet is folded at the dotted line.

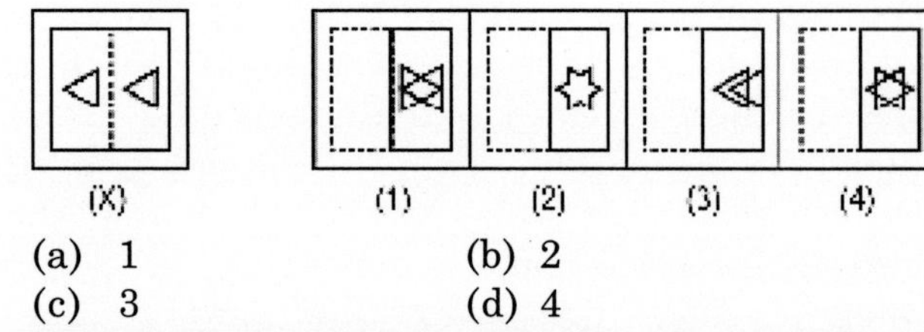

(a) 1 (b) 2
(c) 3 (d) 4

11. Find out from amongst the four alternatives as to how the pattern would appear when the transparent sheet is folded at the dotted line.

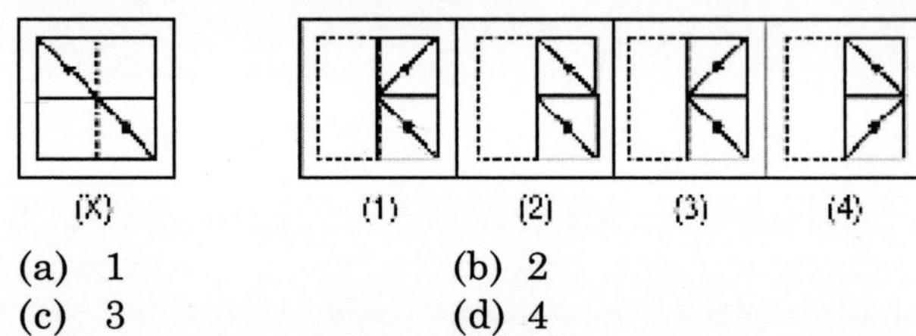

(a) 1 (b) 2
(c) 3 (d) 4

12. Find out from amongst the four alternatives as to how the pattern would appear when the transparent sheet is folded at the dotted line.

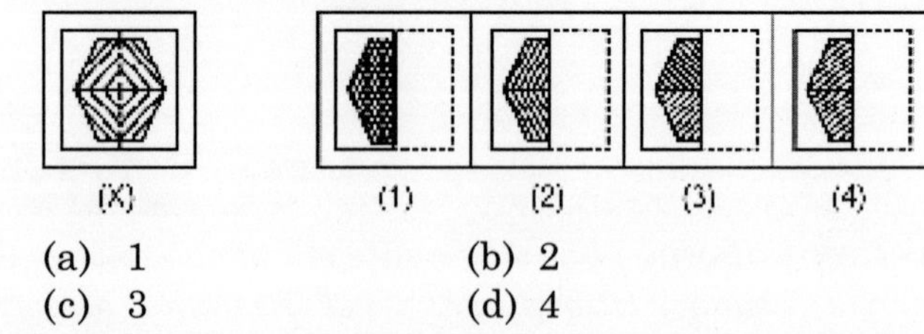

(a) 1 (b) 2
(c) 3 (d) 4

13. Find out from amongst the four alternatives as to how the pattern would appear when the transparent sheet is folded at the dotted line.

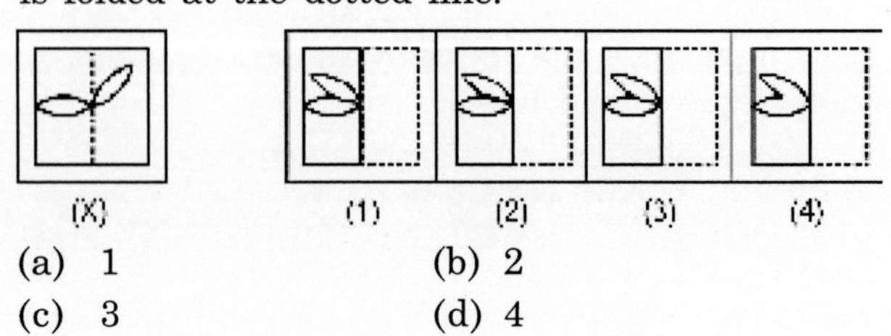

(a) 1 (b) 2
(c) 3 (d) 4

14. Find out from amongst the four alternatives as to how the pattern would appear when the transparent sheet is folded at the dotted line.

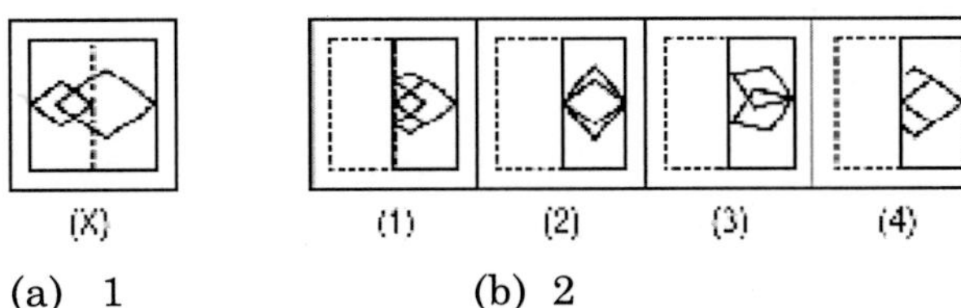

(a) 1 (b) 2
(c) 3 (d) 4

15. Find out from amongst the four alternatives as to how the pattern would appear when the transparent sheet is folded at the dotted line.

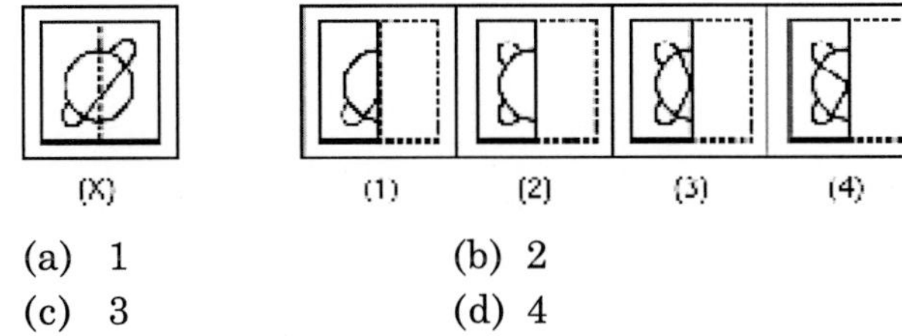

(a) 1 (b) 2
(c) 3 (d) 4

16. Find out from amongst the four alternatives as to how the pattern would appear when the transparent sheet is folded at the dotted line.

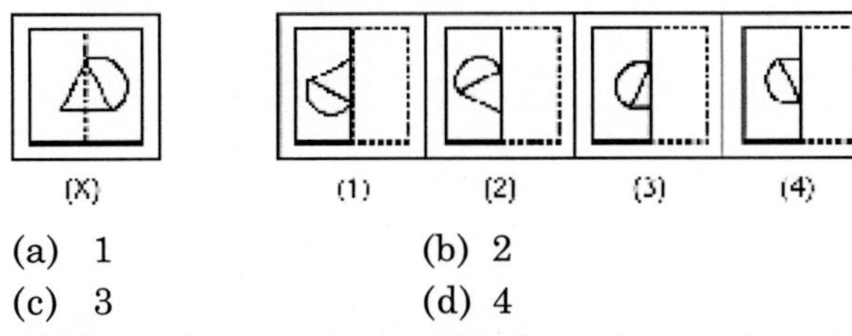

(a) 1 (b) 2
(c) 3 (d) 4

17. Find out from amongst the four alternatives as to how the pattern would appear when the transparent sheet is folded at the dotted line.

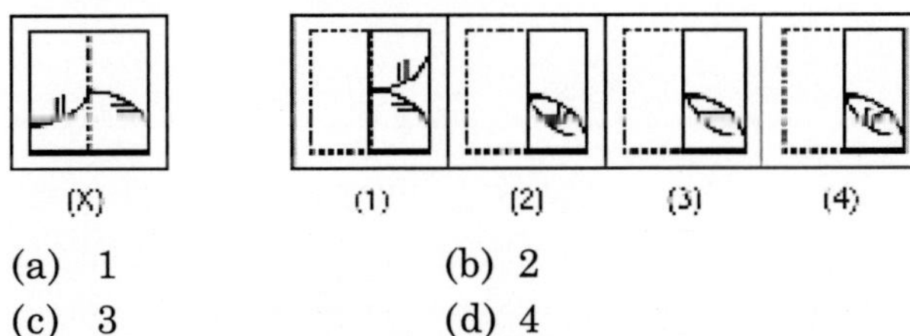

(a) 1 (b) 2
(c) 3 (d) 4

18. Find out from amongst the four alternatives as to how the pattern would appear when the transparent sheet is folded at the dotted line.

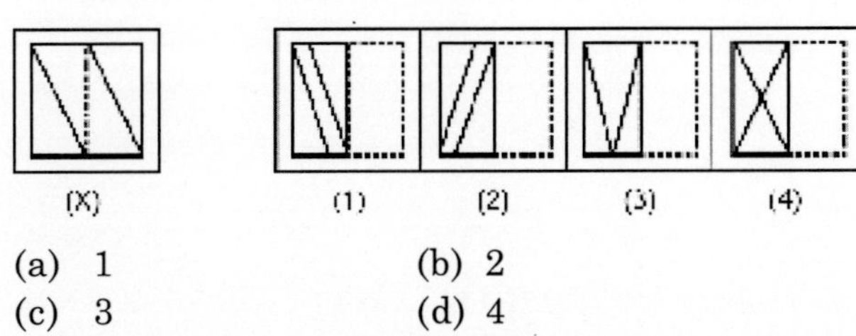

(a) 1 (b) 2
(c) 3 (d) 4

19. Find out from amongst the four alternatives as to how the pattern would appear when the transparent sheet is folded at the dotted line.

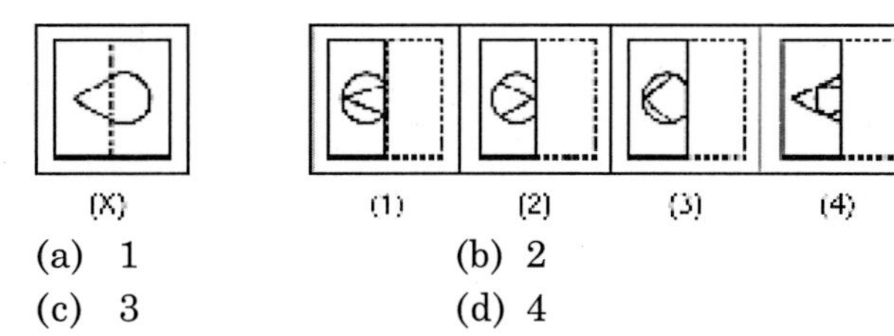

(a) 1 (b) 2
(c) 3 (d) 4

20. Find out from amongst the four alternatives as to how the pattern would appear when the transparent sheet is folded at the dotted line.

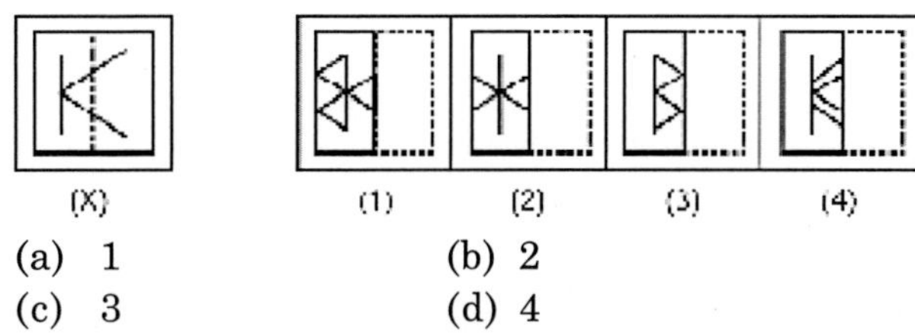

(a) 1 (b) 2
(c) 3 (d) 4

21. Find out from amongst the four alternatives as to how the pattern would appear when the transparent sheet is folded at the dotted line.

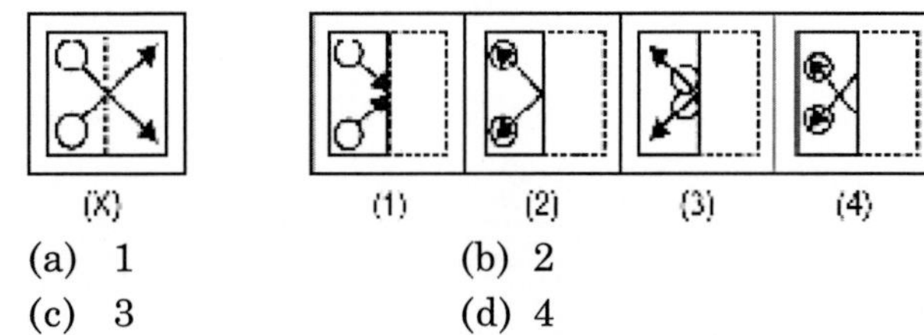

(a) 1 (b) 2
(c) 3 (d) 4

22. Find out from amongst the four alternatives as to how the pattern would appear when the transparent sheet is folded at the dotted line.

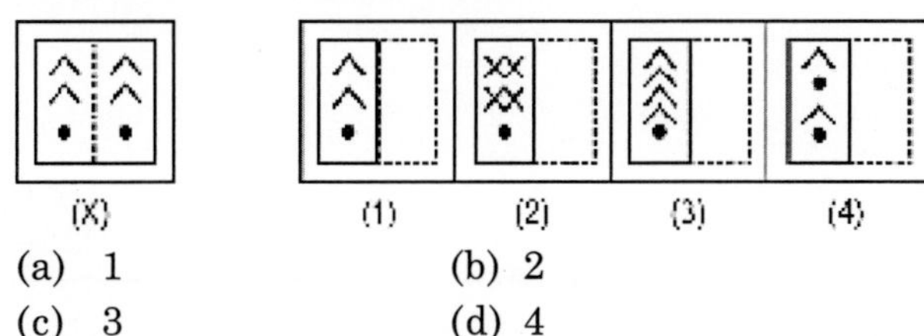

(a) 1 (b) 2
(c) 3 (d) 4

23. Find out from amongst the four alternatives as to how the pattern would appear when the transparent sheet is folded at the dotted line.

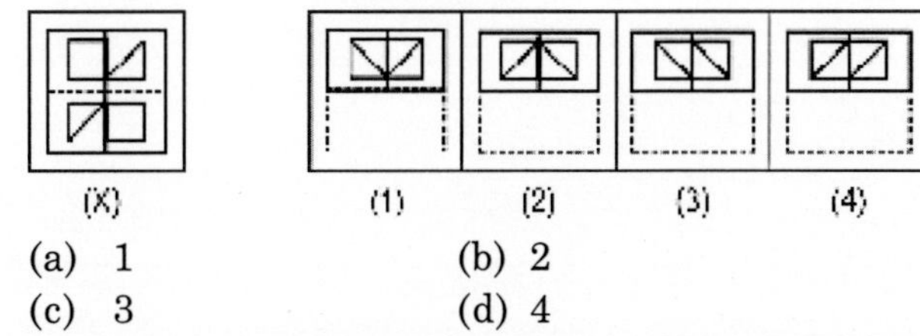

(a) 1 (b) 2
(c) 3 (d) 4

24. Find out from amongst the four alternatives as to how the pattern would appear when the transparent sheet is folded at the dotted line.

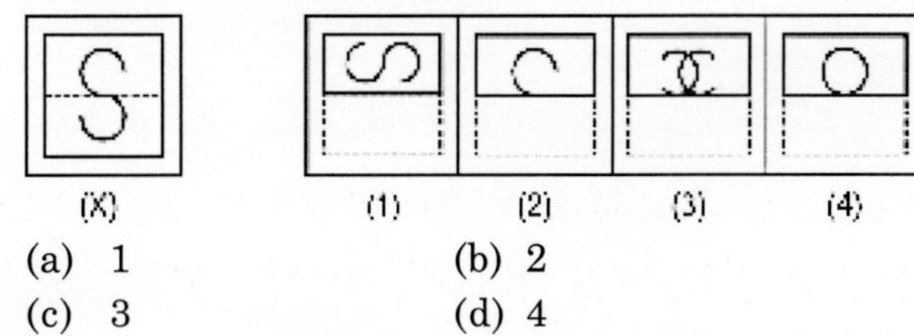

(a) 1 (b) 2
(c) 3 (d) 4

25. Find out from amongst the four alternatives as to how the pattern would appear when the transparent sheet is folded at the dotted line.

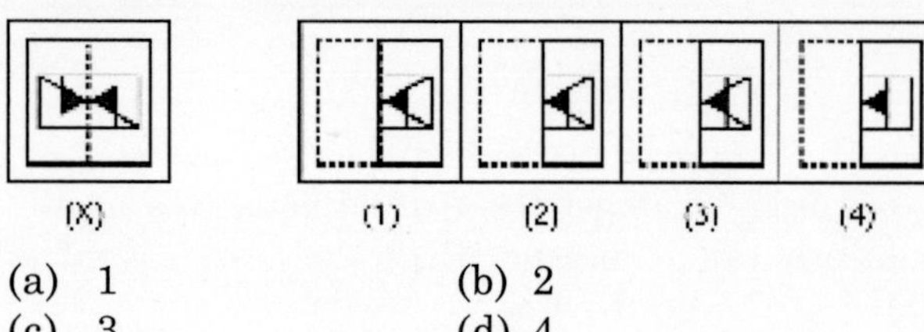

(a) 1 (b) 2
(c) 3 (d) 4

26. Find out from amongst the four alternatives as to how the pattern would appear when the transparent sheet is folded at the dotted line.

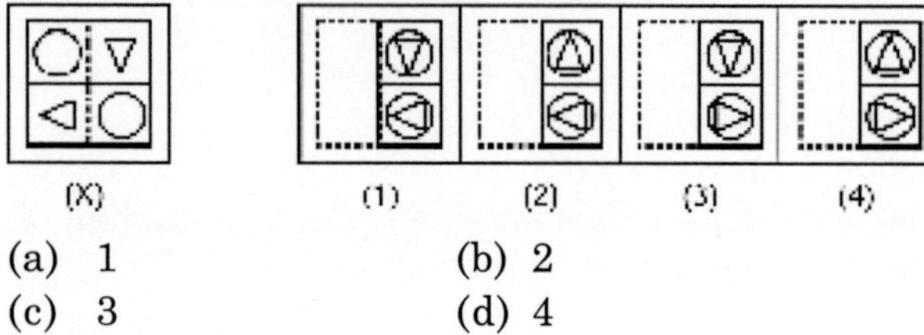

(a) 1 (b) 2
(c) 3 (d) 4

27. Find out from amongst the four alternatives as to how the pattern would appear when the transparent sheet is folded at the dotted line.

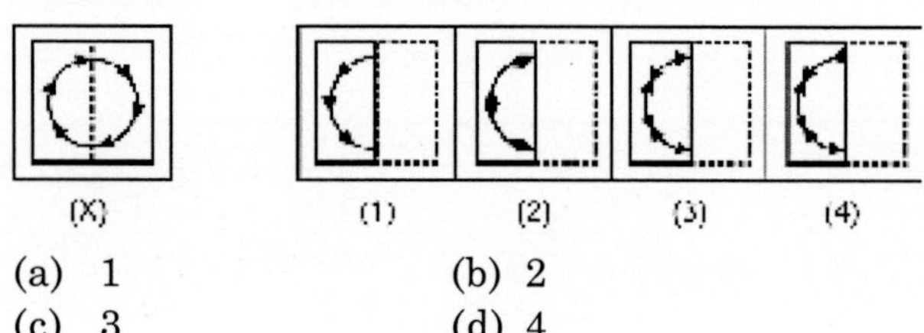

(a) 1 (b) 2
(c) 3 (d) 4

28. Find out from amongst the four alternatives as to how the pattern would appear when the transparent sheet is folded at the dotted line.

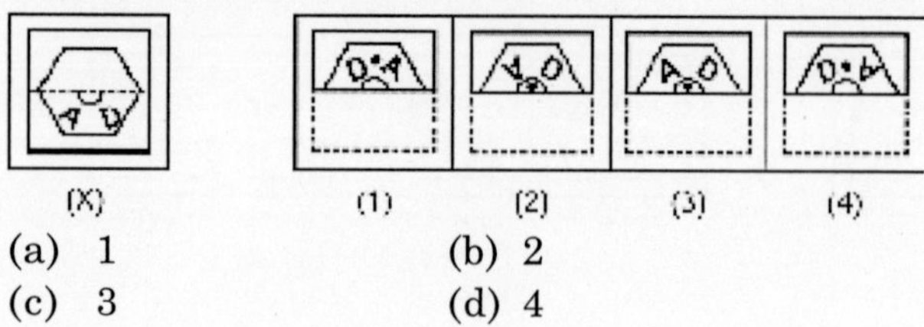

(a) 1 (b) 2
(c) 3 (d) 4

29. Find out from amongst the four alternatives as to how the pattern would appear when the transparent sheet is folded at the dotted line.

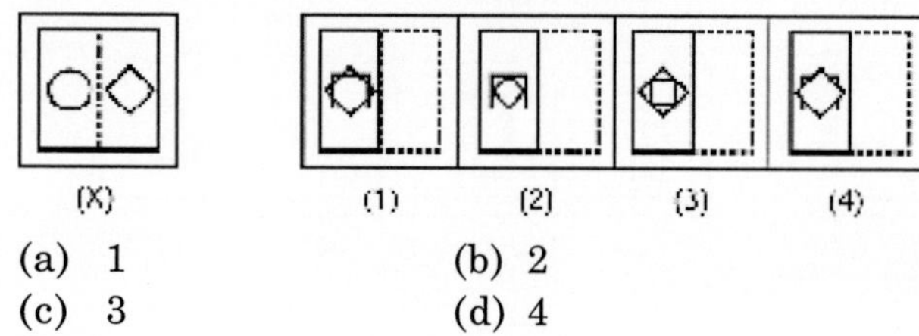

(a) 1 (b) 2
(c) 3 (d) 4

30. Find out from amongst the four alternatives as to how the pattern would appear when the transparent sheet is folded at the dotted line.

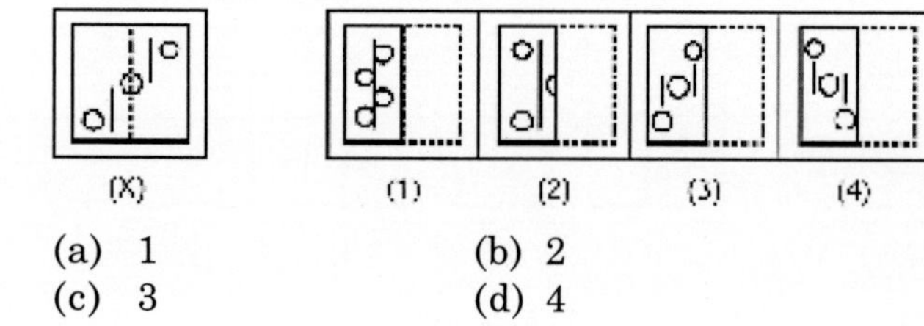

(a) 1 (b) 2
(c) 3 (d) 4

Answer Key

1. (b)	**2.** (a)	**3.** (d)	**4.** (b)	**5.** (d)	**6.** (d)	**7.** (d)	**8.** (c)	**9.** (b)
10. (a)	**11.** (a)	**12.** (b)	**13.** (b)	**14.** (a)	**15.** (d)	**16.** (c)	**17.** (d)	**18.** (d)
19. (a)	**20.** (c)	**21.** (b)	**22.** (a)	**23.** (a)	**24.** (d)	**25.** (c)	**26.** (c)	**27.** (c)
28. (b)	**29.** (a)	**30.** (b)						

Previous Year Questions

1. Find out from amongst the four alternatives as to how the pattern would appear when the transparent sheet is folded at the dotted line.
[NTSE 2012 – Tamilnadu second stage paper]

(X) (1) (2) (3) (4)

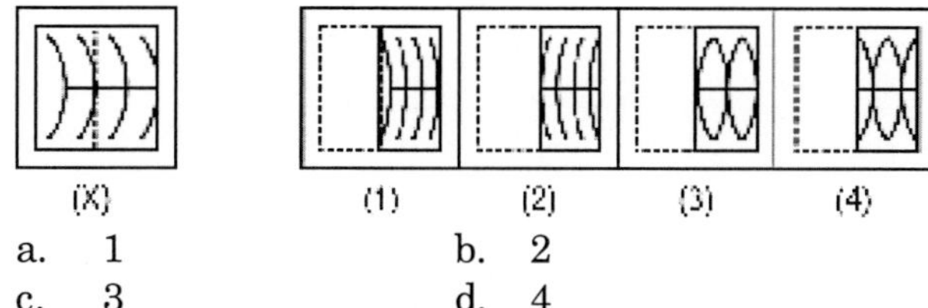

a. 1 b. 2
c. 3 d. 4

2. Find out from amongst the four alternatives as to how the pattern would appear when the transparent sheet is folded at the dotted line.
[NTSE 2007 – Rajasthan second stage paper]

(X) (1) (2) (3) (4)

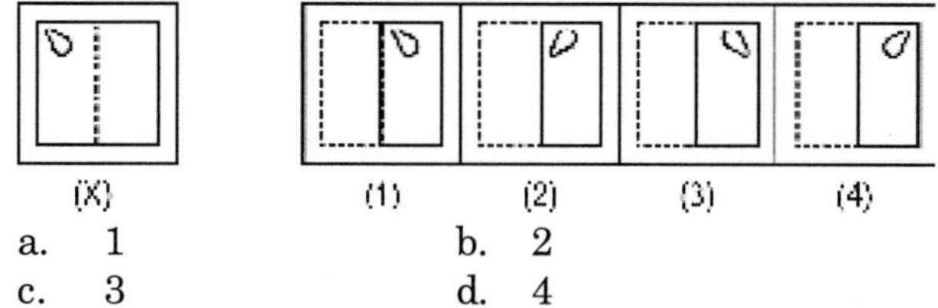

a. 1 b. 2
c. 3 d. 4

3. Find out from amongst the four alternatives as to how the pattern would appear when the transparent sheet is folded at the dotted line.
[NTSE 2003– Bihar second stage paper]

(X) (1) (2) (3) (4)

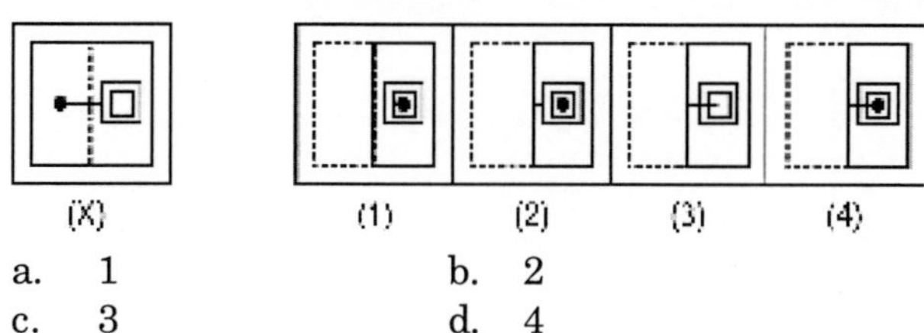

a. 1 b. 2
c. 3 d. 4

4. Find out from amongst the four alternatives as to how the pattern would appear when the transparent sheet is folded at the dotted line.
[NTSE 2002 – Kerala first stage paper]

(X) (1) (2) (3) (4)

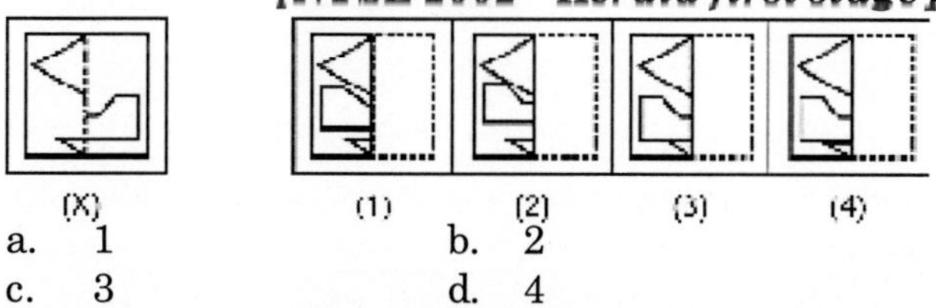

a. 1 b. 2
c. 3 d. 4

5. Find out from amongst the four alternatives as to how the pattern would appear when the transparent sheet is folded at the dotted line.
[NTSE 2001 – UP second stage paper]

(X) (1) (2) (3) (4)

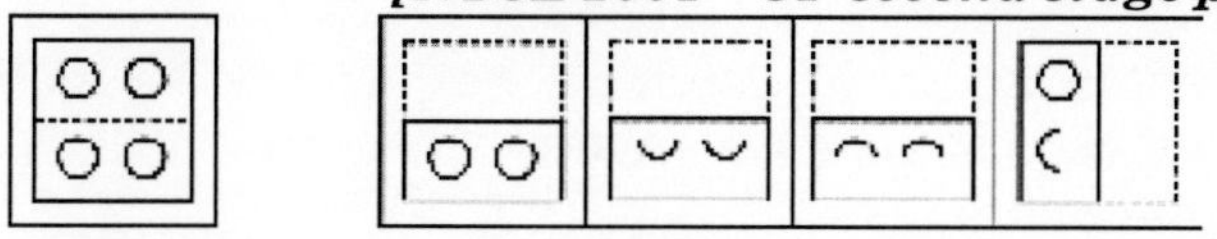

a. 1 b. 2
c. 3 d. 4

6. Find out from amongst the four alternatives as to how the pattern would appear when the transparent sheet is folded at the dotted line.
[NTSE 2003 – Delhi second stage paper]

(X) (1) (2) (3) (4)

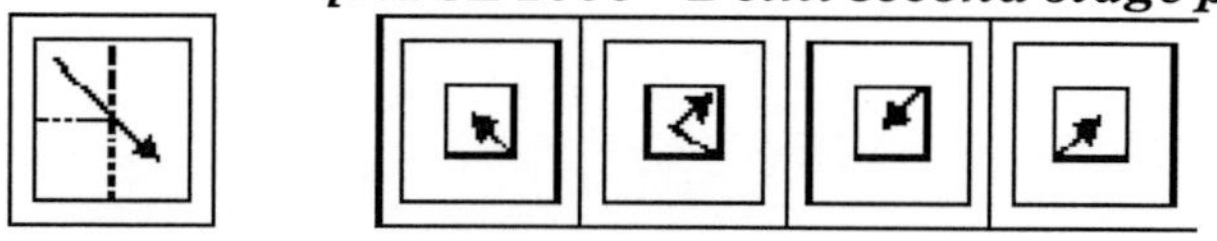

a. 1 b. 2
c. 3 d. 4

7. Find out from amongst the four alternatives as to how the pattern would appear when the transparent sheet is folded at the dotted line.
[NTSE 2003 – Punjab second stage paper]

(X) (1) (2) (3) (4)

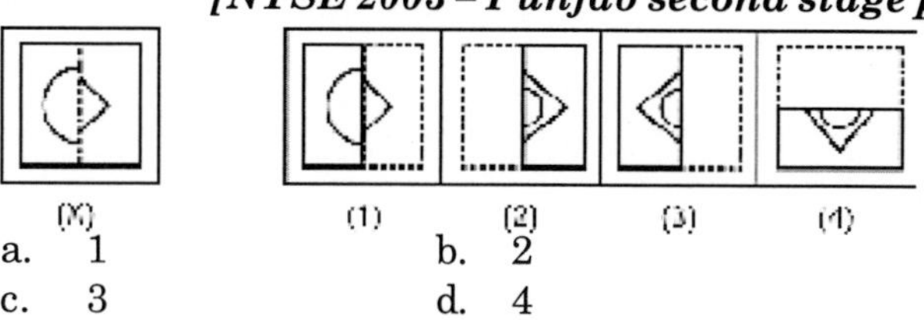

a. 1 b. 2
c. 3 d. 4

8. Find out from amongst the four alternatives as to how the pattern would appear when the transparent sheet is folded at the dotted line.
[NTSE 2012 – Tamilnadu second stage paper]

(X) (1) (2) (3) (4)

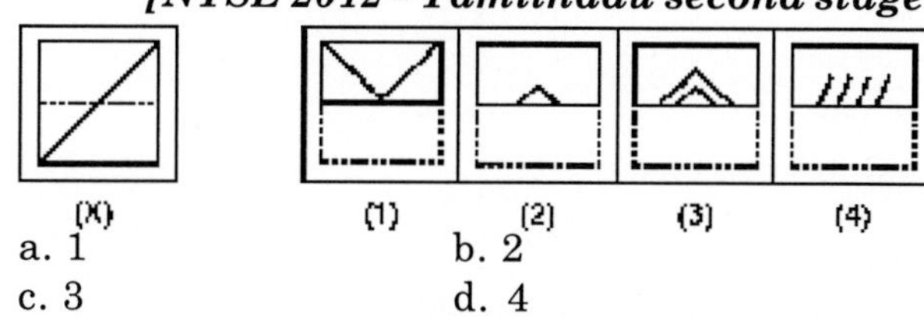

a. 1 b. 2
c. 3 d. 4

9. Find out from amongst the four alternatives as to how the pattern would appear when the transparent sheet is folded at the dotted line.
[NTSE 2012 – MP first stage paper]

(X) (1) (2) (3) (4)

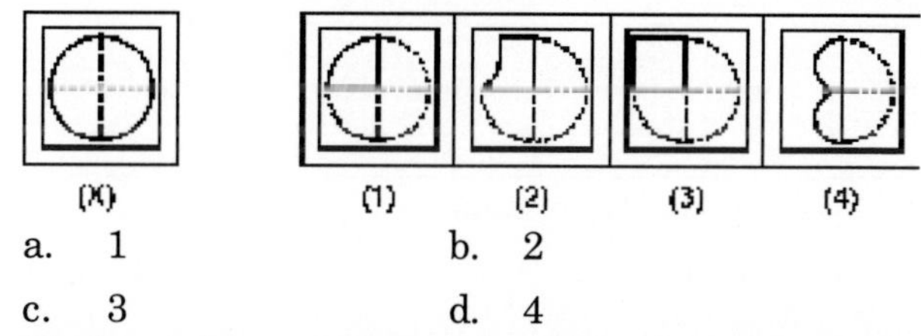

a. 1 b. 2
c. 3 d. 4

10. Find out from amongst the four alternatives as to how the pattern would appear when the transparent sheet is folded at the dotted line.
[NTSE 2012 – Uttrakhand First stage paper]

(X) (1) (2) (3) (4)

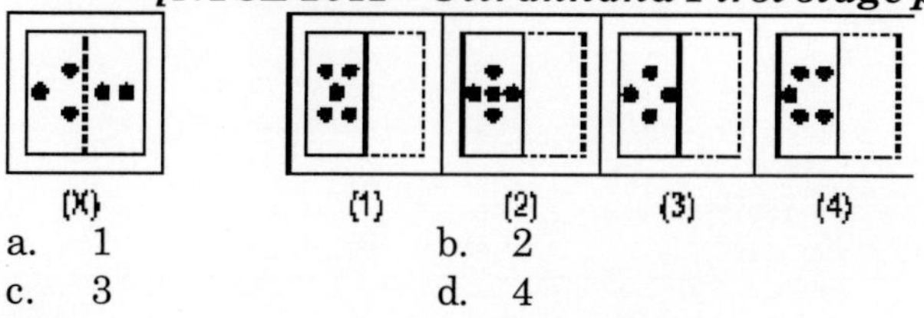

a. 1 b. 2
c. 3 d. 4

Answer Key

1. (c)	**2.** (d)	**3.** (d)	**4.** (c)	**5.** (a)	**6.** (a)	**7.** (c)	**8.** (a)	**9.** (a)	**10.** (c)

UNIT 7

Embedded Figures

Definition : A figure 'A' is called embedded in a figure 'B', if figure B contains figure 'A' as its part.

Many types of problems can be formed on embedded figures. In such type of problems, we have a model figure represented by (X) followed by four alternative figures A, B, C and (D). One has to locate the correct alternative in which figure (X) is embedded. The following example will clarify:

Solved Examples

1. Find out the alternative figure which contains figure (X) as its part.

Model Figure Answer Figure

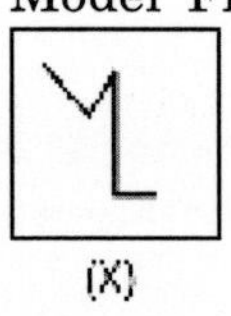

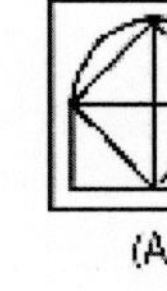
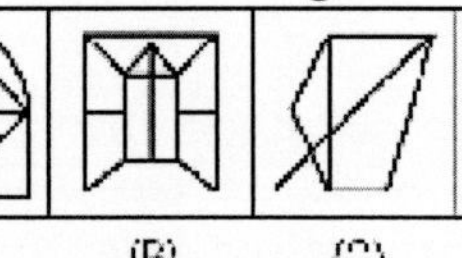

(X) (A) (B) (C) (D)

(a) A (b) B
(c) C (d) D

Solution: Option (b) is correct.

Explanation:

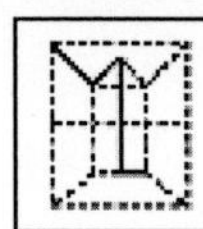

2. Find out the alternative figure which contains figure (X) as its part.

Model Figure Answer Figure

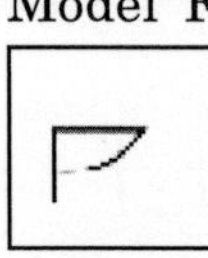
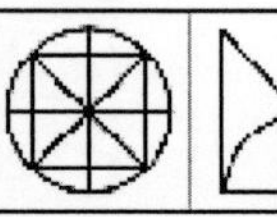
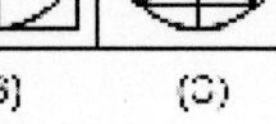
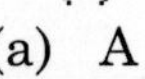
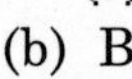

(X) (A) (B) (C) (D)

(a) A (b) B
(c) C (d) D

Solution: Option c) is correct.

Explanation:

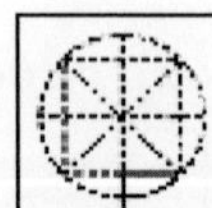

3. Find out the alternative figure which contains figure (X) as its part.

Model Figure Answer Figure

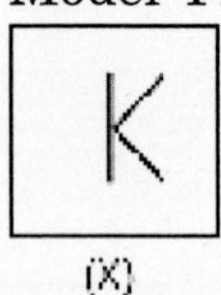
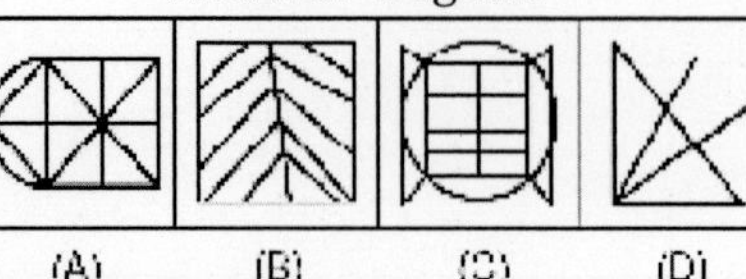

(X) (A) (B) (C) (D)

(a) A (b) B
(c) C (d) D

Solution: Option (a) is correct.

Explanation:

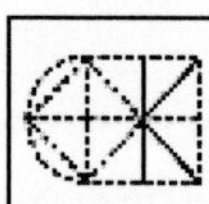

4. Find out the alternative figure which contains figure (X) as its part.

Model Figure Answer Figure

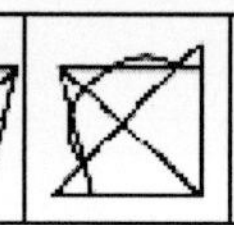
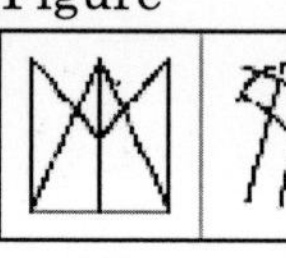

(X) (A) (B) (C) (D)

(a) A (b) B
(c) C (d) D

Solution: Option (a) is correct.

Explanation:

5. Find out the alternative figure which contains figure (X) as its part.

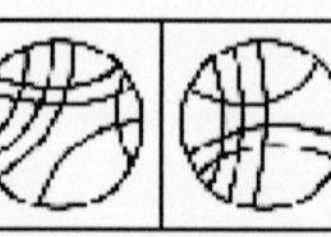
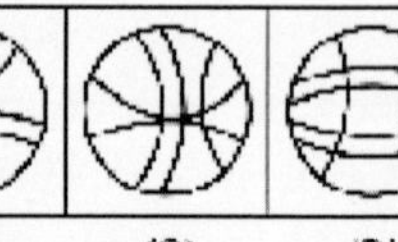

(X) (A) (B) (C) (D)

(a) A (b) B
(c) C (d) D

Solution: Option (c) is correct.

Explanation:

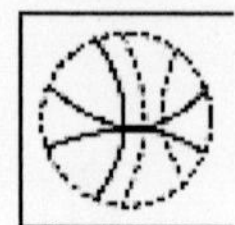

Multiple Choice Questions

☛ *In each of the following questions, you are given a figure (X) followed by four alternative figures (A), (B), (C) and (D) such that figures (X) are embedded in one of them. Trace out the alternative figure which contains fig. (X) as its part.*

1. Find out the alternative figure which contains figure (X) as its part.

Model Figure Answer Figure

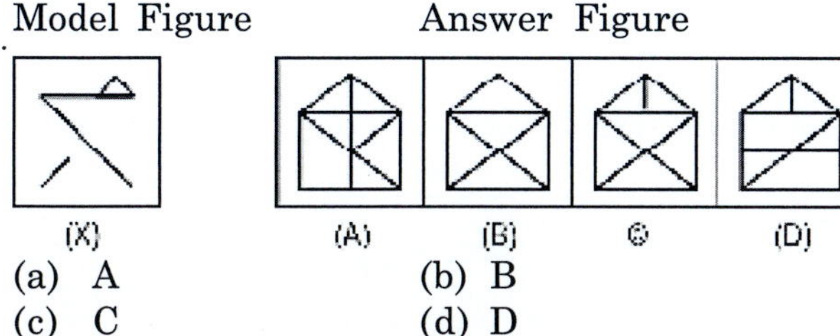

(a) A (b) B
(c) C (d) D

2. Find out the alternative figure which contains figure (X) as its part.

Model Figure Answer Figure

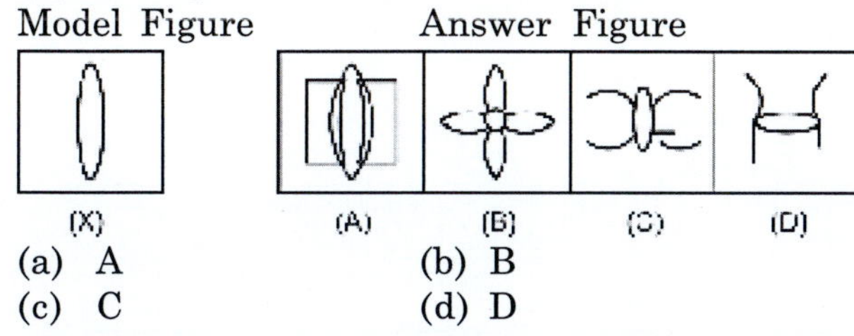

(a) A (b) B
(c) C (d) D

3. Find out the alternative figure which contains figure (X) as its part.

Model Figure Answer Figure

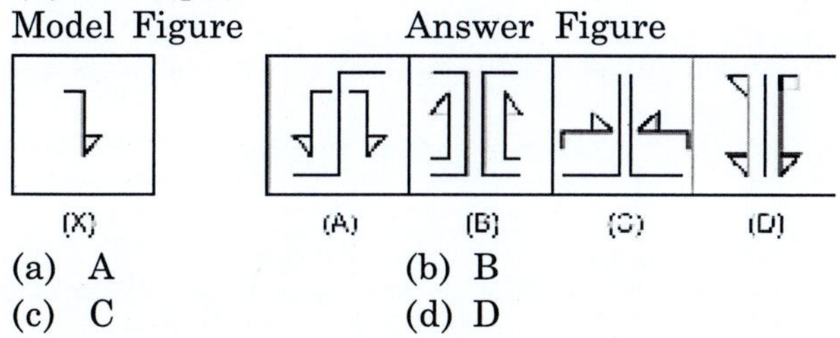

(a) A (b) B
(c) C (d) D

4. Find out the alternative figure which contains figure (X) as its part.

Model Figure Answer Figure

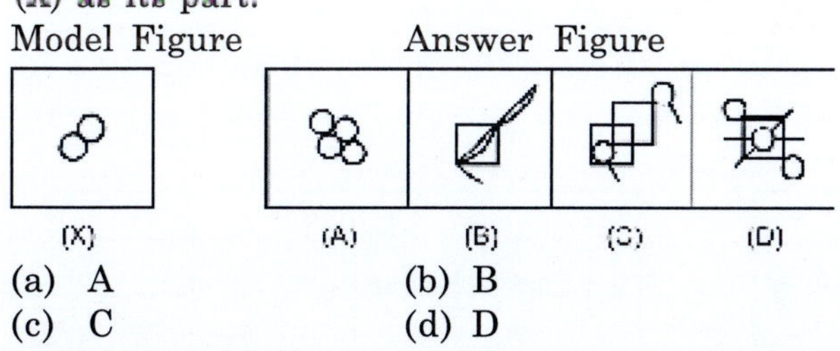

(a) A (b) B
(c) C (d) D

5. Find out the alternative figure which contains figure (X) as its part.

Model Figure Answer Figure

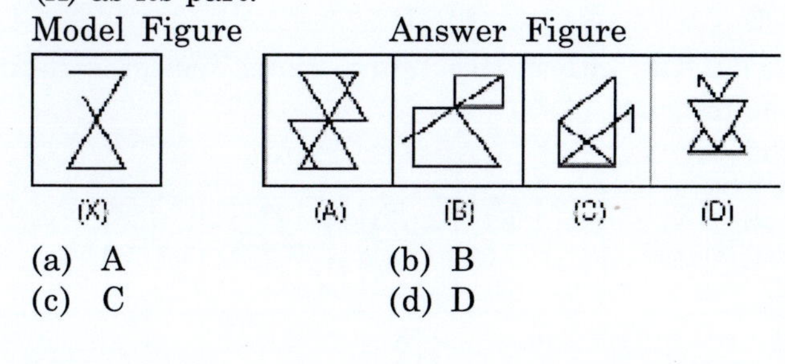

(a) A (b) B
(c) C (d) D

6. Find out the alternative figure which contains figure (X) as its part.

Model Figure Answer Figure

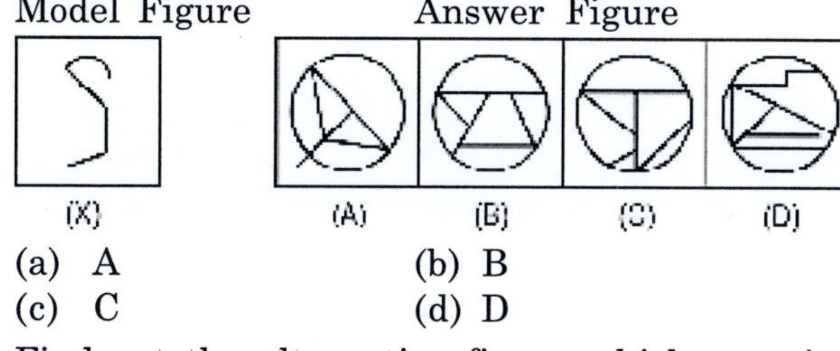

(a) A (b) B
(c) C (d) D

7. Find out the alternative figure which contains figure (X) as its part.

Model Figure Answer Figure

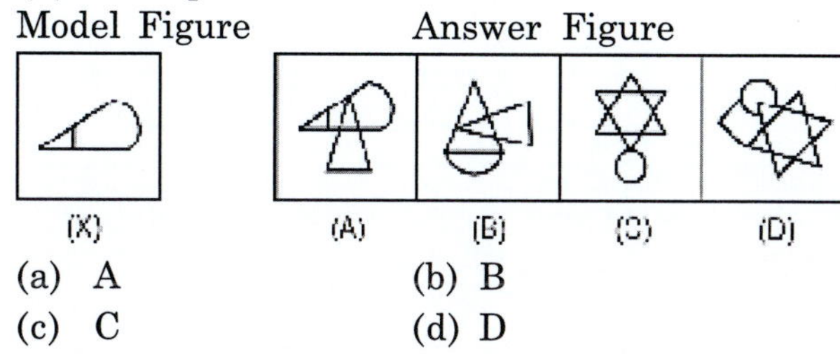

(a) A (b) B
(c) C (d) D

8. Find out the alternative figure which contains figure (X) as its part.

Model Figure Answer Figure

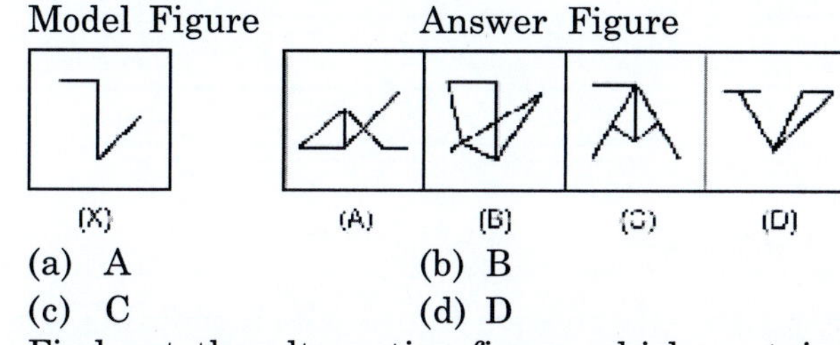

(a) A (b) B
(c) C (d) D

9. Find out the alternative figure which contains figure (X) as its part.

Model Figure Answer Figure

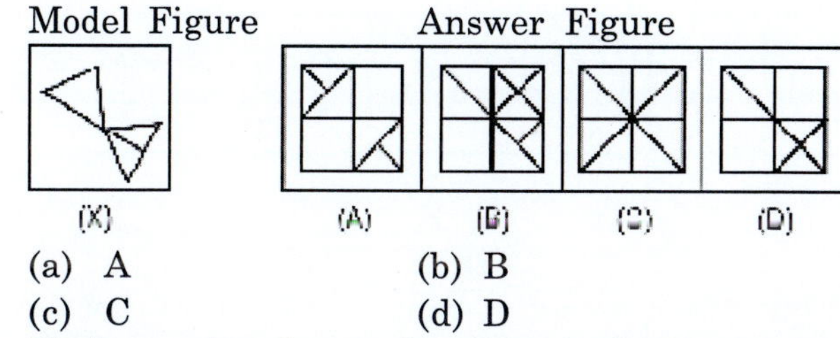

(a) A (b) B
(c) C (d) D

10. Find out the alternative figure which contains figure (X) as its part.

Model Figure Answer Figure

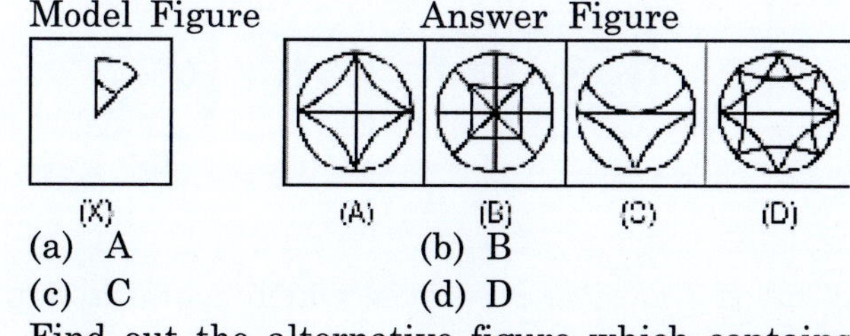

(a) A (b) B
(c) C (d) D

11. Find out the alternative figure which contains figure (X) as its part.

Model Figure Answer Figure

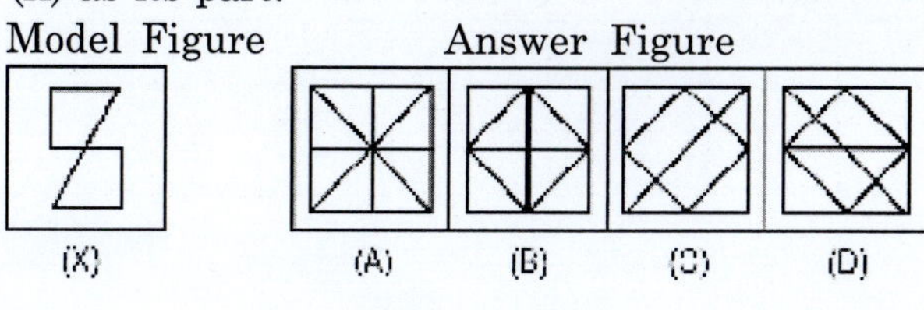

(a) A (b) B
(c) C (d) D

12. Find out the alternative figure which contains figure (X) as its part.

Model Figure Answer Figure

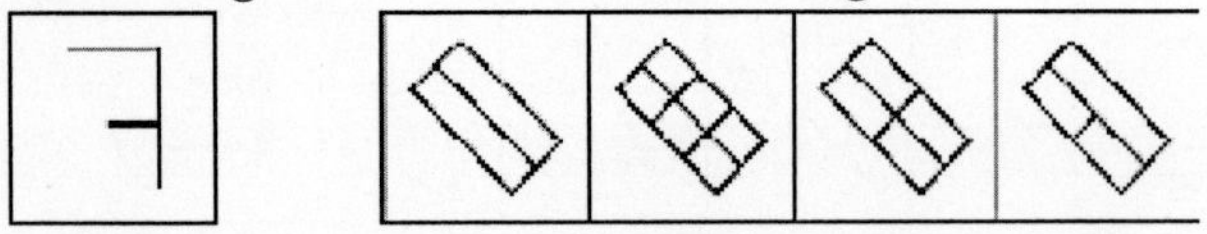

(X) (A) (B) (C) (D)

(a) A (b) B
(c) C (d) D

13. Find out the alternative figure which contains figure (X) as its part.

Model Figure Answer Figure

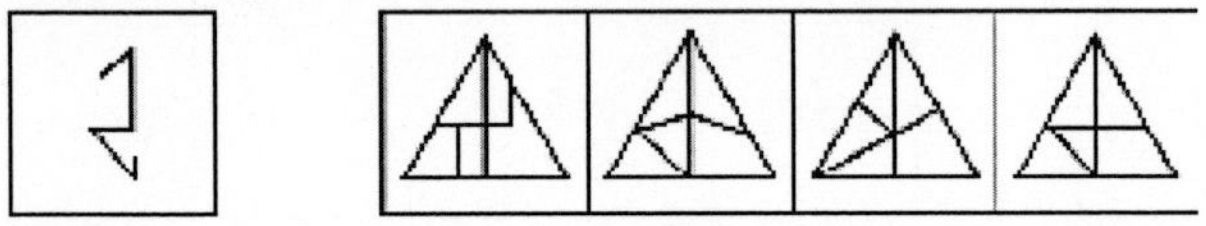

(X) (A) (B) (C) (D)

(a) A (b) B
(c) C (d) D

14. Find out the alternative figure which contains figure (X) as its part.

Model Figure Answer Figure

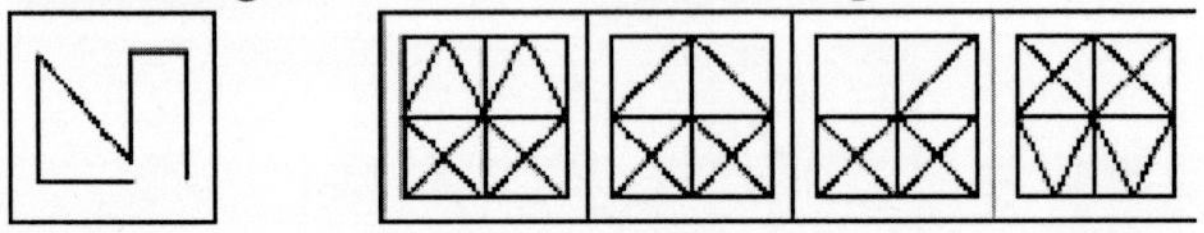

(X) (A) (B) (C) (D)

(a) A (b) B
(c) C (d) D

15. Find out the alternative figure which contains figure (X) as its part.

Model Figure Answer Figure

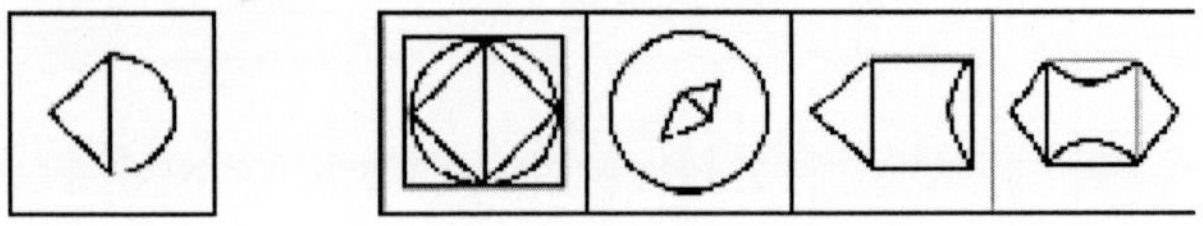

(X) (A) (B) (C) (D)

(a) A (b) B
(c) C (d) D

16. Find out the alternative figure which contains figure (X) as its part.

Model Figure Answer Figure

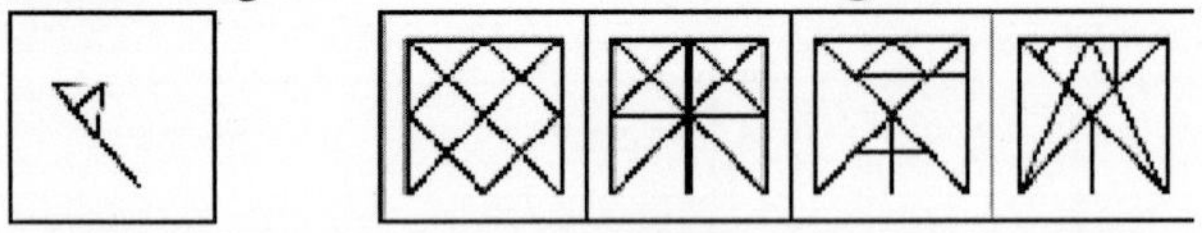

(X) (A) (B) (C) (D)

(a) A (b) B
(c) C (d) D

17. Find out the alternative figure which contains figure (X) as its part.

Model Figure Answer Figure

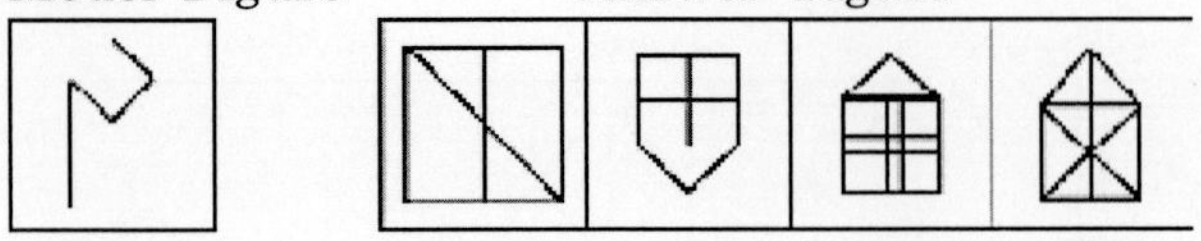

(X) (A) (B) (C) (D)

(a) A (b) B
(c) C (d) D

18. Find out the alternative figure which contains figure (X) as its part.

Model Figure Answer Figure

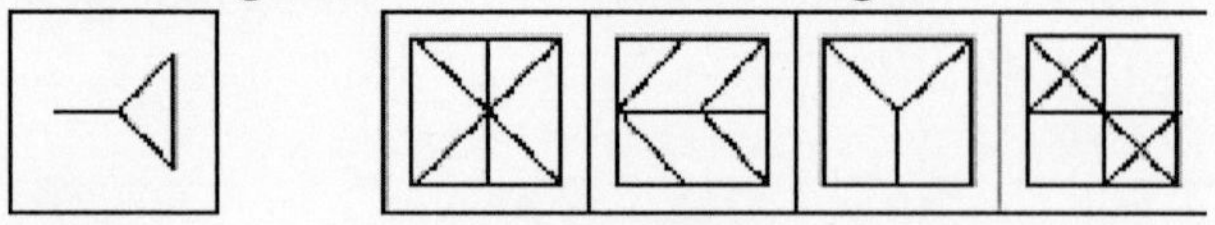

(X) (A) (B) (C) (D)

(a) A (b) B
(c) C (d) D

19. Find out the alternative figure which contains figure (X) as its part.

Model Figure Answer Figure

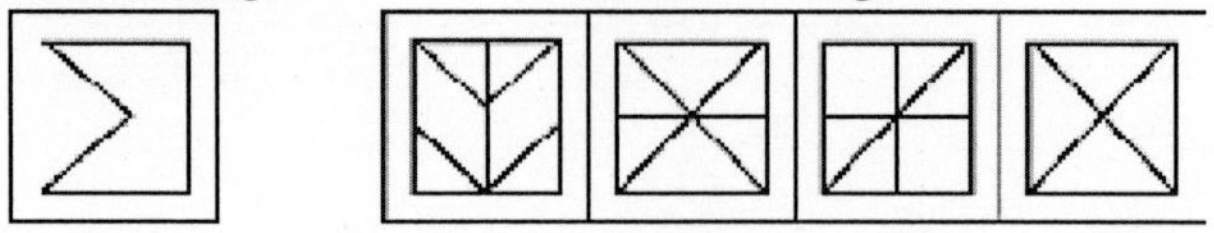

(X) (A) (B) (C) (D)

(a) A (b) B
(c) C (d) D

20. Find out the alternative figure which contains figure (X) as its part.

Model Figure Answer Figure

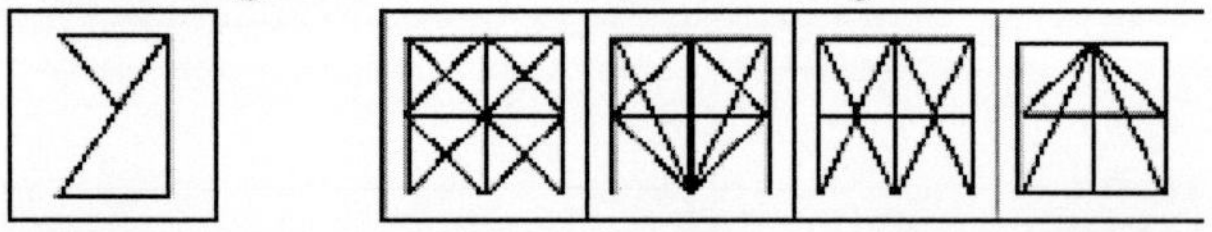

(X) (A) (B) (C) (D)

(a) A (b) B
(c) C (d) D

21. Find out the alternative figure which contains figure (X) as its part.

Model Figure Answer Figure

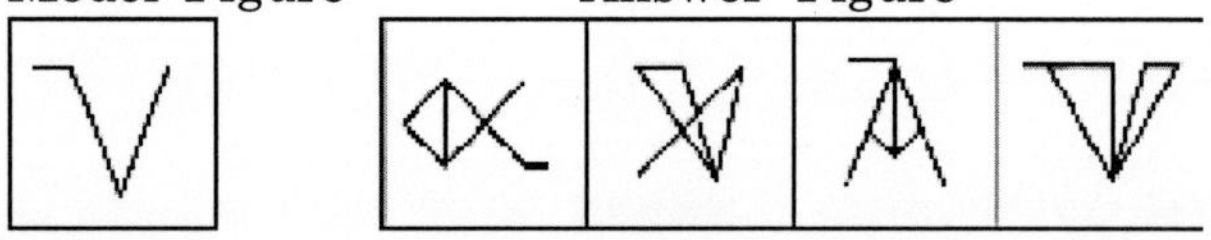

(X) (A) (B) (C) (D)

(a) A (b) B
(c) C (d) D

22. Find out the alternative figure which contains figure (X) as its part.

Model Figure Answer Figure

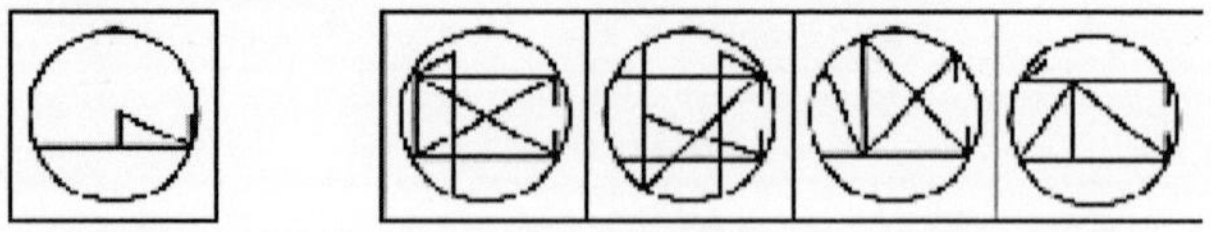

(X) (A) (B) (C) (D)

(a) A (b) B
(c) C (d) D

23. Find out the alternative figure which contains figure (X) as its part.

Model Figure Answer Figure

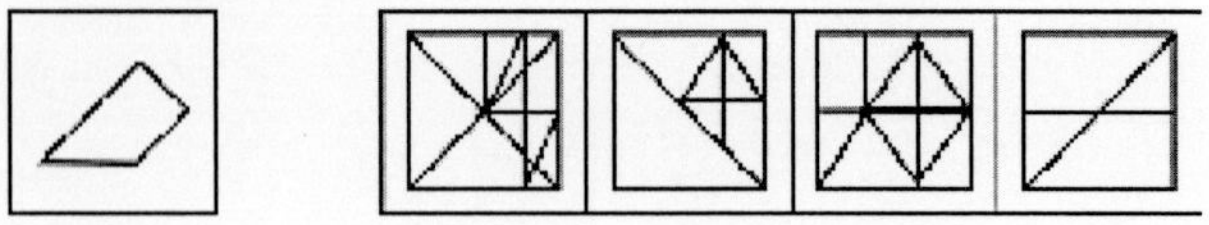

(X) (A) (B) (C) (D)

(a) A (b) B
(c) C (d) D

24. Find out the alternative figure which contains figure (X) as its part.

Model Figure Answer Figure

(a) A (b) B
(c) C (d) D

25. Find out the alternative figure which contains figure (X) as its part.

Model Figure Answer Figure

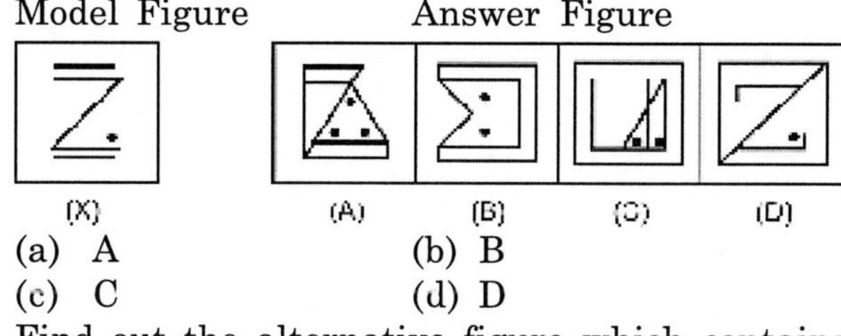

(a) A (b) B
(c) C (d) D

26. Find out the alternative figure which contains figure (X) as its part.

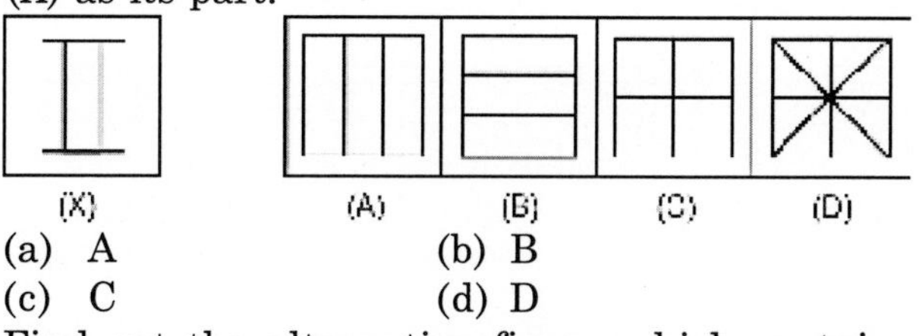

(a) A (b) B
(c) C (d) D

27. Find out the alternative figure which contains figure (X) as its part.

Model Figure Answer Figure

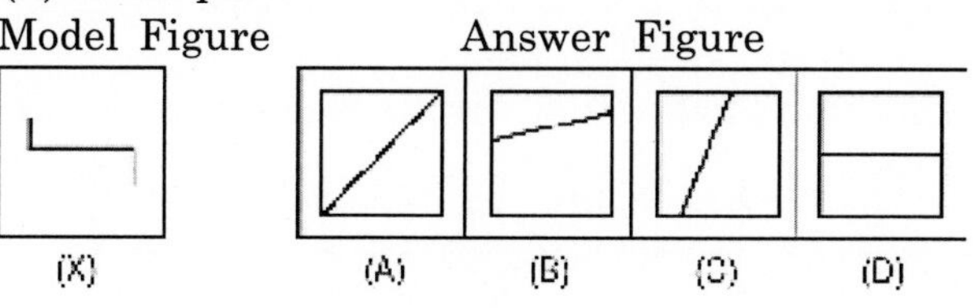

(a) A (b) B
(c) C (d) D

28. Find out the alternative figure which contains figure (X) as its part.

Model Figure Answer Figure

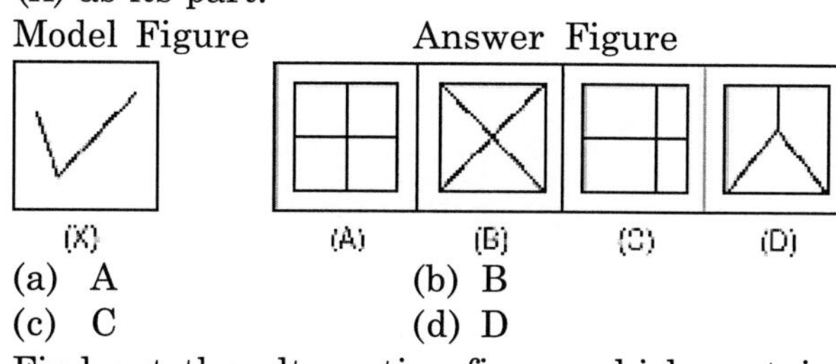

(a) A (b) B
(c) C (d) D

29. Find out the alternative figure which contains figure (X) as its part.

Model Figure Answer Figure

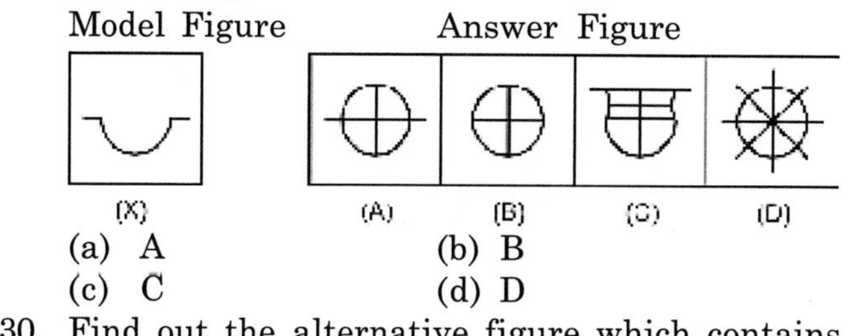

(a) A (b) B
(c) C (d) D

30. Find out the alternative figure which contains figure (X) as its part.

Model Figure Answer Figure

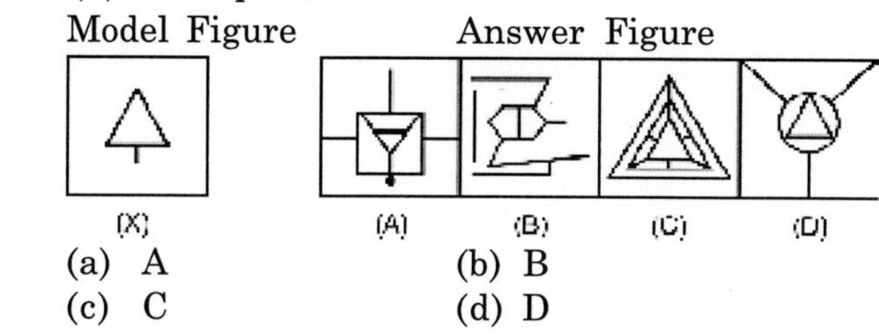

(a) A (b) B
(c) C (d) D

Answer Key

1. (c)	**2.** (c)	**3.** (a)	**4.** (a)	**5.** (a)	**6.** (c)	**7.** (a)	**8.** (b)	**9.** (d)	**10.** (b)
11. (a)	**12.** (c)	**13.** (d)	**14.** (d)	**15.** (a)	**16.** (b)	**17.** (d)	**18.** (b)	**19.** (b)	**20.** (a)
21. (b)	**22.** (d)	**23.** (c)	**24.** (b)	**25.** (d)	**26.** (a)	**27.** (d)	**28.** (b)	**29.** (a)	**30.** (c)

❐

Previous Year Questions

1. Find out the alternative figure which contains figure (X) as its part.

[NTSE 2012 - Punjab first stage Paper]

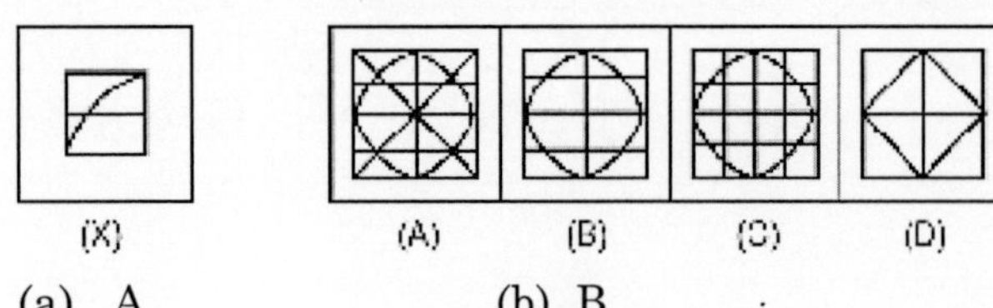

(a) A (b) B
(c) C (d) D

2. Find out the alternative figure which contains figure (X) as its part. ***[NTSE 2003 - MP first stage Paper]***

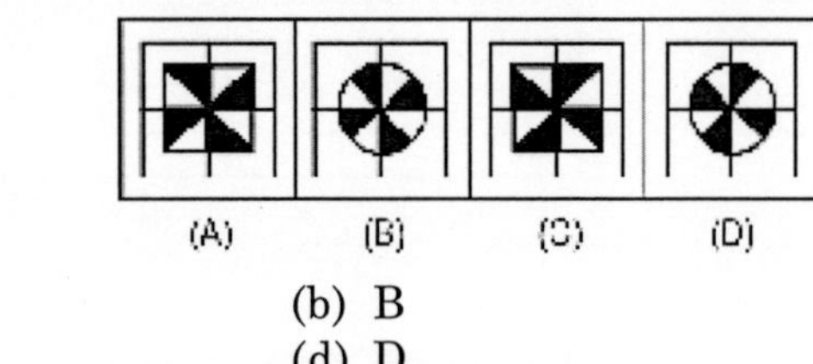

(a) A (b) B
(c) C (d) D

3. Find out the alternative figure which contains figure (X) as its part.

[NTSE 2005– Rajasthan Second stage Paper]

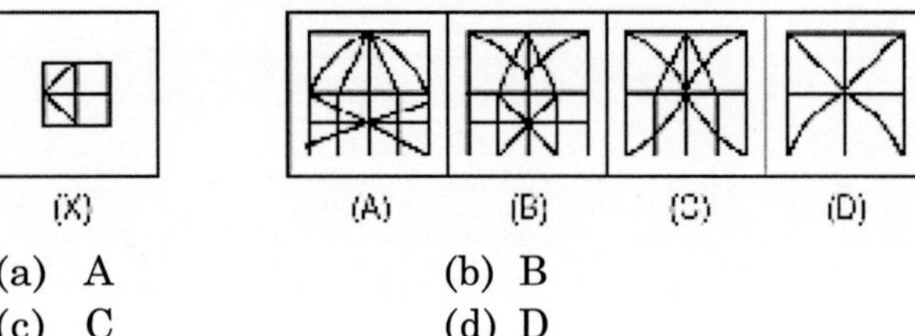

(a) A (b) B
(c) C (d) D

4. Find out the alternative figure which contains figure (X) as its part. ***[NTSE 2003 - Bihar first stage Paper]***

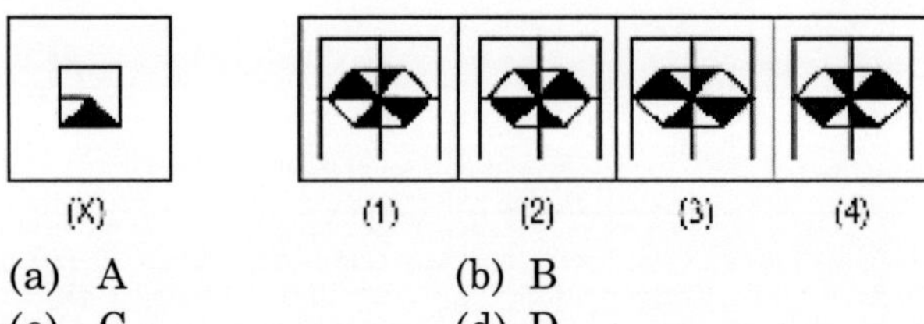

(a) A (b) B
(c) C (d) D

5. Find out the alternative figure which contains figure (X) as its part.

[NTSE 2002 – Karnataka Second stage Paper]

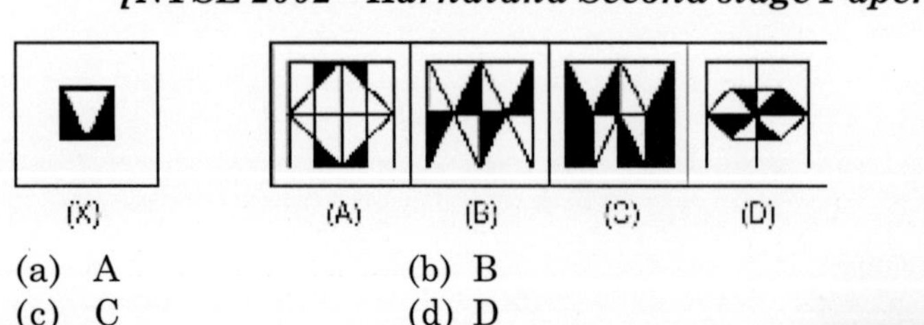

(a) A (b) B
(c) C (d) D

6. Find out the alternative figure which contains figure (X) as its part. ***[NTSE 2005 - Delhi first stage Paper]***

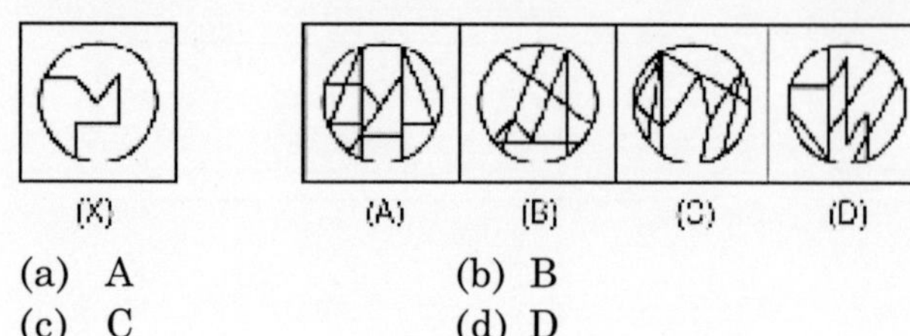

(a) A (b) B
(c) C (d) D

7. Find out the alternative figure which contains figure (X) as its part. ***[NTSE 2012- Delhi first stage Paper]***

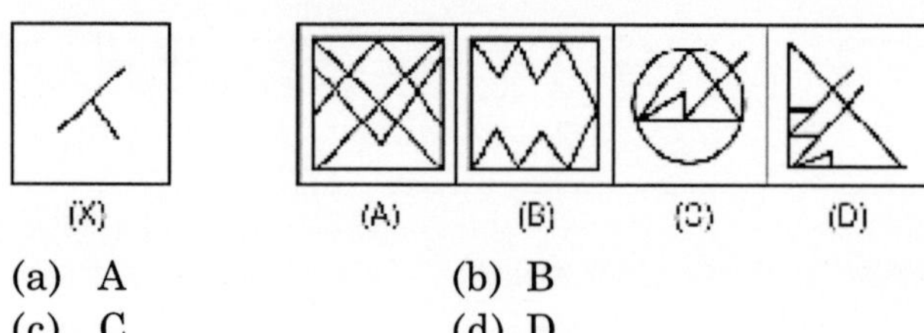

(a) A (b) B
(c) C (d) D

8. Find out the alternative figure which contains figure (X) as its part. ***[NTSE 2004 - UP first stage Paper]***

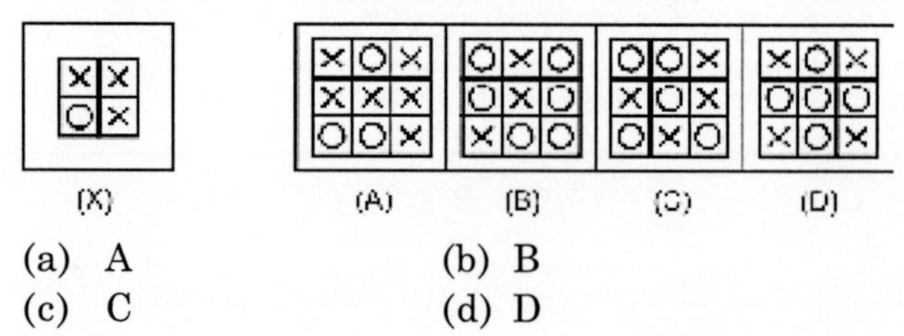

(a) A (b) B
(c) C (d) D

9. Find out the alternative figure which contains figure (X) as its part.

[NTSE 2012 – Tamilnadu Second stage Paper]

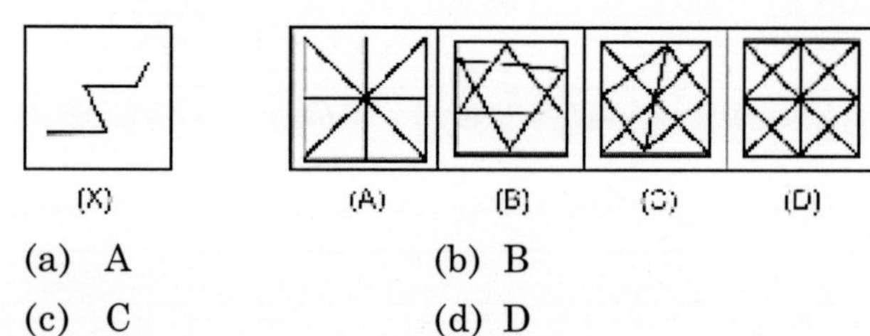

(a) A (b) B
(c) C (d) D

10. Find out the alternative figure which contains figure (X) as its part.

[NTSE 2012 – Uttrakhand First stage Paper]

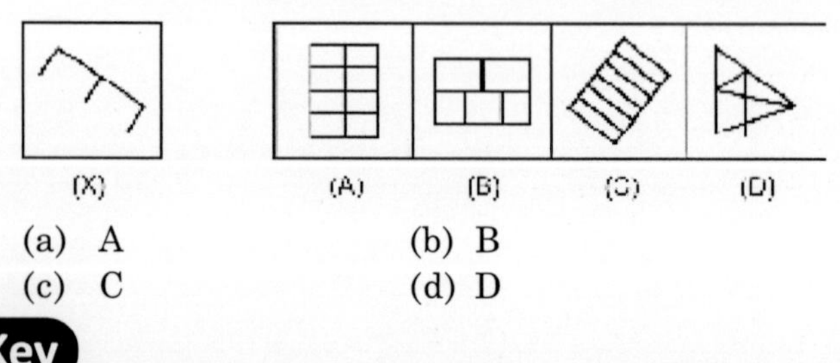

(a) A (b) B
(c) C (d) D

Answer Key

1. (b)	2. (b)	3. (b)	4. (d)	5. (c)	6. (a)	7. (c)	8. (a)	9. (b)	10. (b)

UNIT 8

Dot Fixing Situation

Dot Fixing Situation is for the assessment and resting of students' shrewd observation power. A problem figure is given in which one or more dots are placed in the space enclosed by two or more geometrical figures such as square, rectangle, circle, triangle, pentagon, hexagon, octagon etc. One has to identify the region(s) where the dot is/are situated in the problem figure. Then search for an answer figure in which dots are placed in a similar enclosed area.

Solved Examples

☛ ***Direction to solve (1 to 5):*** From amongst the figures marked (1), (2), (3) and (4), select the figure which satisfies the same conditions of placement of the dots as in figure (X).

1. Select the figure which satisfies the same conditions of placement of the dots as in Figure-X.

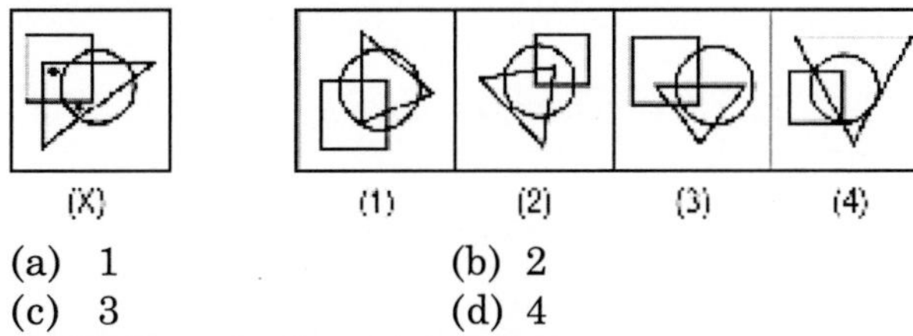

(a) 1 (b) 2
(c) 3 (d) 4

Solution: Option (c) is correct.

Explanation: In figure (X), one of the dots lies in the region common to the square and the triangle and another dot lies in the region common to the circle and the triangle. In each of the alternatives (1), (2) and (4), the region common to the square and the triangle lies within the circle. Therefore, in each of these figures, there is no region common to the square and the triangle only. Only the alternative (3) consists of a region common to the square and the triangle only and another region common to the circle and the triangle only. Hence, figure (3) is the answer.

2. Select the figure which satisfies the same conditions of placement of the dots as in Figure-X.

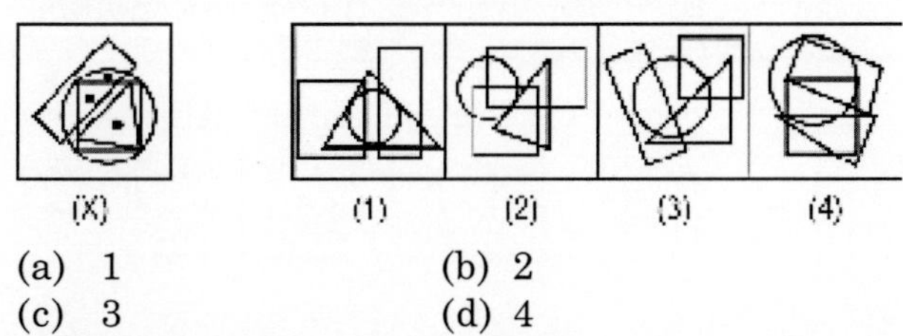

(a) 1 (b) 2
(c) 3 (d) 4

Solution: Option (d) is correct.

Explanation: In figure (X), one of the dots lies in the region common to the circle and the rectangle only; another dot lies in the region common to the circle, the square and the rectangle only and the third dot lies in the region common to the circle, the square and the triangle only. In each of the figures (1) and (3) there is no region common to the circle, the square and the rectangle only and in figure (2), there is no region common to the circle, the square and the triangle only. Only, figure (4) consists of all the three types of regions.

3. Select the figure which satisfies the same conditions of placement of the dots as in Figure-X.

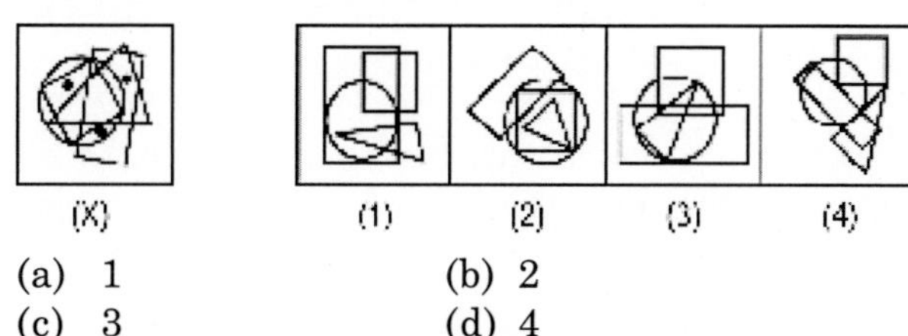

(a) 1 (b) 2
(c) 3 (d) 4

Solution: Option (d) is correct.

Explanation: In figure (X), one of the dots lies in the region common to the circle and the square only; another dot lies in the region common to the circle and the rectangle only and the third dot lies in the region common to the triangle and the rectangle only. In figure (1) there is no region common to the circle and the square only. In figures (2) and (3) there are no. regions common to the triangle and the rectangle only. Only figure (4) consists of all the three types of regions.

4. Select the figure which satisfies the same conditions of placement of the dots as in Figure-X.

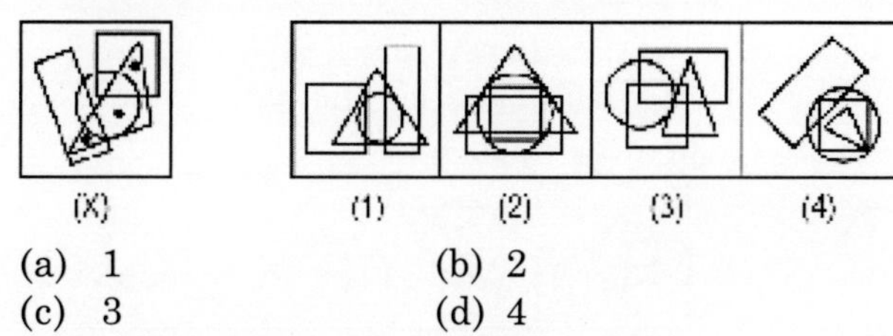

(a) 1 (b) 2
(c) 3 (d) 4

Solution: Option (a) is correct.

Explanation: In figure (X), one of the dots lies in the region common to the square and the triangle only;

another dot lies in the region common to the circle and the triangle only and the third dot lies in the region common to the triangle and the rectangle only. In figure (2), there is no region common to the square and the triangle only. In figure (3), there is no region common to the circle and the triangle only. In figure (4) there is no region common to the triangle and the rectangle only. Only figure (1) consists of all the three types of regions.

5. Select the figure which satisfies the same conditions of placement of the dots as in Figure-X.

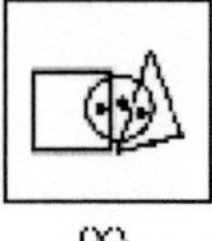
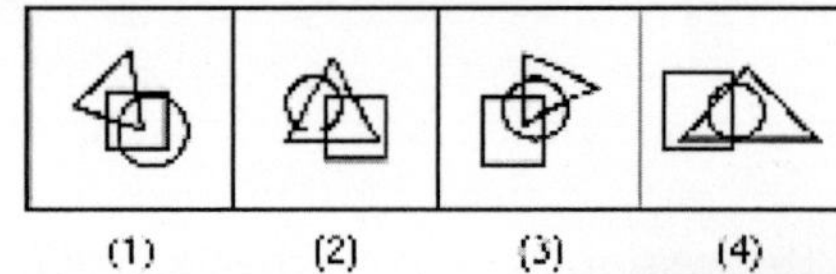

(X) (1) (2) (3) (4)

(a) 1 (b) 2
(c) 3 (d) 4

Solution: Option (c) is correct.

Explanation: In figure (X), one of the dots lies in the region common to the circle and the triangle only; another dot lies in the circle alone and the third dot lies in the region common to the circle and the square only. In figure (1) there is no region common to the circle and the triangle only, in figure (2), there is no region common to the circle and the square and in figure (4), there is no region which lies in the circle alone. Only, figure (3) consists of all the three types of regions.

Multiple Choice Questions

☛ ***Direction to solve (1 to 20):*** From amongst the figures marked (1), (2), (3) and (4), select the figure which satisfies the same conditions of placement of the dots as in figure (X).

1. Select the figure which satisfies the same conditions of placement of the dots as in Figure-X.

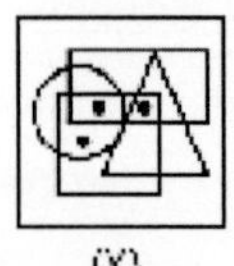
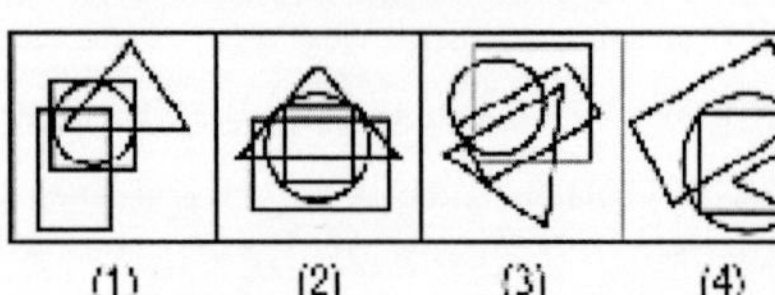

(X) (1) (2) (3) (4)

(a) 1 (b) 2
(c) 3 (d) 4

2. Select the figure which satisfies the same conditions of placement of the dots as in Fig.-X.

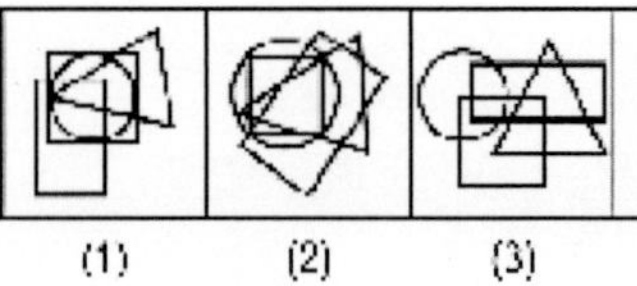

(X) (1) (2) (3) (4)

(a) 1 (b) 2
(c) 3 (d) 4

3. Select the figure which satisfies the same conditions of placement of the dots as in Fig.-X.

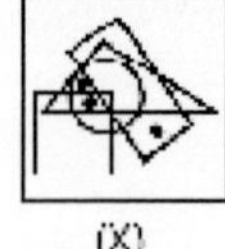

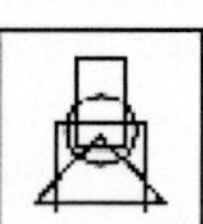
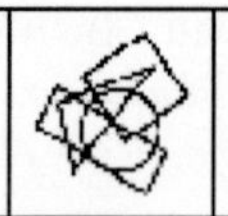
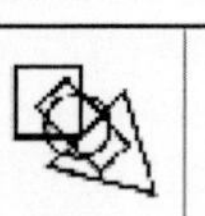
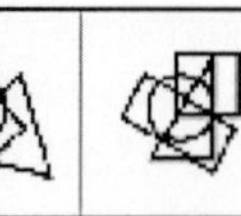

(X) (1) (2) (3) (4)

(a) 1 (b) 2
(c) 3 (d) 4

4. Select the figure which satisfies the same conditions of placement of the dots as in Fig.-X.

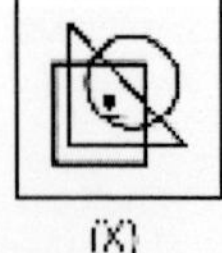
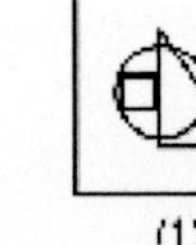
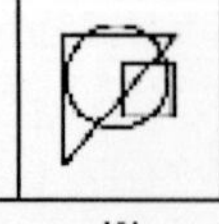
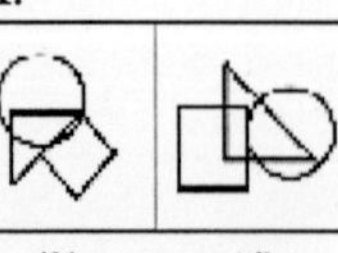

(X) (1) (2) (3) (4)

(a) 1 (b) 2
(c) 3 (d) 4

5. Select the figure which satisfies the same conditions of placement of the dots as in Figure-X.

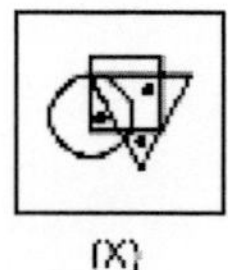
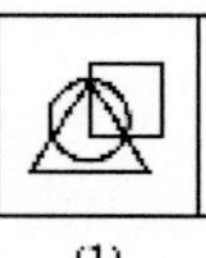
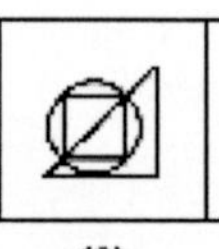
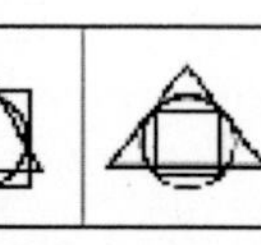

(X) (1) (2) (3) (4)

(a) 1 (b) 2
(c) 3 (d) 4

6. Select the figure which satisfies the same conditions of placement of the dots as in Figure-X.

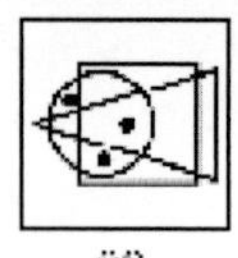

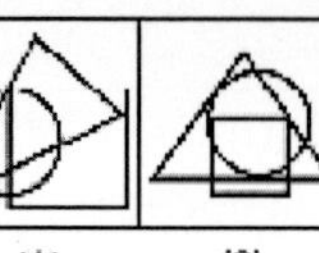
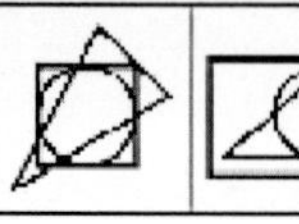

(X) (1) (2) (3) (4)

(a) 1 (b) 2
(c) 3 (d) 4

7. Select the figure which satisfies the same conditions of placement of the dots as in Fig.-X.

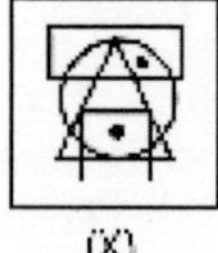
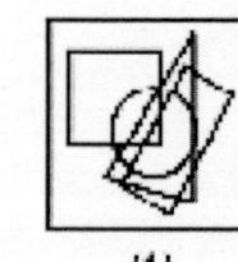
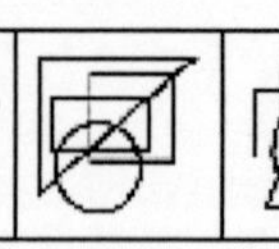
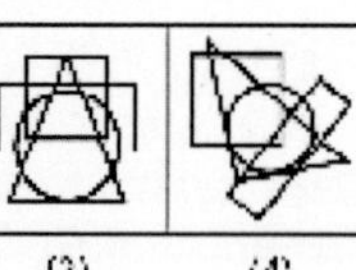

(X) (1) (2) (3) (4)

(a) 1 (b) 2
(c) 3 (d) 4

8. Select the figure which satisfies the same conditions of placement of the dots as in Fig.-X.

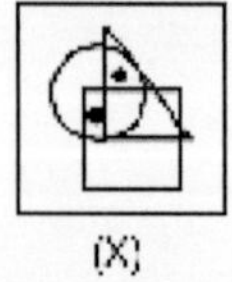
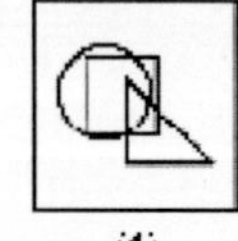

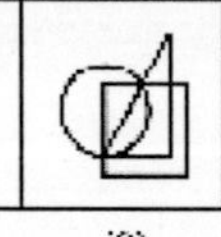
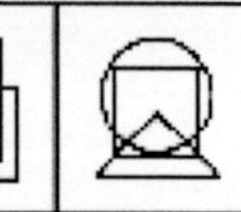

(X) (1) (2) (3) (4)

(a) 1 (b) 2
(c) 3 (d) 4

9. Select the figure which satisfies the same conditions of placement of the dots as in Fig.-X.

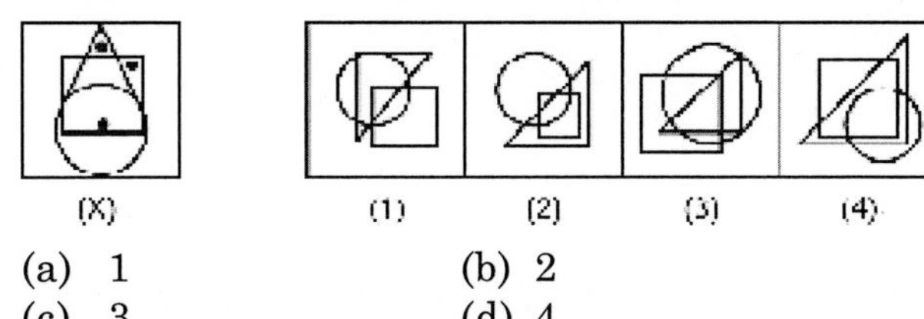

(a) 1 (b) 2
(c) 3 (d) 4

10. Select the figure which satisfies the same conditions of placement of the dots as in Figure-X.

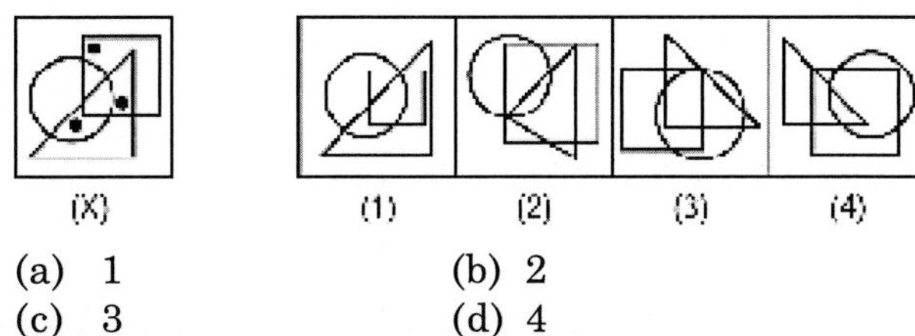

(a) 1 (b) 2
(c) 3 (d) 4

11. Select the figure which satisfies the same conditions of placement of the dots as in Fig.-X.

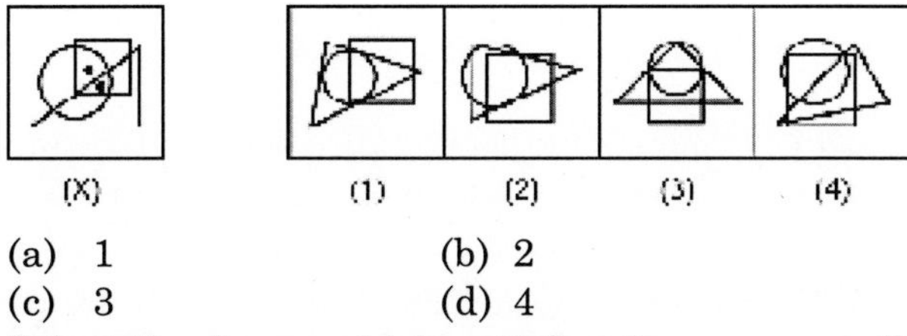

(a) 1 (b) 2
(c) 3 (d) 4

12. Select the figure which satisfies the same conditions of placement of the dots as in Fig.-X.

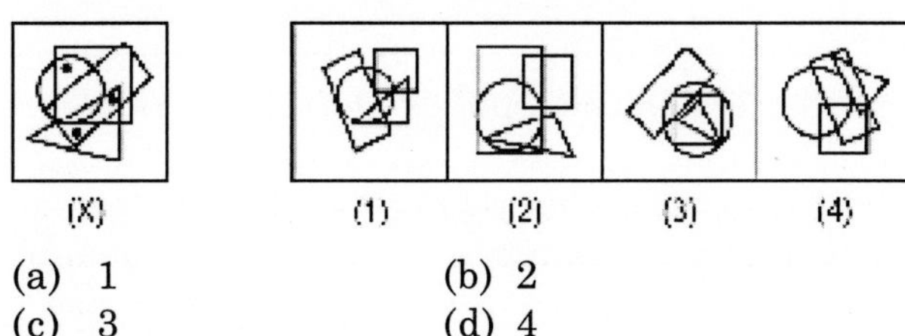

(a) 1 (b) 2
(c) 3 (d) 4

13. Select the figure which satisfies the same conditions of placement of the dots as in Figure-X.

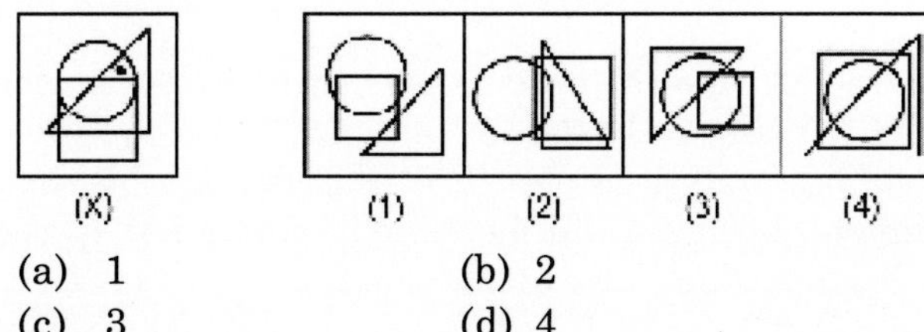

(a) 1 (b) 2
(c) 3 (d) 4

14. Select the figure which satisfies the same conditions of placement of the dots as in Figure-X.

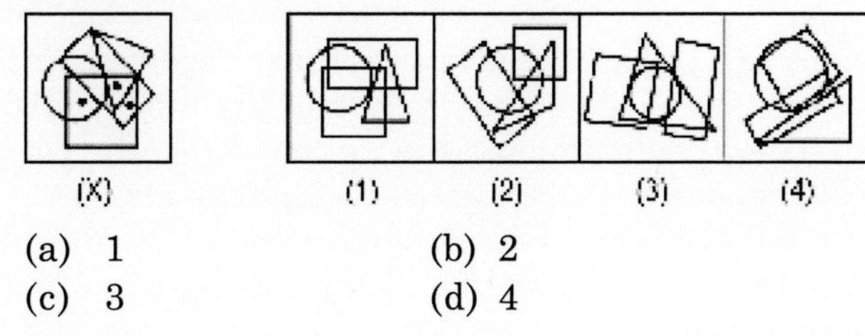

(a) 1 (b) 2
(c) 3 (d) 4

15. Select the figure which satisfies the same conditions of placement of the dots as in Fig.-X.

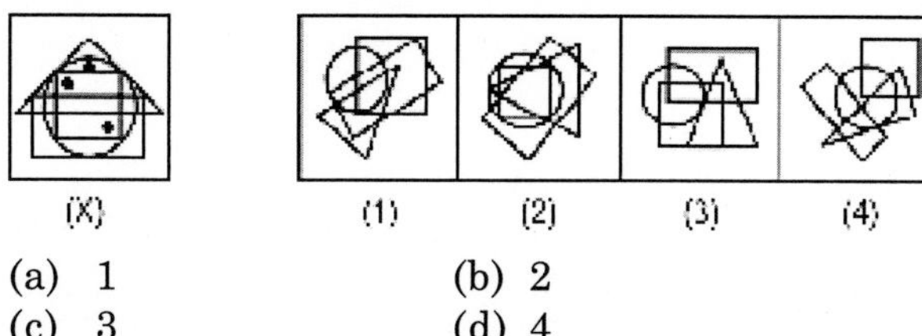

(a) 1 (b) 2
(c) 3 (d) 4

16. Select the figure which satisfies the same conditions of placement of the dots as in Fig.-X.

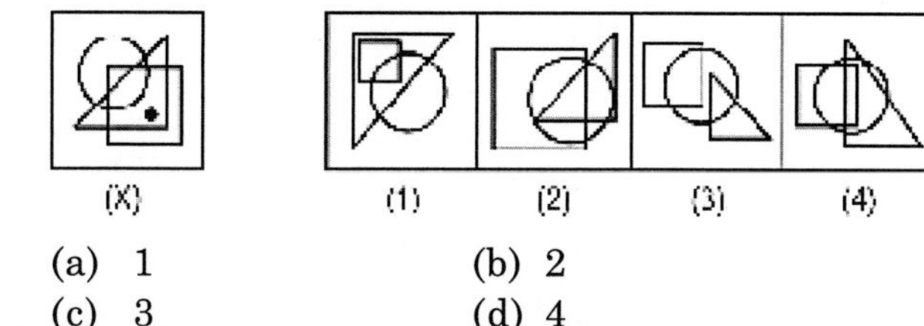

(a) 1 (b) 2
(c) 3 (d) 4

17. Select the figure which satisfies the same conditions of placement of the dots as in Fig.-X.

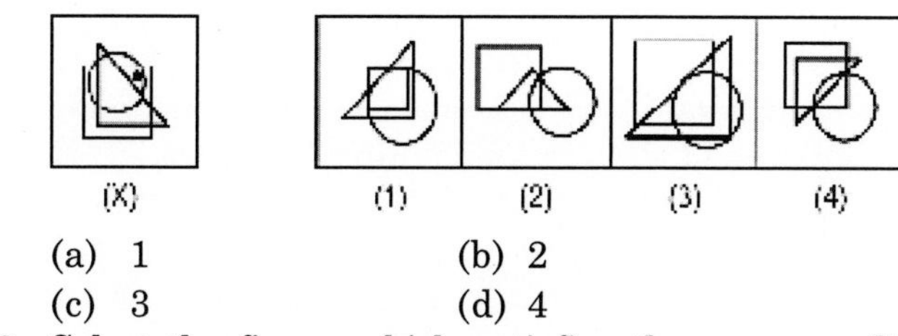

(a) 1 (b) 2
(c) 3 (d) 4

18. Select the figure which satisfies the same conditions of placement of the dots as in Fig.-X.

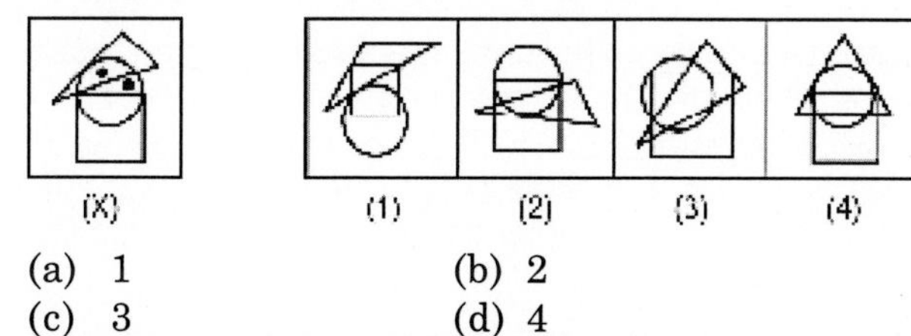

(a) 1 (b) 2
(c) 3 (d) 4

19. Select the figure which satisfies the same conditions of placement of the dots as in Fig.-X.

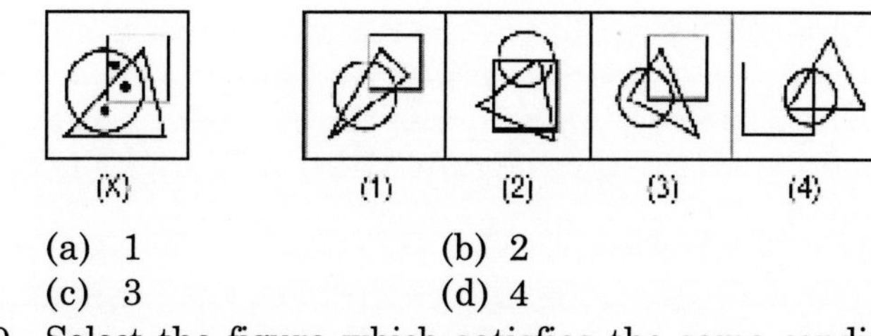

(a) 1 (b) 2
(c) 3 (d) 4

20. Select the figure which satisfies the same conditions of placement of the dots as in Fig.-X.

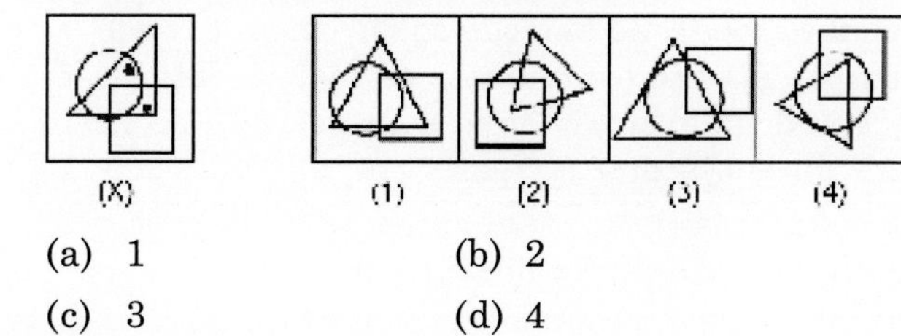

(a) 1 (b) 2
(c) 3 (d) 4

Answer Key

1. (c)	2. (b)	3. (b)	4. (b)	5. (c)	6. (a)	7. (d)	8. (b)	9. (a)	10. (c)	11. (d)
12. (d)	13. (c)	14. (a)	15. (b)	16. (a)	17. (d)	18. (c)	19. (d)	20. (a)		

Explanatory Notes

1. (c)
In figure (X), one of the dots lies in the region common to the circle and the square only; another dot lies in the region common to the circle, the square and the rectangle only; the third dot lies in the region common to the square, the triangle and the rectangle only. In each of the figures (1), (2) and (4), there is no region common to the square, the triangle and the rectangle only. Only figure (3) consists of all the three types of regions.

2. (b)
In figure (X), one of the dots lies in the region common to the circle, the square and the rectangle only; another dot lies in the region common to all the four elements - the circle, the square, the triangle and the rectangle and the third dot lies in the region common to the circle, the triangle and the rectangle only. In figure (1), there is no region common to the circle, the triangle and the rectangle only. In each of the figures (3) and (4) there is no region common to all the four elements - the circle, the square, the triangle and the rectangle. Only figure (2) consists of all the three types of regions.

3. (b)
In figure (X), one of the dots lies in the region common to the circle and the triangle only; another dot lies in the region common to the circle, the square and the triangle only and the third dot lies in the rectangle alone. In figures (1) and (4) there is no region common to the circle and the triangle only. In figure (3) there is no region which lies in the rectangle alone. Only figure (2) contains all the three types of regions.

4. (b)
In figure (X), the dot lies in the region common to all the three figures - square, triangle and circle. Out of the four alternatives, only figure (2) contains a region common to all the three figures. Hence, figure (2) is the answer.

5. (c)
In figure (X), one of the dots lies in the triangle alone; another dot lies in the region common to the square and the triangle only and the third dot lies in the region common to the circle and the square only. In each of the figures (1), (2) and (4), there is no region common to the square and the triangle only. Only figure (3) consists of all the three types of regions.

6. (a)
In figure (X), one of the dots lies in the region common to the circle and the square only; another dot lies in the region common to all the three figures - the circle, the square and the triangle and the third dot lies in the circle alone. In figure (2) there is no region common to the circle and the square only and in each of the figures (3) and (4) there are regions which lie in the circle alone. Only figure (1) consists of all the three types of regions.

7. (d)
In figure (X), one of the dots lies in the region common to the circle and the rectangle only and the other dot lies in the region common to the circle, the square and the triangle only. In each of the figures (1) and (2), there is no region common to the circle and the rectangle only. In figure (3), there is no region common to the circle, the square and the triangle only. Only figure (4) consists of both the types of regions.

8. (b)
In figure (X), one of the dots lies in the region common to the circle and the triangle only and the other dot lies in the region common to the circle and the square only. In each of the figures (1), (3) and (4), there is no region common to the circle and the triangle only. Only figure (2) consists of both the types of regions.

9. (a)
In figure (X), one of the dots lies in the square alone; another dot lies in the triangle alone and the third dot lies in the region common to the circle and the square. In figure (2) there is no region that lies in the square alone; in figure (3) there is no region that lies in the triangle alone and in figure (4) there is no region that lies in the region common to the circle and the square only. Only figure (1) consists of all the three types of regions.

10. (c)
In figure (X), one of the dots lies in the square alone; another dot lies in the region common to the square and the triangle only and the third dot lies in the region common to the circle and the triangle. In figure (1), there is no region which lies in the square alone. In each of the figures (2) and (4), there is no region common to the circle and the triangle only. Only, figure (3) consists of all the three types of regions.

11. (d)
In figure (X), one of the dots lies in the region common to the circle and the square only and the other dot lies in the region common to all the three figures -the circle, the square and the triangle. In each of the alternatives (1), (2) and (3), there is no region common to the square and the circle only. Only figure (4) consists of both the types of regions.

12. (d)
In figure (X), one of the dots lies in the region common to the circle and the square only; another dot lies in the region common to the square, the triangle and the rectangle only and the third dot lies in the region common to the triangle and the rectangle only. In each of the figures (1), (2) and (3) there is no region common to the square, the triangle and the rectangle only. Only figure (4) consists of all the three types of regions.

13. (c)
In figure (X), the dot is contained in the region common to the triangle and the circle only. Out of the four alternatives, only figure (3) contains a region common to the triangle and the circle only.

14. (a)
In figure (X), one of the dots lies in the region common to the circle and the square only; another dot lies in the region common to the square, the triangle and the rectangle only and the third dot lies in the region common to the square and the rectangle only. In figure (2) there is no region common to the square and the rectangle only; in figure (3) there is no region common to the circle and the square only and in figure (4) there is no region common to the square, the triangle and the rectangle only. Only figure (1) consists of all the three types of regions.

15. (b)
In figure (X), one of the dots lies in the region common to the circle and the triangle only; another dot lies in the region common to the circle, the square and the triangle only and the third dot lies in the region common to the circle, the square and the rectangle only. In each of the figures (1) and (3) there is no region common to the circle and the triangle only. In figure (4) there is no region common to the circle, the square and the rectangle only. Only figure (2) consists of all the three types of regions.

16. (a)
In figure (X), the dot is contained in the region common to the triangle and the square only. Out of the four alternatives, only figure (1) contains a region common to the triangle and the square only.

17. (d)
In figure (X), the dot is contained in the region common to the square and the circle only. Out of the four alternatives, only figure (4) contains a region common to the square and the circle only.

18. (c)
In figure (X), one of the dots lies in the region common to the circle and the triangle only and the other dot lies in the circle alone. In each of the two figures (1) and (2), there is no region common to the circle and the triangle only. In figure (4) there is no region which lies in the circle alone. Only figure (3) consists of both the types of regions.

19. (d)
In figure (X), one of the dots lies in the region common to the circle and the triangle only; another dot lies in the region common to all the three figures - the circle, the square and the triangle and the third dot lies in the region common to the circle and the square only. In each of the figures (1) and (3), there is no region common to the circle and the square only and in figure (2), there is no region common to the circle and the triangle only. Only figure (4) consists of all the three types of regions.

20. (a)
In figure (X), one of the dots is placed in the region common to the circle and the triangle only and another dot is placed in the region common to the square and the triangle only. In each of the three alternatives (2), (3) and (4), there is no region common to the square and the triangle only. Only figure (1) consists of both the types of regions.

❐

Previous Year Questions

1. Select the figure which satisfies the same conditions of placement of the dots as in Fig.-X.

[NTSE 2012 – Tamilnadu second stage paper]

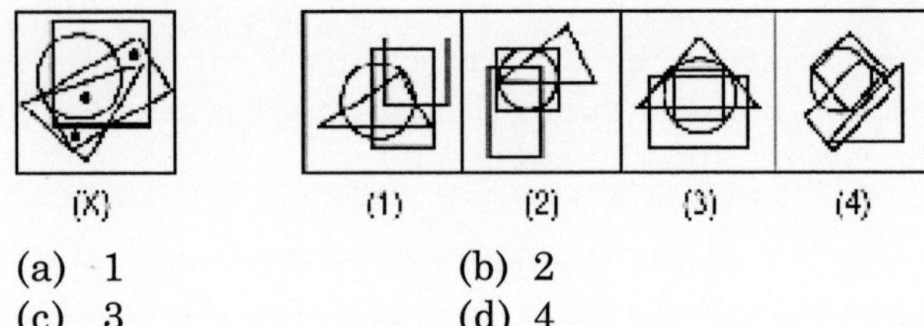

(a) 1 (b) 2
(c) 3 (d) 4

2. Select the figure which satisfies the same conditions of placement of the dots as in Fig.-X.

[NTSE 2012 – UP first stage paper]

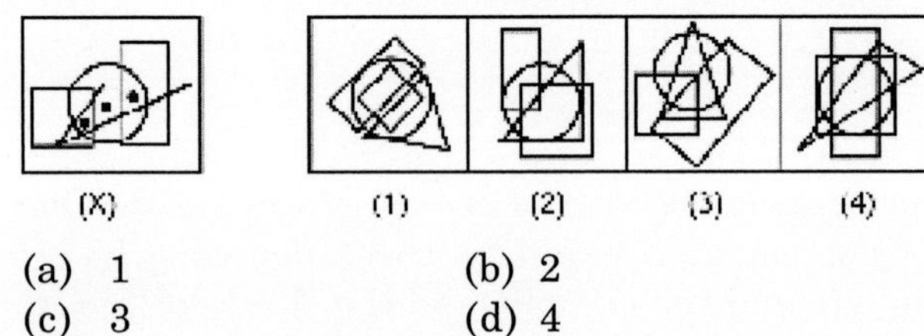

(a) 1 (b) 2
(c) 3 (d) 4

3. Select the figure which satisfies the same conditions of placement of the dots as in Fig.-X.

[NTSE 2007 – Maharashtra Second stage paper]

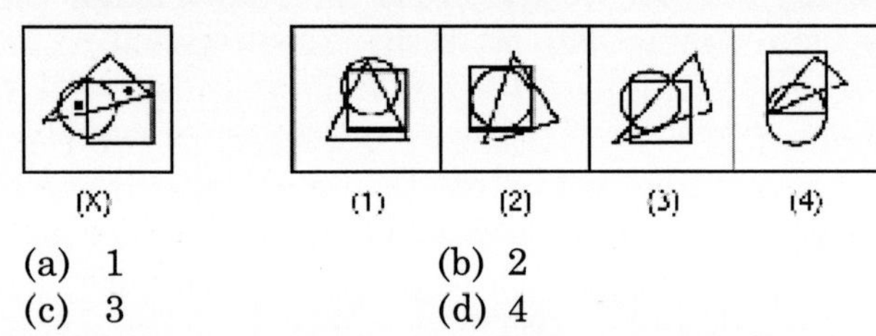

(a) 1 (b) 2
(c) 3 (d) 4

4. Select the figure which satisfies the same conditions of placement of the dots as in Fig.-X.

[NTSE 2005 – Andhra Pradesh second stage paper]

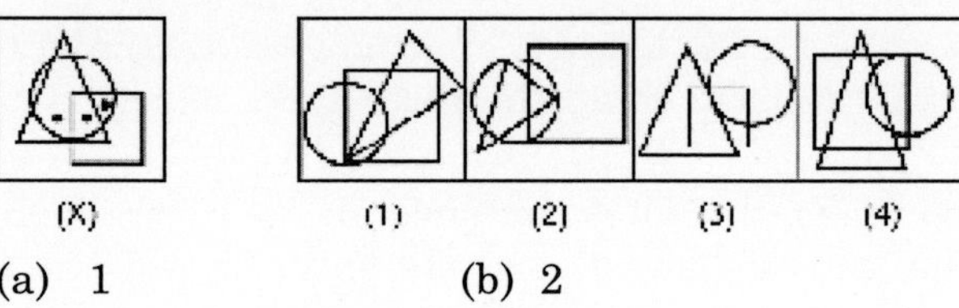

(a) 1 (b) 2
(c) 3 (d) 4

5. Select the figure which satisfies the same conditions of placement of the dots as in Fig.-X.

[NTSE 2012 – Punjab second stage paper]

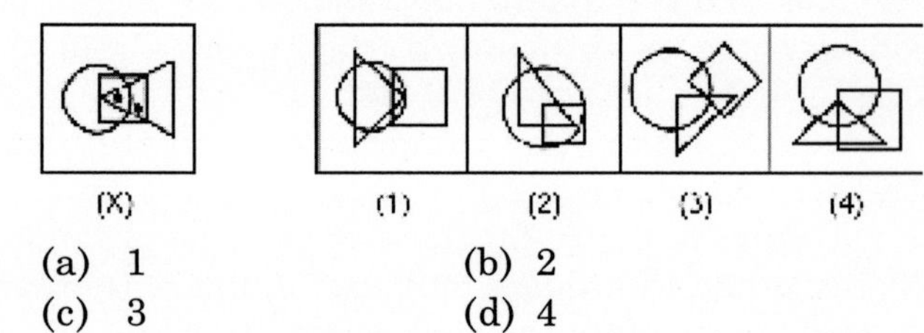

(a) 1 (b) 2
(c) 3 (d) 4

❒

Answer Key

	1. (a)	2. (c)	3. (a)	4. (b)	5. (d)	

Explanatory Notes

1. (a)
In figure (X), one of the dots lies in the region common to the square and the rectangle only; another dot lies in the region common to all the four elements - the circle, the square, the triangle and the rectangle and the third dot lies in the region common to the triangle and the rectangle only. In figure (2) there is no region common to the triangle and the rectangle only. In figure (3) there is no region common to the square and the rectangle only. In figure (4) there is no region common to all the four elements - the circle, the square, the triangle and the rectangle. Only figure (1) consists of all the three types of regions.

2. (c)
In figure (X), one of the dots lies in the region common to the circle, the triangle and the rectangle only; another dot lies in the region common to the circle and the triangle only and the third dot lies in the region common to the circle, the square and the triangle only. In each of the figures (1), (2) and (4) there is no region common to the circle, the triangle and the rectangle only. Only figure (3) consists of all the three types of regions.

3. (a)
In figure (X), one of the dots lies in the region common to the circle and the triangle only and the other dot lies in the region common to the square and the triangle only. In each of the figures (2), (3) and (4), there is no region common to the circle and the triangle only. Only figure (1) consists of both the types of regions.

4. (b)
In figure (X), one of the dots lies in the region common to the circle and the square only; another dot lies in the region common to all the three figures - the circle, the square and the triangle and the third dot lies in the region common to the circle and the triangle only. In each of the alternatives (1), (3) and (4), there is no region common to the circle and the triangle only. Only figure (2) consists of all the three types of regions.

5. (d)
In figure (X), one of the dots lies in the region common to the square and the triangle only and the other dot lies in the region common to all the three figures - the circle, the square and the triangle. In each of the alternatives (1) and (2), there is no region common to the square and the triangle only. In alternative (3), there is no region common to all the three figures. Only, alternative (4) consists of both the types of regions.

❐

UNIT 9

Paper Cutting

In Paper Cutting, we deal with problems related to the analysis of the pattern that is formed when a folded piece of paper is cut in a definite design.

Here, initially, a set of three figures, showing the way in which a given piece of paper is folded, is given. In the first two figures the dotted line refers to the line along which the paper is folded and the arrow indicates the direction of the fold. In the third figure, we see a mark(s) showing the position and the pattern of cut on the folded sheet. Then, finally, the candidate is required to select one figure out of the four given alternatives which would resemble the pattern of the cut of the unfolded paper. Following examples will clarify.

Solved Examples

☛ ***Direction to solve (1 to 4) :*** Each of the following questions consists of a set of three figures X, Y and Z showing a sequence of folding of a piece of paper. Figure (Z) shows the manner in which the folded paper has been cut. These three figures are followed by four answer figures from which you have to choose a figure which would most closely resemble the unfolded form of figure (Z).

1. Choose a figure which would most closely resemble the unfolded form of Figure (Z).

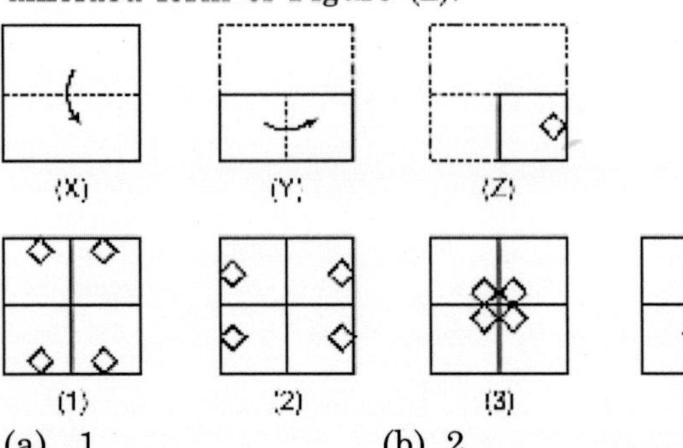

(a) 1 (b) 2
(c) 3 (d) 4

Solution: Option (b) is correct.

2. Choose a figure which would most closely resemble the unfolded form of Figure (Z).

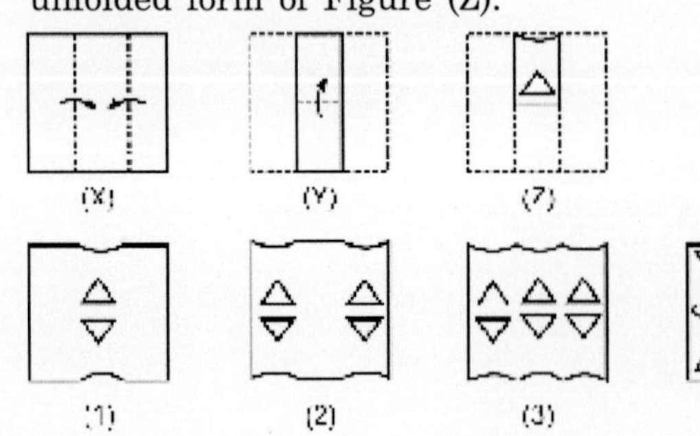

(a) 1 (b) 2
(c) 3 (d) 4

Solution: Option (c) is correct.

3. Choose a figure which would most closely resemble the unfolded form of Figure (Z).

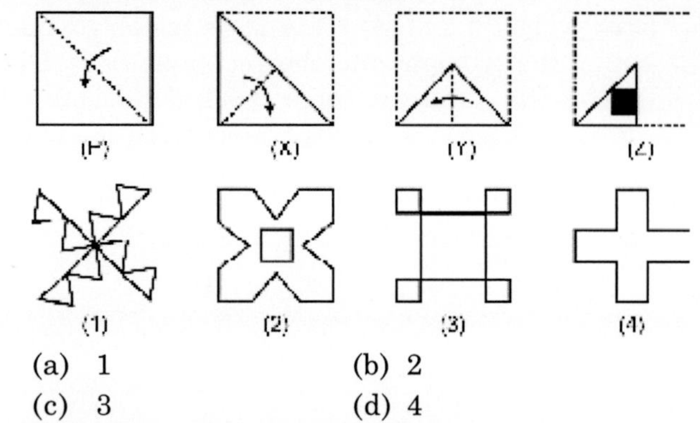

(a) 1 (b) 2
(c) 3 (d) 4

Solution: Option (c) is correct.

4. Choose a figure which would most closely resemble the unfolded form of Figure (Z).

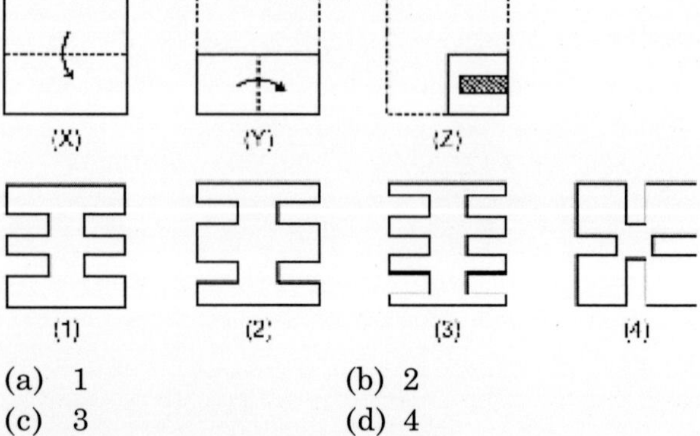

(a) 1 (b) 2
(c) 3 (d) 4

Solution: Option (b) is correct.

5. Choose a figure which would most closely resemble the unfolded form of Figure (Z).

(a) 1 (b) 2
(c) 3 (d) 4

Solution: Option (a) is correct.

Multiple Choice Questions

☛ ***Direction to solve (1 to 40) :*** Each of the following questions consists of a set of three figures X, Y and Z showing a sequence of folding of a piece of paper. Figure (Z) shows the manner in which the folded paper has been cut. These three figures are followed by four answer figures from which you have to choose a figure which would most closely resemble the unfolded form of figure (Z).

1. Choose a figure which would most closely resemble the unfolded form of Figure (Z).

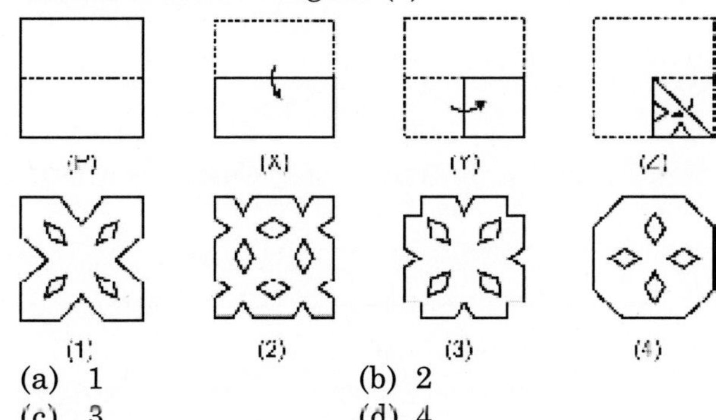

(a) 1 (b) 2
(c) 3 (d) 4

2. Choose a figure which would most closely resemble the unfolded form of Figure (Z).

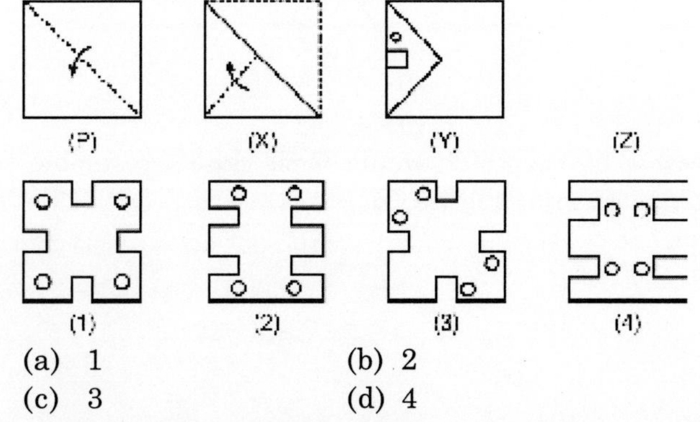

(a) 1 (b) 2
(c) 3 (d) 4

3. Choose a figure which would most closely resemble the unfolded form of Figure (Z).

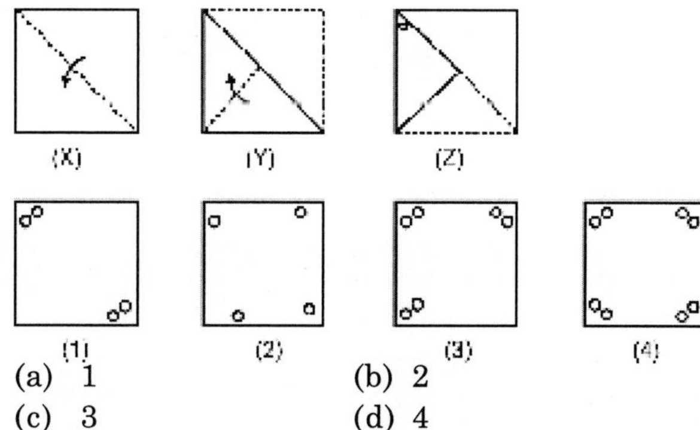

(a) 1 (b) 2
(c) 3 (d) 4

4. Choose a figure which would most closely resemble the unfolded form of Figure (Z).

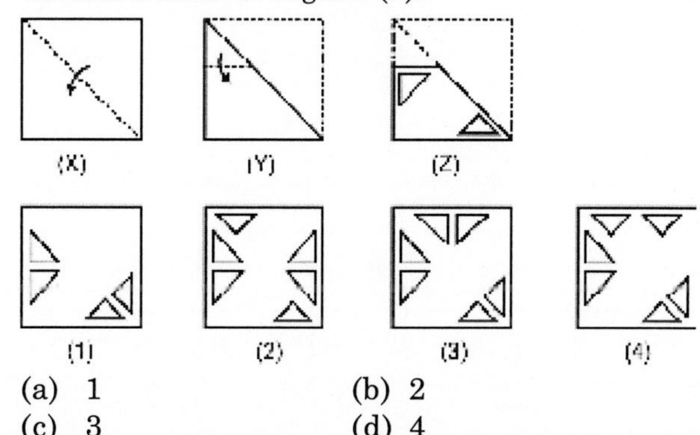

(a) 1 (b) 2
(c) 3 (d) 4

5. Choose a figure which would most closely resemble the unfolded form of Figure (Z).

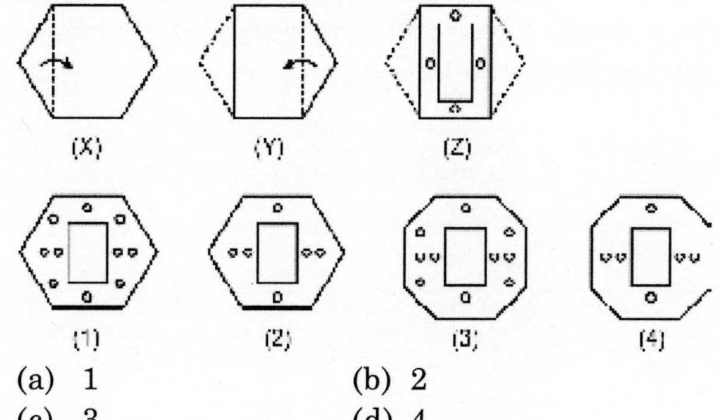

(a) 1 (b) 2
(c) 3 (d) 4

6. Choose a figure which would most closely resemble the unfolded form of Figure (Z).

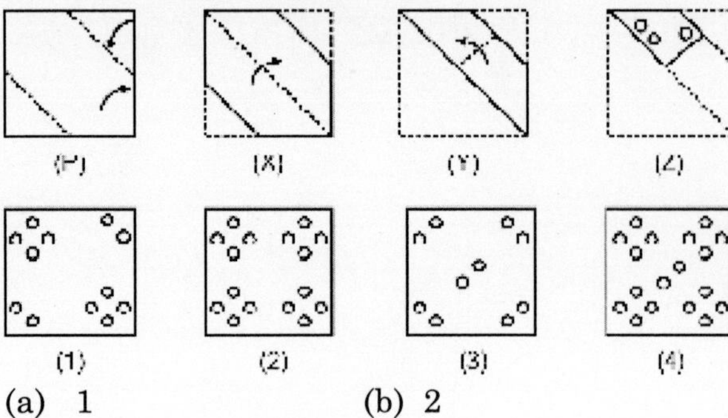

(a) 1 (b) 2
(c) 3 (d) 4

7. Choose a figure which would most closely resemble the unfolded form of Figure (Z).

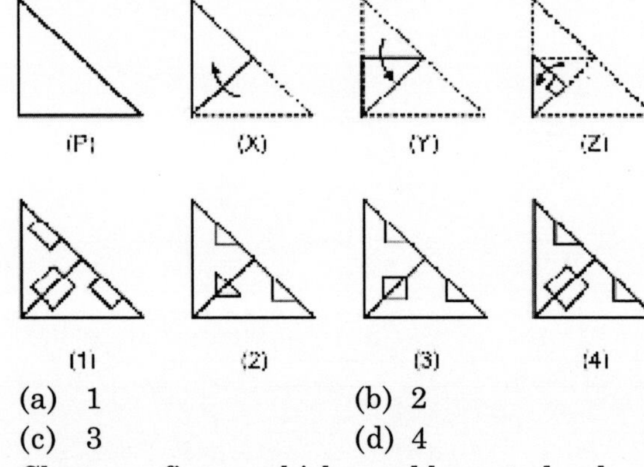

(a) 1 (b) 2
(c) 3 (d) 4

8. Choose a figure which would most closely resemble the unfolded form of Figure (Z).

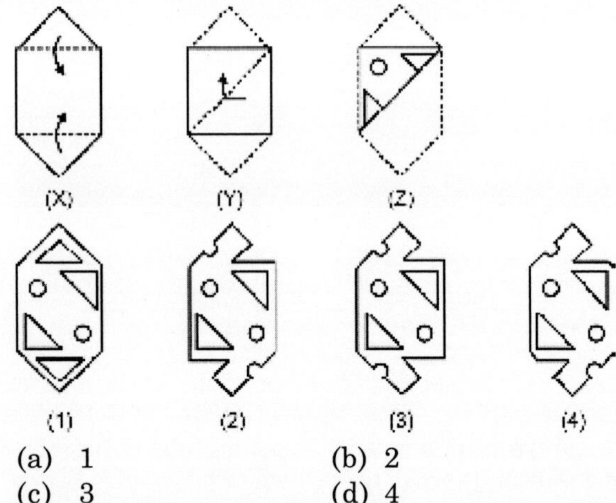

(a) 1 (b) 2
(c) 3 (d) 4

9. Choose a figure which would most closely resemble the unfolded form of Figure (Z).

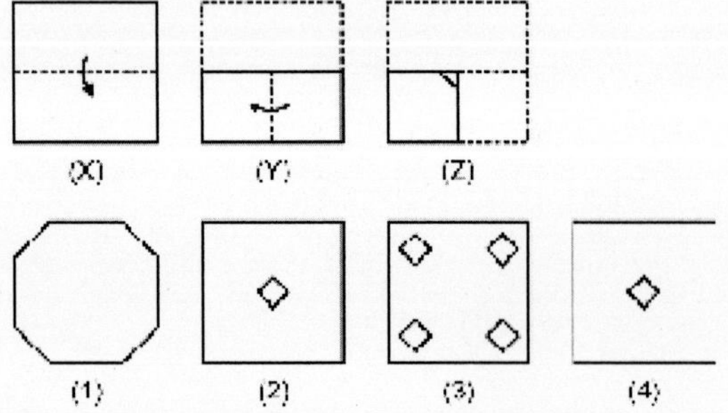

(a) 1 (b) 2
(c) 3 (d) 4

10. Choose a figure which would most closely resemble the unfolded form of Figure (Z).

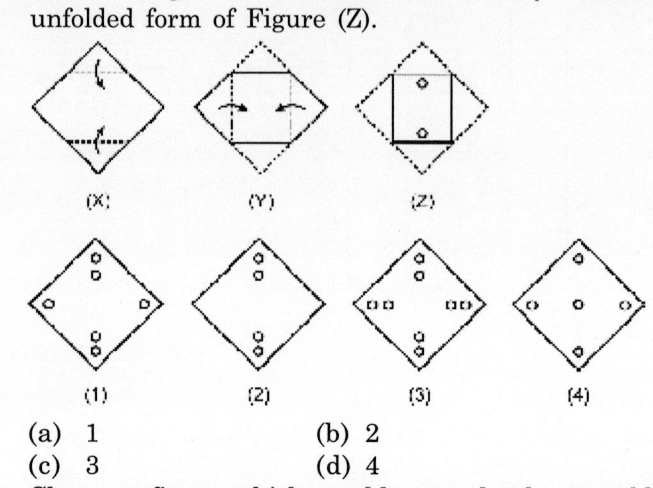

(a) 1 (b) 2
(c) 3 (d) 4

11. Choose a figure which would most closely resemble the unfolded form of Figure (Z).

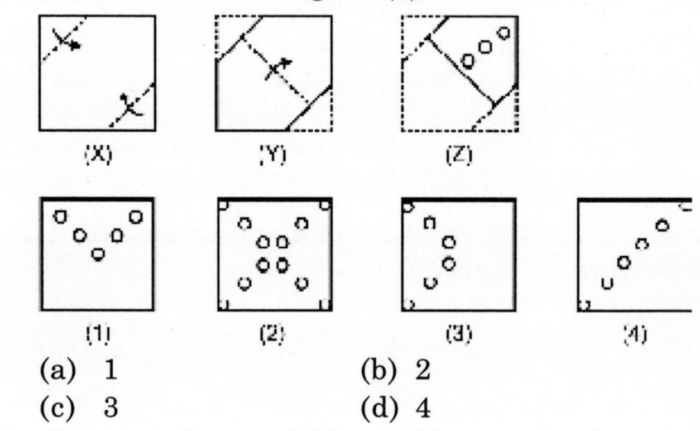

(a) 1 (b) 2
(c) 3 (d) 4

12. Choose a figure which would most closely resemble the unfolded form of Figure (Z).

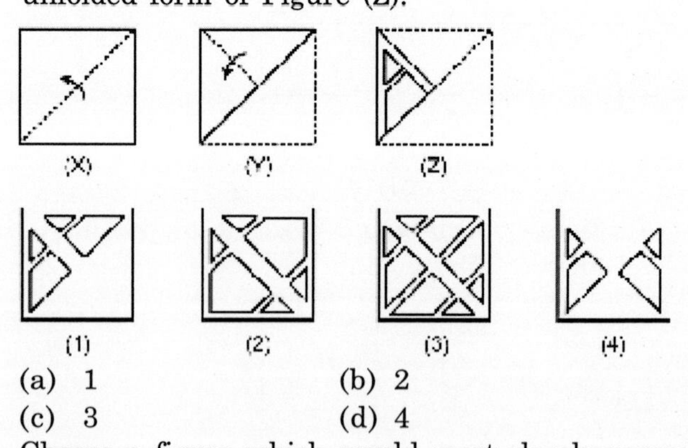

(a) 1 (b) 2
(c) 3 (d) 4

13. Choose a figure which would most closely resemble the unfolded form of Figure (Z).

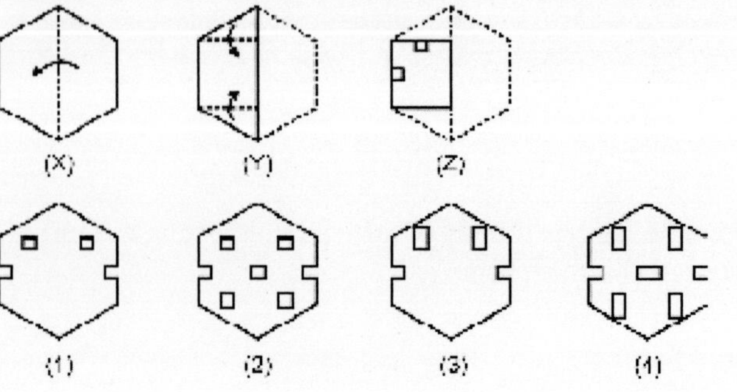

(a) 1 (b) 2
(c) 3 (d) 4

14. Choose a figure which would most closely resemble the unfolded form of Figure (Z).

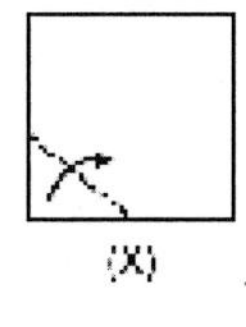

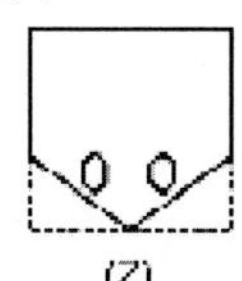

(X) (Y) (Z)

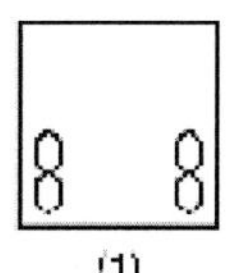
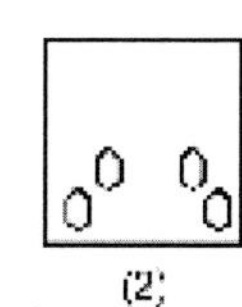
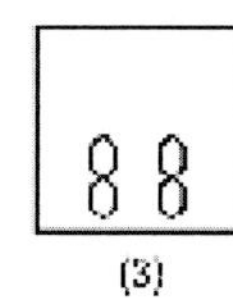
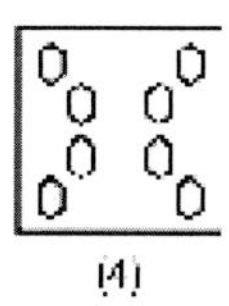

(1) (2) (3) (4)

(a) 1 (b) 2
(c) 3 (d) 4

15. Choose a figure which would most closely resemble the unfolded form of Figure (Z).

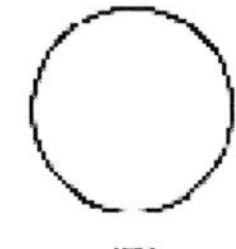
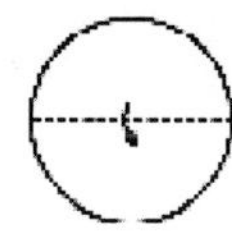
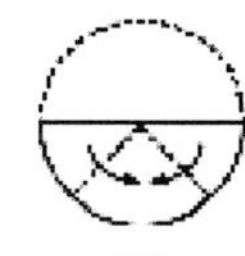
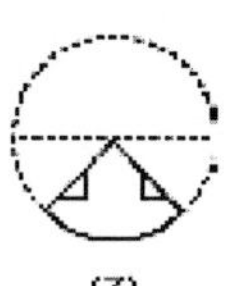

(P) (X) (Y) (Z)

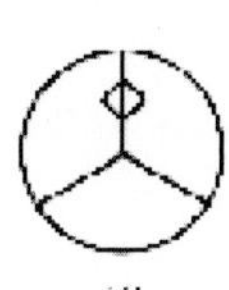
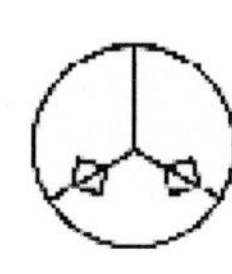
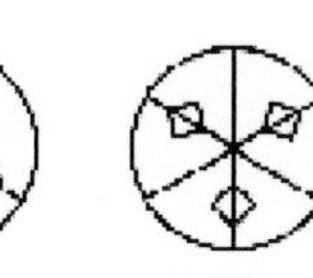
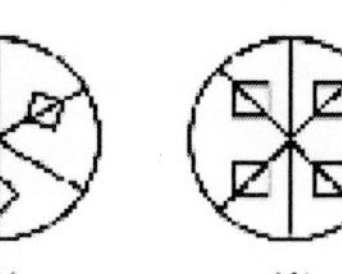

(1) (2) (3) (4)

(a) 1 (b) 2
(c) 3 (d) 4

16. Choose a figure which would most closely resemble the unfolded form of Figure (Z).

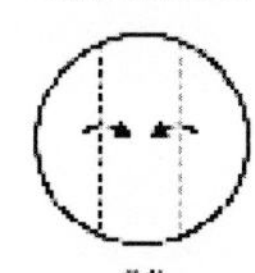
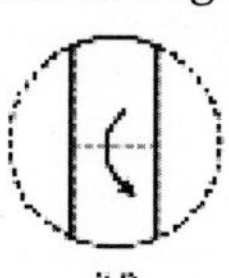
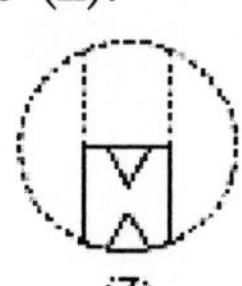

(X) (Y) (Z)

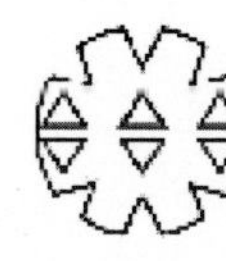

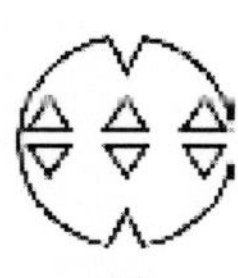

(1) (2) (3) (4)

(a) 1 (b) 2
(c) 3 (d) 4

17. Choose a figure which would most closely resemble the unfolded form of Figure (Z).

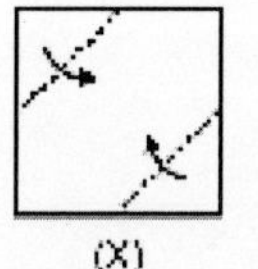
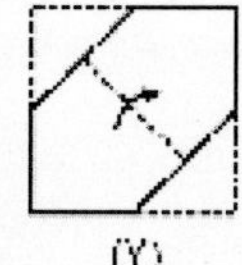
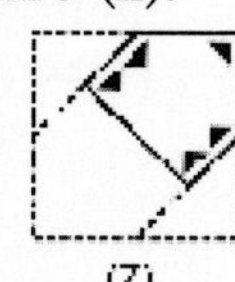

(X) (Y) (Z)

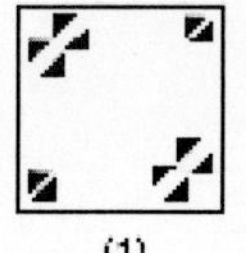

(1) (2) (3) (4)

(a) 1 (b) 2
(c) 3 (d) 4

18. Choose a figure which would most closely resemble the unfolded form of Figure (Z).

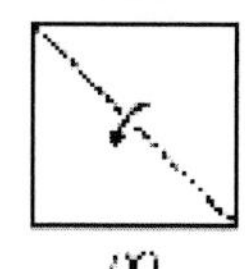
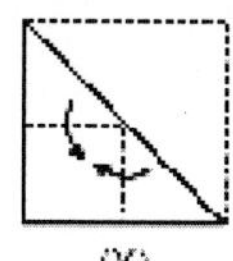
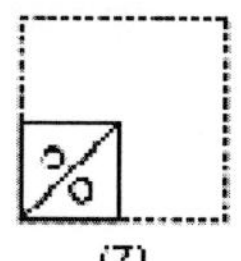

(X) (Y) (Z)

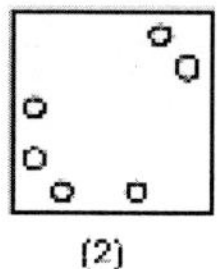
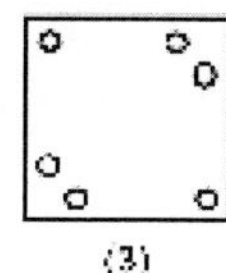
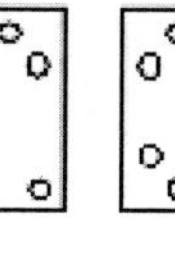
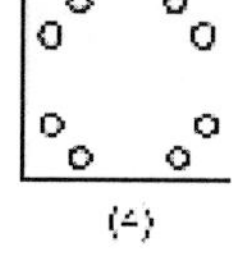

(1) (2) (3) (4)

(a) 1 (b) 2
(c) 3 (d) 4

19. Choose a figure which would most closely resemble the unfolded form of Figure (Z).

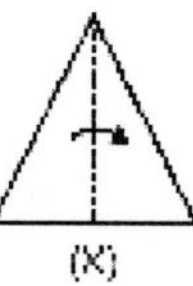
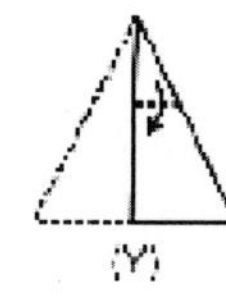
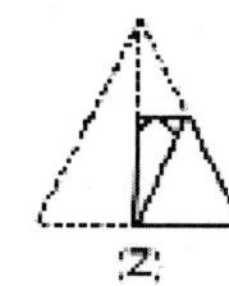

(X) (Y) (Z)

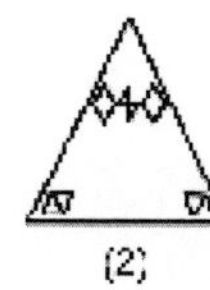
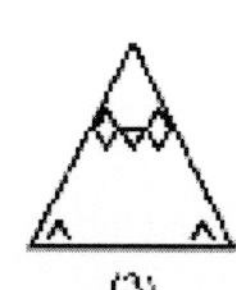
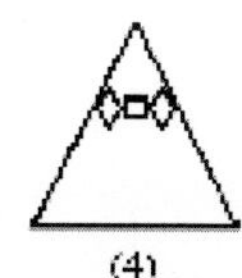

(1) (2) (3) (4)

(a) 1 (b) 2
(c) 3 (d) 4

20. Choose a figure which would most closely resemble the unfolded form of Figure (Z).

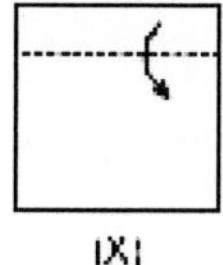
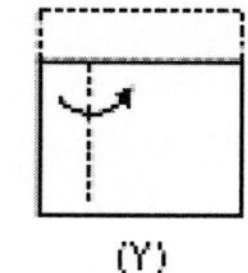
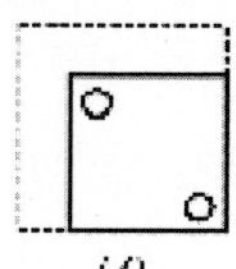

(X) (Y) (Z)

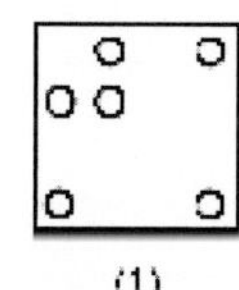
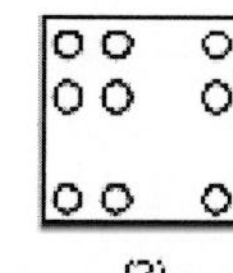
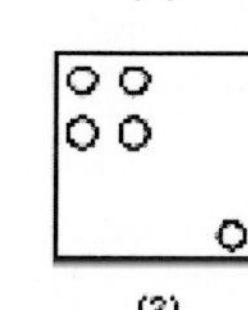
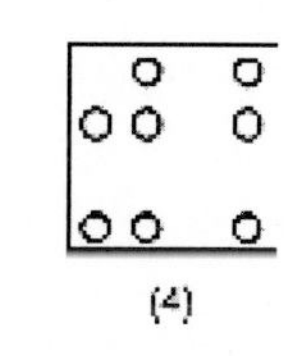

(1) (2) (3) (4)

(a) 1 (b) 2
(c) 3 (d) 4

21. Choose a figure which would most closely resemble the unfolded form of Figure (Z).

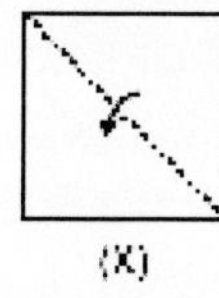
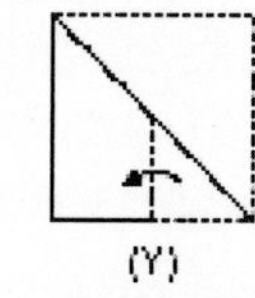
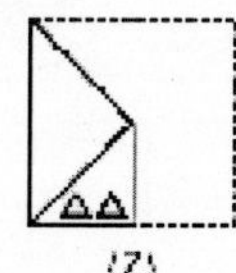

(X) (Y) (Z)

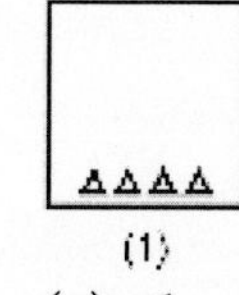
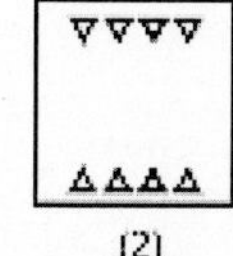
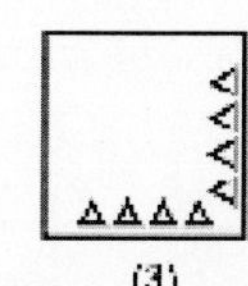
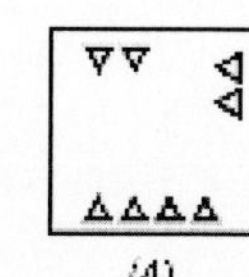

(1) (2) (3) (4)

(a) 1 (b) 2
(c) 3 (d) 4

22. Choose a figure which would most closely resemble the unfolded form of Figure (Z).

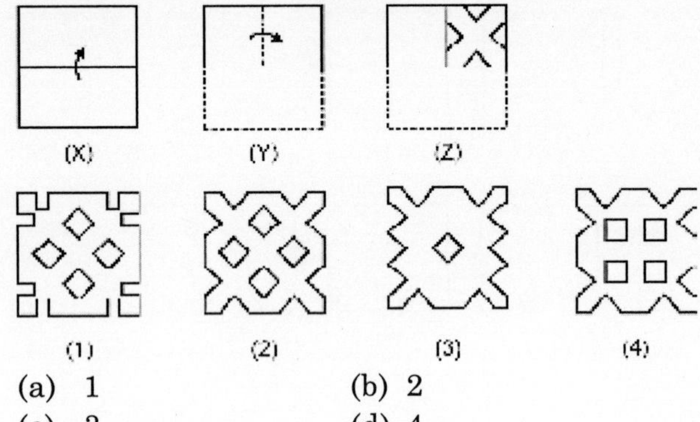

(a) 1 (b) 2
(c) 3 (d) 4

23. Choose a figure which would most closely resemble the unfolded form of Figure (Z).

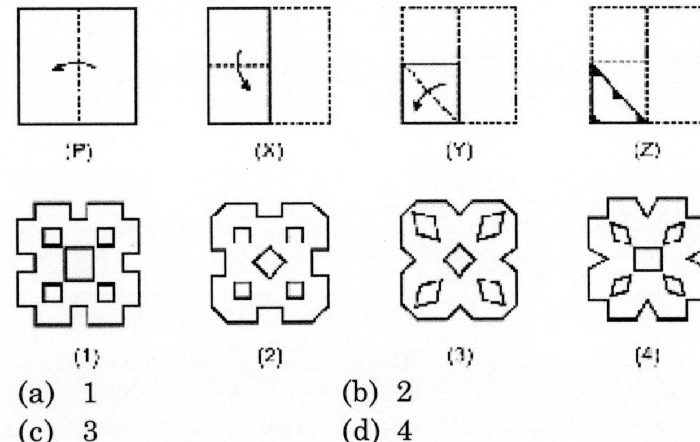

(a) 1 (b) 2
(c) 3 (d) 4

24. Choose a figure which would most closely resemble the unfolded form of Figure (Z).

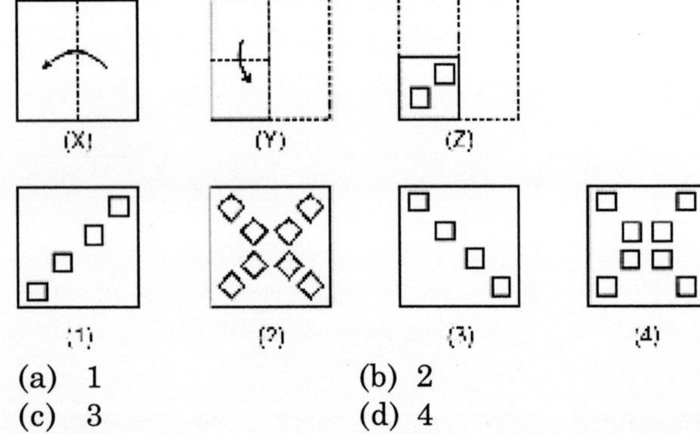

(a) 1 (b) 2
(c) 3 (d) 4

25. Choose a figure which would most closely resemble the unfolded form of Figure (Z).

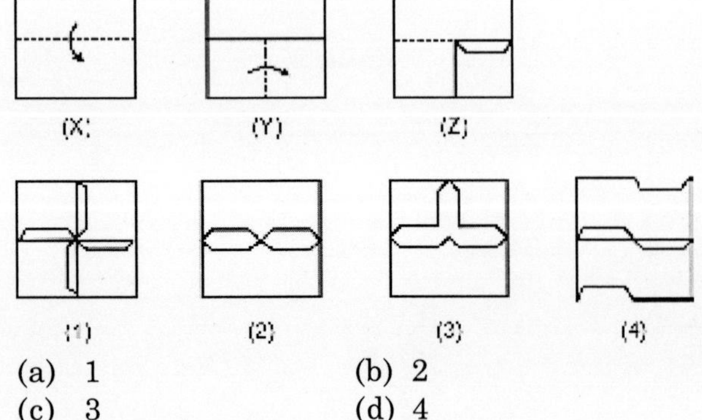

(a) 1 (b) 2
(c) 3 (d) 4

26. Choose a figure which would most closely resemble the unfolded form of Figure (Z).

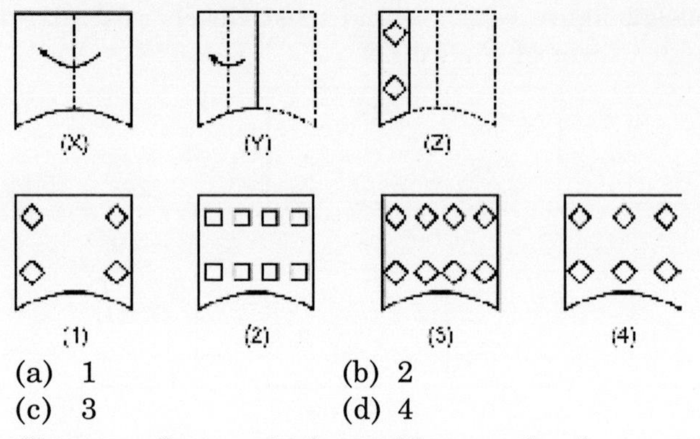

(a) 1 (b) 2
(c) 3 (d) 4

27. Choose a figure which would most closely resemble the unfolded form of Figure (Z).

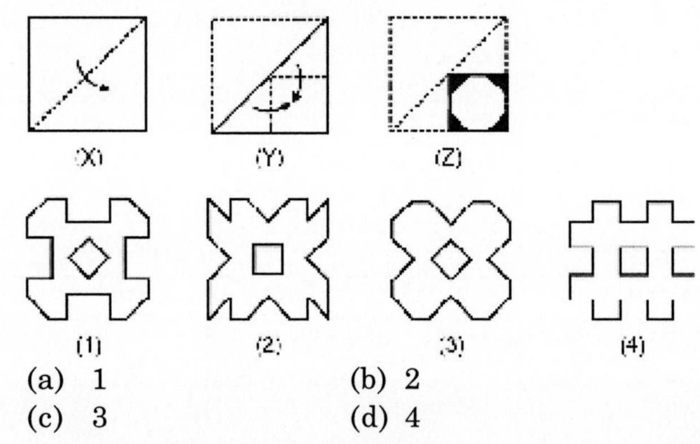

(a) 1 (b) 2
(c) 3 (d) 4

28. Choose a figure which would most closely resemble the unfolded form of Figure (Z).

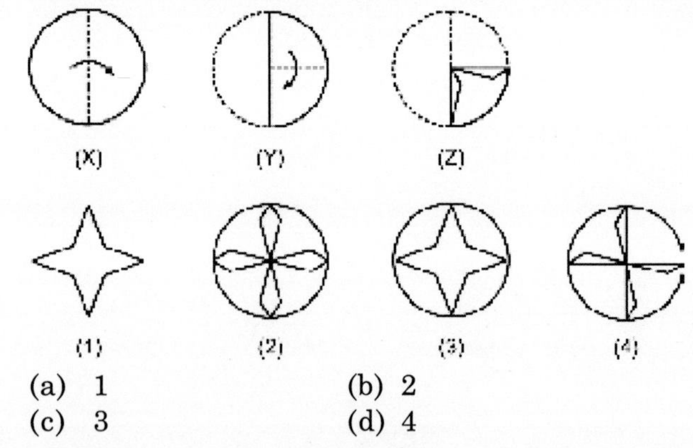

(a) 1 (b) 2
(c) 3 (d) 4

29. Choose a figure which would most closely resemble the unfolded form of Figure (Z).

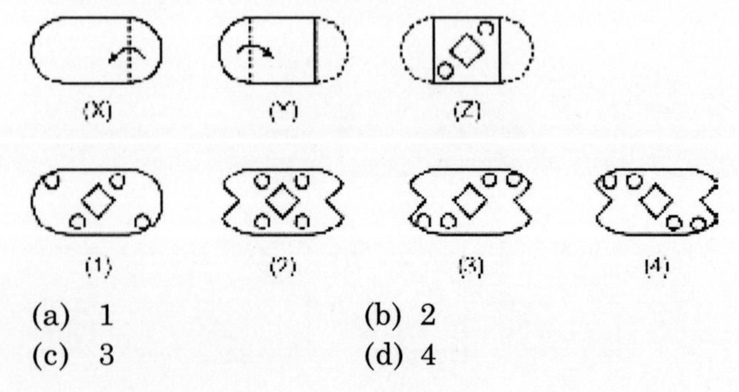

(a) 1 (b) 2
(c) 3 (d) 4

30. Choose a figure which would most closely resemble the unfolded form of Figure (Z).

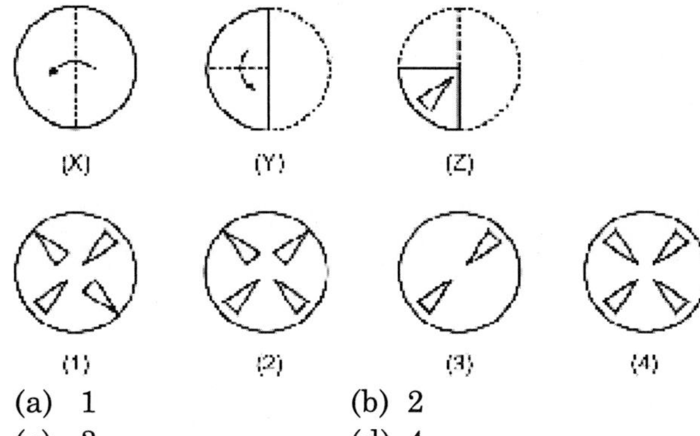

(a) 1 (b) 2
(c) 3 (d) 4

31. Choose a figure which would most closely resemble the unfolded form of Figure (Z).

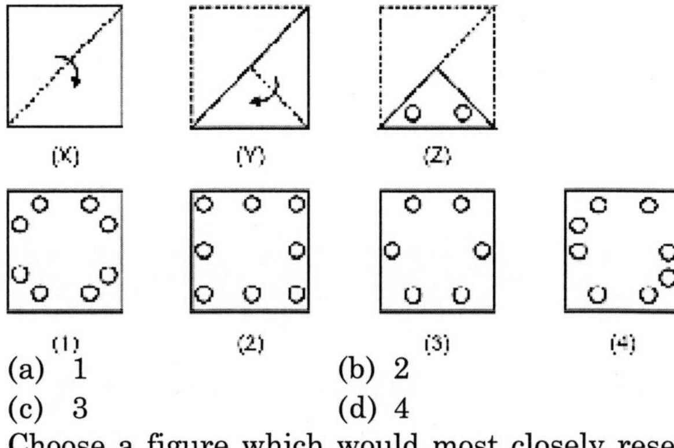

(a) 1 (b) 2
(c) 3 (d) 4

32. Choose a figure which would most closely resemble the unfolded form of Figure (Z).

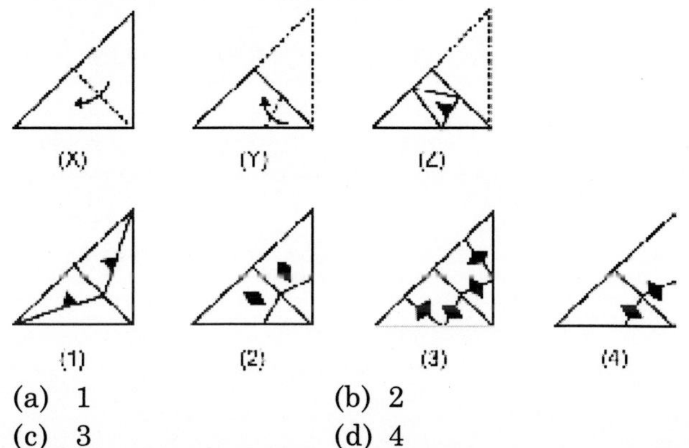

(a) 1 (b) 2
(c) 3 (d) 4

33. Choose a figure which would most closely resemble the unfolded form of Figure (Z).

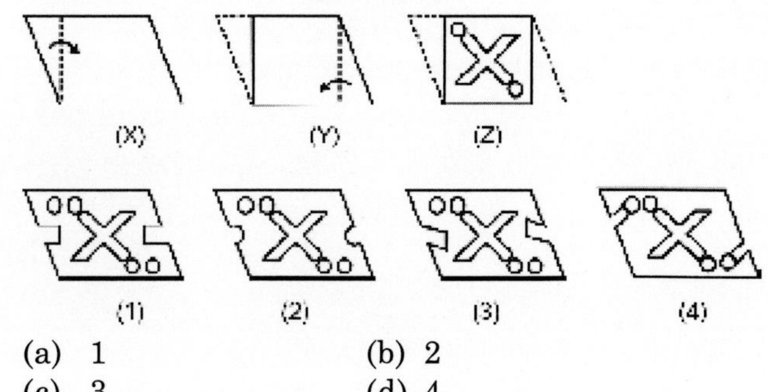

(a) 1 (b) 2
(c) 3 (d) 4

34. Choose a figure which would most closely resemble the unfolded form of Figure (Z).

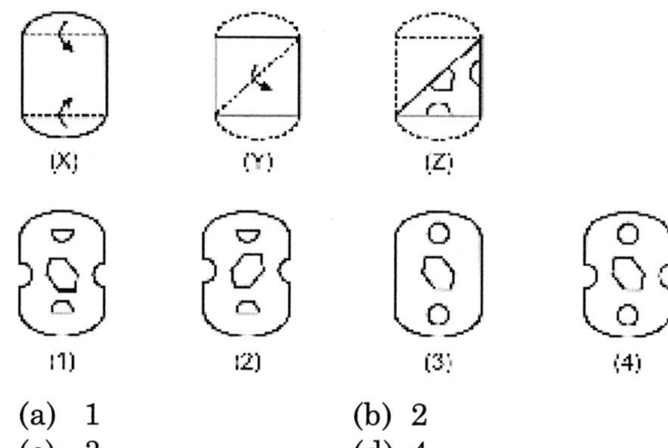

(a) 1 (b) 2
(c) 3 (d) 4

35. Choose a figure which would most closely resemble the unfolded form of Figure (Z).

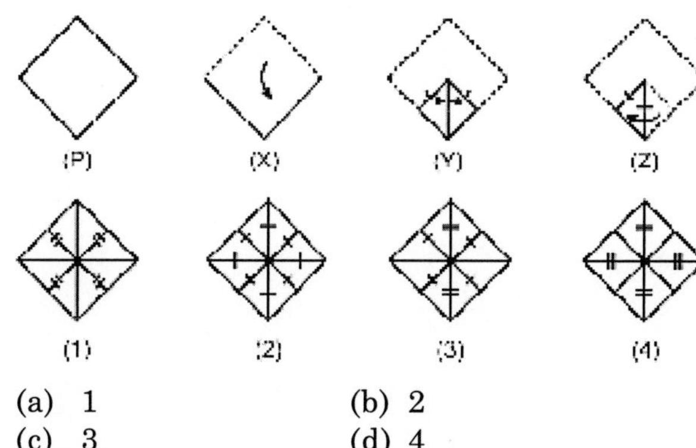

(a) 1 (b) 2
(c) 3 (d) 4

36. Choose a figure which would most closely resemble the unfolded form of Figure (Z).

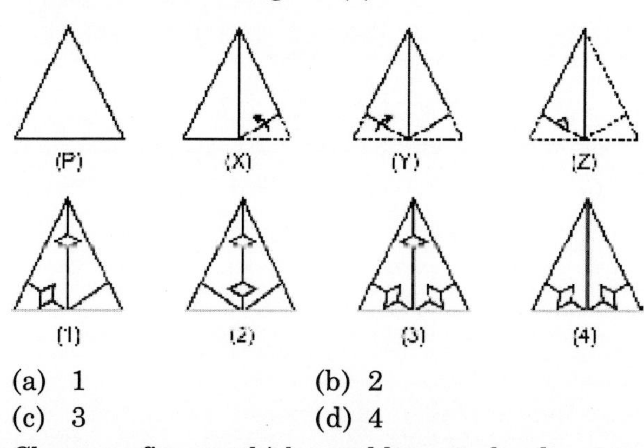

(a) 1 (b) 2
(c) 3 (d) 4

37. Choose a figure which would most closely resemble the unfolded form of Figure (Z).

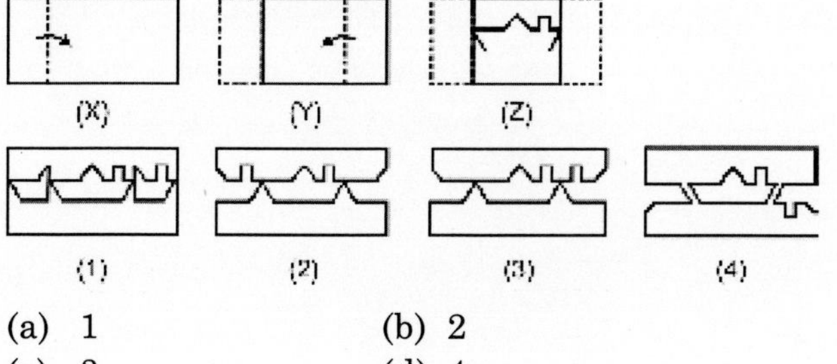

(a) 1 (b) 2
(c) 3 (d) 4

38. Choose a figure which would most closely resemble the unfolded form of Figure (Z).

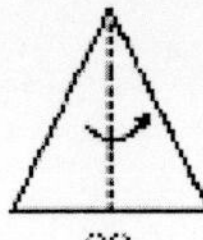
(X)
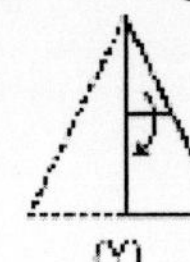
(Y)
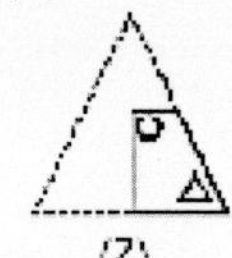
(Z)

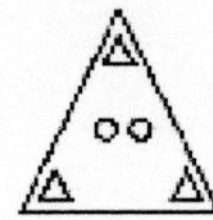
(1)
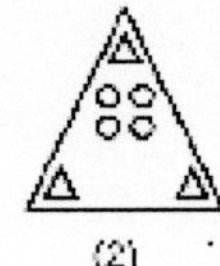
(2)
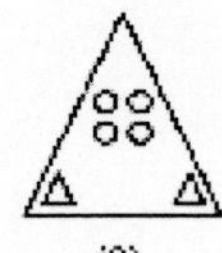
(3)
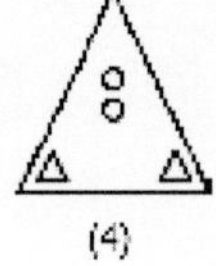
(4)

(a) 1 (b) 2
(c) 3 (d) 4

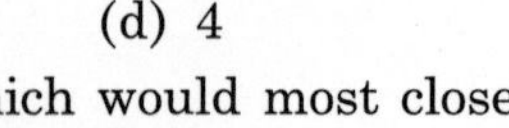

39. Choose a figure which would most closely resemble the unfolded form of Figure (Z).

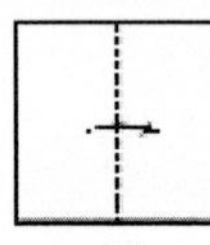
(X)
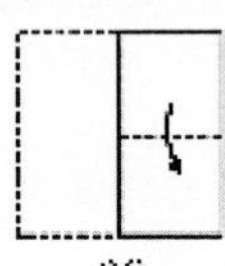
(Y)

(Z)

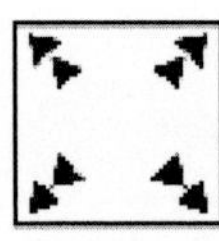
(1)
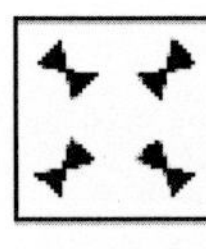
(2)
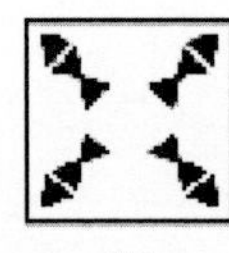
(3)
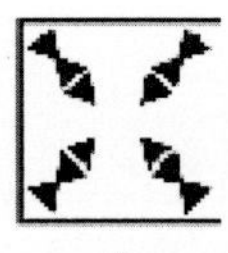
(4)

(a) 1 (b) 2
(c) 3 (d) 4

40. Choose a figure which would most closely resemble the unfolded form of Figure (Z).

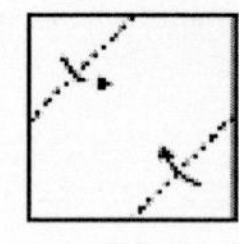
(X)
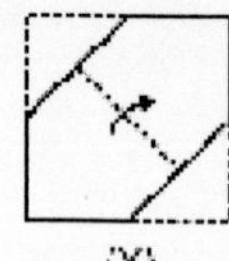
(Y)
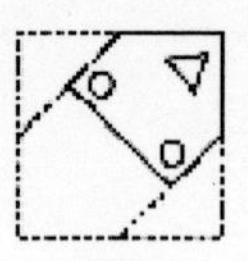
(Z)

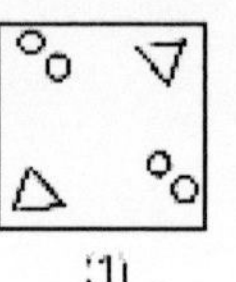
(1)
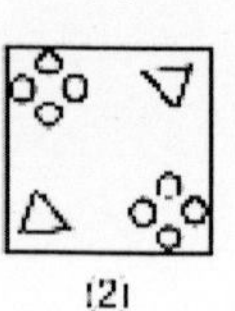
(2)
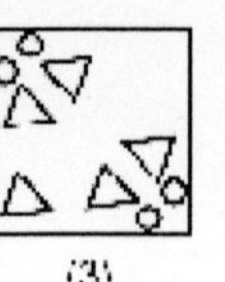
(3)
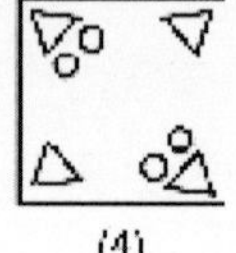
(4)

(a) 1 (b) 2
(c) 3 (d) 4

Answer Key

1. (b)	**2.** (c)	**3.** (a)	**4.** (c)	**5.** (b)	**6.** (b)	**7.** (a)	**8.** (d)	**9.** (b)	**10.** (b)
11. (d)	**12.** (b)	**13.** (c)	**14.** (b)	**15.** (d)	**16.** (d)	**17.** (b)	**18.** (d)	**19.** (a)	**20.** (c)
21. (c)	**22.** (b)	**23.** (c)	**24.** (d)	**25.** (b)	**26.** (c)	**27.** (c)	**28.** (b)	**29.** (c)	**30.** (d)
31. (a)	**32.** (d)	**33.** (d)	**34.** (d)	**35.** (b)	**36.** (d)	**37.** (c)	**38.** (c)	**39.** (c)	**40.** (b)

Previous Year Questions

1. Choose a figure which would most closely resemble the unfolded form of Figure (Z).
[NTSE 2002 - Gujarat first stage paper]

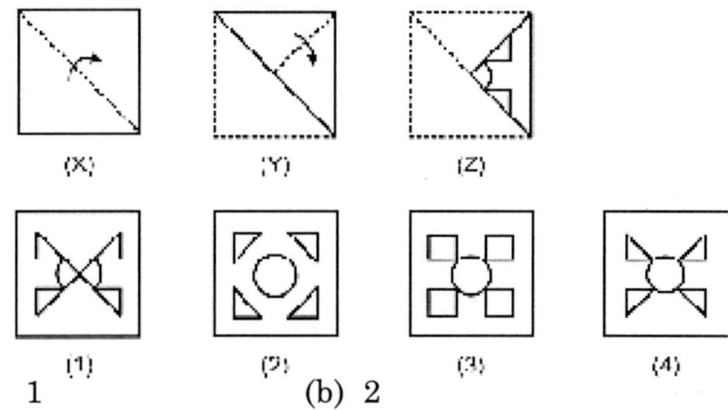

(a) 1 (b) 2
(c) 3 (d) 4

2. Choose a figure which would most closely resemble the unfolded form of Figure (Z).
[NTSE 2012 - Punjab first stage paper]

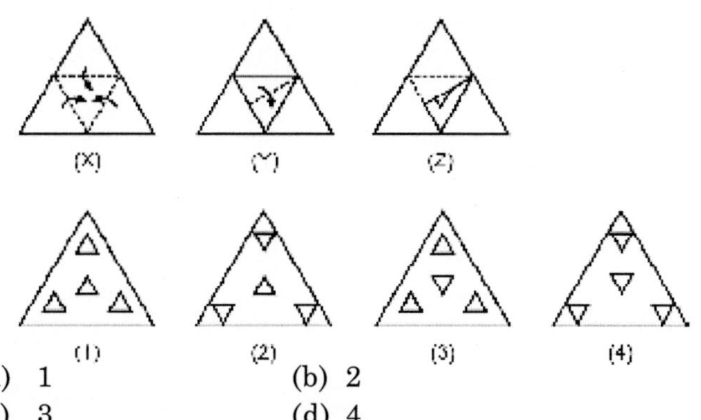

(a) 1 (b) 2
(c) 3 (d) 4

3. Choose a figure which would most closely resemble the unfolded form of Figure (Z).
[NTSE 2003 - MP second stage paper]

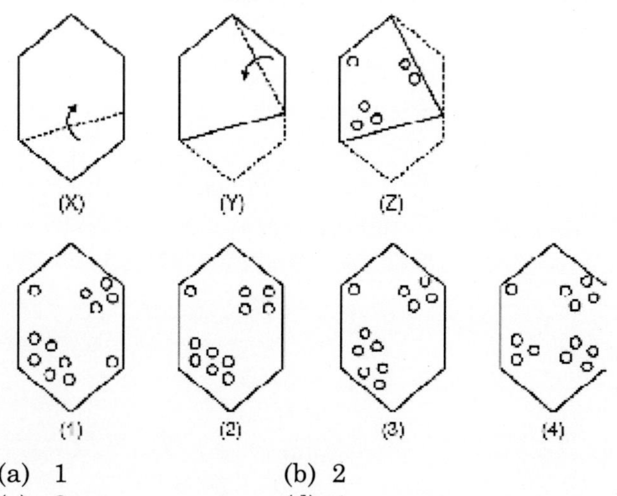

(a) 1 (b) 2
(c) 3 (d) 4

4. Choose a figure which would most closely resemble the unfolded form of Figure (Z).
[NTSE 2004 - Gujarat first stage paper]

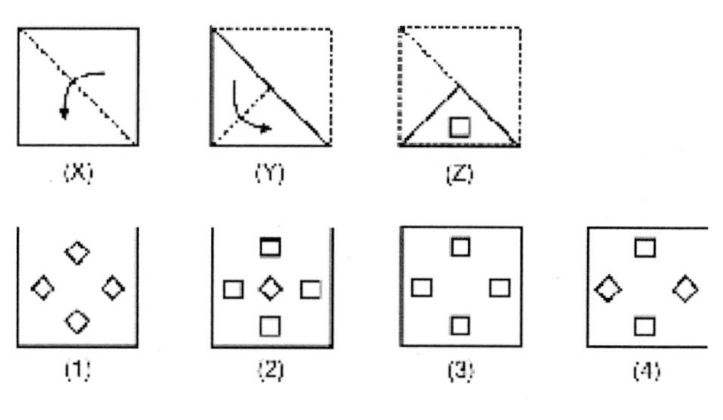

(a) 1 (b) 2
(c) 3 (d) 4

5. Choose a figure which would most closely resemble the unfolded form of Figure (Z).
[NTSE 2006 - Kerala first stage paper]

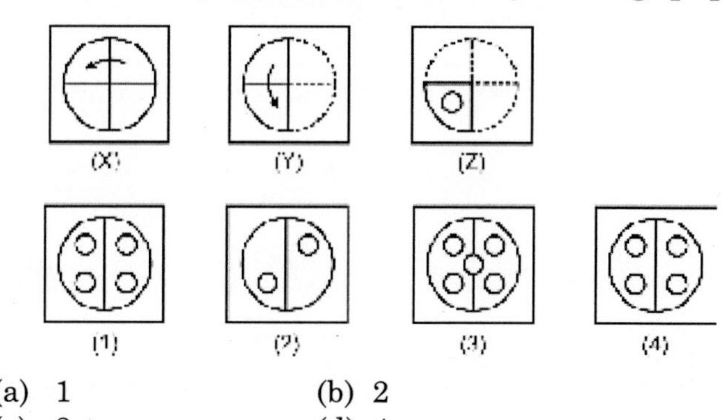

(a) 1 (b) 2
(c) 3 (d) 4

6. Choose a figure which would most closely resemble the unfolded form of Figure (Z).
[NTSE 2000 - Maharashtra second stage paper]

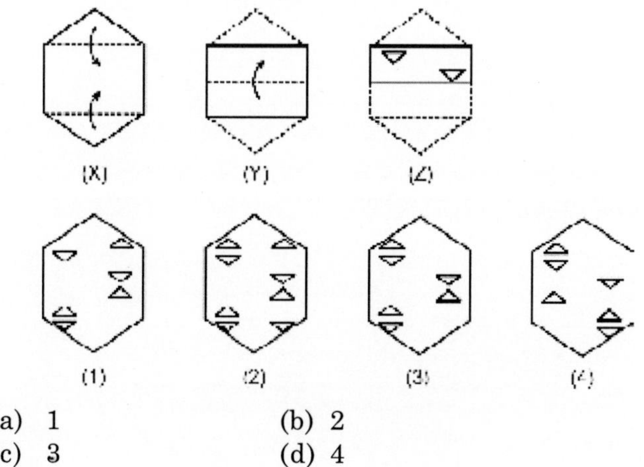

(a) 1 (b) 2
(c) 3 (d) 4

7. Choose a figure which would most closely resemble the unfolded form of Figure (Z).

[NTSE 2005 - Delhi first stage paper]

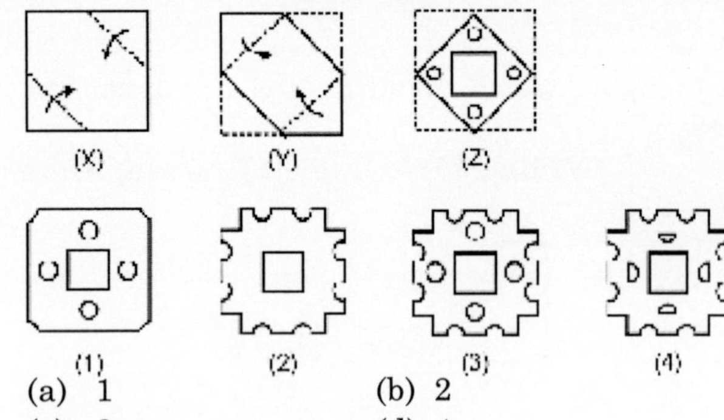

(a) 1 (b) 2
(c) 3 (d) 4

8. Choose a figure which would most closely resemble the unfolded form of Figure (Z).

[NTSE 2006 - Bihar second stage paper]

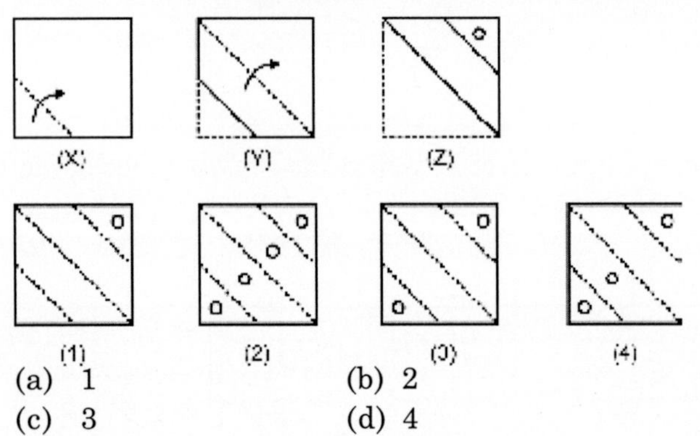

(a) 1 (b) 2
(c) 3 (d) 4

9. Choose a figure which would most closely resemble the unfolded form of Figure (Z).

[NTSE 2001 - UP first stage paper]

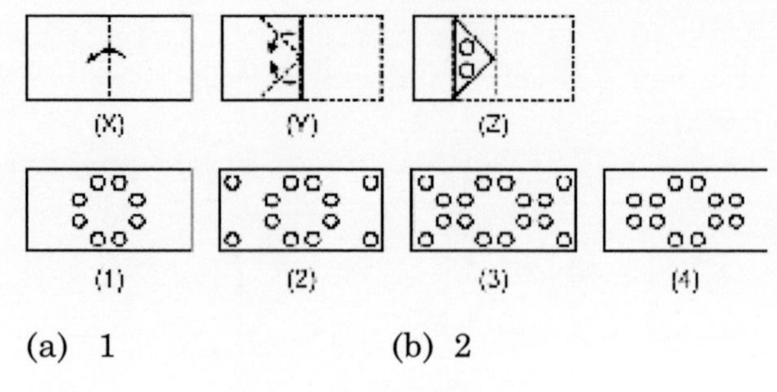

(a) 1 (b) 2
(c) 3 (d) 4

10. Choose a figure which would most closely resemble the unfolded form of Figure (Z).

[NTSE 2012 - Delhi second stage paper]

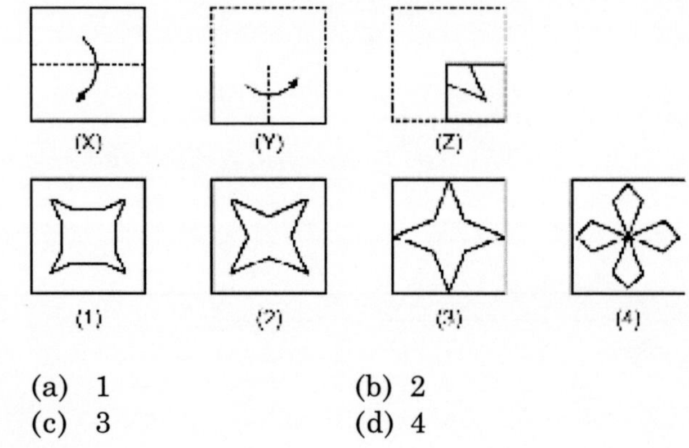

(a) 1 (b) 2
(c) 3 (d) 4

Answer Key

1. (c)	**2.** (c)	**3.** (c)	**4.** (c)	**5.** (d)	**6.** (c)	**7.** (c)	**8.** (a)	**9.** (a)	**10.** (b)

UNIT 10

Water Images

Definition: *T*he reflection of an object, as seen in water, is called its water image. It is the inverted image obtained by turning the object upside down.

Water Images of Capital Letters

Letters	A	∀	G	Ә	M	W	S	Ƨ	Y	⅄
Water Images	B	B	H	H	N	И	T	⊥	Z	Σ
Letters	C	C	I	I	O	O	U	∩		
Water Images	D	D	J	ᒣ	P	ь	V	Λ		
Letters	E	E	K	K	Q	Ọ	W	M		
Water Images	F	Ⅎ	L	Γ	R	ꓤ	X	X		

Notes :

- The letters whose water images remain unchanged are:
  C, D, E, H, I, K, O and X
- Certain words which have identical water images are: KICK, KID, CHIDE, HIKE, CODE, CHICK

Water Images of Small Letters

Letters	a	ɐ	g	ƃ	m	ɯ	s	ɘ	y	ʎ
Water Images	b	p	h	ɥ	n	u	t	ɟ	z	ƨ
Letters	c	c	i	!	o	o	u	n		
Water Images	d	q	j	!	p	b	v	ʌ		
Letters	e	ɐ	k	ʞ	q	d	w	ʍ		
Water Images	f	ɟ	l	l	r	ɹ	x	x		

Water Images of Numbers

Letters	0	1	2	3	4	5	6	7	8	9
Water Images	0	⇂	Ƨ	Ɛ	߂	ϛ	ɘ	⅃	8	6

Solved Examples

1. Choose the correct water image of the given figure (X) from amongst the four alternatives.

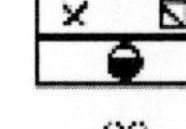

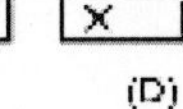

(X) (A) (B) (C) (D)

(a) A (b) B
(c) C (d) D

Solution: Option (c) is correct.

2: Choose the correct water image of the given figure (X) from amongst the four alternatives.

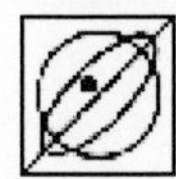

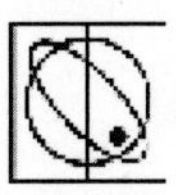

(X) (A) (B) (C) (D)

(a) A (b) B
(c) C (d) D

Solution: Option (b) is correct.

3. Choose the alternative which closely resembles the water image of the given combination.

TUceh69

(A) ɐɐɥɘɔUT **(B)** ɐɐɥɘcUT
(C) TUɔɘɥɐɘ **(D)** ⊥∩ɔɘɥɐɐ

(a) A (b) B
(c) C (d) D

Solution: Option (d) is correct.

4. Choose the alternative which closely resembles the water image of the given combination.

XYZO48SX

(A) X2840ZYX **(B)** X⅄ZO߂8ƧX
(C) X28ЬOZYX **(D)** X28߂OZ⅄X

(a) A (b) B
(c) C (d) D

Solution: Option (b) is correct.

Multiple Choice Questions

☛ ***Direction to solve (1 to 15):*** *In each of the following questions, choose the water image of the Fig. (X) from amongst the four alternatives (A), (B), (C) and (D) given along with it.*

1. Choose the alternative which closely resembles the water image of the given combination.

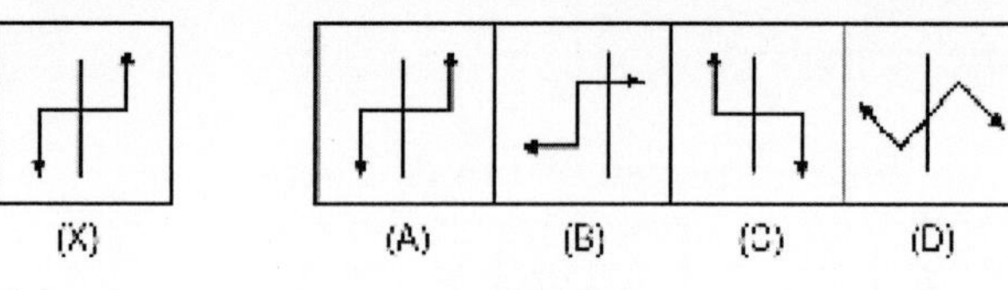

(a) A (b) B
(c) C (d) D

2. Choose the alternative which closely resembles the water image of the given combination.

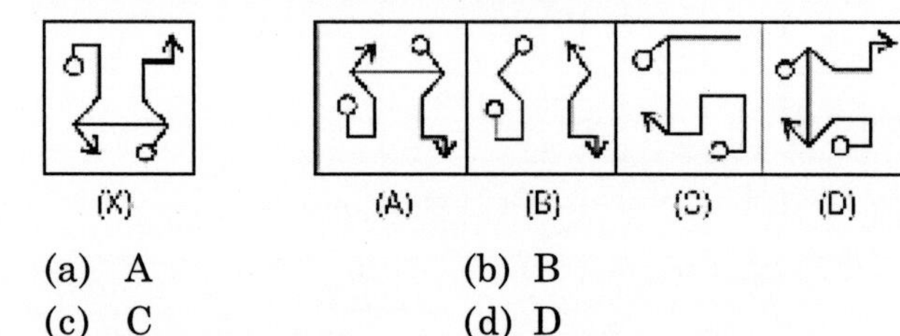

(a) A (b) B
(c) C (d) D

3. Choose the alternative which closely resembles the water image of the given combination.

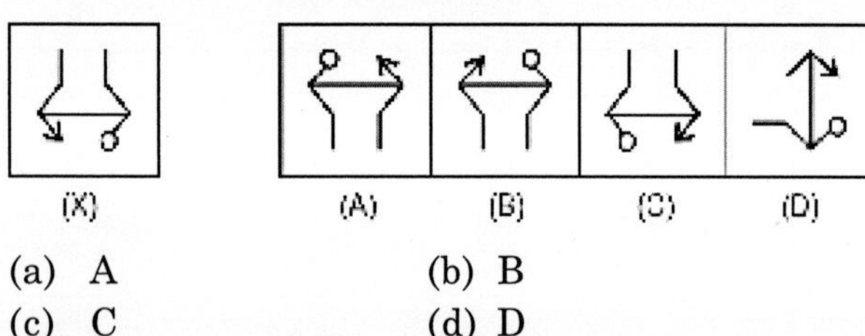

(a) A (b) B
(c) C (d) D

4. Choose the alternative which closely resembles the water image of the given combination.

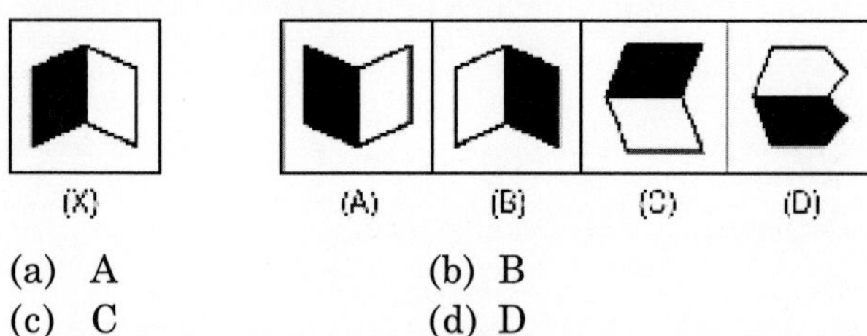

(a) A (b) B
(c) C (d) D

5. Choose the alternative which closely resembles the water image of the given combination.

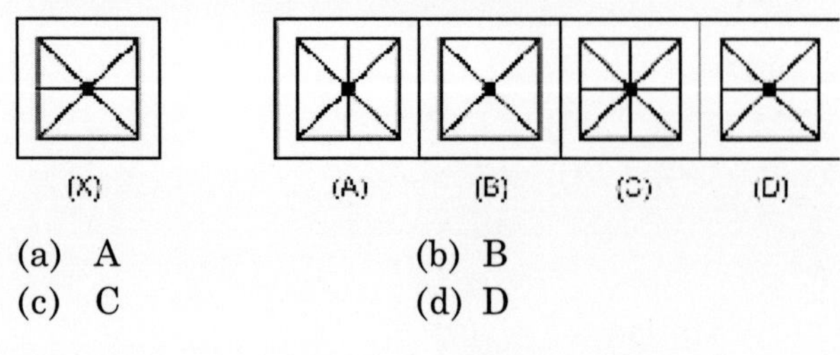

(a) A (b) B
(c) C (d) D

6. Choose the alternative which closely resembles the water image of the given combination.

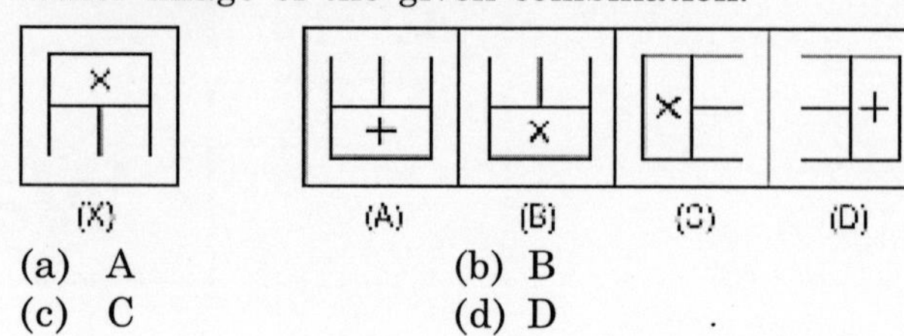

(a) A (b) B
(c) C (d) D

7. Choose the alternative which closely resembles the water image of the given combination.

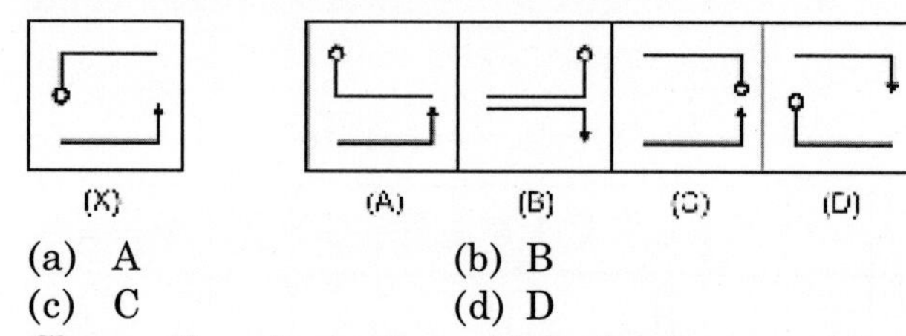

(a) A (b) B
(c) C (d) D

8. Choose the alternative which closely resembles the water image of the given combination.

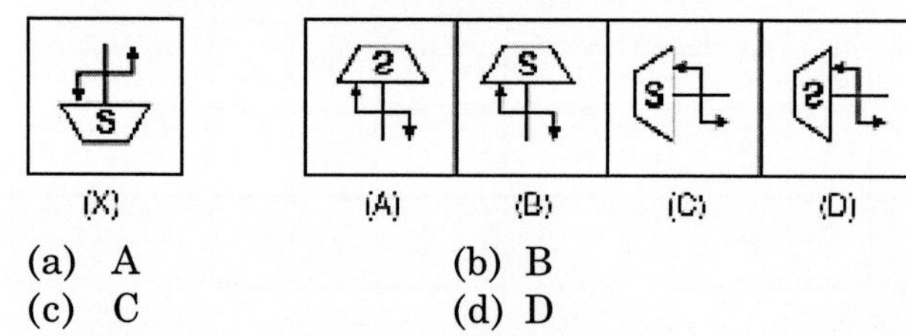

(a) A (b) B
(c) C (d) D

9. Choose the alternative which closely resembles the water image of the given combination.

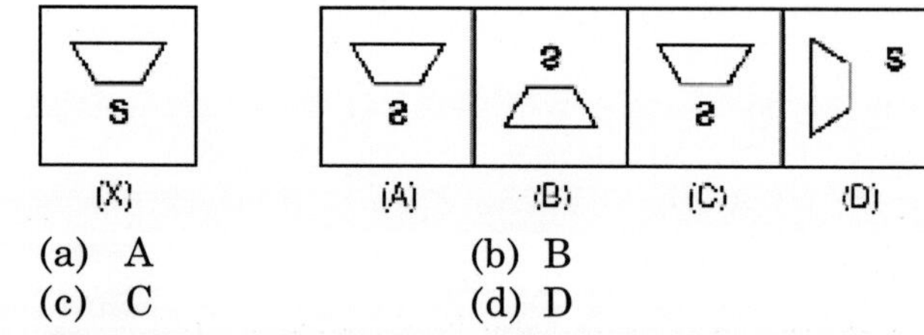

(a) A (b) B
(c) C (d) D

10. Choose the alternative which closely resembles the water image of the given combination.

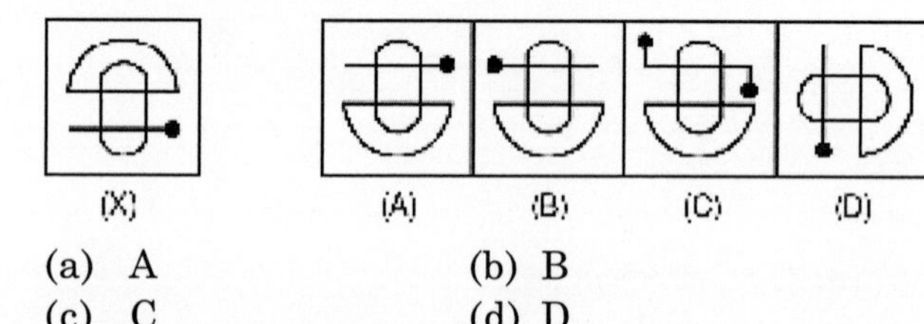

(a) A (b) B
(c) C (d) D

11. Choose the alternative which closely resembles the water image of the given combination.

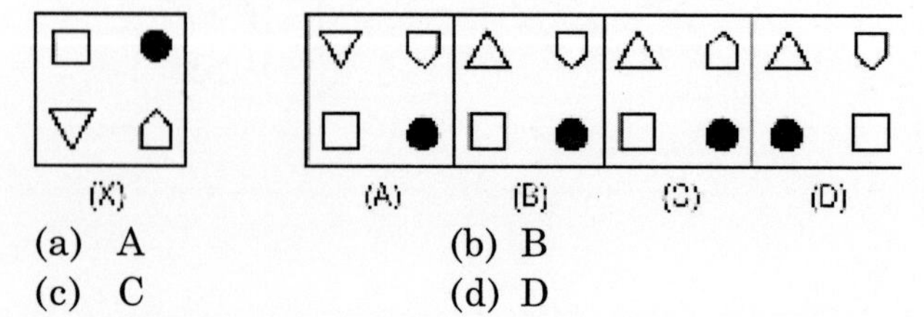

(a) A (b) B
(c) C (d) D

12. Choose the alternative which closely resembles the water image of the given combination.

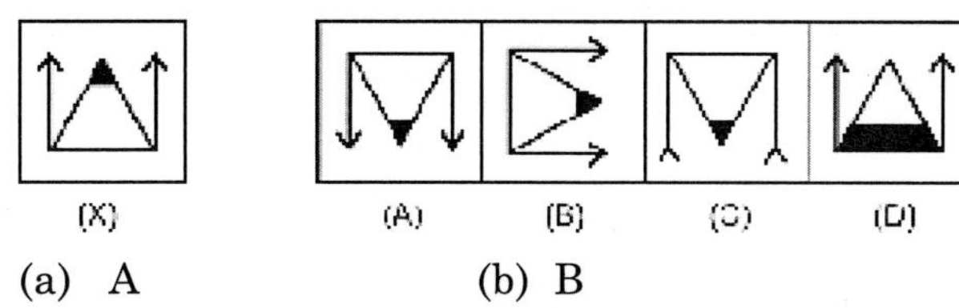

(a) A (b) B
(c) C (d) D

13. Choose the alternative which closely resembles the water image of the given combination.

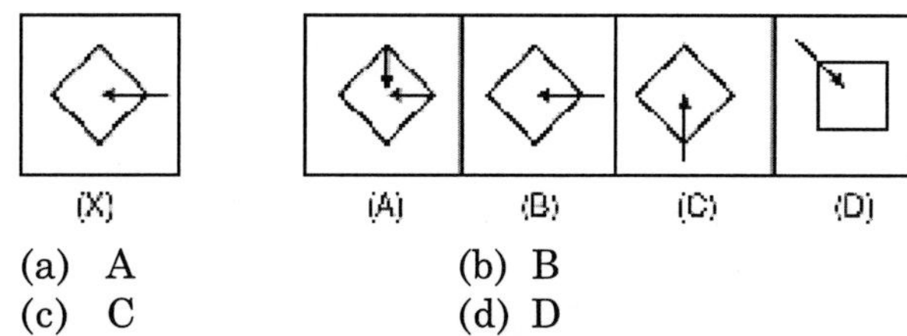

(a) A (b) B
(c) C (d) D

14. Choose the alternative which closely resembles the water image of the given combination.

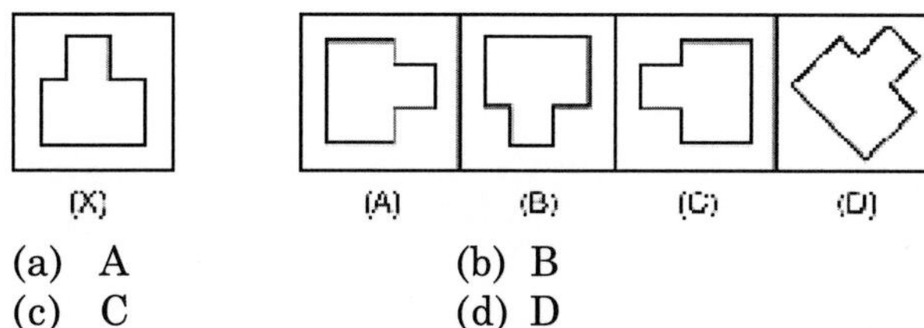

(a) A (b) B
(c) C (d) D

15. Choose the alternative which closely resembles the water image of the given combination.

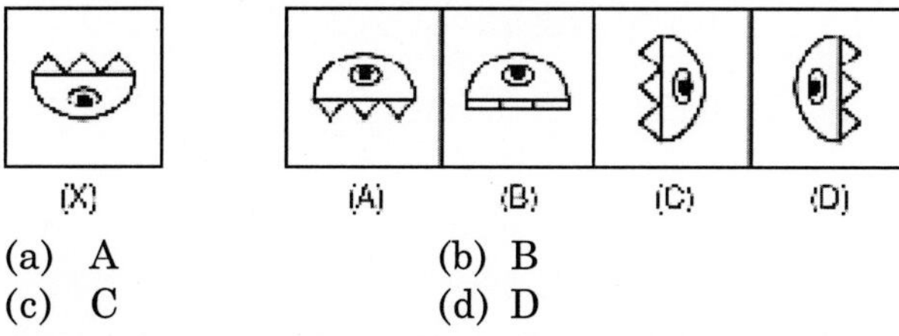

(a) A (b) B
(c) C (d) D

☛ ***Direction to solve (16 to 30):*** *In each of the following questions, you are given a combination of alphabets and/ or numbers followed by four alternatives (A), (B), (C) and (D). Choose the alternative which closely resembles the water image of the given combination.*

16. Choose the alternative which closely resembles the water image of the given combination.

CDEF

(A) CDEⅎ **(B) CDEF**
(C) FEDC **(D) ƆDƎꟻ**

(a) A (b) B
(c) C (d) D

17. Choose the alternative which closely resembles the water image of the given combination.

XYZ

(A) XʎZ **(B) XʎƧ**
(C) XZY **(D) ZYX**

(a) A (b) B
(c) C (d) D

18. Choose the alternative which closely resembles the water image of the given combination.

01234

(A) 0⅂ՇƐᔭ **(B) 43210**
(C) 01324 **(D) 0ՇƐᔭ**

(a) A (b) B
(c) C (d) D

19. Choose the alternative which closely resembles the water image of the given combination.

CHICK

(A) Ↄ H I CꓘI **(B) Ↄ H I Ↄ ꓘ**
(C) KCIHC **(D) CHICK**

(a) A (b) B
(c) C (d) D

20. Choose the alternative which closely resembles the water image of the given combination.

CODE

(A) CODF **(B) FDOC**
(C) Ↄ OᗡƎ **(D) Ↄ OᗡƎ**

(a) A (b) B
(c) C (d) D

21. Choose the alternative which closely resembles the water image of the given combination.

HIKE

(A) HIKE **(B) EKIH**
(C) H IꓘƎ **(D) HIKƎ**

(a) A (b) B
(c) C (d) D

22. Choose the alternative which closely resembles the water image of the given combination.

CHIDE

(A) Ↄ HIᗡƎ **(B) CHIᗡƎ**
(C) EDIHC **(D) CHIDE**

(a) A (b) B
(c) C (d) D

23. Choose the alternative which closely resembles the water image of the given combination.

SUBHAM

(A) ƧՈᗺHꓯW **(B) Ƨ ՈᗺHAW**
(C) ƧՈBHꓯW **(D) MAHBUS**

(a) A (b) B
(c) C (d) D

24. Choose the alternative which closely resembles the water image of the given combination.

U4P15B7

(A) Ոᔭb⅃ƧBꓶ **(B) Ոᔭdl ƧBꓶ**
(C) Ոᔭb⅃ƧBꓶ **(D) Ոᔭb ⅃ƧBꓶ**

(a) A (b) B
(c) C (d) D

25. Choose the alternative which closely resembles the water image of the given combination.

    96FSH52

    (A) ƐɘFƧHƐƧ (B) 69FƧHƧƧ

    (C) ɘɘFƧHƐƧ (D) 69FƧHƧƐ

    (a) A (b) B
    (c) C (d) D

26. Choose the alternative which closely resembles the water image of the given combination.

    US91Q4M5W3

    (A) ∩Ƨ9⅂Ó4MƧWƐ (B) ∩Ƨ6⅂Ó4MƧM3

    (C) ∩S9⅂Ó4MƧWƐ (D) ∩Ƨ9⅂Ó4MƧM3

    (a) A (b) B
    (c) C (d) D

27. Choose the alternative which closely resembles the water image of the given combination.

    rise

    (A) ɼᴉƨɘ (B) esir

    (C) ɿiƨɔ (D) ɘƨiɿ

    (a) A (b) B
    (c) C (d) D

28. Choose the alternative which closely resembles the water image of the given combination.

    BK50RP62

    (A) BꓘƧ0ꓤbƐƧ (B) BKƧ0ꓤbƐƧ

    (C) BKƧ0ꓤbɘƧ (D) BKS0ꓤbɘƧ

    (a) A (b) B
    (c) C (d) D

29. Choose the alternative which closely resembles the water image of the given combination.

    NhRqS y

    (A) NᖰꓤdƧ ʎ (B) ИԿꓤdƧ ʎ

    (C) ИᖰꓤdƧ ʎ (D) ИᖰꓤdƧ ʎ

    (a) A (b) B
    (c) C (d) D

30. Choose the alternative which closely resembles the water image of the given combination.

    MNOP

    (A) WИOb (B) PONM

    (C) WИOb (D) MNOP

    (a) A (b) B
    (c) C (d) D

Answer Key

1. (c)	**2.** (a)	**3.** (b)	**4.** (a)	**5.** (d)	**6.** (b)	**7.** (d)	**8.** (a)	**9.** (b)	**10.** (a)
11. (b)	**12.** (a)	**13.** (b)	**14.** (b)	**15.** (a)	**16.** (a)	**17.** (b)	**18.** (d)	**19.** (d)	**20.** (a)
21. (a)	**22.** (d)	**23.** (c)	**24.** (c)	**25.** (c)	**26.** (d)	**27.** (a)	**28.** (b)	**29.** (d)	**30.** (c)

Previous Year Questions

1. Choose the correct water image of the given figure (X) from amongst the four alternatives.
[NTSE 2012 - Delhi first stage paper]

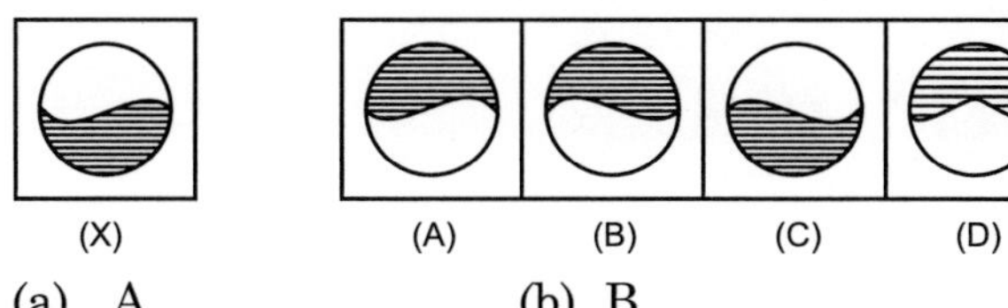

(a) A (b) B
(c) C (d) D

2. Choose the correct water image of the given figure (X) from amongst the four alternatives.
[NTSE 2006 - Karnataka first stage paper]

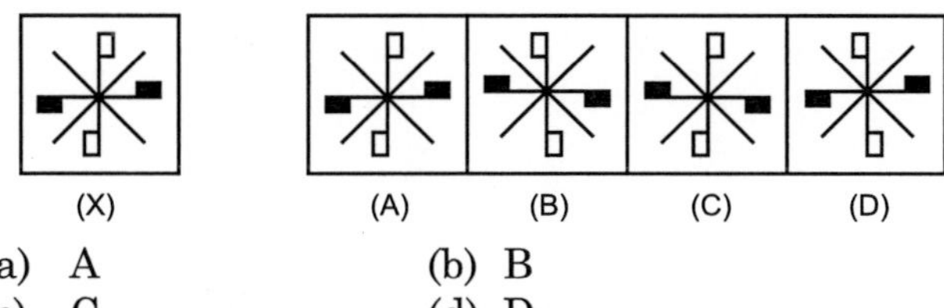

(a) A (b) B
(c) C (d) D

3. Choose the correct water image of the given figure (X) from amongst the four alternatives.
[NTSE 2007 - Gujarat first stage paper]

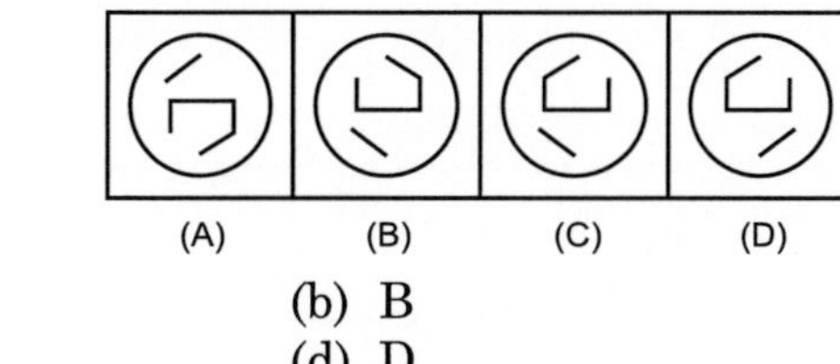

(a) A (b) B
(c) C (d) D

4. Choose the correct water image of the given figure (X) from amongst the four alternatives.
[NTSE 2007 - Gujarat first stage paper]

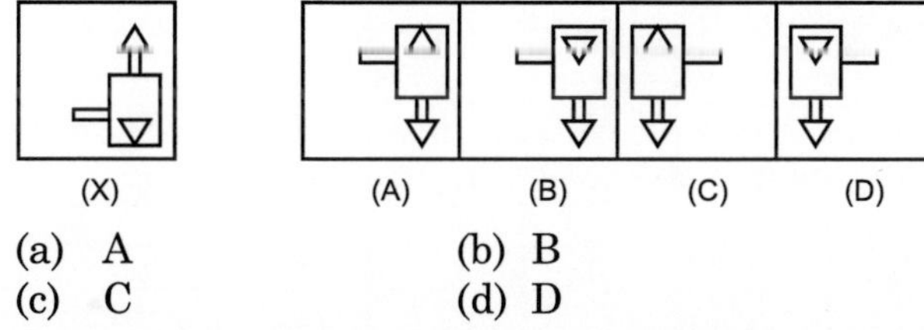

(a) A (b) B
(c) C (d) D

5. Choose the correct water image of the given figure (X) from amongst the four alternatives.
[NTSE 2012 - West Bengal first stage paper]

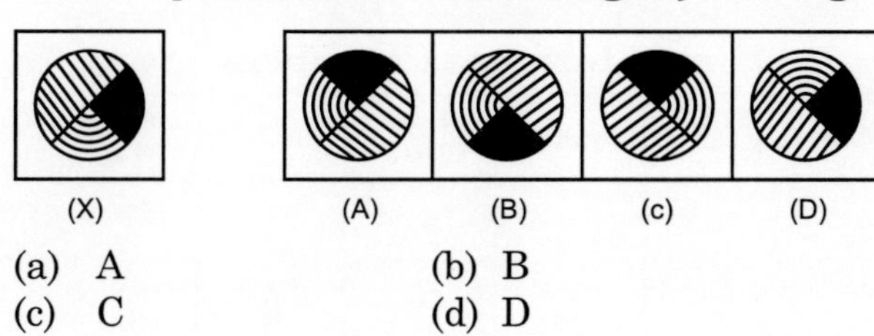

(a) A (b) B
(c) C (d) D

6. Choose the alternative which closely resembles the water image of the given combination.
[NTSE 2012 - UP first stage paper]

BANKING

(A) ƏNIKИAꓭ **(B) BAИKIИG**
(C) BANKING **(D) ꓭAИ⋊IИG**

(a) A (b) B
(c) C (d) D

7. Choose the alternative which closely resembles the water image of the given combination.
[NTSE 2012 - Rajasthan first stage paper]

INCOME

(A) IИCOWE **(B) EWOCИI**
(C) ƎMOƆИI **(D) INCOME**

(a) A (b) B
(c) C (d) D

8. Choose the alternative which closely resembles the water image of the given combination.
[NTSE 2005 - Maharashtra first stage paper]

497680

(A) ɥ9ꓶ680 **(B) 4eꓕ980**
(C) ɥeꓕ980 **(D) ɥe7980**

(a) A (b) B
(c) C (d) D

9. Choose the alternative which closely resembles the water image of the given combination.
[NTSE 2000 - Kerala first stage paper]

012345

(A) 0ꞁƧƐɥƧ **(B) ƧɥƐƧꞁ0**
(C) Ƨ4ƐƧꞁ0 **(D) 0ꞁƧƐɥƧ**

(a) A (b) B
(c) C (d) D

10. Choose the alternative which closely resembles the water image of the given combination.
[NTSE 2012 - UP first stage paper]

AB12C3

(A) ƐƆƧꞁꓭA **(B) Aꓭꞁ2Ɔ3**
(C) ∀ꓭꞁƧC3 **(D) Aꓭ12C3**

(a) A (b) B
(c) C (d) D

Answer Key

1. (b)	**2.** (b)	**3.** (d)	**4.** (a)	**5.** (d)
6. (b)	**7.** (a)	**8.** (a)	**9.** (a)	**10.** (c)

UNIT 11

Mirror Images

Definition: The image of an object, as seen in a mirror, is called its mirror reflection or mirror image. In a mirror image, the right part of an object appears at the left side and vice-versa, but the upper and lower parts remains the same.

Observe the following mirror images:

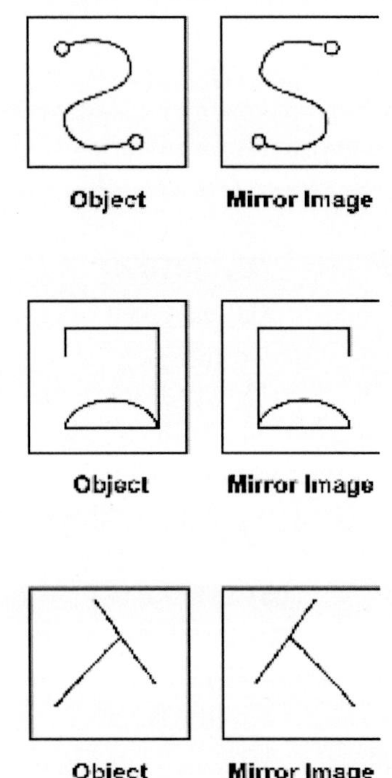

Lateral Inversion: In such an image, the right side of the object appears on the left side and vice-versa. A mirror image is therefore said to be laterally inverted and the phenomenon is called Lateral Inversion.

Mirror Images of Capital Letters

Letters	Mirror Image	Letters	Mirror Image	Letters	Mirror Image
A	A	J	ᒐ	S	Ƨ
B	ᗺ	K	ꓘ	T	T
C	Ɔ	L	⅃	U	U
D	ᗡ	M	M	V	V
E	Ǝ	N	И	W	W
F	ꟻ	O	O	X	X
G	Ә	P	ꟼ	Y	Y
H	H	Q	Ϙ	Z	Ƹ
I	I	R	Я		

Mirror Images of Small Letters

Letters	Mirror Image	Letters	Mirror Image	Letters	Mirror Image
a	ɒ	j	į	s	ƨ
b	d	k	ʞ	t	ƚ
c	ɔ	l	l	u	u
d	b	m	m	v	v
e	ɘ	n	n	w	w
f	ᖷ	o	o	x	x
g	ϱ	p	q	y	γ
h	ʜ	q	p	z	ƹ
I	I	r	ɿ	.	.

Mirror Images of Numbers

Numbers	Mirror Image	Numbers	Mirror Image	Numbers	Mirror Image
1	Ɩ	4	ᔨ	7	Ƭ
2	ᘔ	5	ᘕ	8	8
3	Ɛ	6	∂	9	୧

Solved Examples

1. Choose the alternative which closely resembles the mirror image of the given combination.

MIRROR-images

(1) MIЯЯOЯ-images **(2)** segami-ЯOЯЯIM

(3) segami-ЯOЯЯIW **(4)** segami-ЯOЯЯIM

(a) 1 (b) 2
(c) 3 (d) 4

Solution: Option (b) is correct.

2. Choose the alternative which closely resembles the mirror image of the given combination.

WANTEDth420

(1) WAИTƎDtht420 **(2)** WAИTEDht420

(3) 024htDƎTNAW **(4)** 024htDƎTИAW

(a) 1 (b) 2
(c) 3 (d) 4

Solution: Option (c) is correct.

3. Choose the correct mirror image of the given figure (X) from amongst the four alternatives.

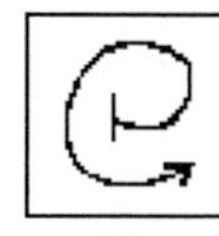

(X) (A) (B) (C) (D)

(a) 1 (b) 2
(c) 3 (d) 4

Solution: Option c) is correct.

4. Choose the correct mirror image of the given figure (X) from amongst the four alternatives.

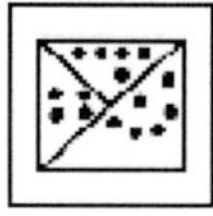
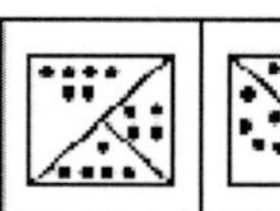
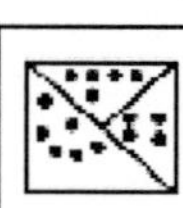
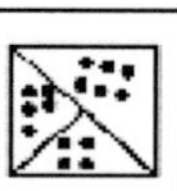
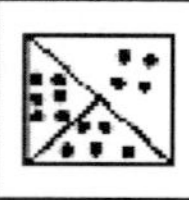

(X) (A) (B) (C) (D)

(a) 1 (b) 2
(c) 3 (d) 4

Solution: Option b) is correct.

Multiple Choice Questions

☛ ***Direction to solve (1 to 15):*** *In each of the following questions you are given a combination of alphabets and/ or numbers followed by four alternatives (1), (2), (3) and (4). Choose the alternative which closely resembles the mirror image of the given combination.*

1. **UTZFY6KH**

(1) HK9YƎZTU **(2)** UTZƎY9KH

(3) HK6YFZTU **(4)** Hꓘ6YƎZTU

(a) 1 (b) 2
(c) 3 (d) 4

2. **AN54WMG3**

(1) ƐGMW4ƧNA **(2)** ƐGMW4ƧNA

(3) 3GMW4ƧNA **(4)** ƎGMW4ƧNA

(a) 1 (b) 2
(c) 3 (d) 4

3. **SUPERVISOR**

(1) ЯOSIVЯƎPUS **(2)** SUPERVISOR

(3) RSOUPSERIV **(4)** SUPERVIOSR

(a) 1 (b) 2
(c) 3 (d) 4

4. **MAGAZINE**

(1) MAGAZIИƎ **(2)** ƎNIZAGAM

(3) MAGAZIИƎ **(4)** ƎNIZAGAM

(a) 1 (b) 2
(c) 3 (d) 4

5. **DL 9CG4 7 28**

(1) DJ 9CG4 7 28 **(3)** 82 7 4GC9 LD

(2) 82 7 4GC9 JD **(4)** 82 7 4GC9 JD

(a) 1 (b) 2
(c) 3 (d) 4

6. **PAINTED**

(1) DƎTNIAꟼ **(3)** DƎTNIAꟼ

(2) DƎTNIAꟼ **(4)** DETNIAꟼ

(a) 1 (b) 2
(c) 3 (d) 4

7. **NATIONAL**

(1) LANOITAN **(3)** LANOITAИ

(2) LANOITAN **(4)** LAИOITAИ

(a) 1 (b) 2
(c) 3 (d) 4

8. **GEOGRAPHY**

(1) YHꟼAЯGOƎG **(2)** YHPARGOEG

(3) YHꟼAЯGOƎG **(4)** YHꟼAЯGOƎG

(a) 1 (b) 2
(c) 3 (d) 4

9. **BR4AQ16HI**

   (1) IH∂1QAᔭЯᗺ (2) IH61QA4RB
   (3) IH6 1QA4Яᗺ (4) IH9⇂QAᔭЯᗺ

   (a) 1 (b) 2
   (c) 3 (d) 4

10. **247596**

    (1) 695742 (2) ɘ95ƚ4Ƨ
    (3) ƧᔭƚƧƏƏ (4) ɘ9ƨ7ᔭƧ

    (a) 1 (b) 2
    (c) 3 (d) 4

11. NiCaRaGuA

    (1) AuGaRaCin (2) AnӘaЯaƆiИ
    (3) AnӘaЯaƆiИ (4) AuӘaЯaƆiИ

    (a) 1 (b) 2
    (c) 3 (d) 4

12. COLONIAL

    (1) LAINOLOC (2) ⅃AINOLOϽ
    (3) ΓAIИOΓOC (4) ⅃AIИO⅃OϽ

    (a) 1 (b) 2
    (c) 3 (d) 4

13. **1 9 6 5 I NDOPAK**

    (1) ꓘAꟼOᗡИ I ƨ 6 9 ⇂
    (2) ꟼAꓘ I ИᗡO⇂ ƨ 6 9
    (3) ꓘAꟼOᗡИ I ƨ 9 6 ⇂
    (4) ꓘAꟼOᗡИ I ƨ ə 9 ⇂

    (a) 1 (b) 2
    (c) 3 (d) 4

14. **EMANATE**

    (1) ƎWⱯNⱯꓕƎ (2) ƎTANAMƎ
    (3) ETANAME (4) EATEMAN

    (a) 1 (b) 2
    (c) 3 (d) 4

15. KALINGA261B

    (1) KⱯLINGⱯZ6⇂B
    (2) B162AGNILAK
    (3) B261KALINGA
    (4) ᗺ⇂ƍƧAӘИI⅃Aꓘ

    (a) 1 (b) 2
    (c) 3 (d) 4

☛ ***Direction to solve (16 to 30):*** *In each of the following questions, choose the correct mirror images of the given image of the Fig.(X) from amongst the four alternatives (1), (2), (3) and (4) given along with it.*

16. Choose the correct mirror image of the given figure (X) from amongst the four alternatives.

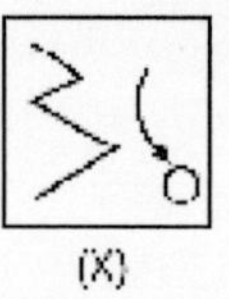

(X) (1) (2) (3) (4)

(a) 1 (b) 2
(c) 3 (d) 4

17. Choose the correct mirror image of the given figure (X) from amongst the four alternatives.

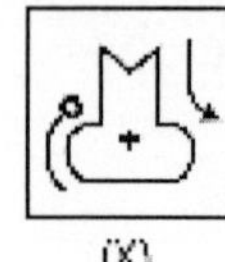 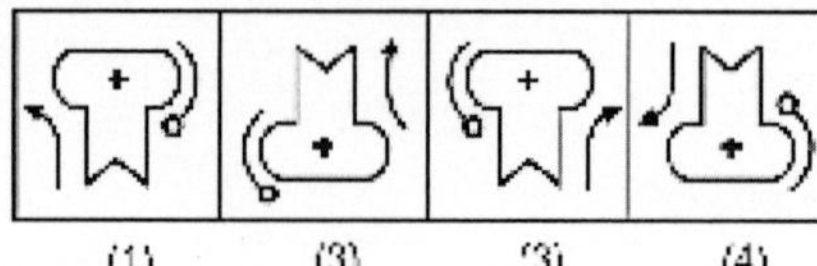

(X) (1) (3) (3) (4)

(a) 1 (b) 2
(c) 3 (d) 4

18. Choose the correct mirror image of the given figure (X) from amongst the four alternatives.

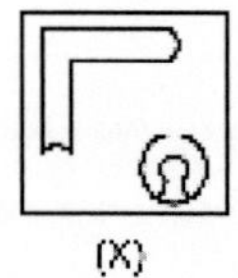 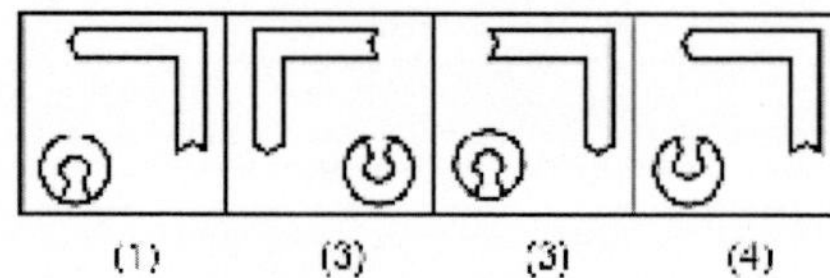

(X) (1) (3) (3) (4)

(a) 1 (b) 2
(c) 3 (d) 4

19. Choose the correct mirror image of the given figure (X) from amongst the four alternatives.

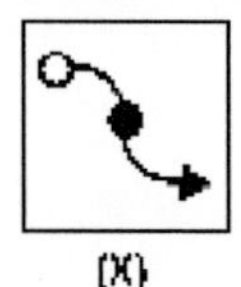 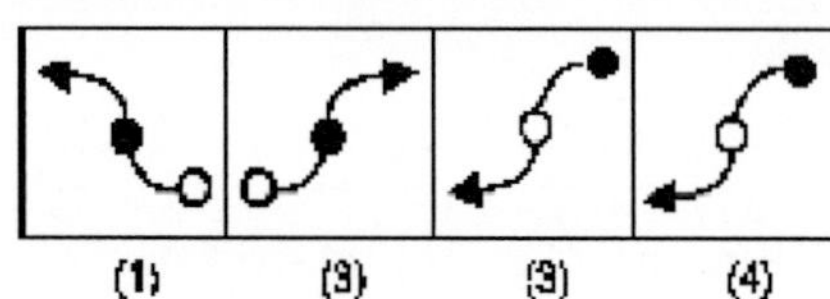

(X) (1) (3) (3) (4)

(a) 1 (b) 2
(c) 3 (d) 4

20. Choose the correct mirror image of the given figure (X) from amongst the four alternatives.

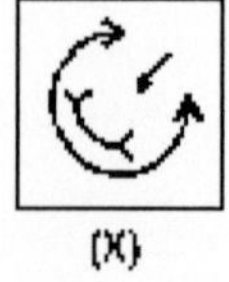 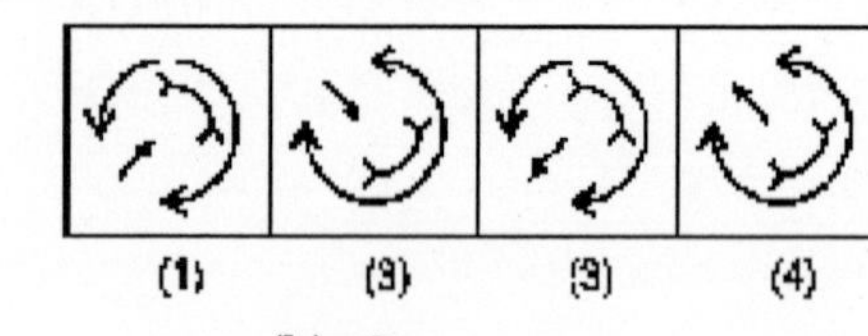

(X) (1) (3) (3) (4)

(a) 1 (b) 2
(c) 3 (d) 4

21. Choose the correct mirror image of the given figure (X) from amongst the four alternatives.

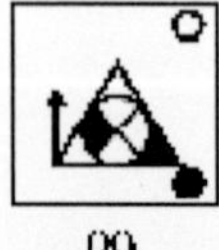 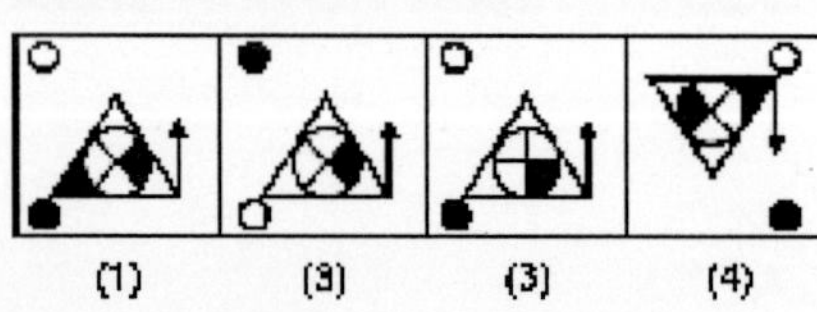

(X) (1) (3) (3) (4)

(a) 1 (b) 2
(c) 3 (d) 4

22. Choose the correct mirror image of the given figure (X) from amongst the four alternatives.

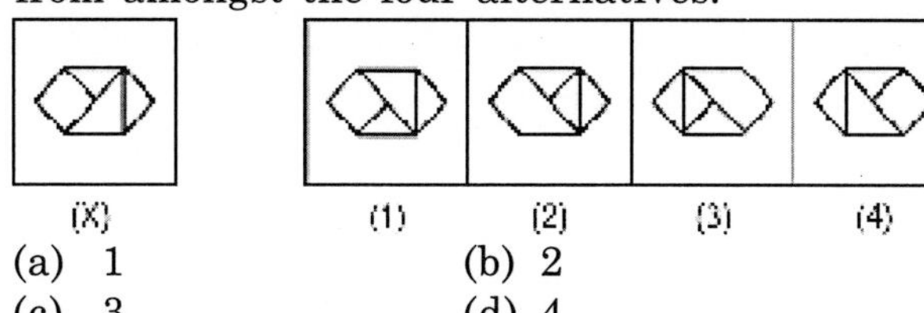

(a) 1 (b) 2
(c) 3 (d) 4

23. Choose the correct mirror image of the given figure (X) from amongst the four alternatives.

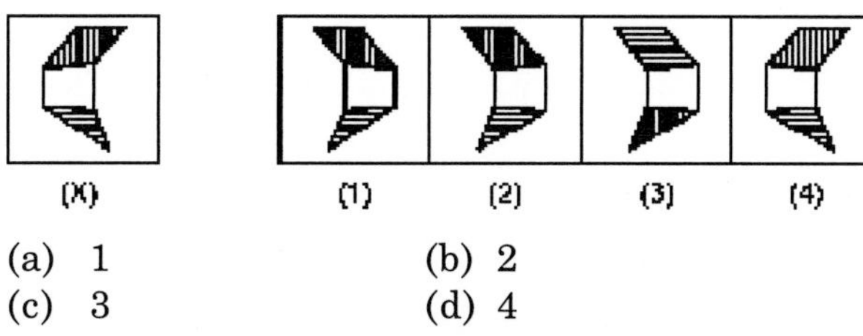

(a) 1 (b) 2
(c) 3 (d) 4

24. Choose the correct mirror image of the given figure (X) from amongst the four alternatives.

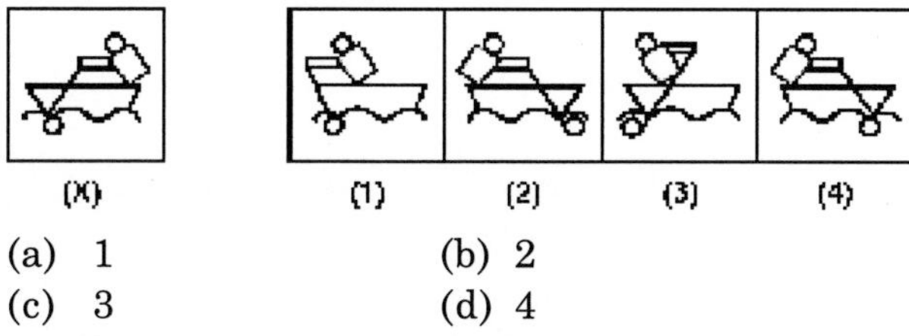

(a) 1 (b) 2
(c) 3 (d) 4

25. Choose the correct mirror image of the given figure (X) from amongst the four alternatives.

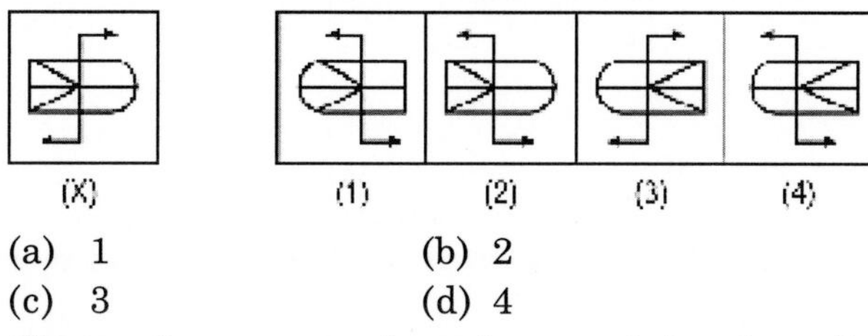

(a) 1 (b) 2
(c) 3 (d) 4

26. Choose the correct mirror image of the given figure (X) from amongst the four alternatives.

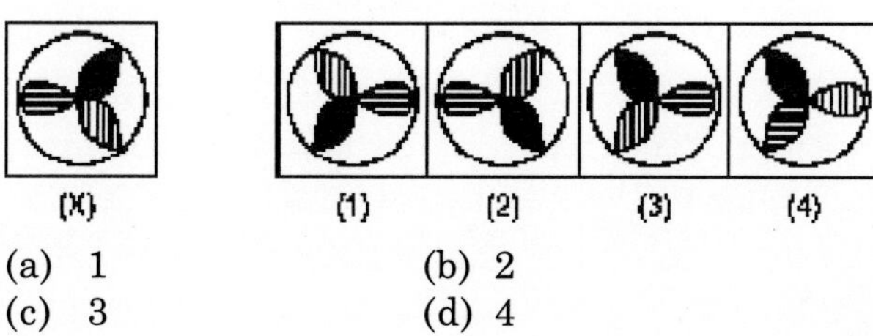

(a) 1 (b) 2
(c) 3 (d) 4

27. Choose the correct mirror image of the given figure (X) from amongst the four alternatives.

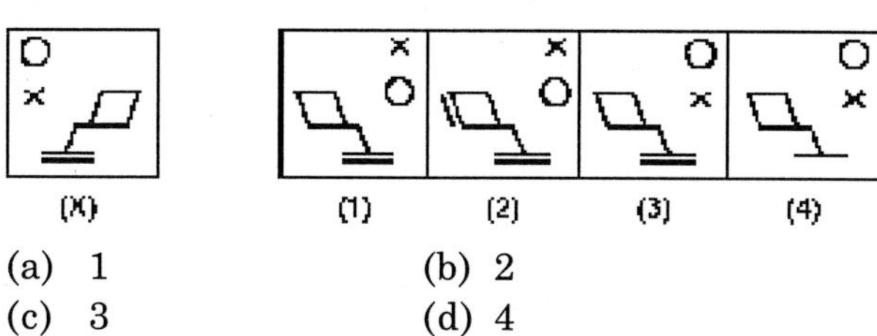

(a) 1 (b) 2
(c) 3 (d) 4

28. Choose the correct mirror image of the given figure (X) from amongst the four alternatives.

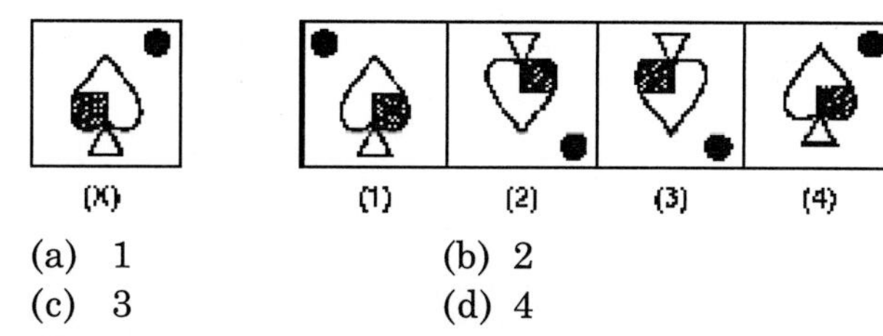

(a) 1 (b) 2
(c) 3 (d) 4

29. Choose the correct mirror image of the given figure (X) from amongst the four alternatives.

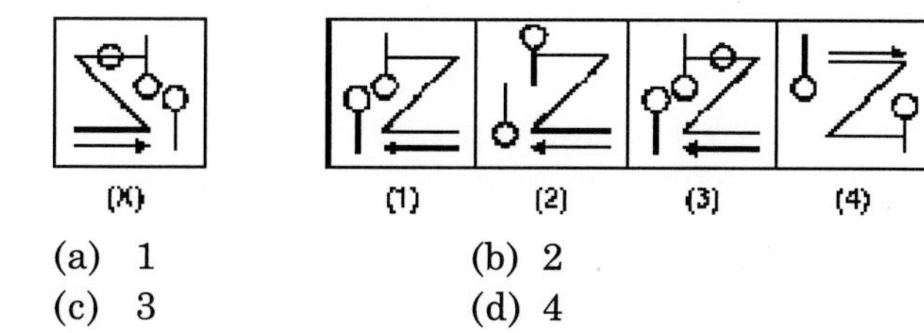

(a) 1 (b) 2
(c) 3 (d) 4

30. Choose the correct mirror image of the given figure (X) from amongst the four alternatives.

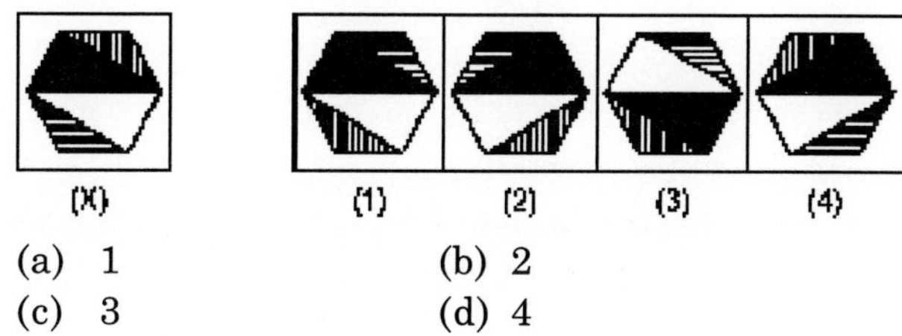

(a) 1 (b) 2
(c) 3 (d) 4

Answer Key

1. (d)	**2.** (b)	**3.** (a)	**4.** (d)	**5.** (c)	**6.** (b)	**7.** (b)	**8.** (a)	**9.** (a)	**10.** (d)
11. (d)	**12.** (d)	**13.** (d)	**14.** (b)	**15.** (d)	**16.** (c)	**17.** (d)	**18.** (a)	**19.** (c)	**20.** (b)
21. (a)	**22.** (d)	**23.** (a)	**24.** (d)	**25.** (d)	**26.** (c)	**27.** (c)	**28.** (a)	**29.** (c)	**30.** (d)

❐

Previous Year Questions

1. Choose the correct mirror image of the given figure (X) from amongst the four alternatives.
[NTSE 2002 - Gujarat first stage paper]

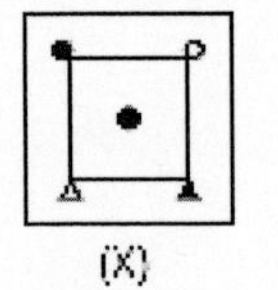
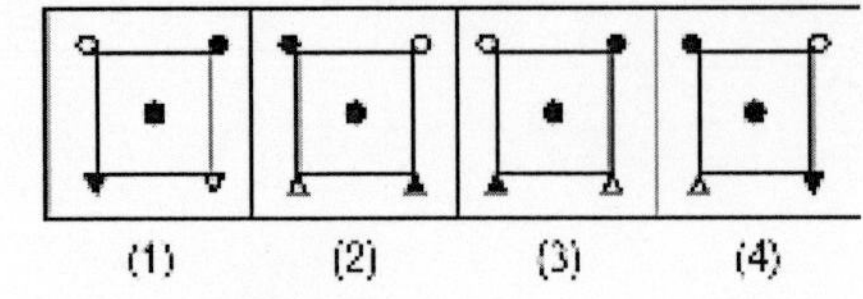

(X) (1) (2) (3) (4)

(a) 1 (b) 2
(c) 3 (d) 4

2. Choose the correct mirror image of the given figure (X) from amongst the four alternatives.
[NTSE 2006 - Kerala first stage paper]

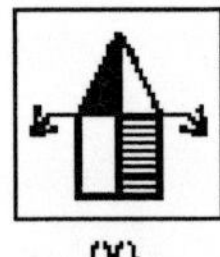
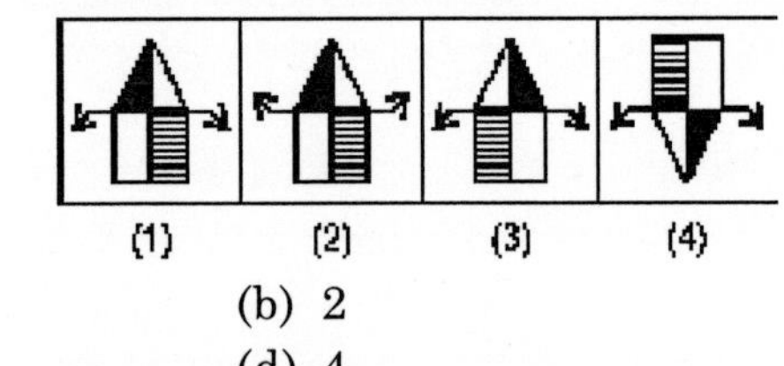

(X) (1) (2) (3) (4)

(a) 1 (b) 2
(c) 3 (d) 4

3. Choose the correct mirror image of the given figure (X) from amongst the four alternatives.
[NTSE 2002 – West Bengal second stage paper]

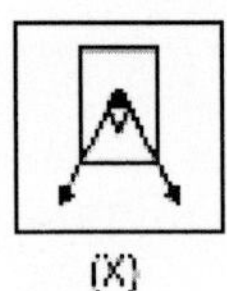
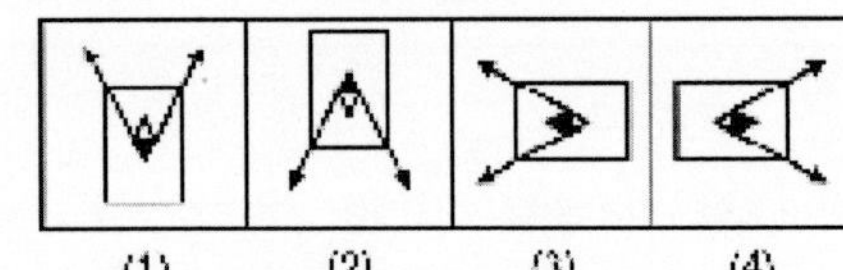

(X) (1) (2) (3) (4)

(a) 1 (b) 2
(c) 3 (d) 4

4. Choose the correct mirror image of the given figure (X) from amongst the four alternatives.
[NTSE 2001 - Punjab first stage paper]

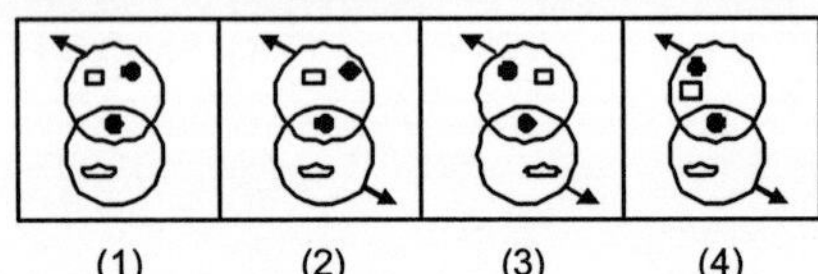

(X) (1) (2) (3) (4)

(a) 1 (b) 2
(c) 3 (d) 4

5. Choose the correct mirror image of the given figure (X) from amongst the four alternatives.
[NTSE 2012 - Delhi first stage paper]

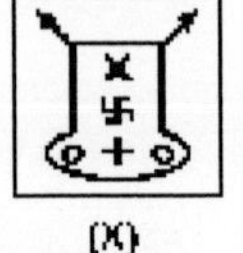
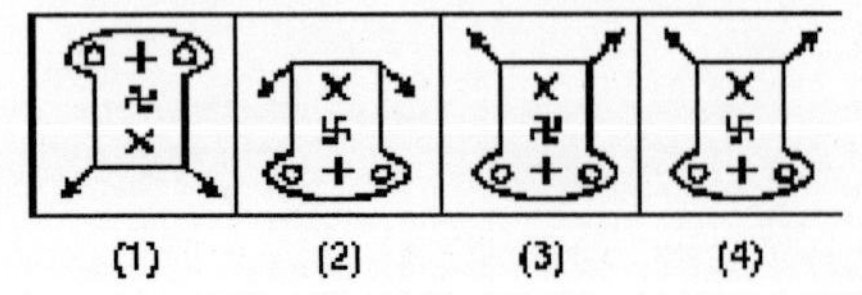

(X) (1) (2) (3) (4)

(a) 1 (b) 2
(c) 3 (d) 4

6. Choose the alternative which closely resembles the mirror image of the given combination.
[NTSE 2003 - Maharashtra second stage paper]

HINDUSTANcho1
(1) HIИDUƧTAИɔhoꞁ
(2) ꞁohɔИATƧUDИIH
(3) HIИDUƧTAИɔhoꞁ
(4) ꞁohɔИATƧUDИIH

(a) 1 (b) 2
(c) 3 (d) 4

7. Choose the alternative which closely resembles the mirror image of the given combination.
[NTSE 2007 - Bihar first stage paper]

DAEWOO-matiz
(1) ᗡAƎWOO-matiz (2) zitam-OOMƎAD
(3) ᗡAƎMOO-matiz (4) zitam-OOWƎAᗡ

(a) 1 (b) 2
(c) 3 (d) 4

8. Choose the alternative which closely resembles the mirror image of the given combination.
[NTSE 2003 - UP second stage paper]

CERELONPIII
(1) IIIꟼИO⅃ƎЯƎƆ (2) IIIꟼИO⅃ƎЯƎC
(3) ƆƎЯƎ⅃OИꟼIII (4) ƆƎЯƎLOИꟼIII

(a) 1 (b) 2
(c) 3 (d) 4

9. Choose the alternative which closely resembles the mirror image of the given combination.
[NTSE 2004 - Maharashtra first stage paper]

DL3N 8956
(1) ᗡ⅃ƐИ8ɘ2ɘ (2) ɘ2ɘ8NƐ⅃ᗡ
(3) ᗡ⅃ƐИ8ɘ2ɘ (4) ɘ2ɘ8NƐ⅃D

(a) 1 (b) 2
(c) 3 (d) 4

10. Choose the alternative which closely resembles the mirror image of the given combination.
[NTSE 2003 - Punjab first stage paper]

TOWHIM
(1) TOWHIM (2) WIHMOT
(3) MIHWOT (4) TOMHIW

(a) 1 (b) 2
(c) 3 (d) 4

Answer Key

1. (c)	2. (c)	3. (b)	4. (b)	5. (c)	6. (b)	7. (d)	8. (a)	9. (b)	10. (c)

UNIT 12

Cubes and Dice

Dice is a cube. In cube there are 6 faces. Some important points are given below:

1. There are 6 faces in the cube - ABCG, GCDE, DEFH, BCDH, AGEF and ABHF.

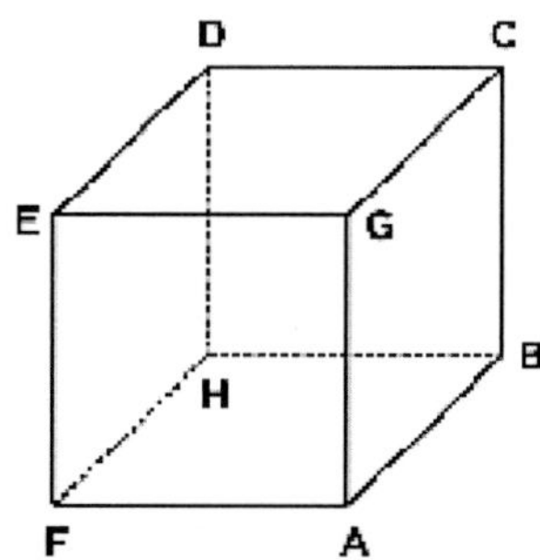

2. Always four faces are adjacent to one face.
3. Opposite of ABCG is DEFH and so on.
4. CDEG is the upper face of the cube.
5. ABHF is the bottom of the cube.

Rules on Dice

Rule No. 1: Two opposite faces cannot be adjacent to each other.

Example: Two different positions of a dice are shown below. Which number will appear on the face opposite to the face with number 4?

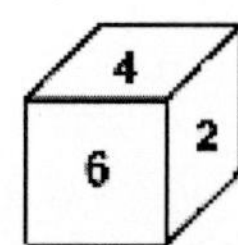

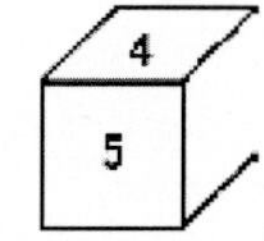

Solution: Faces with four numbers 6, 2, 5 and 3 are adjacent of to the face with No. 4.

Hence the faces with no. 6, 2, 5 and 3 cannot be opposite to the face with no. 4.

Therefore the remaining face with no.1 will be the opposite of the face with no. 4.

Rule No. 2: If two different positions of a dice are shown and one of the two common faces is in the same position then of the remaining faces will be opposite to each other.

Example: Two different positions of a dice are shown below.

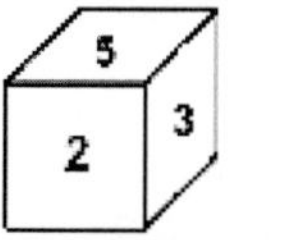

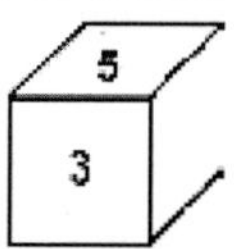

Here in both shown positions two faces 5 and 3 are common.

The remaining faces are 2 and 4.

Hence both the number on the face opposite to the face with number 2 is 4.

Rule No. 3: If in two different positions of a dice, the position of a common face is the same, then each of the opposite faces of the remaining faces will be in the same position.

Example:

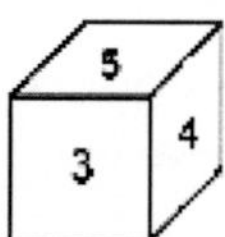

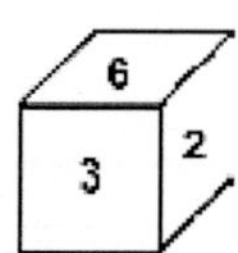

Here in both positions common (3) is same.

Therefore, opposite of 5 is 6 and opposite of 4 is 2.

Rule No. 4: If in two different positions of a dice, the position of the common face is not the same, then opposite face of the common face will be that which is not shown on any face in these two positions. Besides, the opposite faces of the remaining faces will not be the same.

Example:

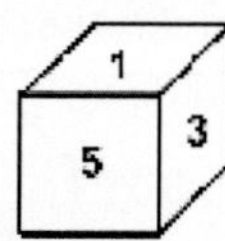

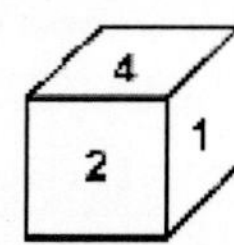

Here in two positions of a dice, the face with number 1 is not in the same position.

The face with number 6 is not shown.

Hence the face opposite to the face with number 1 is 6.

Besides the opposite face of 3 will be the face with number 2 and opposite face to face 5 will be the face with number 1.

Solved Examples

1. Two positions of a dice are shown below. Which number will appear on the face opposite to the face with the number 5?

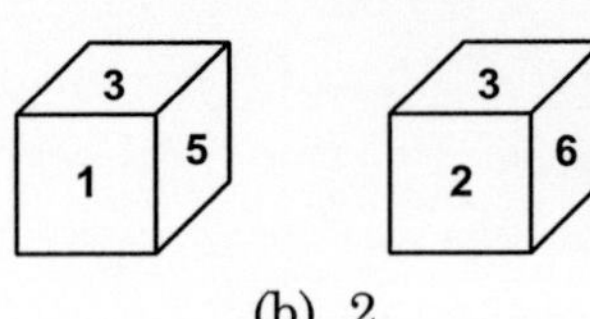

(a) 2/6 (b) 2
(c) 6 (d) 4

Solution: Option c) is correct.
Explanation: According to the rule number (3), common faces with number 3 are in same positions. Hence the number of the opposite face to the face with number 5 will be 6.

2. How many points will be on the face opposite the face which contains 2 points ?

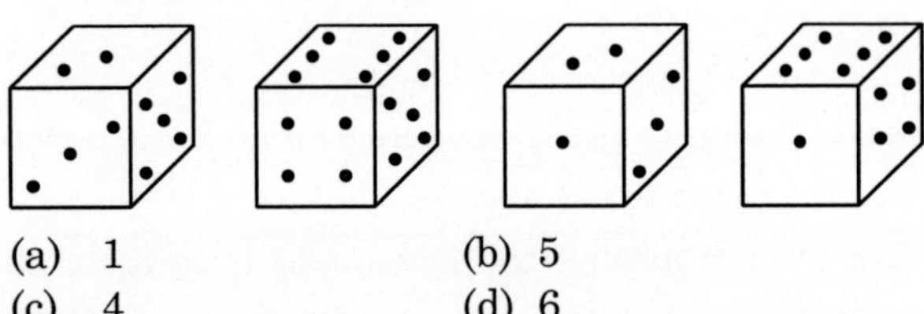

(a) 1 (b) 5
(c) 4 (d) 6

Solution: Option d) is correct.
Explanation: In first two positions of dice one common face containing 5 is same. Therefore according to rule number (3) the face opposite to the face which contains 2 points will contains 6 points.

3. Two positions of a dice are shown below. When number '1' is on the top. What number will be at the bottom?

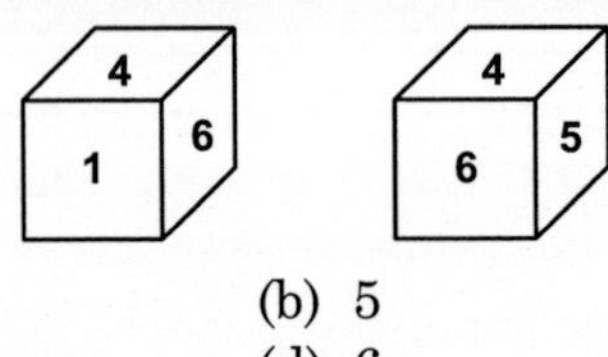

(a) 3 (b) 5
(c) 2 (d) 6

Solution: Option (b) is correct.
Explanation: According to the rule (2) when 'one' is at the top, then 5 will be at the bottom.

4. Which number is on the face opposite to 6?

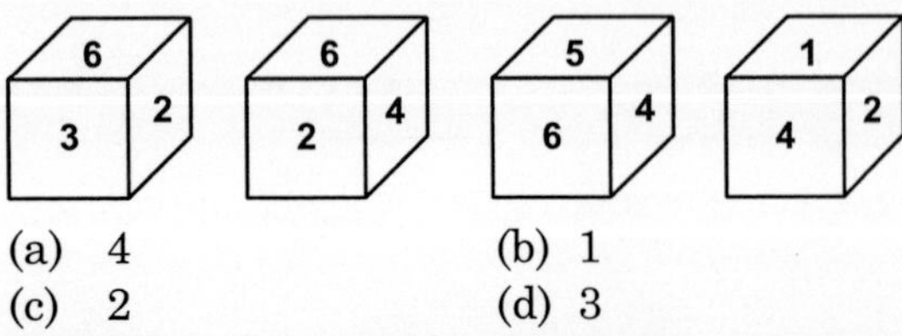

(a) 4 (b) 1
(c) 2 (d) 3

Solution: Option (b) is correct.
Explanation: As the numbers 2, 3, 4 and 5 are adjacent to 6. Hence the number on the face opposite to 6 is 1.

5. Here two positions of a dice are shown. If there are two dots in the bottom, then how many dots will be on the top?

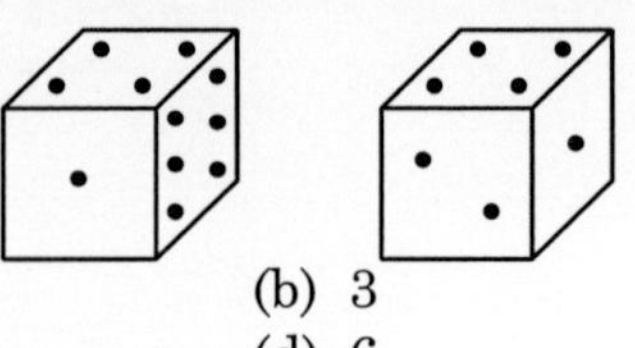

(a) 2 (b) 3
(c) 5 (d) 6

Solution: Option (c) is correct.
Explanation: Here the common faces with 4 dots are in same positions.
Hence 2 will be opposite to 5.

Construction of Boxes

The details of the cube formed when a sheet is folded to form a box are as follows :

Form I

In this case: 1 lies opposite 5
2 lies opposite 4
3 lies opposite 6

Form II

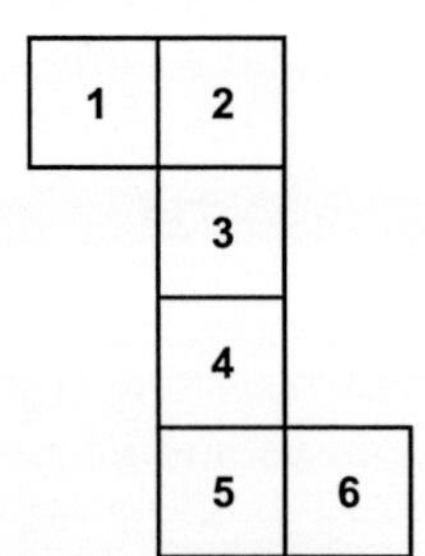

In this case: 1 lies opposite 6
2 lies opposite 4
3 lies opposite 5

Form III

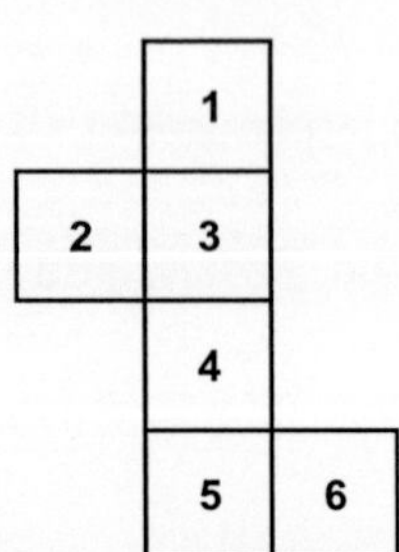

In this case: 1 lies opposite 4
2 lies opposite 6
3 lies opposite 5

Form IV

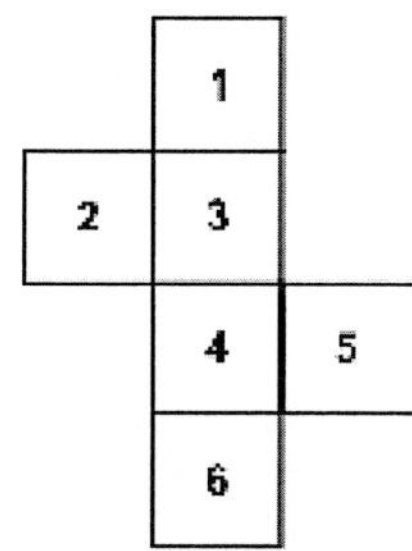

In this case: 1 lies opposite 4
2 lies opposite 5
3 lies opposite 6

Form V

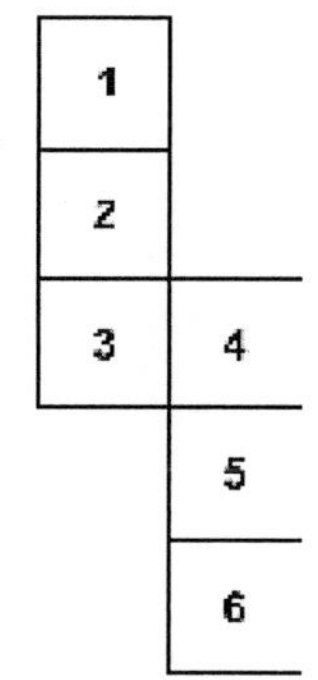

In this case: 1 lies opposite 3
2 lies opposite 5
4 lies opposite 6

Form VI

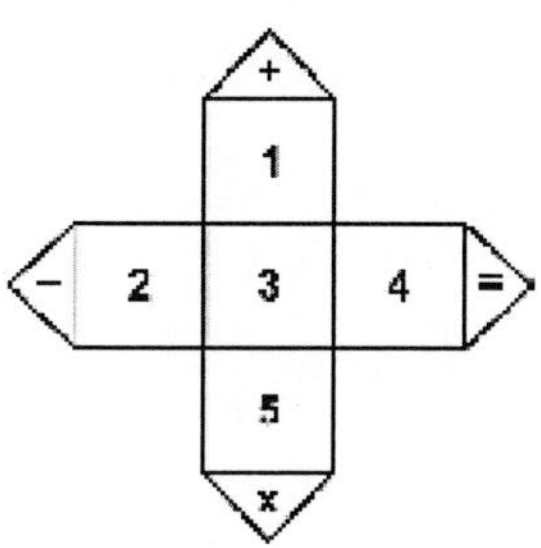

In this case:

will be the one of the faces of the cube and will lie opposite 3, 2 will lie opposite 4, 1 will lie opposite 5

Form VII

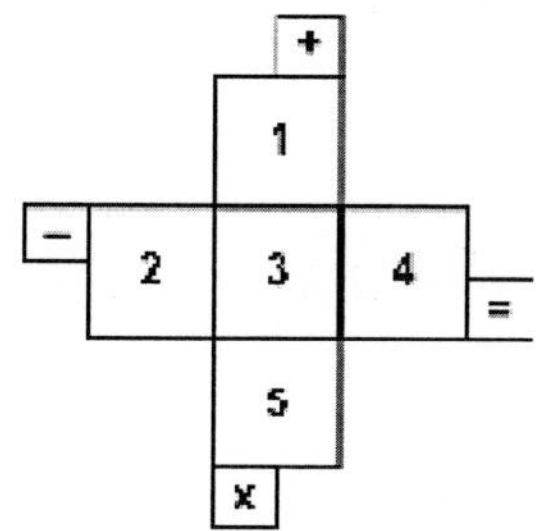

In this case:

will be the one of the faces of the cube and will lie opposite 3, 2 will lie opposite 4, 1 will lie opposite 5

Form VIII

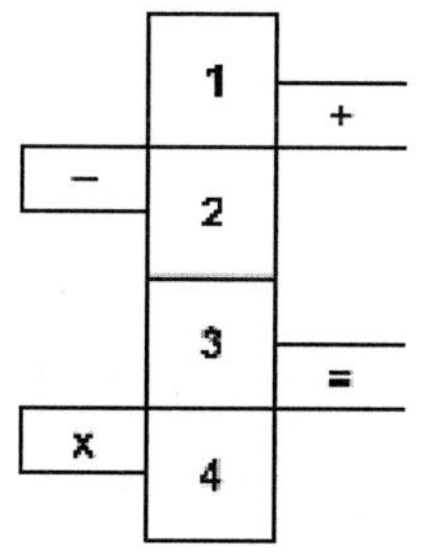

In this case:

and are two faces of the cube that lie opposite to each other. 1 lies opposite 3, 2 lies opposite 4

Solved Examples

1. How many dots lie opposite to the face having three dots, when the given figure is folded to form a cube?

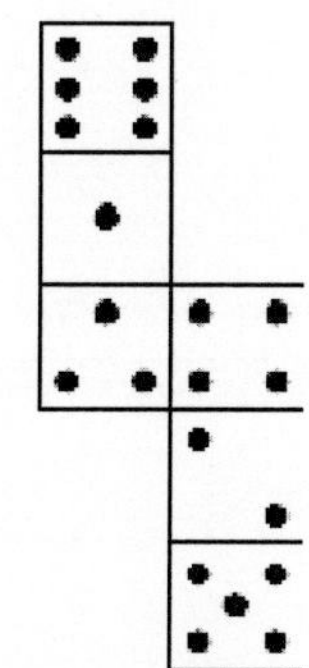

(a) 2 (b) 4
(c) 5 (d) 6

Solution: Option (d) is correct.

Explanation: The given figure is similar to Form V. Therefore, when this figure is folded to form a cube then the face bearing six dots will lie opposite the face bearing three dots.

2. Choose the box that is similar to the box formed from the given sheet of paper (X).

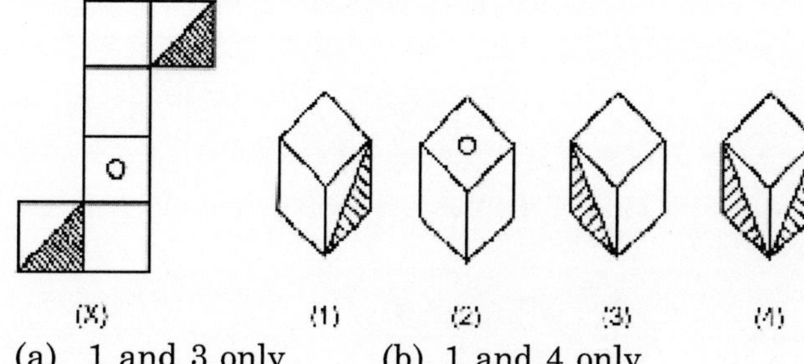

(a) 1 and 3 only (b) 1 and 4 only
(c) 2 and 4 only (d) 3 and 4 only

Solution: Option (a) is correct.

Explanation: The figure (X) is similar to Form II. So, when the sheet shown in figure (X) is folded to form a cube the two half-shaded faces lie opposite to each other, the face bearing a circle lies opposite to one of the two blank faces and the two remaining blank faces lie opposite to each other. Therefore, the cubes shown in figure (4) which has the two half-shaded faces adjacent to each other cannot be formed by folding the sheet shown in figure (X). Also, the cube shown in figure (2) has the face bearing a circle adjacent to two blank faces. This is not possible since there is one blank face opposite to the circle and one blank face opposite to the third blank face. Hence, only the cubes in figures (1) and (3) can be formed.

3. Choose the box that is similar to the box formed from the given sheet of paper (X).

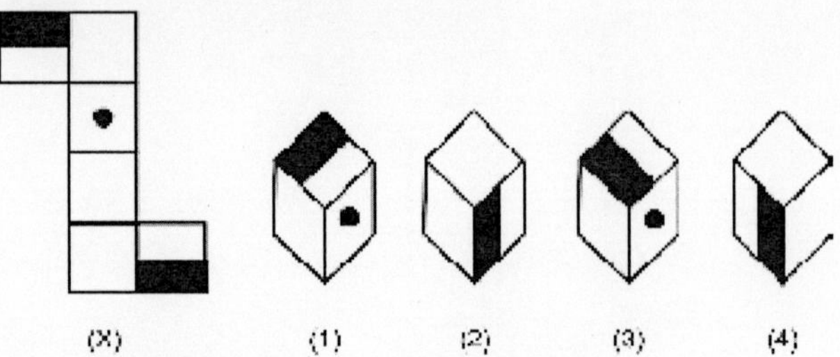

(a) 1 and 2 only (b) 2 and 3 only
(c) 2 and 4 only (d) 1, 2, 3 and 4

Solution: Option (d) is correct.

Explanation: The figure (X) is similar to **Form II**. So, when a cube is formed by folding the sheet shown in figure (X), then the two half-shaded faces lie opposite to each other and one of the three blank faces appears opposite to the face bearing a dot. Clearly, each one of the four cubes shown in figures (1), (2), (3) and (4) can be formed by folding the sheet shown in figure (X).

Multiple Choice Questions

1. From the positions of a cube shown below, which letter will be on the face opposite to face with 'A'?

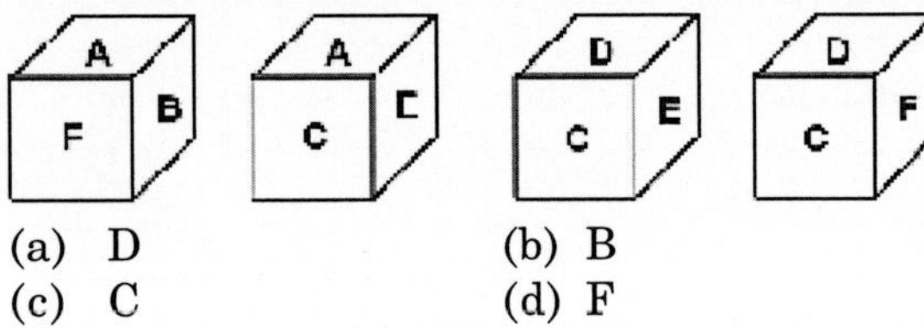

(a) D (b) B
(c) C (d) F

2. Two positions of a dice are shown below. When 3 points are at the bottom, how many points will be at the top?

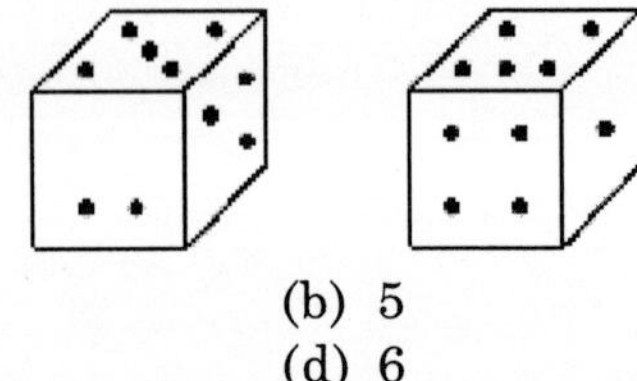

(a) 2 (b) 5
(c) 4 (d) 6

3. Observe the dots on the dice (one to six dots) in the following figures. How many dots are contained on the face opposite to the face containing four dots?

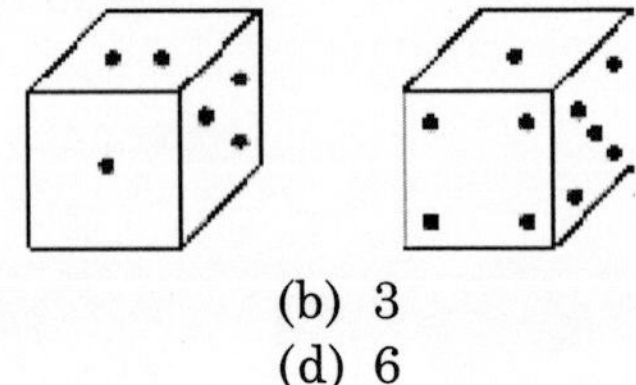

(a) 2 (b) 3
(c) 5 (d) 6

4. Here 4 positions of a cube are shown. Which sign will be opposite to '+' ?

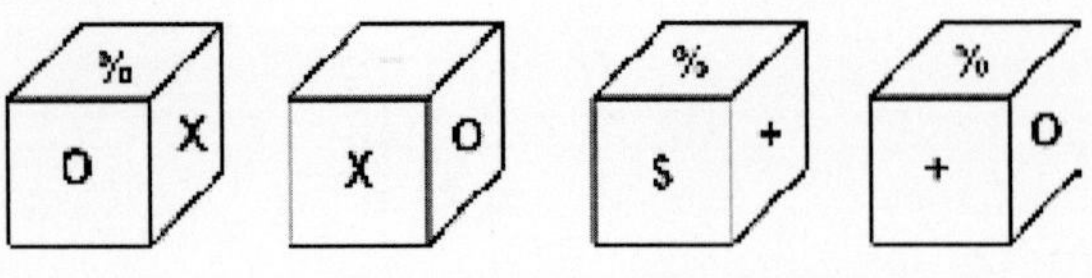

(a) % (b) -
(c) x (d) $

5. From the four positions of a dice given below, find the colour which is opposite to yellow?

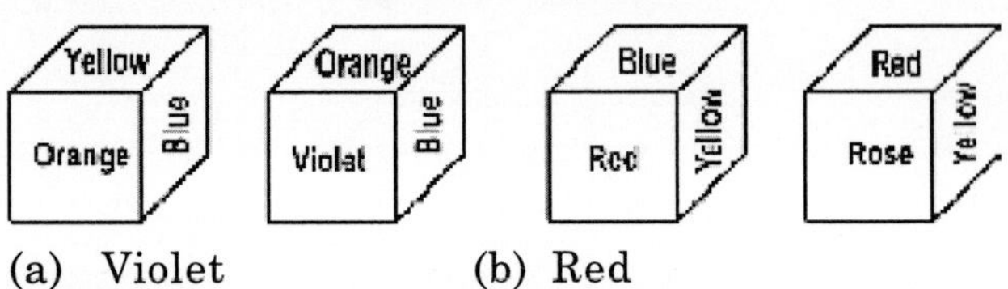

(a) Violet (b) Red
(c) Rose (d) Blue

6. When the digit 5 is on the bottom then which number will be on its upper surface?

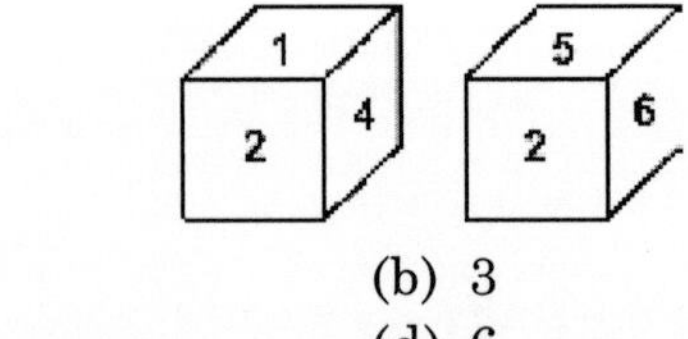

(a) 1 (b) 3
(c) 4 (d) 6

7. How many points will be on the face opposite to the face which contains 3 points?

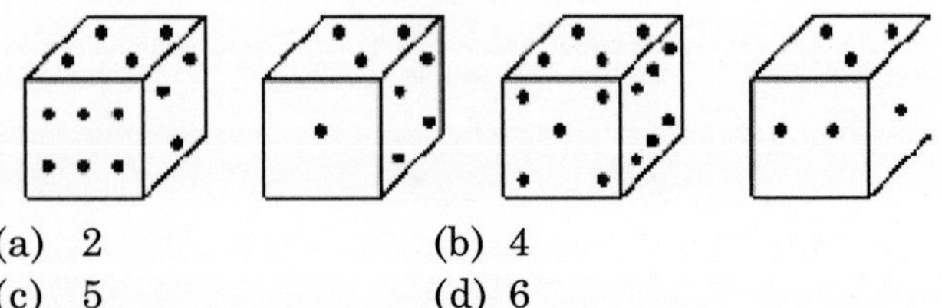

(a) 2 (b) 4
(c) 5 (d) 6

8. Two positions of a cube with its surfaces numbered are shown below. When the surface 4 touches the bottom, what surface will be on the top?

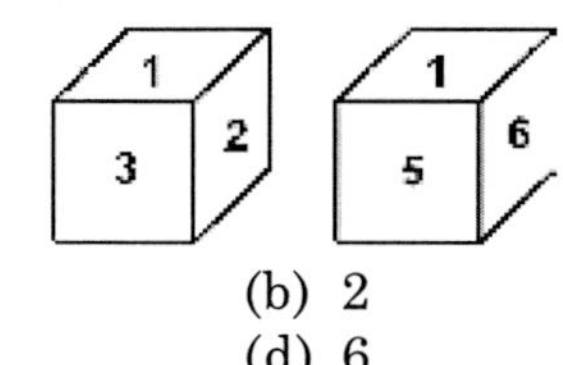

(a) 1 (b) 2
(c) 5 (d) 6

9. Two positions of a dice are shown below. How many points will be on the top when 2 points are at the bottom?

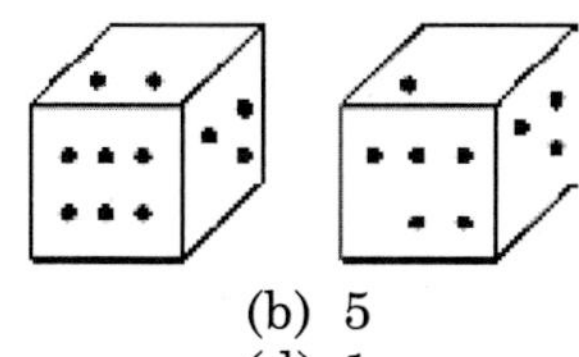

(a) 6 (b) 5
(c) 4 (d) 1

10. Which symbol will be on the face opposite to the face with symbol * ?

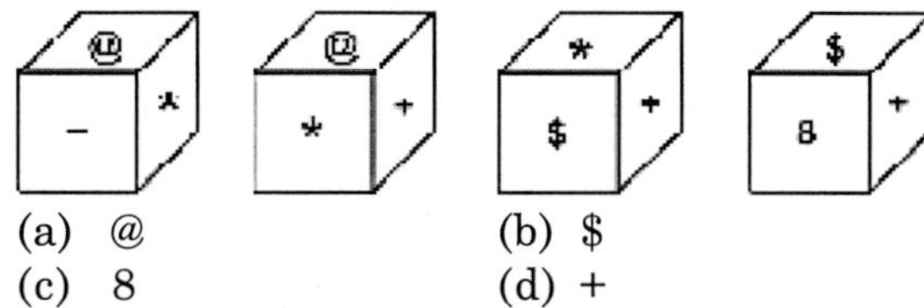

(a) @ (b) $
(c) 8 (d) +

11. Which digit will appear on the face opposite to the face with number 4?

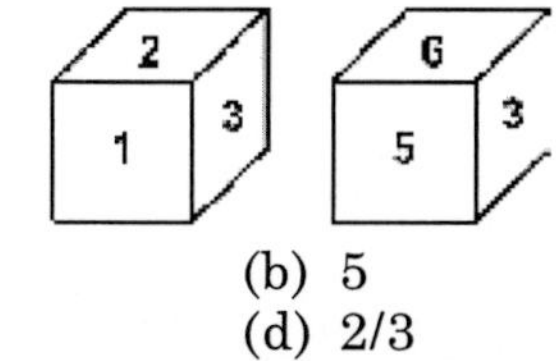

(a) 3 (b) 5
(c) 6 (d) 2/3

12. Two positions of dice are shown below. How many points will appear on the opposite to the face containing 5 points?

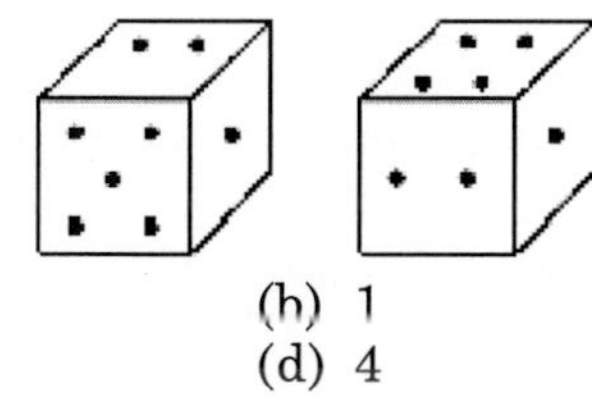

(a) 3 (b) 1
(c) 2 (d) 4

☛ ***Direction to solve (13 to 17):*** *Six dice with upper faces erased are as shows.*

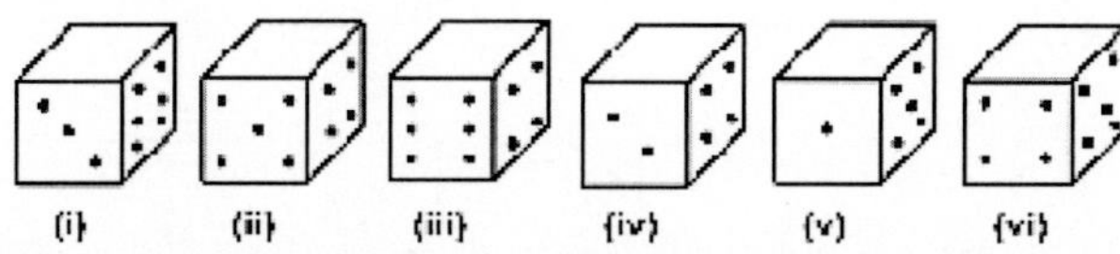

The sum of the numbers of dots on the opposite face is 7.

13. If even numbered dice have even number of dots on their top faces, then what would be the total number of dots on the top faces of their dice?
(a) 12 (b) 14
(c) 18 (d) 24

14. If the odd numbered dice have even number of dots on their top faces, then what would be the total number of dots on the top faces of their dice?
(a) 8 (b) 10
(c) 12 (d) 14

15. If dice (I), (II) and (III) have even number of dots on their bottom faces and the dice (IV), (V) and (VI) have odd number of dots on their top faces, then what would be the difference in the total number of top faces between these two sets?
(a) 0 (b) 2
(c) 4 (d) 6

16. If the even numbers of dice have odd number of dots on their top faces and odd numbered dice have even of dots on their bottom faces, then what would be the total number of dots on their top faces?
(a) 12 (b) 14
(c) 16 (d) 18

17. If the dice (I), (II) and (III) have even number of dots on their bottom faces, then what would be the total number of dots on their top faces?
(a) 7 (b) 11
(c) 12 (d) 14

☛ ***Directions:*** *The sheet of paper shown in the figure (X) given on the left hand side, in each problem, is folded to form a box. Choose from amongst the alternatives (1), (2), (3) and (4), the boxes that are similar to the box that will be forme(d)*

18. Choose the box that is similar to the box formed from the given sheet of paper (X).

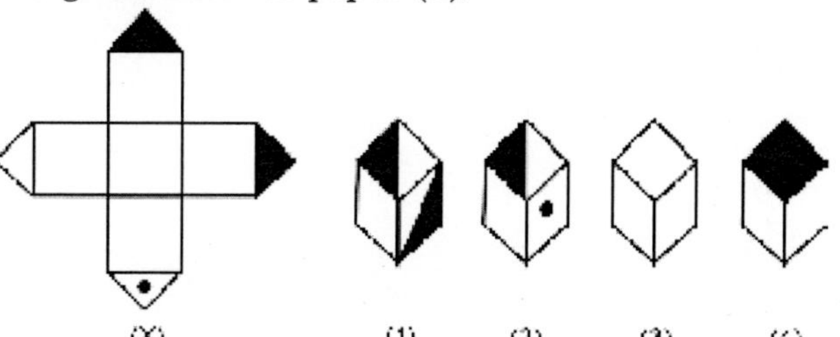

(a) 1 and 2 only (b) 2 and 4 only
(c) 2 and 3 only (d) 1 and 4 only

19. Choose the box that is similar to the box formed from the given sheet of paper (X).

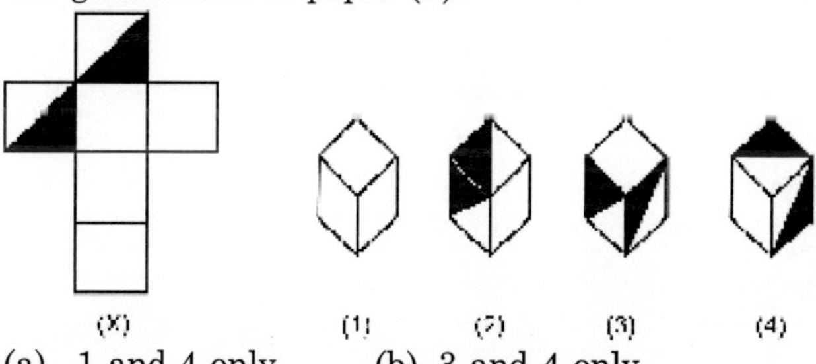

(a) 1 and 4 only (b) 3 and 4 only
(c) 1 and 2 only (d) 2 and 3 only

20. Choose the box that is similar to the box formed from the given sheet of paper (X).

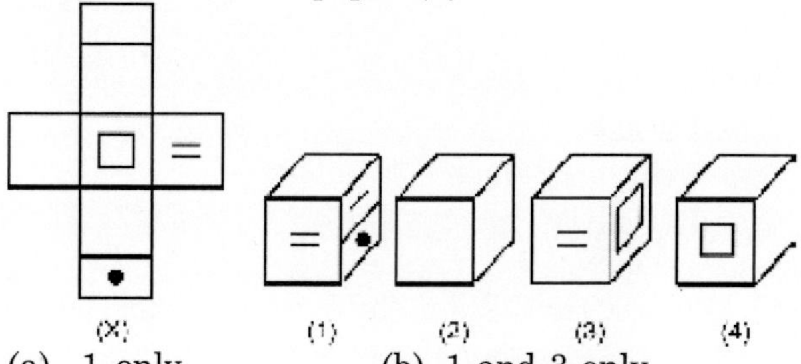

(a) 1 only (b) 1 and 3 only
(c) 1, 3 and 4 only (d) 1, 2, 3 and 4

21. Choose the box that is similar to the box formed from the given sheet of paper (X).

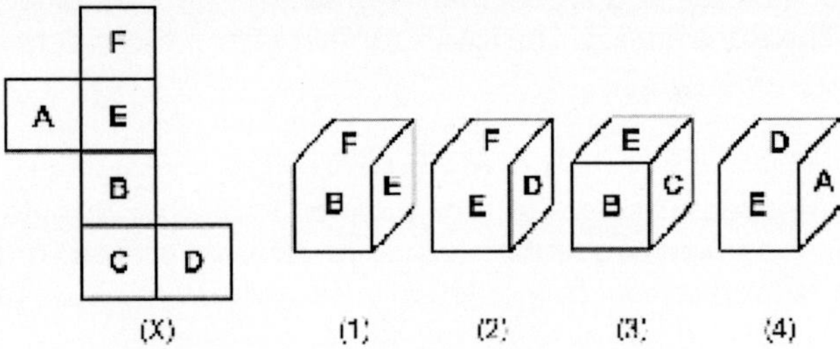

(a) 1 only (b) 2 only
(c) 1 and 3 only (d) 1, 2, 3 and 4 only

22. Choose the box that is similar to the box formed from the given sheet of paper (X).

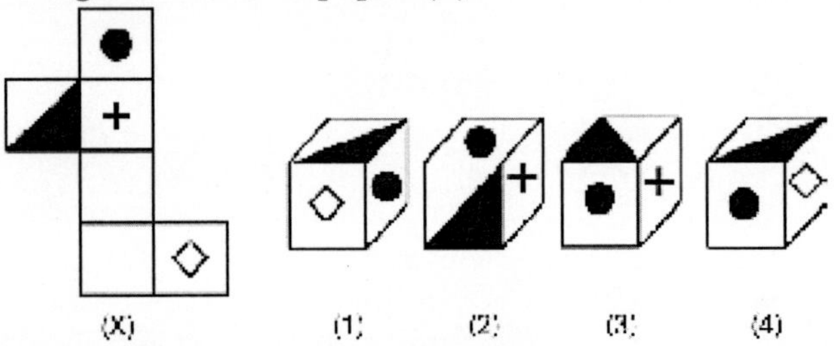

(a) 1 only (b) 2 only
(c) 3 only (d) 4 only

23. Choose the box that is similar to the box formed from the given sheet of paper (X).

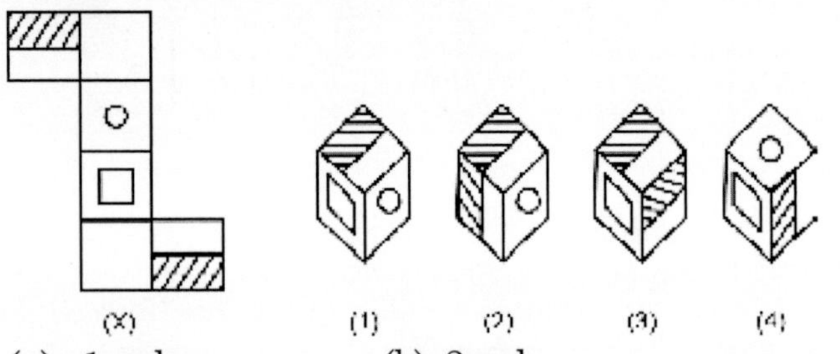

(a) 1 only (b) 2 only
(c) 3 only (d) 4 only

24. Choose the box that is similar to the box formed from the given sheet of paper (X).

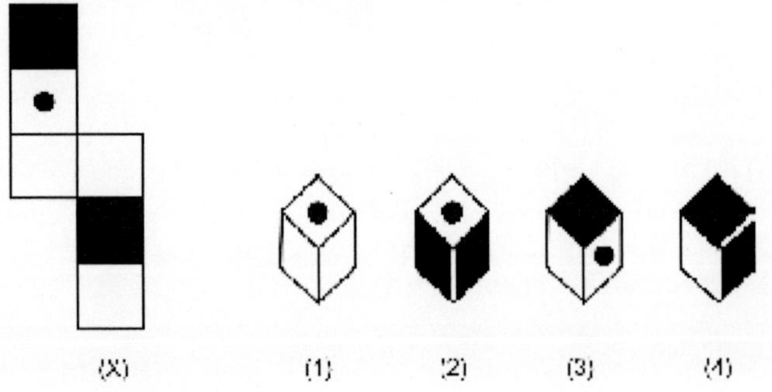

(a) 2 and 3 only
(b) 1, 3 and 4 only
(c) 2 and 4 only
(d) 1 and 4 only

25. Choose the box that is similar to the box formed from the given sheet of paper (X).

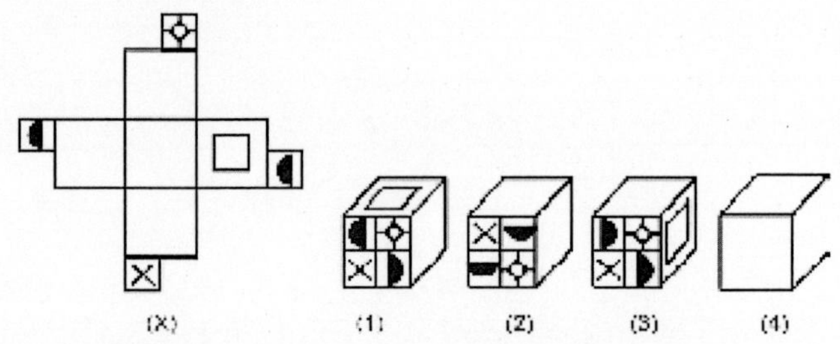

(a) 1, 2 and 3 only (b) 2 and 3 only
(c) 1, 3 and 4 only (d) 2, 3 and 4 only

26. Choose the box that is similar to the box formed from the given sheet of paper (X).

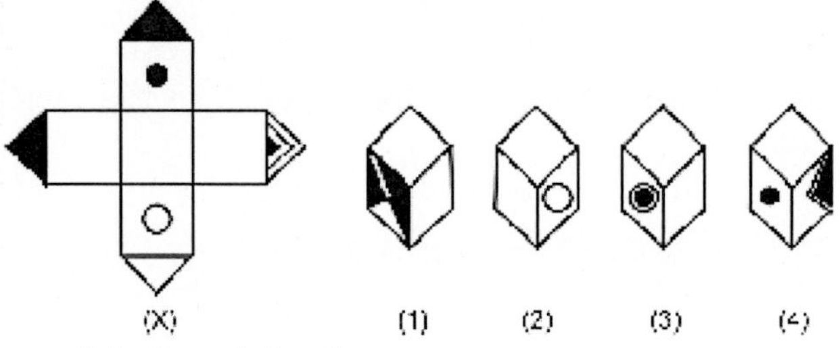

(a) 1 and 2 only
(b) 1, 2 and 3 only
(c) 1 and 3 only
(d) 1, 2, 3 and 4

27. Choose the box that is similar to the box formed from the given sheet of paper (X).

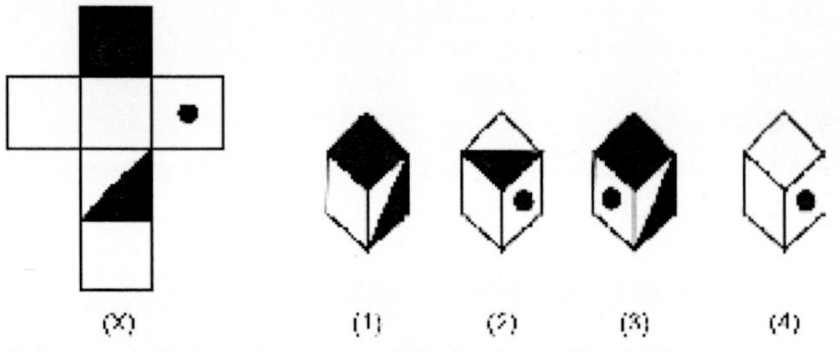

(a) 1 and 3 only (b) 2, 3 and 4 only
(c) 2 only (d) 3 and 4 only

28. Choose the box that is similar to the box formed from the given sheet of paper (X).

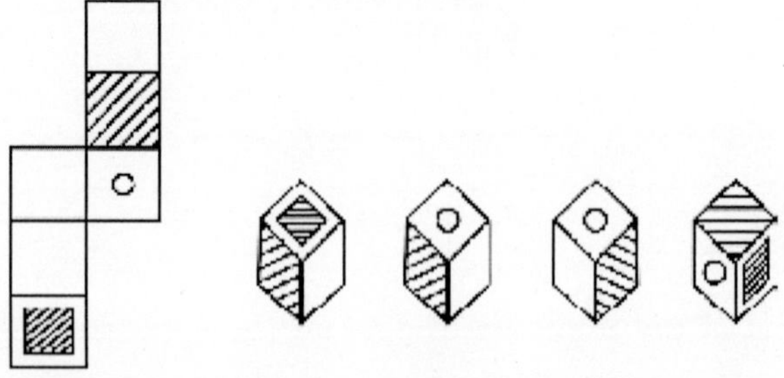

(a) 1 and 2 only (b) 1, 2 and 4 only
(c) 1 and 4 only (d) 1, 2 and 3 only

29. Choose the box that is similar to the box formed from the given sheet of paper (X).

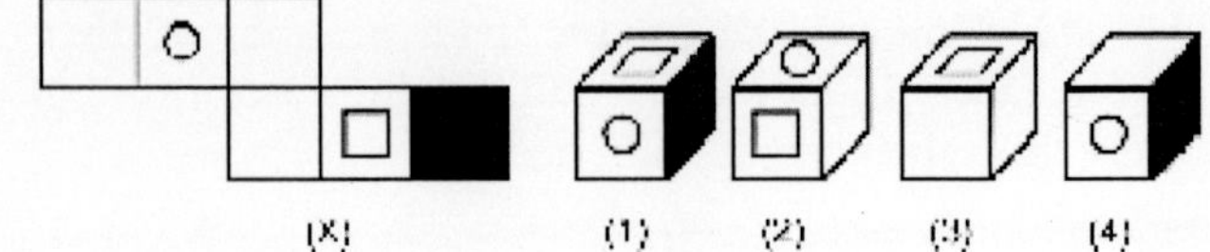

(a) 1 and 2 only (b) 2, 3 and 4 only
(c) 4 only (d) 3 and 4 only

30. Choose the box that is similar to the box formed from the given sheet of paper (X).

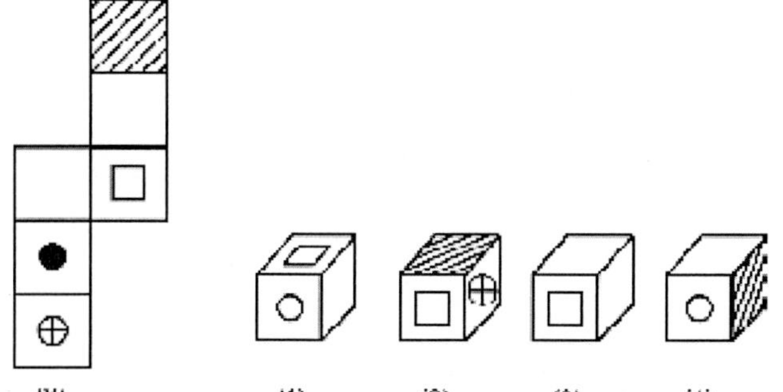

(a) 1 only (b) 2 and 3 only
(c) 1 and 3 only (d) 1, 2 and 4 only

31. Which of the following finished patterns can be obtained from the piece of cardboard (X) shown below?

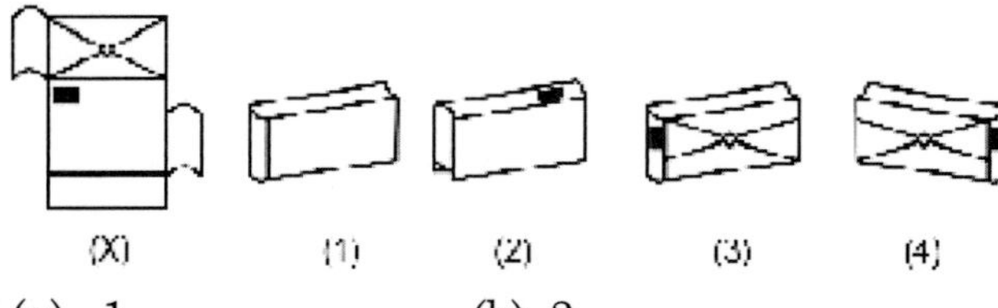

(a) 1 (b) 2
(c) 3 (d) 4

32. Choose the box that is similar to the box formed from the given sheet of paper (X).

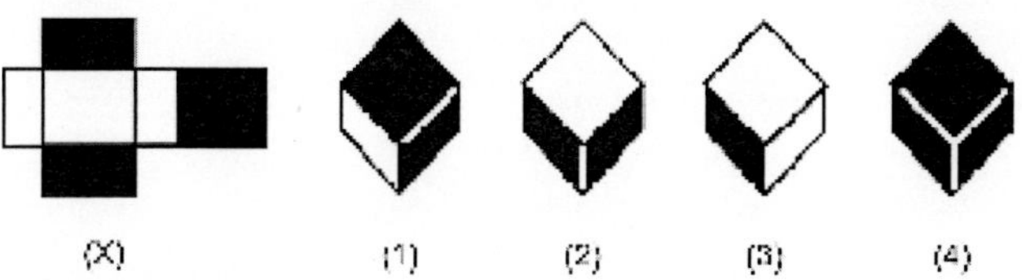

(a) 1 and 3 only (b) 2 and 4 only
(c) 3 and 4 only (d) 1 and 4 only

33. Choose the box that is similar to the box formed from the given sheet of paper (X).

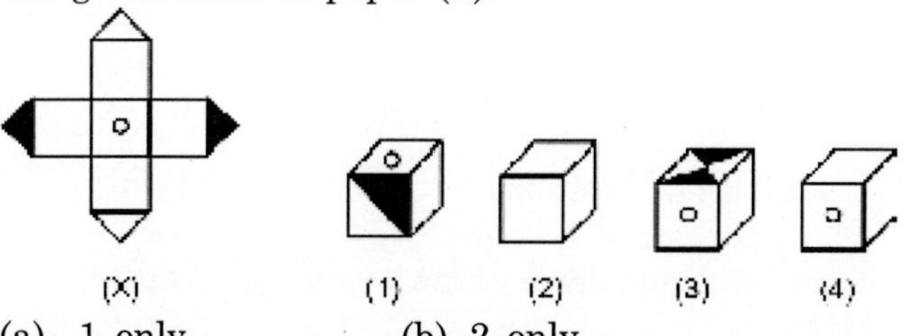

(a) 1 only (b) 2 only
(c) 3 only (d) 4 only

34. When the following figure is folded to form a cube, how many dots lie opposite the face bearing five dots?

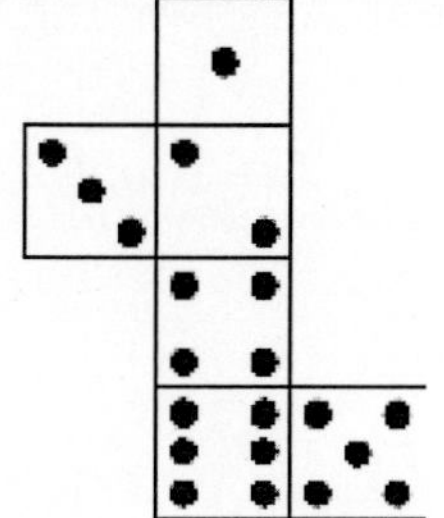

(a) 1 (b) 2
(c) 3 (d) 4

35. Choose the box that is similar to the box formed from the given sheet of paper (X).

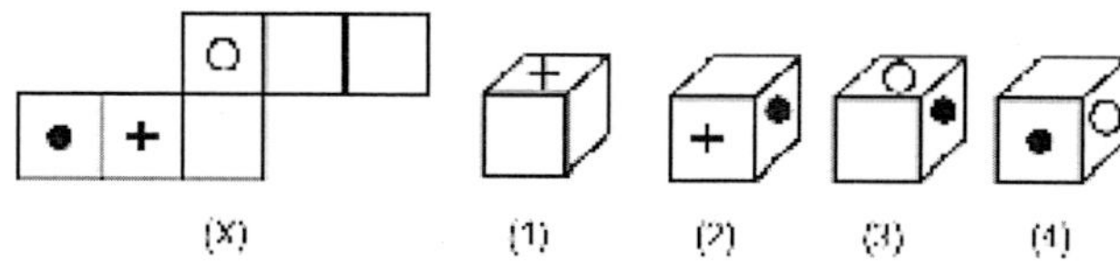

(a) 1 only (b) 1, 2 and 3 only
(c) 2 and 3 only (d) 1, 2, 3 and 4

36. Choose the box that is similar to the box formed from the given sheet of paper (X).

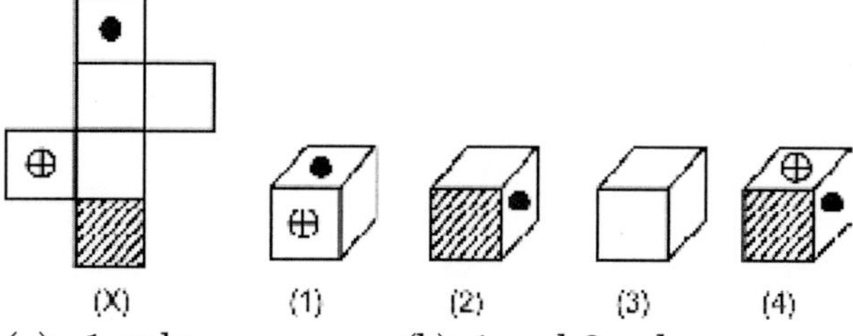

(a) 1 only (b) 1 and 3 only
(c) 1, 3 and 4 only (d) 1, 2, 3 and 4

37. Choose the box that is similar to the box formed from the given sheet of paper (X).

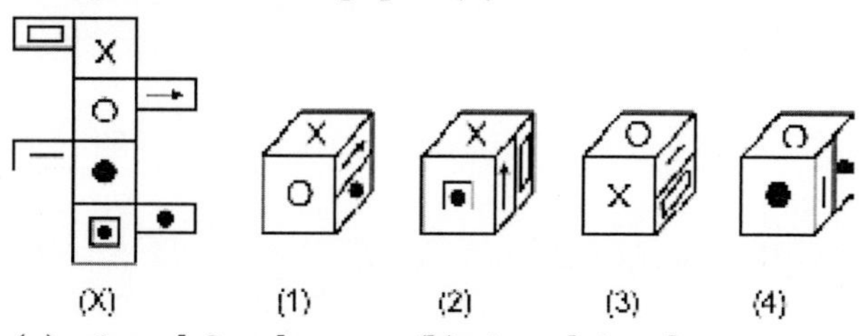

(a) 1 and 2 only (b) 1 and 3 only
(c) 3 and 4 only (d) 1, 2, 3 and 4

38. Observe the dots on a dice (one to six dots) in the following figures. How many dots are contained on the face opposite to that containing four dots?

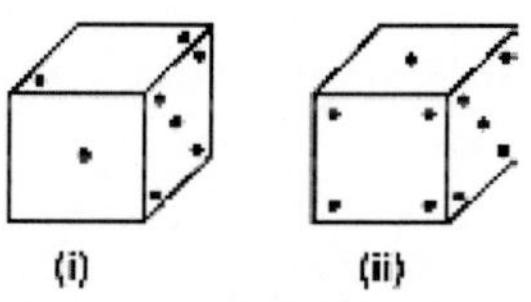

(a) 2 (b) 3
(c) 6 (d) Cannot be determined

39. Three different positions of a dice are shown below. How many dots lie opposite 2 dots?

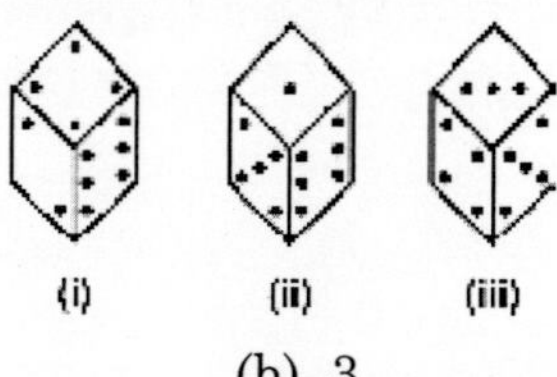

(a) 1 (b) 3
(c) 5 (d) 6

40. The six faces of a dice have been marked with alphabets A, B, C, D, E and F respectively. This dice is rolled down three times. The three positions are shown as:

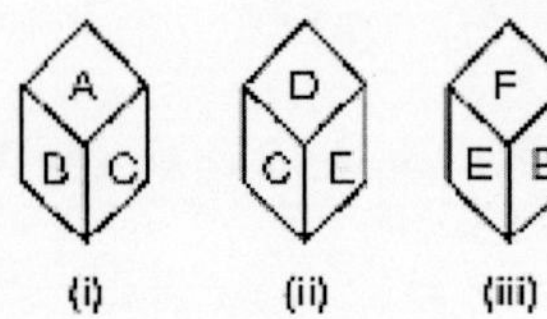

Find the alphabet opposite (A)

(a) C (b) D
(c) E (d) F

41. Three positions of a dice are given. Based on them find out which number is found opposite the number 2 in the given cube.

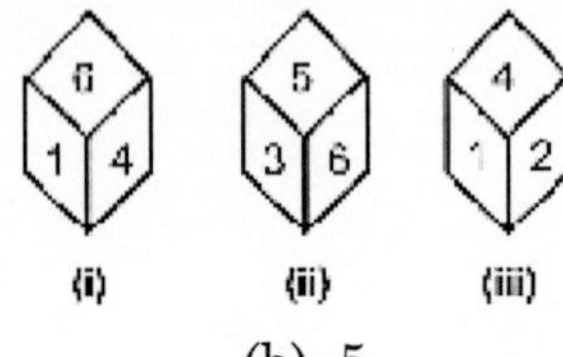

(a) 6 (b) 5
(c) 3 (d) 1

42. A dice is thrown four times and its four different positions are shown below. Find the number on the face opposite the face showing 2.

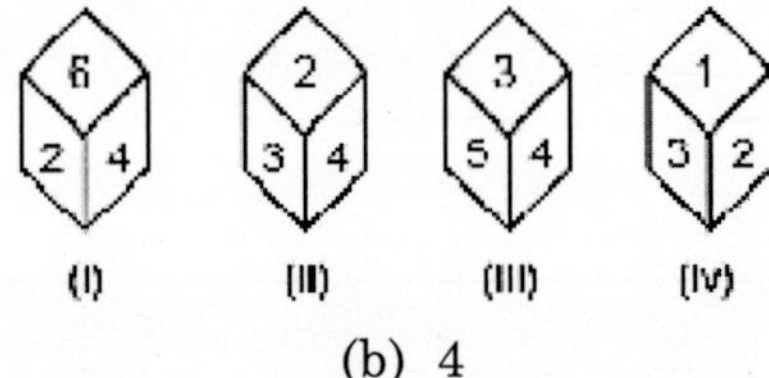

(a) 3 (b) 4
(c) 5 (d) 6

43. Three different positions X, Y and Z of a dice are shown in the figures given below. Which number lies at the bottom face in position X?

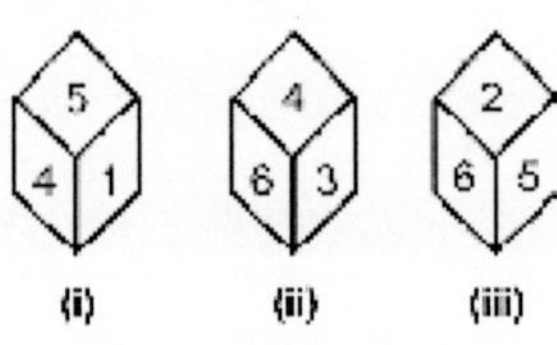

(a) 2 (b) 3
(c) 6 (d) Cannot be determined

44. A dice is numbered from 1 to 6 in different ways. If 2 is opposite to 3 and adjacent to 4 and 6, then which of the following statements is necessarily true?
 (a) 1 is opposite to 5
 (b) 4 is opposite to 6
 (c) 4 is adjacent to 2 and 6
 (d) 1 is adjacent to 2 and 3

45. Two positions of a dice are shown below. When number 1 is on the top, what number will be at the bottom?

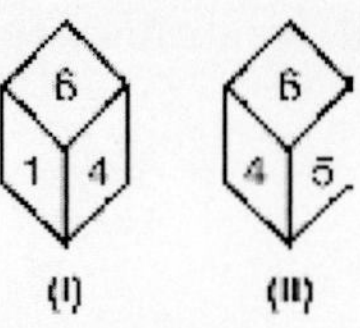

(a) 2 (b) 3
(c) 5 (d) Cannot be determined

46. Two positions of a block are shown below: When six is at the bottom, what number will be at the top?

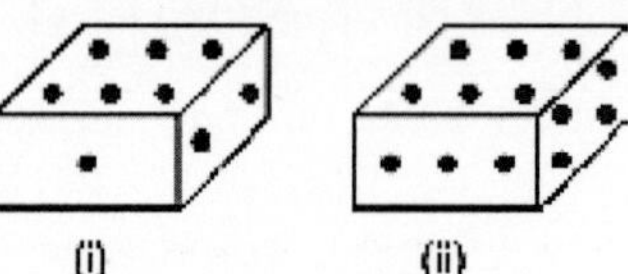

(a) 1 (b) 2
(c) 4 (d) 5

47. Two positions of a dice are shown below. When 2 is at the bottom, what number will be at the top?

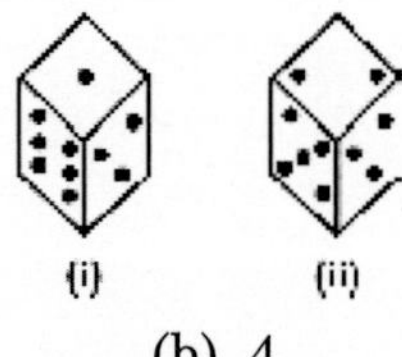

(a) 6 (b) 4
(c) 1 (d) 5

48. A dice is numbered from 1 to 6 in different ways. If 1 is opposite to 5 and 2 is opposite to 3, then
 (a) 4 is adjacent to 3 and 6
 (b) 2 is adjacent to 4 and 6
 (c) 4 is adjacent to 5 and 6
 (d) 6 is adjacent to 3 and 4

49. Two positions of a block are shown below. When 2 is at the bottom, which number will be at the top?

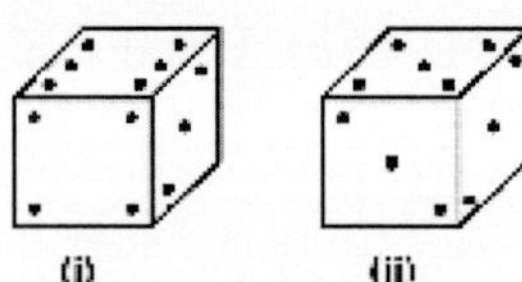

(a) 1 (b) 4
(c) 6 (d) Cannot be determined

50. Three different positions X, Y and Z of a dice are shown in the figures given below. Which numbers are hidden behind the numbers 6 and 5 in the position Z?

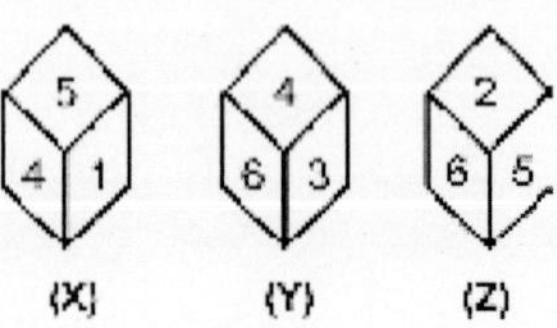

(a) 1 and 4 (b) 1 and 3
(c) 4 and 3 (d) 1 and 2

Answer Key

1. (a)	**2.** (c)	**3.** (a)	**4.** (c)	**5.** (a)	**6.** (a)	**7.** (c)	**8.** (a)	**9.** (d)	**10.** (c)
11. (a)	**12.** (d)	**13.** (c)	**14.** (a)	**15.** (d)	**16.** (c)	**17.** (b)	**18.** (c)	**19.** (a)	**20.** (c)
21. (b)	**22.** (b)	**23.** (a)	**24.** (b)	**25.** (d)	**26.** (a)	**27.** (c)	**28.** (b)	**29.** (d)	**30.** (c)
31. (a)	**32.** (a)	**33.** (d)	**34.** (c)	**35.** (d)	**36.** (a)	**37.** (b)	**38.** (a)	**39.** (c)	**40.** (c)
41. (a)	**42.** (c)	**43.** (b)	**44.** (d)	**45.** (c)	**46.** (d)	**47.** (c)	**48.** (b)	**49.** (c)	**50.** (b)

Explanatory Notes

1. (a)
The letters of the adjacent faces to the face with letter A, are B, F, C and E. Hence D is the letter of the face opposite to the face with letters A.

2. (c)
According to the rule (2) when 3 points are at the bottom, 4 points will be at the top.

3. (a)
Here one of the two common faces (5) is in the same position, then according to the rule no (2) the remaining face with the 4 dots will be opposite to face with dots 2.

4. (c)
From position I and III common face with % is in the same position. Hence, according to rule (3) opposite is x.

5. (a)
The colours adjacent to yellow are orange, blue, red and rose. Hence violet will be opposite to yellow.

6. (a)
According to the rule number (3), common faces with number 2 are in same positions. Hence when the digit 5 is on the bottom, 1 will be on the upper surface.

7. (c)
The adjacent faces to the face with 3 points have 2, 1, 4 and 6 points. Hence on the face which is opposite to the face which contains 3 points, there will be 5 points.

8. (a)
In these two positions one common face with number 1 is in the same position. Hence, according to the rule number (3), 2 is opposite 6 and 3 is opposite to 5. Therefore, opposite to 4 is 1.

9. (d)
In these two positions of a dice, one common face having points 3 is in the same position. Hence, according to rule (3), there will be 4 points on the required face.

10. (c)
The symbols of the adjacent faces to the face with symbol * are @, -, + and $. Hence, the required symbol is 8.

11. (a)
Here the common faces with number 3, are in same positions. Hence 6 is opposite to 2 and 5 is opposite to 1. Therefore 4 is opposite to 3.

12. (d)
In these two positions one of the common faces having 1 point is in the same position. Therefore according to rule number (2), there will be 4 points on the required face.

13. (c)
Even numbered dice are: (II), (IV) and (VI)
No. of dots on the top face of (II) dice = 6
No. of dots on the top face of (IV) dice = 6
and no. of dots on the top face of (VI) dice = 6
Therefore, required total no. of dots
= 6 + 6 + 6 = 18

14. (a)
Odd numbered dice are: (II), (III) and (V)
No. of dots on the top faces of these dice are 2, 2 and 4 respectively.
Required total no. of dots = 2 + 2 + 4 = 8

15. (d)
No. of faces on the top faces of the dice (I), (II) and (III) are 5, 1 and 5 respectively.
Therefore, total of these numbers = 5 + 1 + 5
= 11
No. of dots on the top faces of the dice (IV), (V) and (VI) are 1, 3 and 1 respectively.
Therefore, total of these numbers = 1 + 3 + 1 = 5
Required difference = 11 – 5 = 6

16. (c)
No. of dots on the top faces of the dice (II), (IV) and (VI) are 1, 1 and 1 respectively.
No. of dots on the top faces of the dice (I), (III) and (V) are 5, 5 and 3 respectively.
Required total no. of dots = 5 + 5 + 3 + 1 + 1 + 1 = 16

17. (b)
No. of dots on the top faces of dice (I), (II) and (III) are 5, 1 and 5 respectively.
Required total no. of dots = 5 + 1 + 5 = 11

18. (c)
The figure (X) is similar to the Form VI. So, when a cube is formed by folding the sheet shown in figure (X), then is one of the faces of the cube. However, the cube in figure (1) has two such faces and figure (4) has a face which is completely shaded. So, these two cubes cannot be formed. Hence, only the cubes in figures (2) and (3) can be formed.

19. (a)
The figure (X) is similar to the Form I. So, when the sheet shown in figure (X) is folded to form a cube, one of the two half-shaded faces lies opposite to one of the blank faces and the other half-shaded face lies opposite to another blank face. The two remaining blank faces lie opposite to each other. Thus, both the cubes shown in figures (1) and (4) can be formed when the sheet shown in figure (X) is folded. Also, though the cubes shown in figures (2) and (3) have faces that can appear adjacent to each other but the cube formed by folding the sheet in figure (X) cannot be rotated to form either of the two. Hence, the cubes in figures (2) and (3) cannot be formed.

20. (c)
When the sheet in figure (X) is folded, then one of the faces of the cube formed will be of the form 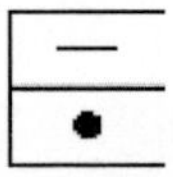 and this face will lie opposite the face bearing a square. Also, one of the blank faces lies opposite another blank face and the third blank face lies opposite the face bearing an '=' sign. Clearly, all the three blank faces cannot appear adjacent to each other. So, the cube shown in figure (2) which has all the three blank faces adjacent to each other cannot be formed. Hence, only the cubes shown in figures A, C and D can be formed.

21. (b)
The figure (X) is similar to the Form III. So, when the sheet in figure (X) is folded to form a cube, then 'F' appears opposite 'B', 'E' appears opposite 'C' and 'A' appears opposite 'D' Therefore, the cube in figure (1) which shows 'F' adjacent to 'B', the cube in figure (3) which shows 'E' adjacent to 'C', and the cube in figure (4) which shows 'A' adjacent to 'D' cannot be formed. Hence, only the cube in figure (2) can be formed.

22. (b)
The figure (X) is similar to the Form III. So, when the sheet in figure (X) is folded to form a cube, the half-shaded face appears opposite to the face bearing a rhombus, the face with a black circle appears opposite to one of the two blank faces and the face with a '+' sign appears opposite to the other blank face. Clearly, the cubes shown in figures (1) and (4) cannot be formed since they have the half-shaded face adjacent to the face bearing the rhombus. Also, though the cube shown in figure (3) has faces that can appear adjacent to each other yet the cube formed by folding the sheet in figure (X) cannot be rotated to form figure (3). Hence, the cube in figure (3) cannot be formed. Thus, only the cube shown in figure (2) can be formed.

23. (a)
The figure (X) is similar to the Form II. So, when the sheet shown in figure (X) is folded to form a cube, the two half-shaded faces lie opposite to each other, the face bearing a square lies opposite to one of the two blank faces and the face bearing a circle lies opposite to the other blank face. Therefore, the cubes shown in figures (2) and (3) which have the two half-shaded faces adjacent to each other, cannot be formed by folding the sheet shown in figure (X). Also, though the cube shown in figure (4) has faces that can appear adjacent to each other yet the cube formed by folding the sheet in figure (X) cannot be rotated to form the cube in figure (4). Hence, only the cube in figure (1) can be formed.

24. (b)
The figure (X) is similar to the Form V. So, when the sheet in figure (X) is folded to form a cube, the face bearing a dot lies opposite to one of the shaded faces. Therefore, the cube shown in figure (2) which has both the shaded faces adjacent to the face bearing the dot, cannot be formed. Hence, the cubes shown in figures (1), (2) and (4) can be formed.

25. (d)
The figure (X) is similar to the Form VII. So, when a cube is formed by folding the sheet shown in figure (X), the figure 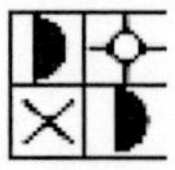 is one of the faces of the cube and this face lies opposite to a blank face. Also, a face bearing a square lies opposite to another blank face. The remaining two blank faces lie opposite to each other. Clearly, in the cube shown in figure (1), the face consisting of the four symbols is not the same as formed (as shown above). Hence, the cube in figure (1) cannot be formed.

26. (a)
The figure (X) is similar to the Form VI. So, when a cube is formed by folding the sheet shown in figure (X), the figure  is one of the faces of the cube and this face lies opposite to a blank face. Also, a face bearing a circle lies opposite to one bearing a dot. Clearly, this cube does not have faces as shown in the cubes in figures (3) and (4). Hence, only the cubes shown in figures (1) and (2) can be formed.

27. (c)
The figure (X) is similar to the Form I. So, when the sheet in figure (X) is folded to form a cube, the completely shaded face lies opposite to the half shaded face. Therefore, the cubes shown in figures (1) and (3) which have the completely shaded face adjacent to the half-shaded face cannot be formed. Since Fig (4) doesn't have at-least one shaded face, it cannot be formed. Hence, only the cubes in figure (2) can be formed.

28. (b)
The figure (X) is similar to the Form V. So, when the sheet shown in figure (X) is folded to form a cube, the shaded face lies opposite to one of the blank faces, the face bearing a circle lies opposite to another blank face and the face bearing a shaded square lies opposite to the third blank face. Thus, each one of the cubes shown in figures (1), (2) and (4) can be formed. Also, though

the cube shown in figure (3) has faces that can appear adjacent to each other but the cube formed by folding the sheet in figure (X) cannot be rotated to form figure (3). Hence, the cube in figure (3) cannot be formed.

29. (d)
The figure (X) is similar to the Form V. So, when the sheet in figure (X) is folded to form a cube, the face bearing a square lies opposite to the face bearing a circle. Therefore, the cubes shown in figures (1) and (2) which have the faces bearing the square and the circle adjacent to each other cannot be formed. Hence, only the cubes in figures (3) and (4) can be formed.

30. (c)
The figure (X) is similar to Form V. So, when the sheet shown in figure (X) is folded to form a cube, the face with shading lies opposite to the face bearing a square, the face bearing a dot lies opposite to a blank face and the face bearing a circle (with a '+' sign inside it) lies opposite to another blank face. The cubes in figures (2) and (4) have the shaded face adjacent to the face bearing a square. Therefore, the cubes in these two figures cannot be formed. Hence, only cubes in figures (1) and (3) can be formed.

31. (a)
The pattern on figure (X) and also the fact that the faces are rectangle, indicate that only figure (1) can be obtained by folding figure (X).

32. (a)
The figure (X) is similar to Form I. So, when the sheet shown in figure (X) is folded to form a box (cuboid), the two rectangular-shaded faces lie opposite to each other, two rectangular white faces lie opposite to each other and the two square shaped faces (one shaded and the other white) lie opposite to each other. Clearly, the cuboids shown in figures (2) and (4) cannot be formed as in each of the two cuboids the two shaded rectangular faces appear adjacent to each other. So, only the cuboids in figures (1) and (3) can be formed.

33. (d)
The figure (X) is similar to the Form VI. So, when the cube is formed by folding the sheet shown in figure (X), then is one of the faces of the cube and this face lies opposite to the face bearing a circle. Also, one of the blank faces lies opposite to another blank face and yet another blank face lies opposite to the fourth blank face. Thus, out of the four blank faces, no three faces can appear adjacent to each other.
Clearly, the cube in figure (1) cannot be formed since there is no face of the type , the cube in figure (2) cannot be formed since it shows three blank faces adjacent to each other and the cube in figure (3) cannot be formed since the face 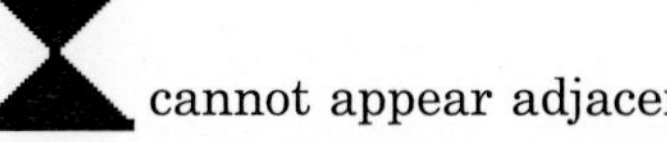 cannot appear adjacent to the face bearing the circle. Hence, only the cube in figure (4) can be formed.

34. (c)
The given figure is similar to Form III. Therefore, when this figure is folded to form a cube, the face bearing three dots will lie opposite the face bearing five dots.

35. (d)
The figure (X) is similar to the Form V. So, when the sheet in figure (X) is folded to form a cube, the face bearing a dot appears opposite to a blank face, the face bearing a '+' sign appears opposite to another blank face and the face bearing a circle appears opposite to the third blank face. Clearly, all the four cubes shown in figures (1), (2), (3) and (4) can be formed.

36. (a)
The figure (X) is similar to Form IV. So, when the sheet shown in figure (X) is folded to form a cube, the face bearing the dot lies opposite to the shaded face, the face bearing a circle (with '+' sign inside it) lies opposite to a blank face and the remaining two blank faces lie opposite to each other. Clearly, the cubes shown in figures (2) and (4) cannot be formed since they have the shaded face adjacent to the face bearing a dot and the cube shown in figure (3) cannot be formed since it shows all the three blank faces adjacent to each other. Hence, only the cube shown in figure (1) can be formed.

37. (b)
The figure (X) is similar to the Form VIII. So, when a cube is formed by folding the sheet shown in figure (X), the figures and are the two faces and these two faces lie opposite to each other. Also, the face bearing the 'x' sign lies opposite the face bearing the black circle and the face bearing the white circle lies opposite the face bearing the square (having a dot inside it). Now, the cubes in figures (2) and (4) consist of faces which are not formed when the sheet in figure (X) is folded. Hence, these two cubes are not formed. Therefore, only the cubes in figures (1) and (3) are formed.

38. (a)
We shall assume the dice in figure (ii) to be rotated so that the 5 dots appear at the same position as in figure (i) i.e. on RHS face (i.e. on face II as per activity 1) and 1 dot appears at the same position as in fig; (i) i.e. on Front face (i.e. on face I). Then, from the two figures, 2 dots appear on the top face (i.e. on face V) and 4 dots appear on the Bottom face (i.e. on face VI).
Since, these two faces are opposite to each other, therefore, two dots are contained on the face opposite to that containing four dots.

39. (c)
From figures (ii) and (iii), we conclude that 1, 6, 3 and 4 dots lie adjacent to 5 dots. Therefore, 2 dots must lie

opposite 5 dots. Conversely, 5 dots must lie opposite 2 dots.

40. (c)
From figures (ii) and (iii), we conclude that the alphabets C, D, B and F appear adjacent to the alphabet E. Therefore, the alphabet A appears opposite E. Conversely, E appears opposite A.

41. (a)
From figures (i) and (ii), we conclude that the numbers 1, 4, 3 and 5 lie adjacent to the number 6. Clearly, the number 2 lies opposite 6 and conversely 6 lies opposite 2.

42. (c)
From figures (i), (ii) and (iv) we conclude that 6, 4, 3 and 1 lie adjacent to 2. Hence, 5 must lie opposite 2.

43. (b)
From positions X and Y we conclude that 1, 5, 6 and 3 lie adjacent to 4. Therefore, 2 must lie opposite 4. From positions Y and Z we conclude that 4, 3, 2 and 5 lie adjacent to 6. Therefore, 1 must lie opposite 6. Thus, 2 lies opposite 4, 1 lies opposite 6 and consequently 5 lies opposite 3.
As analysed above, the number on the face opposite 5 is 3. In position X, since 5 lies on the top, therefore 3 must lie at the bottom face.

44. (d)
If 2 is opposite to 3, then 1 cannot lie opposite to either of the two numbers - 2 or 3. Hence, 1 is necessarily adjacent to both 2 and 3.

45. (c)
Number 6 is common to both the positions of the dice. We assume the dice in figure (ii) to be rotated so that 6 remains on the top face (i.e. face V as per activity 1) and the number 4 in figure (ii) moves to the FR-RH face (i.e. face I) as in figure (i), then 5 will move to the RR-RH face (i.e. face II). Clearly, 5 (which lies on face II) and 1 (which lies on face IV) will be opposite to each other. So, when 1 is on the top, then 5 will be at the bottom.

46. (d)
From figures (i) and (ii) we conclude that the number 1, 2, 3 and 4 appear adjacent to 6. Thus, the number 5 will appear opposite 6. Therefore, when six is at the bottom, then 5 will be at the top.

47. (c)
Number 3 is common to both the figures (i) and (ii). The dice in figure (ii) is assumed to be rotated so that 3 remains on the FR-RH face (i.e. face I as per activity 1) and the numbers 5 and 2 move to the faces hidden behind the numbers 6 and 1 respectively [in figure (i)]. Thus, the combined figure will have 3 on FR-RH face (i.e. face I), 5 on RR-RH face (i.e. face II), 2 on Bottom face (i.e. face VI), 1 on the Top face (i.e. face V) and 6 on FR-LH face (i.e. face IV). Clearly, 2 lies opposite 1. Hence, when 2 is at the bottom, then 1 will be at the top.

48. (b)
If 1 is opposite to 5 and 2 is opposite to 3, then 4 definitely lies opposite to 6. Therefore, 2 cannot lie opposite to any of the two numbers - 4 or 6. Hence, 2 necessarily lies adjacent to both 4 and 6.

49. (c)
Number 3 is common to the two positions of the block. We assume the block in figure (ii) to be rotated so that 3 appears at the same position as in figure (i) i.e. on RHS face (i.e. on face II as per activity 1) and the numbers 5 and 2 move to the faces hidden behind the numbers 4 and 6 respectively [in figure (i)]. Thus, the combined figure will have 3 on RHS face (i.e. face II), 4 on the Front face (i.e. face I), 6 on the Top face (i.e. face V), 5 on the Rear face (i.e. face III) and 2 on the Bottom face (i.e. face VI). Clearly, when 2 is at the bottom; then 6 is at the top.

50. (b)
From positions X and Y we conclude that 1, 5, 6 and 3 lie adjacent to 4. Therefore, 2 must lie opposite 4. From positions Y and Z we conclude that 4, 3, 2 and 5 lie adjacent to 6. Therefore, 1 must lie opposite 6. Thus, 2 lies opposite 4, 1 lies opposite 6 and consequently 5 lies opposite 3.
As analysed above, the number opposite 6 is 1 and the number opposite 5 is 3. Therefore, the numbers hidden behind the numbers 6 and 5 in position Z (these are the numbers opposite 5 and 6 respectively) are 1 and 3.

❒

Previous Year Questions

1. Four usual dice are thrown on the ground. The total of numbers on the top faces of these four dice is 13 as the top faces showed 4, 3, 1 and 5 respectively. What is the total of the faces touching the ground?

   [NTSE 2002 - Gujarat first stage paper]

   (a) 12 (b) 13
   (c) 15 (d) Cannot be determined

2. The four different positions of a dice are given below. Find the number on the face opposite the face showing 6?

   [NTSE 2012 - Delhi first stage paper]

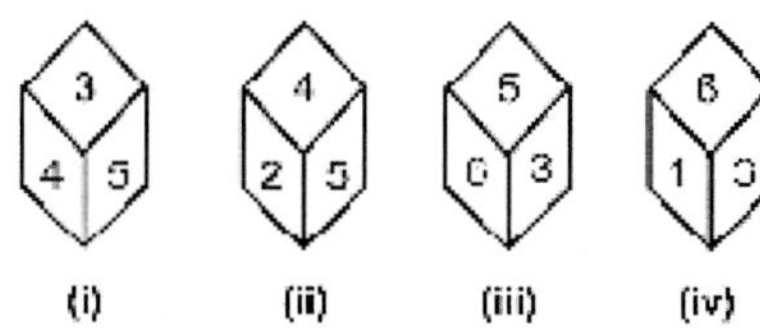

   (a) 1 (b) 2
   (c) 4 (d) 5

3. Two positions of a dice with 1 to 6 dots on its sides are shown below. If the dice is resting on the side with three dots, what will be number of dots on the side at the top?

   [NTSE 2007 – Punjab first stage paper]

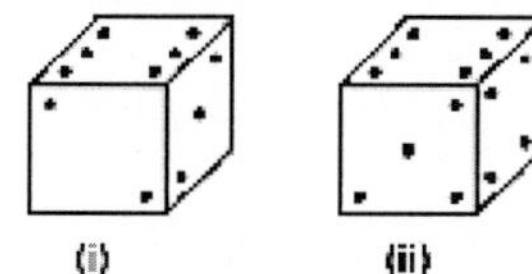

   (a) 1 or 5 (b) 2
   (c) 3 (d) 5

4. A dice is numbered from 1 to 6 in different ways. If 1 is adjacent to 2, 4 and 6, then which of the following statements is necessarily true?

   [NTSE 2012 - UP first stage paper]

   (a) 2 is opposite to 6
   (b) 1 is adjacent to 3
   (c) 3 is adjacent to 5
   (d) 3 is opposite to 5

5. A cube has six different symbols drawn over its six faces. The symbols are dot, circle, triangle, square, cross and arrow. Three different positions of the cube are shown in figures X, Y, and Z. Which symbol occurs at the bottom of figure(Y)?

   [NTSE 2005 – Andhra Pradesh first stage paper]

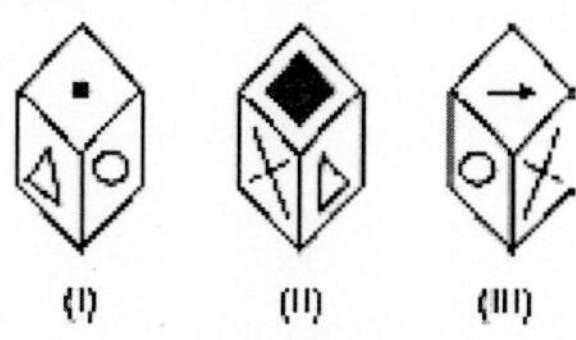

   (a) Arrow (b) Triangle
   (c) Circle (d) Dot

6. Which number is on the face opposite 4, if the four different positions of a dice are as shown in the figure given below?

   [NTSE 2012 - Haryana second stage paper]

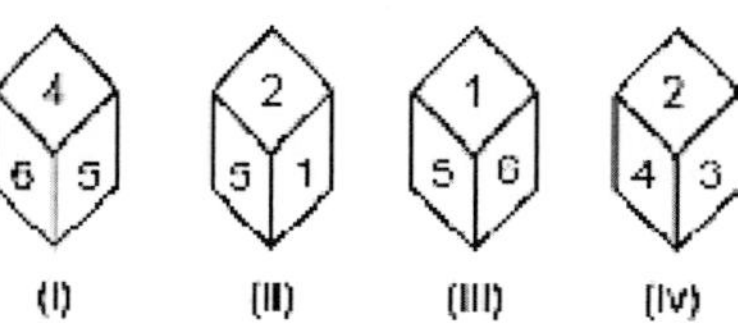

   (a) 5 (b) 3
   (c) 2 (d) 1

7. How many dots are there on the dice face opposite the one with three dots?

   [NTSE 2000 - Tamilnadu first stage paper]

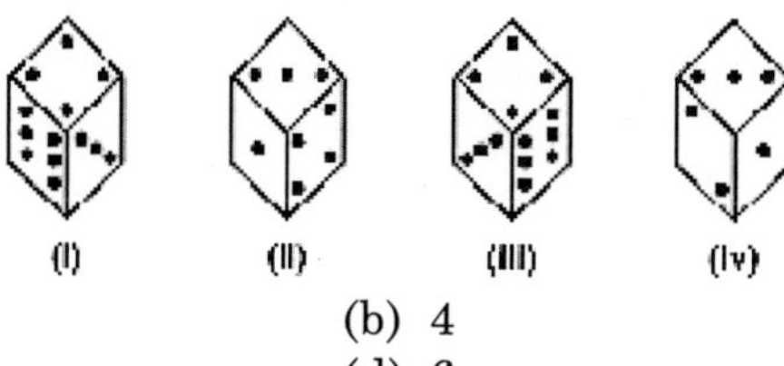

   (a) 2 (b) 4
   (c) 5 (d) 6

8. Two positions of a dice are shown below. When there are two dots at the bottom, the number of dots at the top will be

   [NTSE 2003 - Karnataka first stage paper]

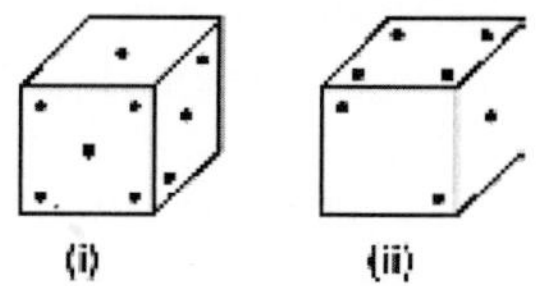

   (a) 3 (b) 5
   (c) 6 (d) Cannot be determined

9. Two positions of a dice are shown below. If the face with 1 dot is at the bottom, then the number of dots on the top is:

   [NTSE 2007 - Maharashtra second stage paper]

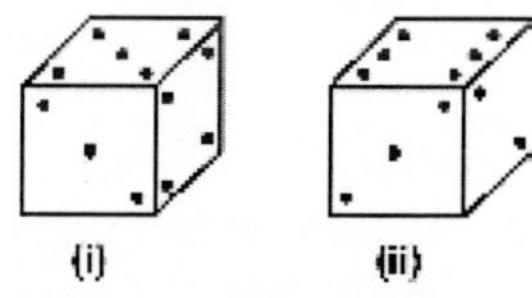

   (a) 2 (b) 3
   (c) 4 (d) 5

10. Amongst the following figures, find the correct one, if it is known that the total number of dots on opposite faces of the cube shown is always 7.

    [NTSE 2000 - Delhi first stage paper]

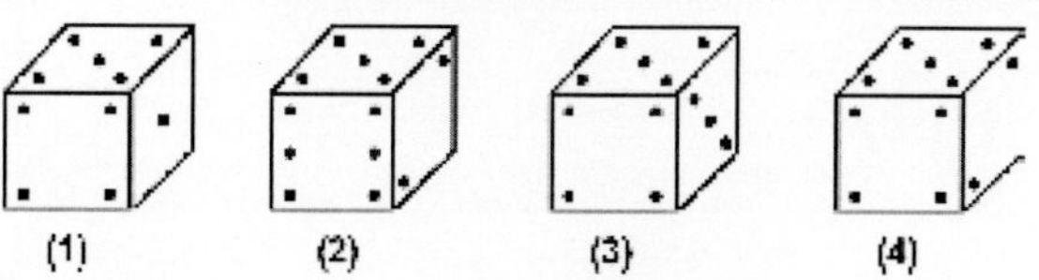

    (a) Figure 1 (b) Figure 2
    (c) Figure 3 (d) Figure 4

Answer Key

1. (c)	**2.** (c)	**3.** (a)	**4.** (c)	**5.** (c)	**6.** (d)	**7.** (c)	**8.** (a)	**9.** (b)	**10.** (a)

Explanatory Notes

1. (c)
In a usual dice, the sum of the numbers on any two opposite faces is always 7. Thus, 1 is opposite 6, 2 is opposite 5 and 3 is opposite 4.
Consequently, when 4, 3, 1 and 5 are the numbers on the top faces, 3, 4, 6 and 2 respectively are the numbers on the face touching the ground. The total of these numbers = 3 + 4 + 6 + 2 = 15

2. (c)
From figures (i), (ii) and (iii), we conclude that 3, 4, 2 and 6 lie adjacent to 5. Therefore, 1 must lie opposite 5.
From figures (i), (iii) and (iv), we conclude that 4, 5, 6 and 1 lie adjacent to 3. Therefore, 2 must lie opposite 3. Now, we have 1 opposite 5 and 2 opposite 3. Hence, 4 must lie opposite 6.

3. (a)
From figures (i) and (ii) we conclude that 2, 6 and 4 dots appear adjacent to 3 dots. Hence, either 1 or 5 dots may appear opposite 3 dots. Thus, if the dice is resting on the side with three dots, then the number of dots on the side at the top is either 1 or 5.

4. (c)
If 1 is adjacent to 2, 4 and 6 then either 3 or 5 lies opposite to 1. So, the numbers 3 and 5 cannot lie opposite to each other. Hence, 3 is adjacent to 5 (necessarily)

5. (c)
From figures X and Y, we conclude that dot, circle, square and cross lie adjacent to the triangle. Therefore, the arrow must lie opposite the triangle. From figures X and Z, we conclude that dot, triangle, arrow and cross lie adjacent to the circle. Therefore, the square must lie opposite the circle. Thus, the arrow lies opposite the triangle, the square lies opposite the circle and consequently, the cross lies opposite the dot.
Since the square lies at the top of figure (Y) and the circle lies opposite the square (as analysed above), so the circle occurs at the bottom of fig. (Y).

6. (d)
From figures (i) and (iv) we conclude that 6, 5, 2 and 3 lie adjacent to 4. It follows that 1 lies opposite 4.

7. (c)
From figures (i), (ii) and (iv), we conclude that 6, 4,1 and 2 dots appear adjacent to 3 dots. Clearly, there will be 5 dots on the face opposite the face with 3 dots.

8. (a)
Number 1 is common to both the positions of the dice. We assume the dice in fig. (ii) to be rotated so that 1 dot moves to the top face (i.e. face V as per activity 1) i.e. to the same position as in fig. (i) and 2 and 4 dots move to the faces hidden behind the faces with 3 and 5 dots respectively. Thus, the combined figure will have 1 dot on the Top (i.e. on face V), 5 dots on Front face (i.e. on face I), 3 dots on RHS face (i.e. face II), 4 dots on the Rear face (i.e. face III) and 2 dots on the LHS face (i.e. face IV). Clearly, 3 dots lie on the face opposite the face having 2 dots. Therefore, when there are 2 dots at the bottom, the number of dots at the top will be 3.

9. (b)
From figures (i) and (ii), we conclude that 5, 4, 6 and 2 dots appear adjacent to 3 dots. Therefore, 1 dot must appear opposite 3 dots. Thus, if the face with 1 dot is at the bottom, then the face with 3 dots will appear on the top.

10. (a)
Since the total number of dots on opposite faces is always 7, therefore 1 dot must lie opposite 6 dots, 2 dots must lie opposite 5 dots and 3 dots must lie opposite 4 dots. In each of the two figures (2) and (4), 2 dots appear adjacent to 5 dots, and in fig. (3), 3 dots appear adjacent to 4 dots. Hence, these figures are incorrect. Therefore/only figure (1) is correct.

❐

UNIT 13

Pattern Perception

In the problems based on pattern perception, a figure following a set sequence or pattern is given. A part of the figure, generally a quarter, is left blank. The candidate is then required to select a part out of the four given alternatives, which best fits into the blank space of the problem.

Solved Examples

☛ ***Directions to solve (1 to 5):*** *In each of the following questions, select a figure from amongst the four alternatives, which when placed in the blank space of figure (X) would complete the pattern.*

1. Identify the figure that completes the pattern.

(a) 1 (b) 2
(c) 3 (d) 4

Solution: Option (c) is correct.

Explanation:

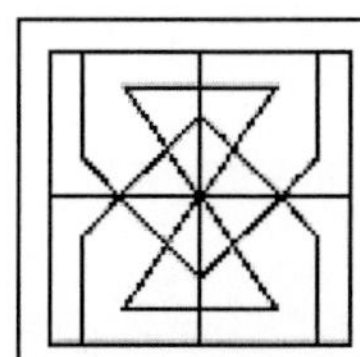

2. Identify the figure that completes the pattern.

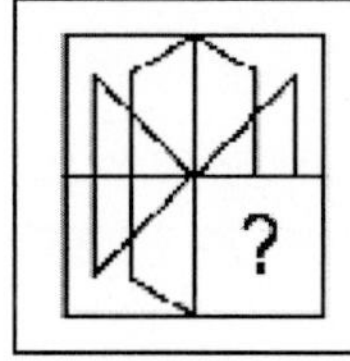
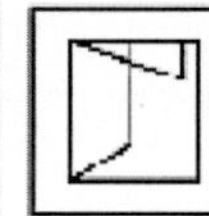
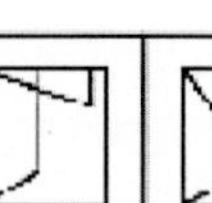
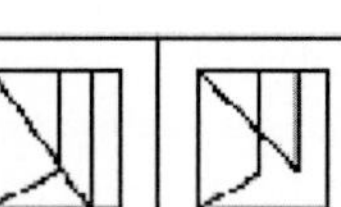

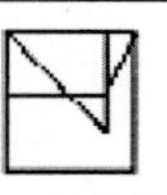

(X) (1) (2) (3) (4)

(a) 1 (b) 2
(c) 3 (d) 4

Solution: Option c) is correct.

Explanation:

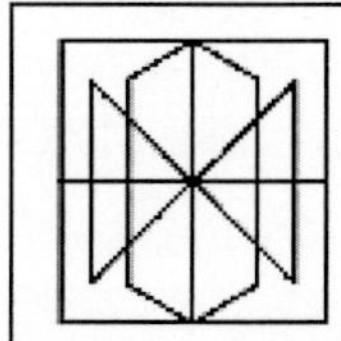

3. Identify the figure that completes the pattern.

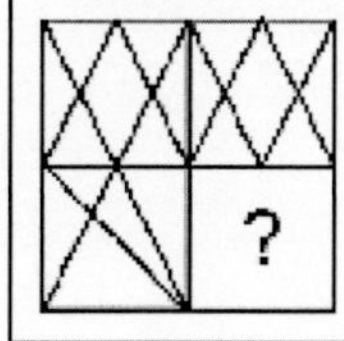
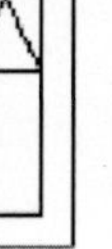
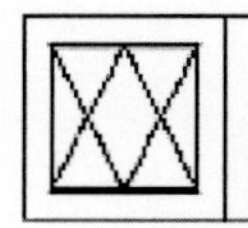
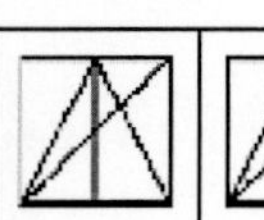
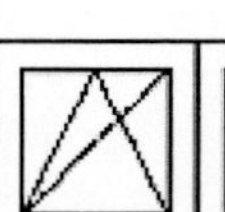
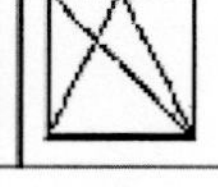
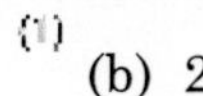

(X) (1) (2) (3) (4)

(a) 1 (b) 2
(c) 3 (d) 4

Solution: Option c) is correct.

Explanation:

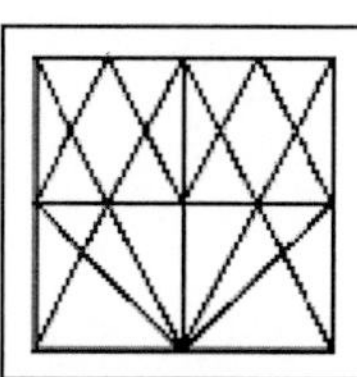

4. Identify the figure that completes the pattern.

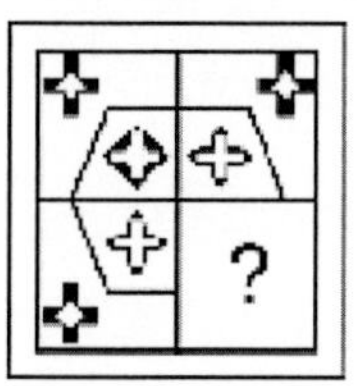

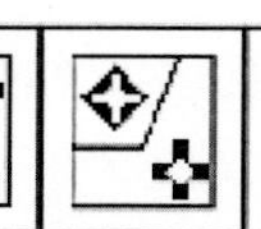
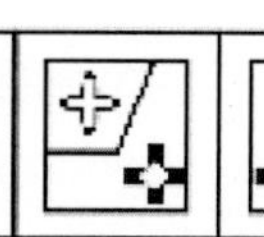
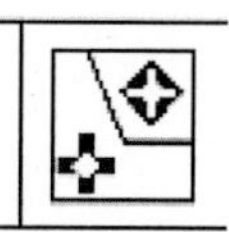

(X) (1) (2) (3) (4)

(a) 1 (b) 2
(c) 3 (d) 4

Solution: Option (b) is correct.

Explanation:

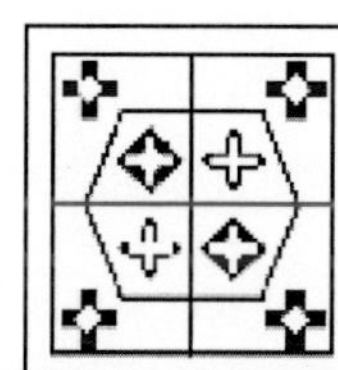

5. Identify the figure that completes the pattern.

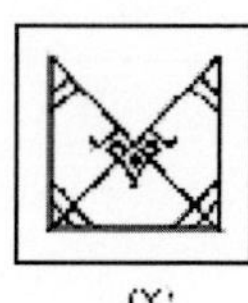
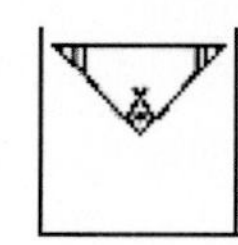
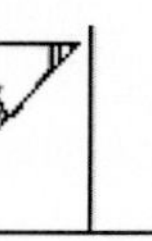
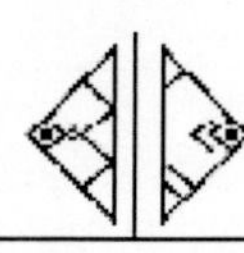
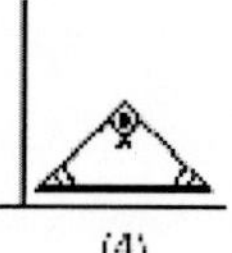

(X) (1) (2) (3) (4)

(a) 1 (b) 2
(c) 3 (d) 4

Solution: Option (d) is correct.

Explanation:

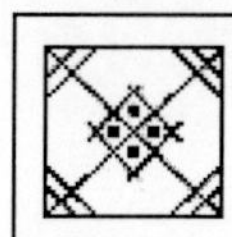

Multiple Choice Questions

☛ *In each of the following questions, select a figure from amongst the four alternatives, which when placed in the blank space of figure (X) would complete the pattern.*

1. Identify the figure that completes the pattern

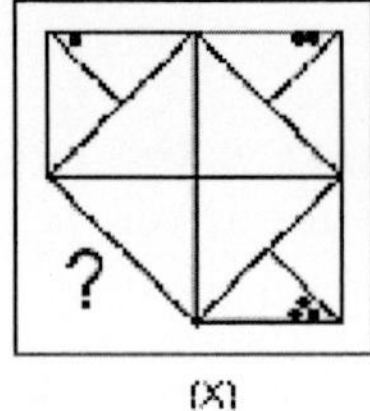
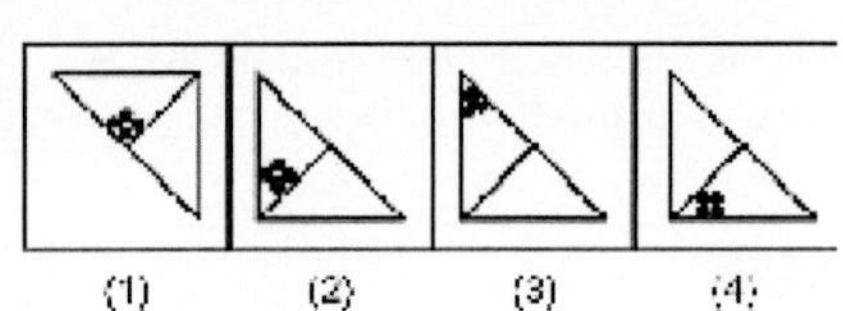

(X) (1) (2) (3) (4)

(a) 1 (b) 2
(c) 3 (d) 4

2. Identify the figure that completes the pattern

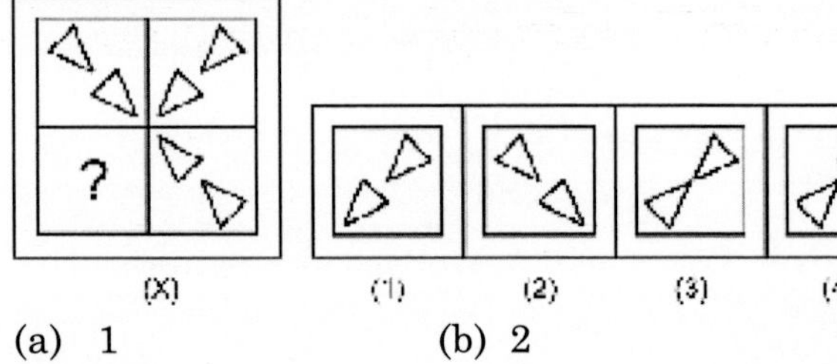

(X) (1) (2) (3) (4)

(a) 1 (b) 2
(c) 3 (d) 4

3. Identify the figure that completes the pattern

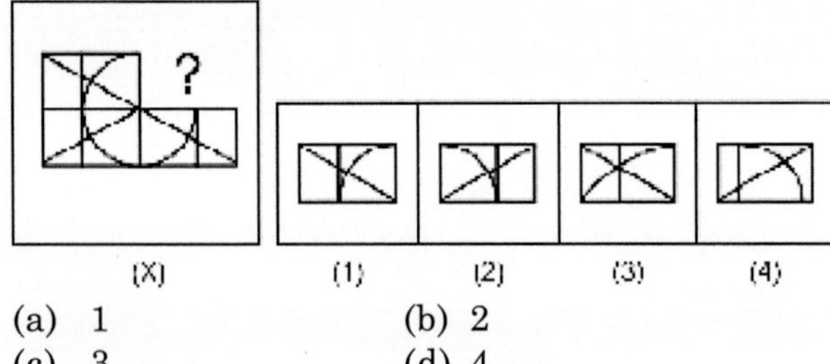

(X) (1) (2) (3) (4)

(a) 1 (b) 2
(c) 3 (d) 4

4. Identify the figure that completes the pattern

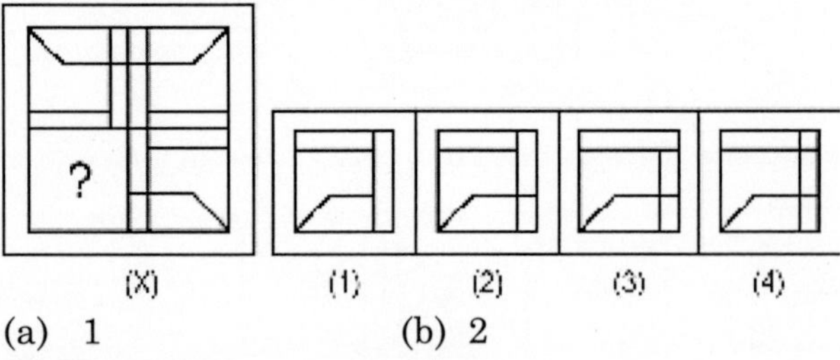

(X) (1) (2) (3) (4)

(a) 1 (b) 2
(c) 3 (d) 4

5. Identify the figure that completes the pattern

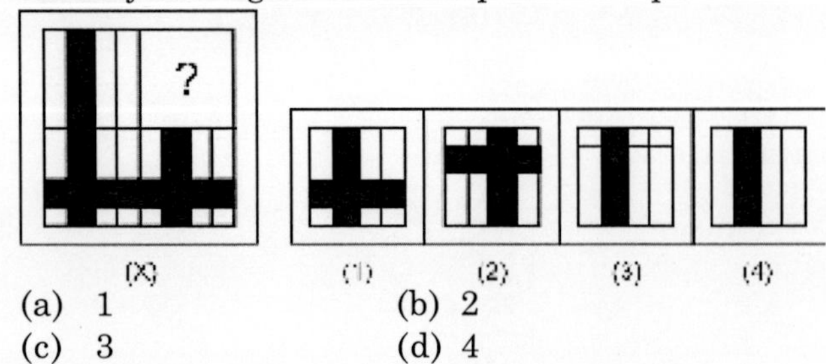

(X) (1) (2) (3) (4)

(a) 1 (b) 2
(c) 3 (d) 4

6. Identify the figure that completes the pattern

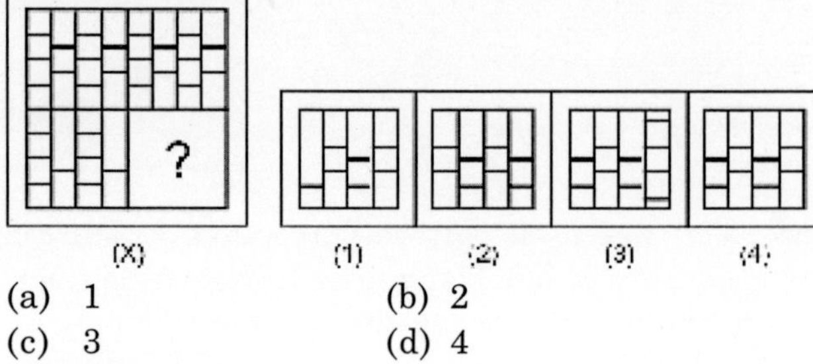

(X) (1) (2) (3) (4)

(a) 1 (b) 2
(c) 3 (d) 4

7. Identify the figure that completes the pattern.

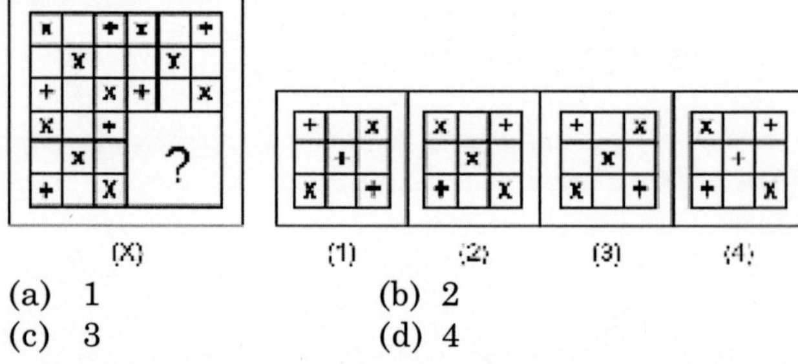

(X) (1) (2) (3) (4)

(a) 1 (b) 2
(c) 3 (d) 4

8. Identify the figure that completes the pattern.

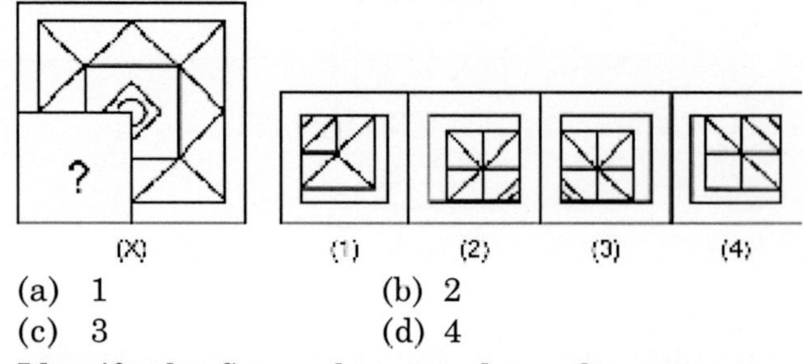

(X) (1) (2) (3) (4)

(a) 1 (b) 2
(c) 3 (d) 4

9. Identify the figure that completes the pattern.

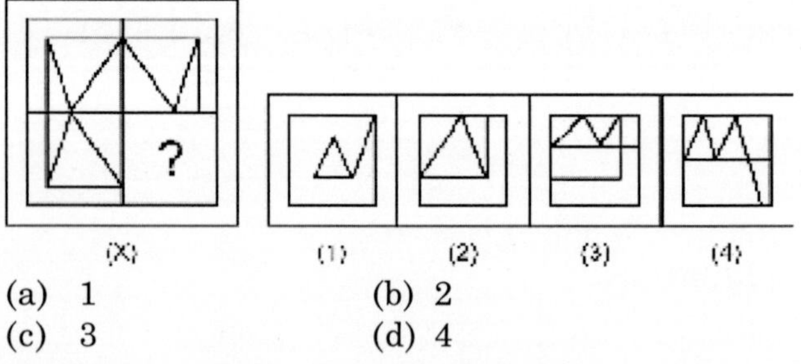

(X) (1) (2) (3) (4)

(a) 1 (b) 2
(c) 3 (d) 4

10. Identify the figure that completes the pattern.

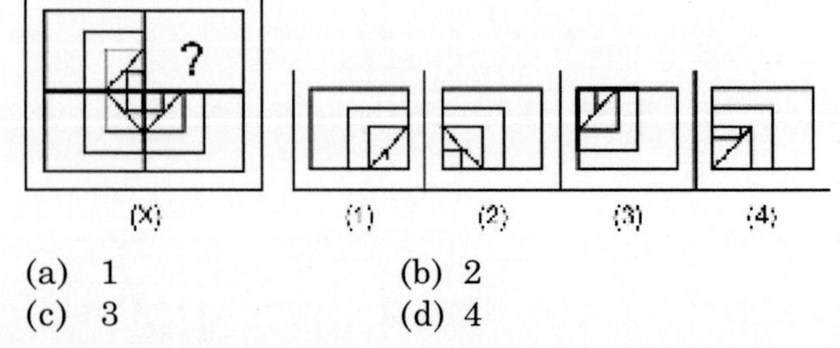

(X) (1) (2) (3) (4)

(a) 1 (b) 2
(c) 3 (d) 4

11. Identify the figure that completes the pattern.

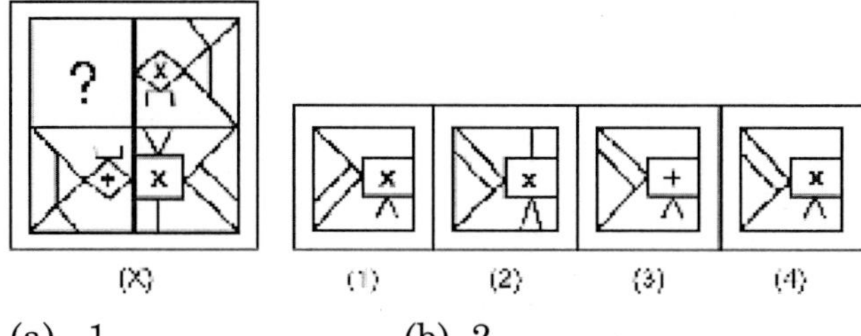

(a) 1 (b) 2
(c) 3 (d) 4

12. Identify the figure that completes the pattern.

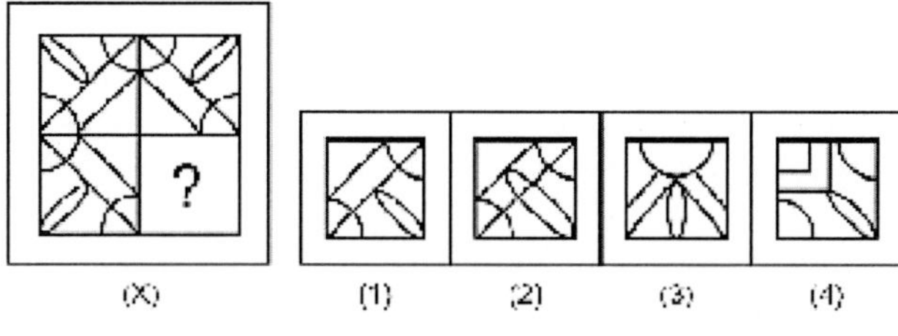

(a) 1 (b) 2
(c) 3 (d) 4

13. Identify the figure that completes the pattern.

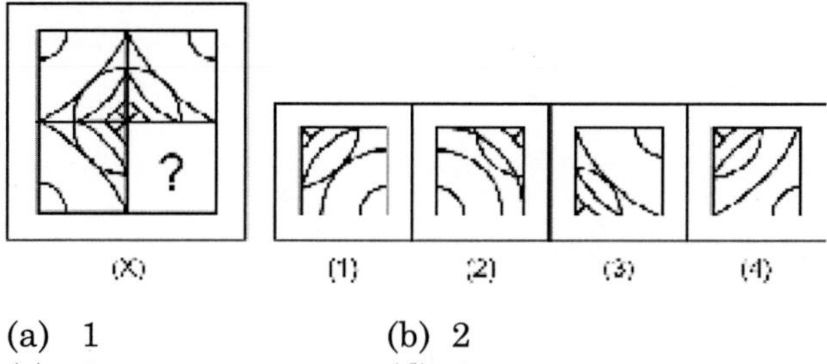

(a) 1 (b) 2
(c) 3 (d) 4

14. Identify the figure that completes the pattern.

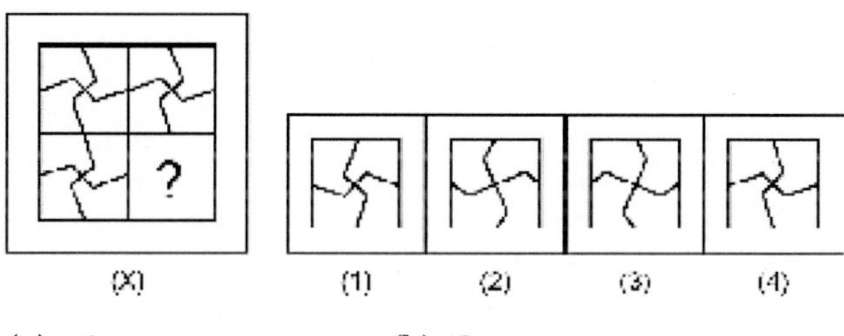

(a) 1 (b) 2
(c) 3 (d) 4

15. Identify the figure that completes the pattern.

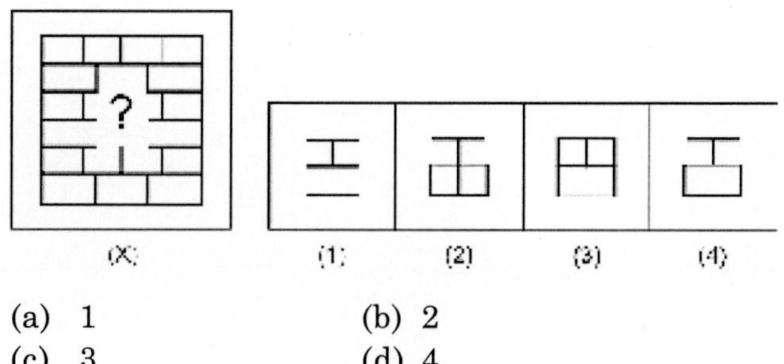

(a) 1 (b) 2
(c) 3 (d) 4

16. Identify the figure that completes the pattern.

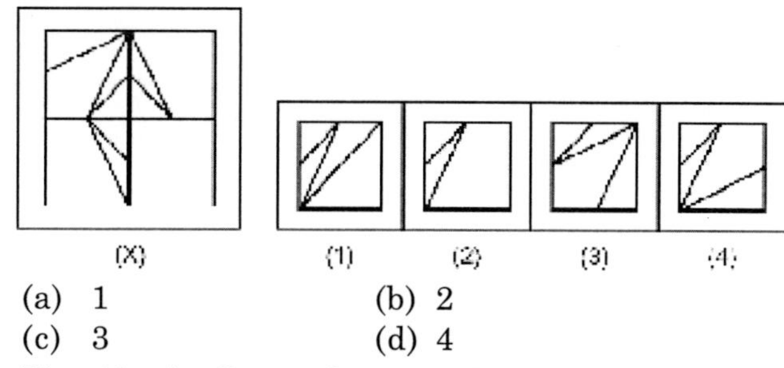

(a) 1 (b) 2
(c) 3 (d) 4

17. Identify the figure that completes the pattern.

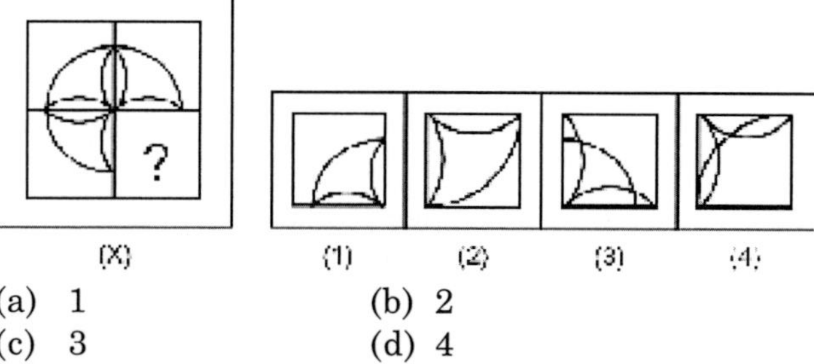

(a) 1 (b) 2
(c) 3 (d) 4

18. Identify the figure that completes the pattern.

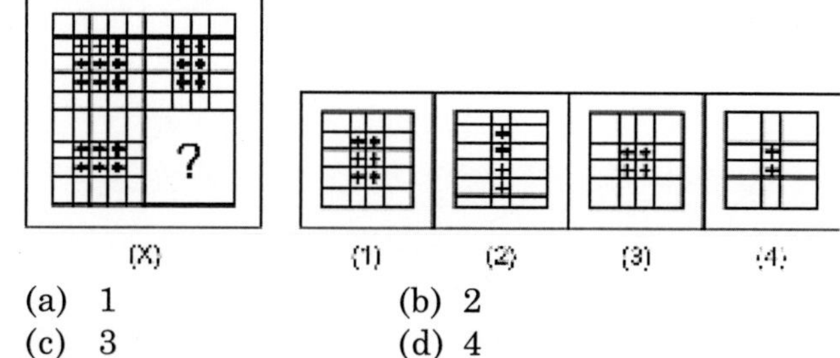

(a) 1 (b) 2
(c) 3 (d) 4

19. Identify the figure that completes the pattern.

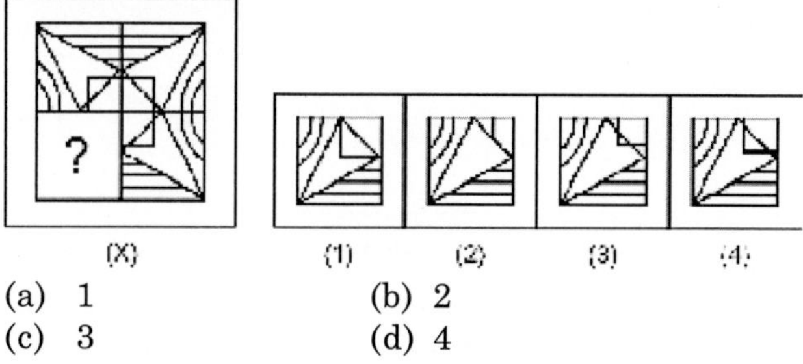

(a) 1 (b) 2
(c) 3 (d) 4

20. Identify the figure that completes the pattern.

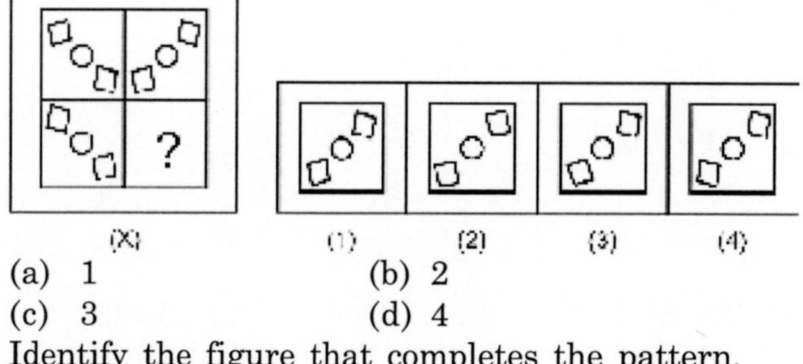

(a) 1 (b) 2
(c) 3 (d) 4

21. Identify the figure that completes the pattern.

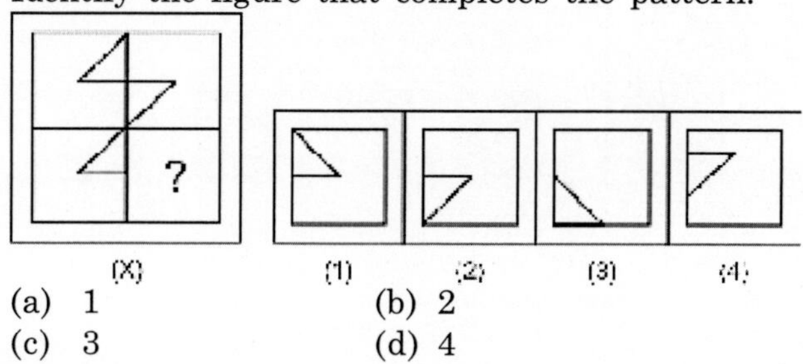

(a) 1 (b) 2
(c) 3 (d) 4

22. Identify the figure that completes the pattern.

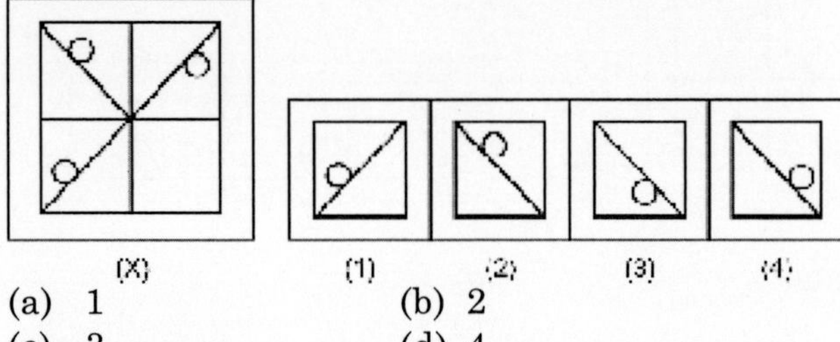

(a) 1
(b) 2
(c) 3
(d) 4

23. Identify the figure that completes the pattern.

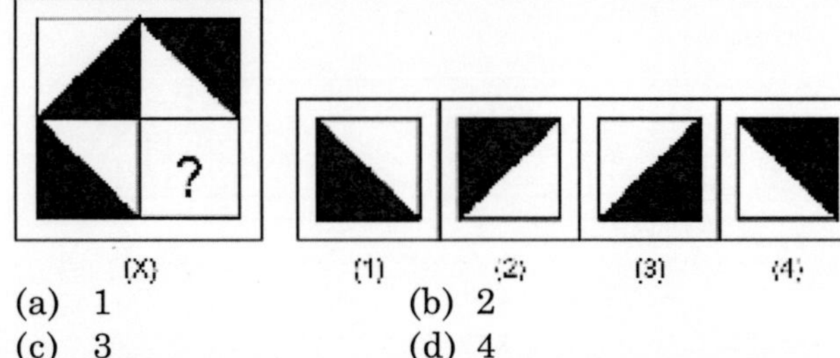

(a) 1
(b) 2
(c) 3
(d) 4

24. Identify the figure that completes the pattern.

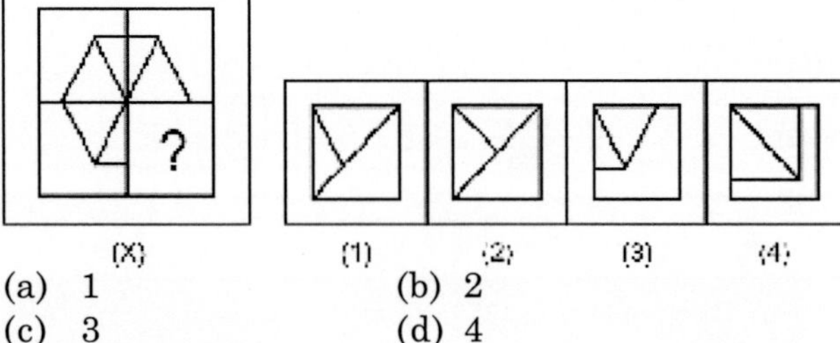

(a) 1
(b) 2
(c) 3
(d) 4

25. Identify the figure that completes the pattern.

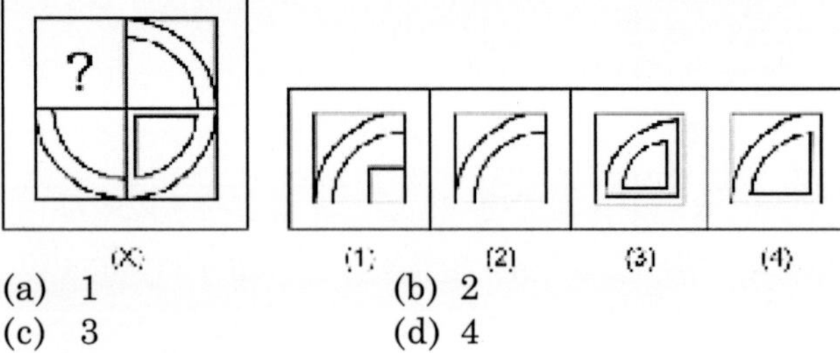

(a) 1
(b) 2
(c) 3
(d) 4

26. Identify the figure that completes the pattern.

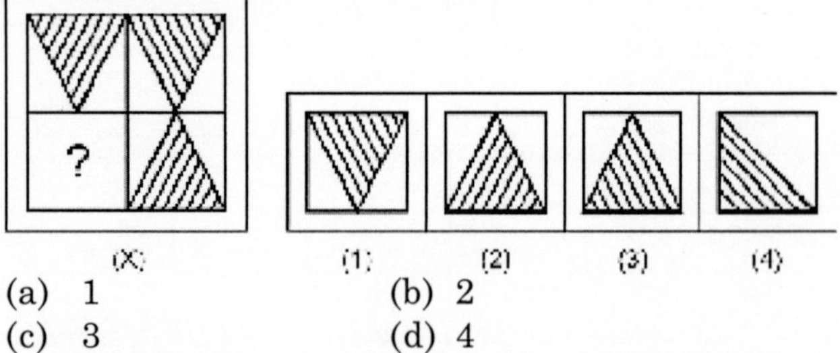

(a) 1
(b) 2
(c) 3
(d) 4

27. Identify the figure that completes the pattern.

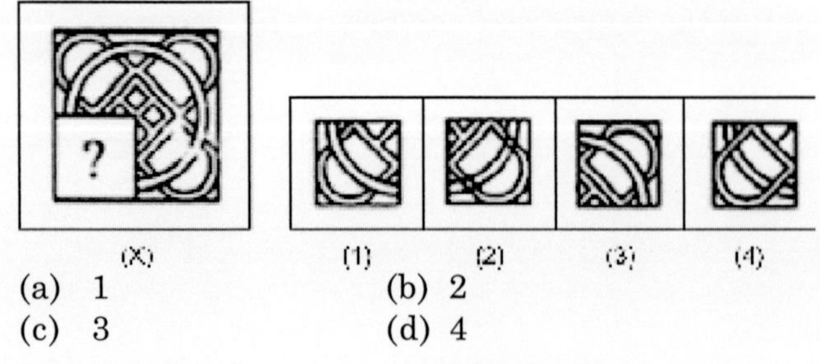

(a) 1
(b) 2
(c) 3
(d) 4

28. Identify the figure that completes the pattern.

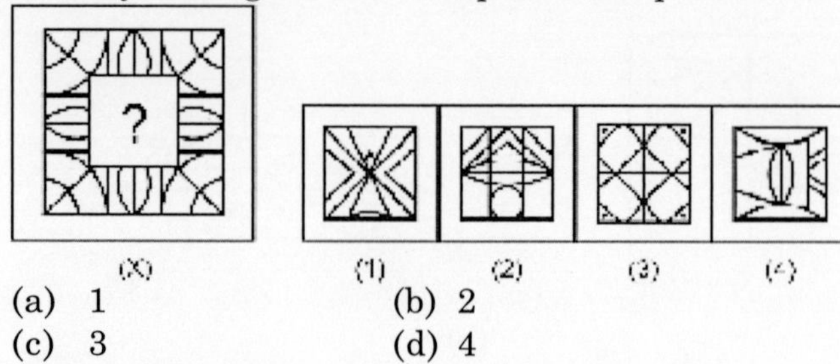

(a) 1
(b) 2
(c) 3
(d) 4

29. Identify the figure that completes the pattern.

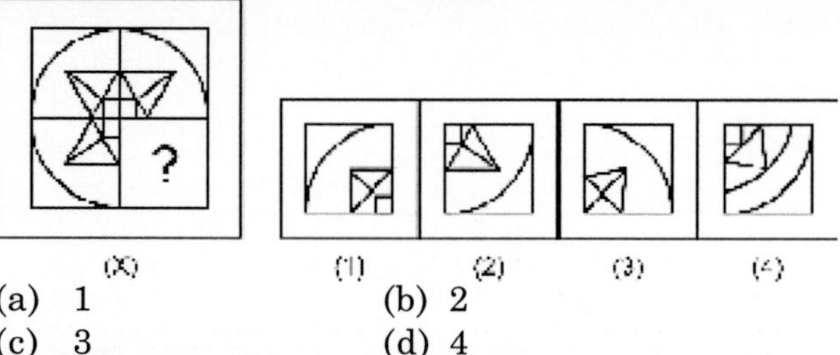

(a) 1
(b) 2
(c) 3
(d) 4

30. Identify the figure that completes the pattern.

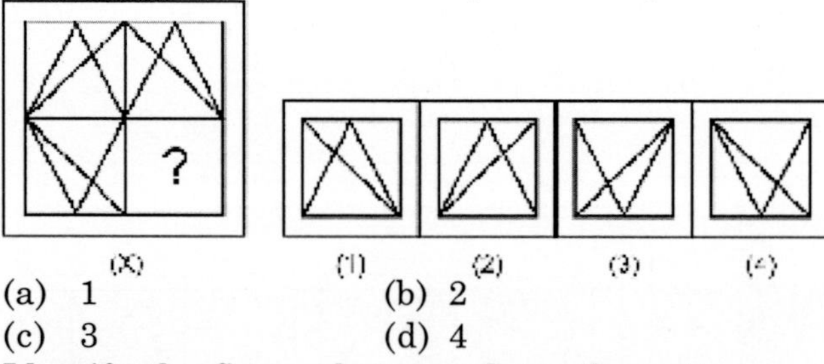

(a) 1
(b) 2
(c) 3
(d) 4

31. Identify the figure that completes the pattern.

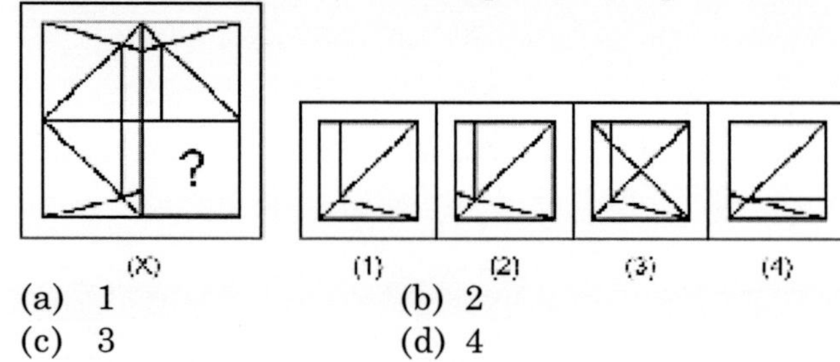

(a) 1
(b) 2
(c) 3
(d) 4

32. Identify the figure that completes the pattern.

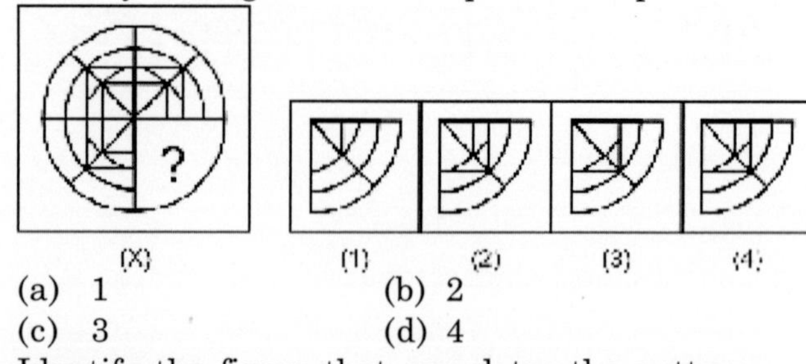

(a) 1
(b) 2
(c) 3
(d) 4

33. Identify the figure that completes the pattern.

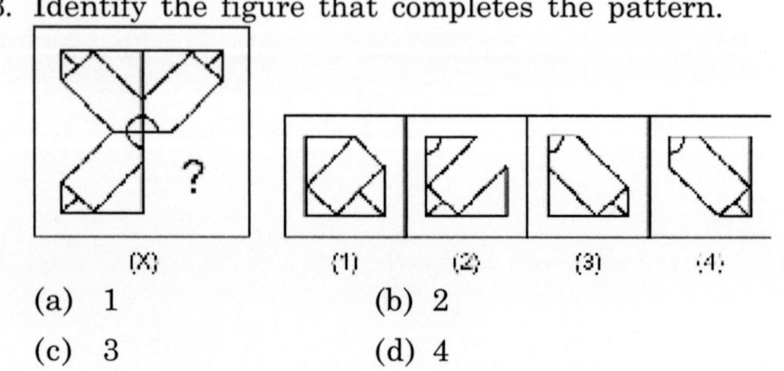

(a) 1
(b) 2
(c) 3
(d) 4

34. Identify the figure that completes the pattern.

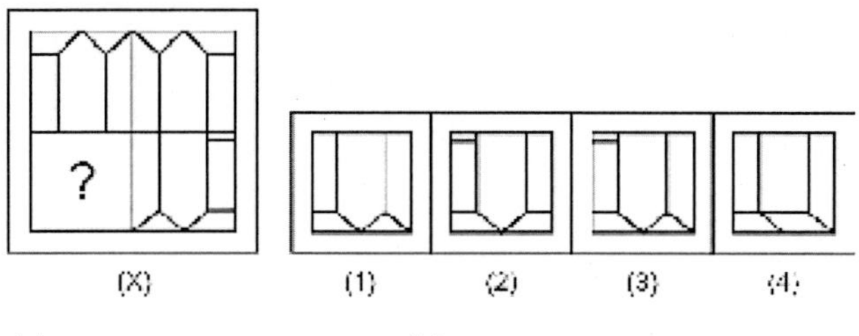

(a) 1 (b) 2
(c) 3 (d) 4

35. Identify the figure that completes the pattern.

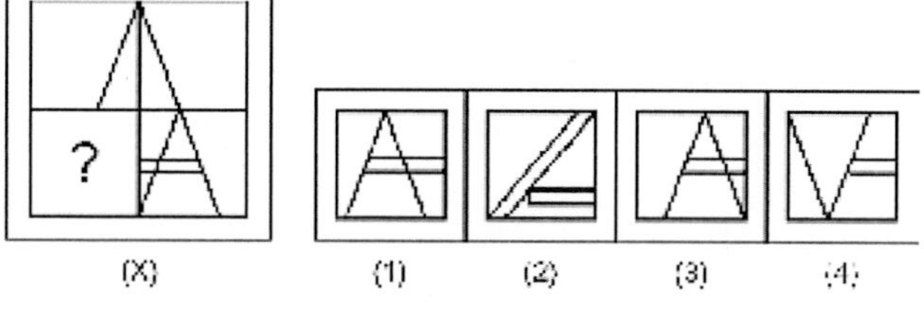

(a) 1 (b) 2
(c) 3 (d) 4

Answer Key

1. (d)	**2.** (d)	**3.** (b)	**4.** (b)	**5.** (d)	**6.** (d)	**7.** (b)	**8.** (c)	**9.** (b)	**10.** (b)
11. (b)	**12.** (a)	**13.** (c)	**14.** (d)	**15.** (d)	**16.** (d)	**17.** (a)	**18.** (c)	**19.** (d)	**20.** (c)
21. (b)	**22.** (c)	**23.** (b)	**24.** (c)	**25.** (d)	**26.** (c)	**27.** (c)	**28.** (c)	**29.** (b)	**30.** (c)
31. (b)	**32.** (d)	**33.** (c)	**34.** (c)	**30.** (c)	**31.** (b)	**32.** (d)	**33.** (c)	**34.** (c)	**35.** (c)

Explanatory Notes

1. (d)

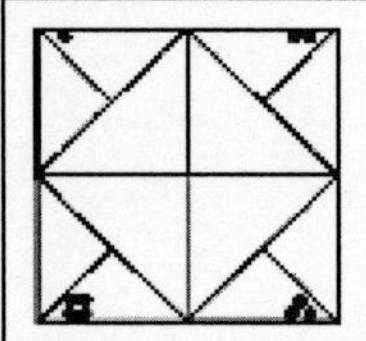

2. (d)

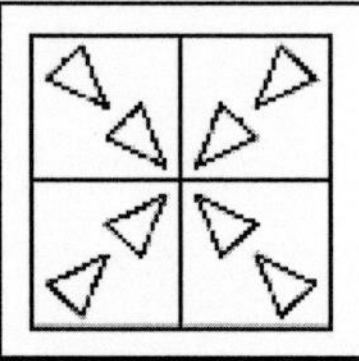

3. (b)

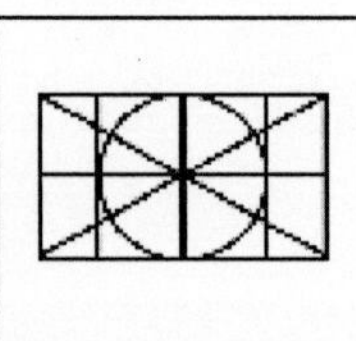

4. (b)

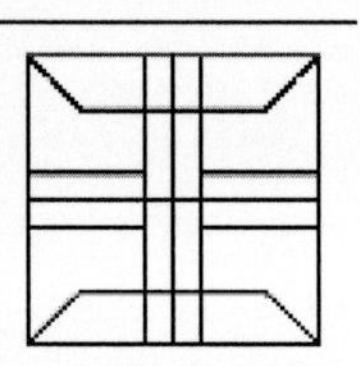

5. (d)

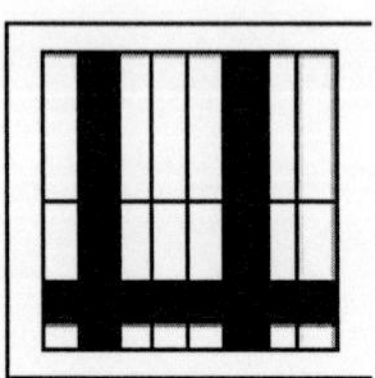

6. (d)

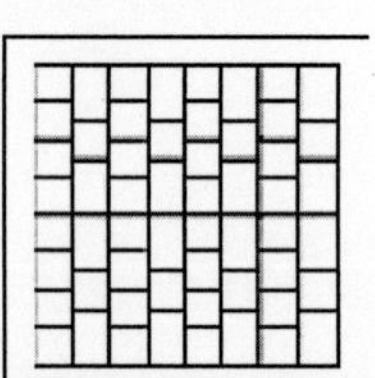

7. (b)

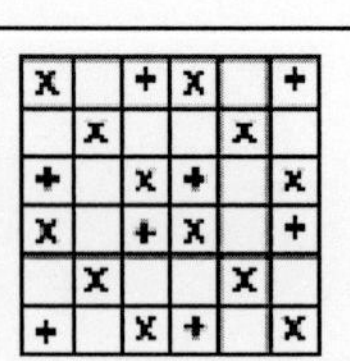

8. (c)

9. (b)

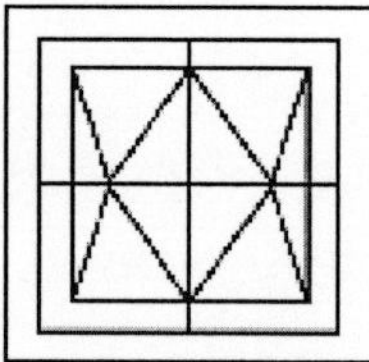

10. (b)

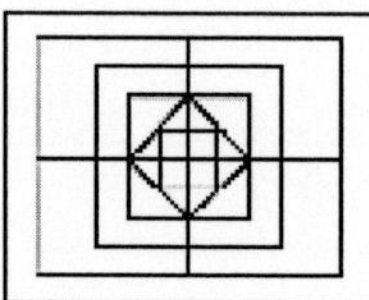

11. (b)

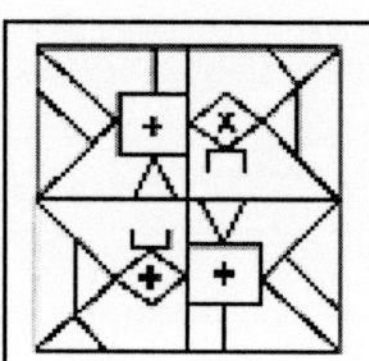

12. (a)

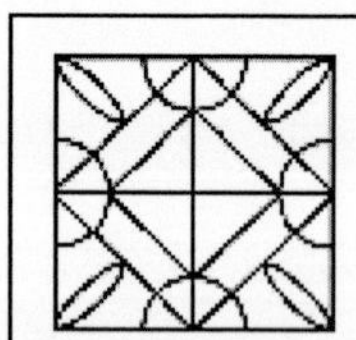

13. (c)

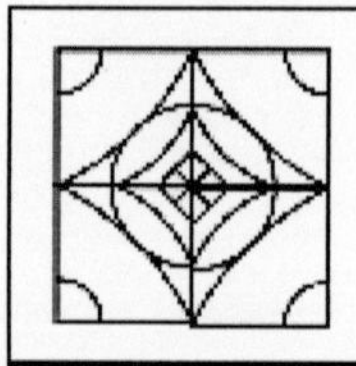

14. (d)

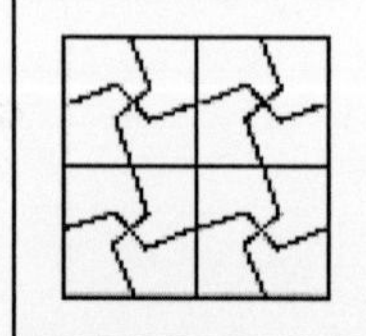

15. (d)

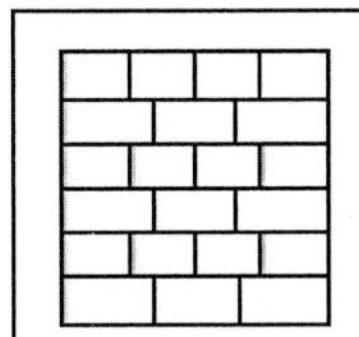

16. (d)

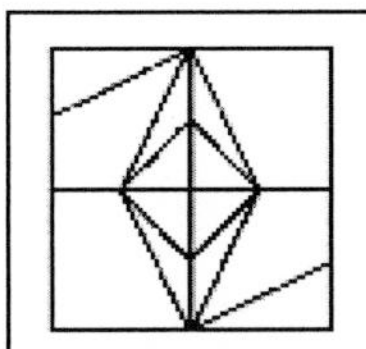

17. (a)

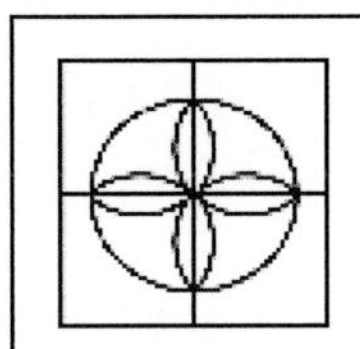

18. (c)

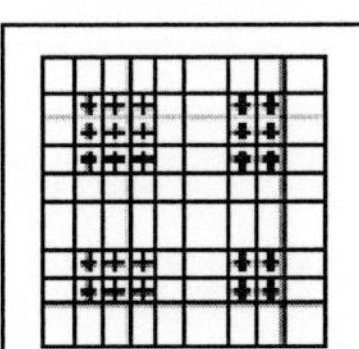

19. (d)

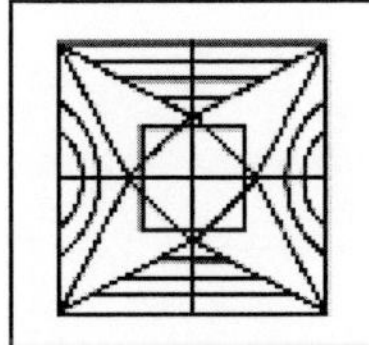

20. (c)

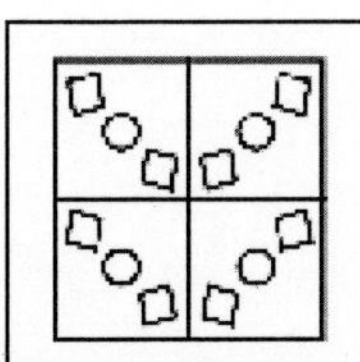

21. (b)

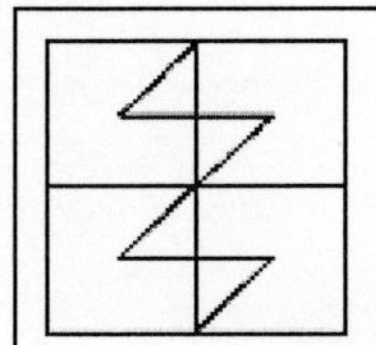

22. (c)

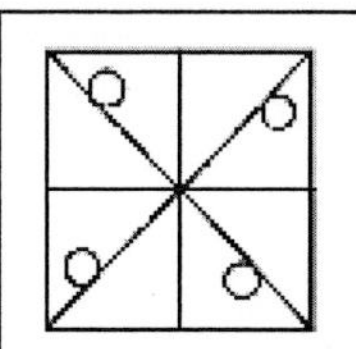

23. (b)

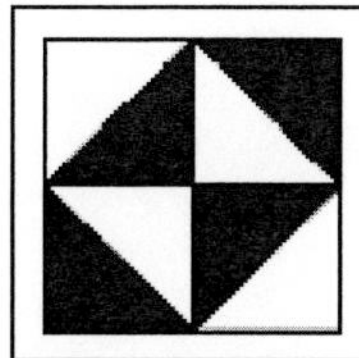

24. (c)

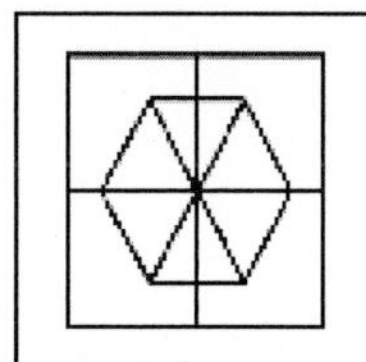

25. (d)

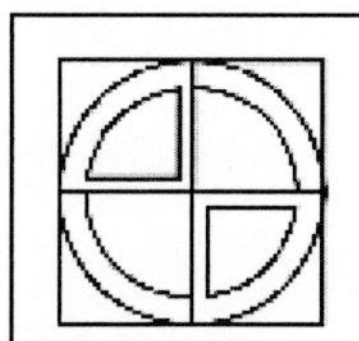

26. (c)

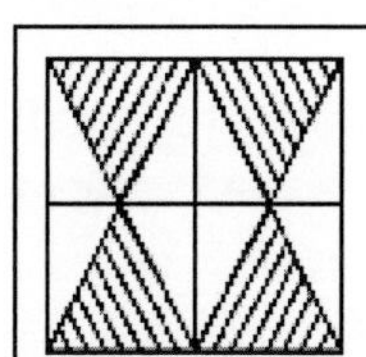

27. (c)

28. (c)

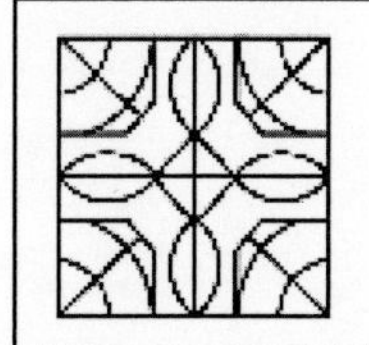

29. (b)

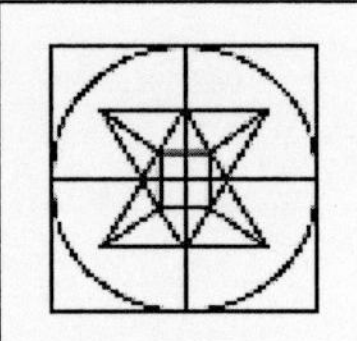

30. (c)

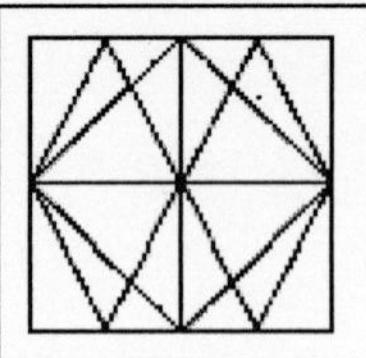

31. (b)

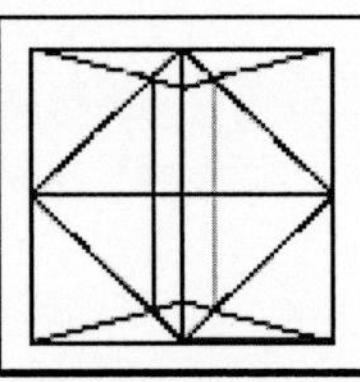

32. (d)

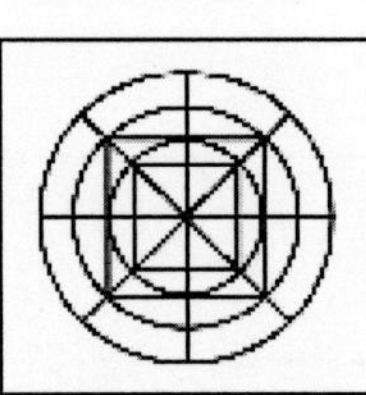

33. (c)

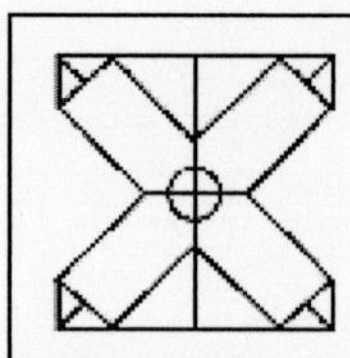

34. (c)

35. (c)

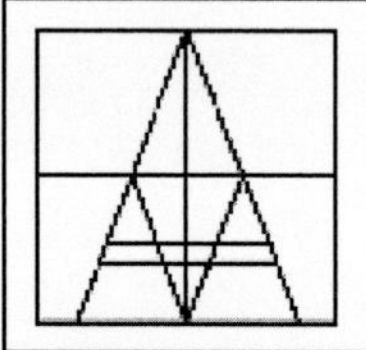

Previous Year Questions

☛ *In each of the following questions, select a figure from amongst the five alternatives, which when placed in the blank space of problem figure would complete the pattern.*

1. Identify the figure that completes the pattern.
[NTSE 2005 - UP first stage paper]

Problem Figure

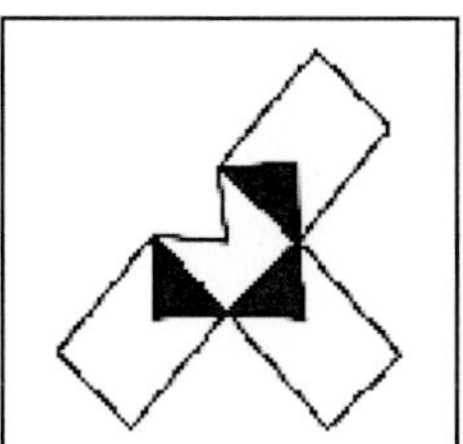

Answer Figures

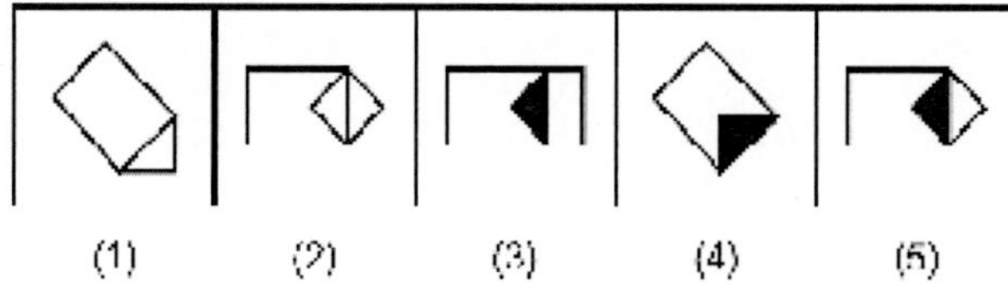

(a) 1 (b) 2
(c) 3 (d) 4
(e) 5

2. Identify the figure that completes the pattern.
[NTSE 2001 - Karnataka second stage paper]

Problem Figure

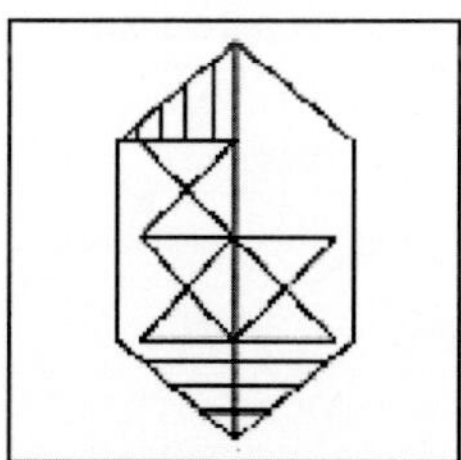

Answer Figures

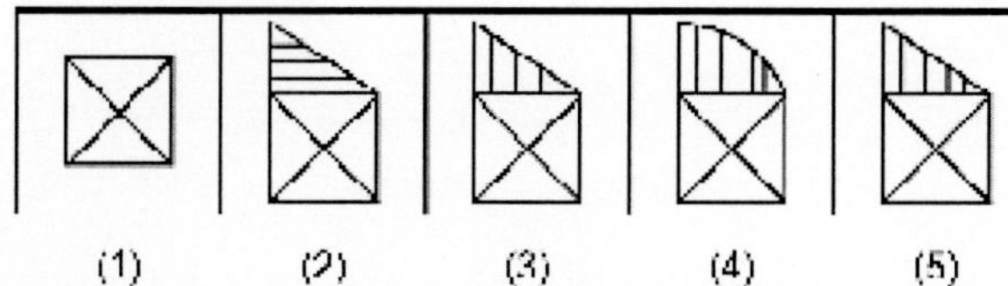

(a) 1 (b) 2
(c) 3 (d) 4
(e) 5

3. Identify the figure that completes the pattern.
[NTSE 2003 - Punjab second stage paper]

Problem Figure

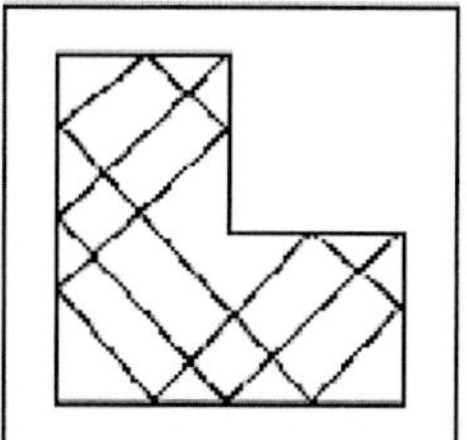

Answer Figures

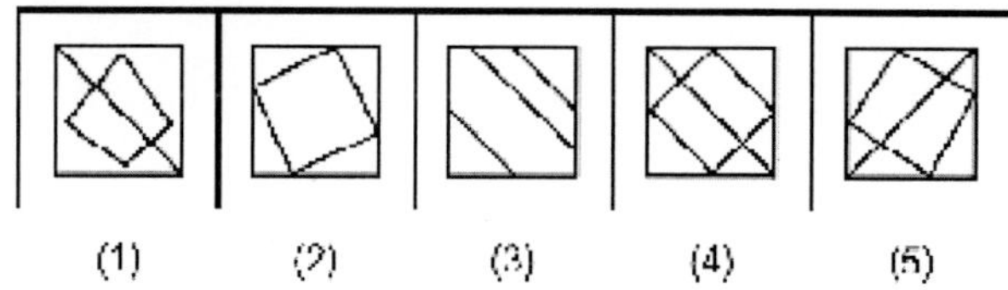

(a) 1 (b) 2
(c) 3 (d) 4
(e) 5

4. Identify the figure that completes the pattern.
[NTSE 2004 - Gujarat first stage paper]

Problem Figure

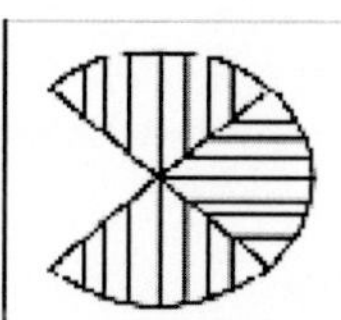

Answer Figures

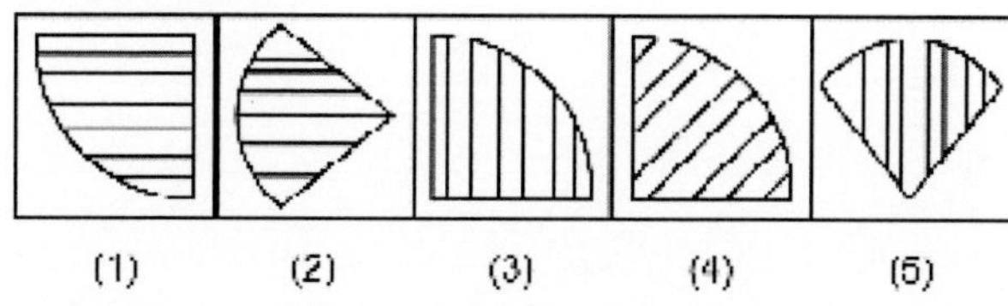

(a) 1 (b) 2
(c) 3 (d) 4
(e) 5

5. Identify the figure that completes the pattern.
[NTSE 2002 - Maharashtra second stage paper]

Problem Figure

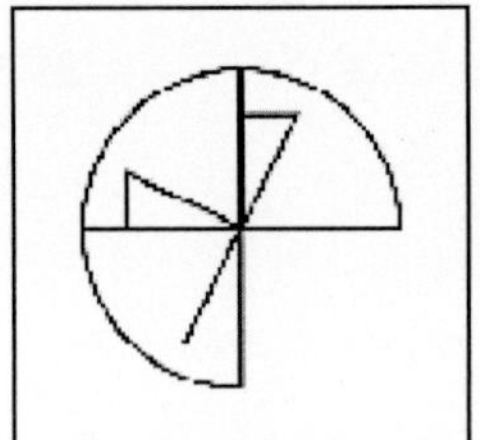

Answer Figures

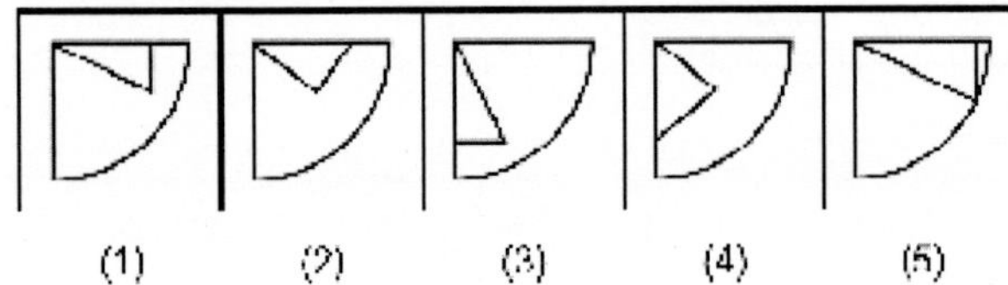

(a) 1 (b) 2
(c) 3 (d) 4
(e) 5

6. Identify the figure that completes the pattern
[NTSE 2012 - Bihar first stage paper]

Problem Figure

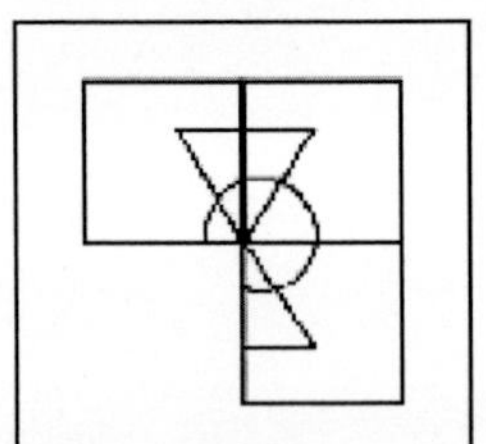

Answer Figures

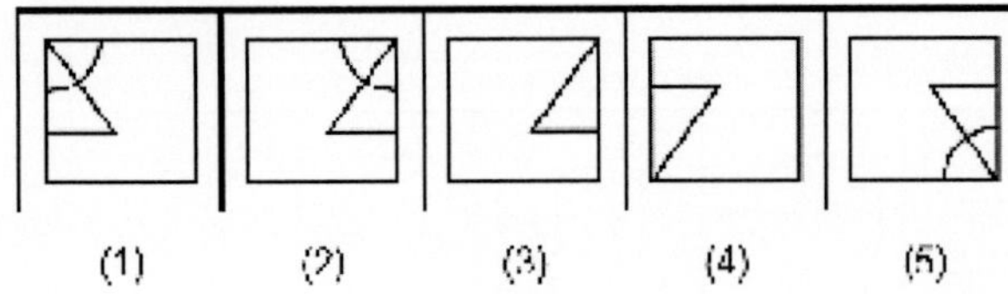

(a) 1 (b) 2
(c) 3 (d) 4
(e) 5

7. Identify the figure that completes the pattern.
[NTSE 2012 - Kerala first stage paper]

Problem Figure

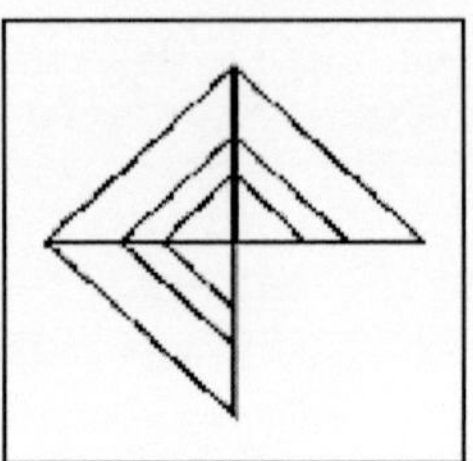

Answer Figures

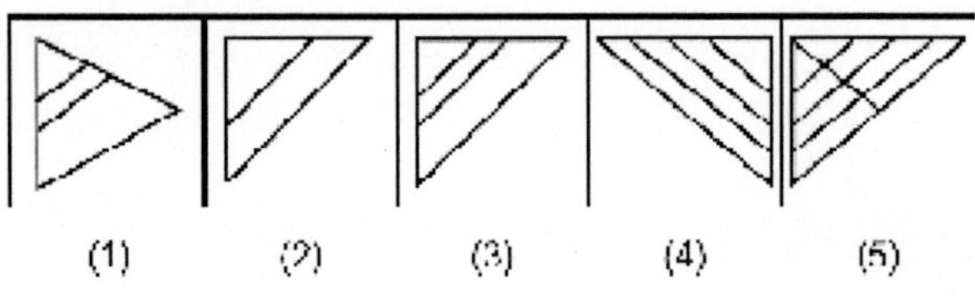

(a) 1 (b) 2
(c) 3 (d) 4
(e) 5

8. Identify the figure that completes the pattern.
[NTSE 2012 - Delhi first stage paper]

Problem Figure

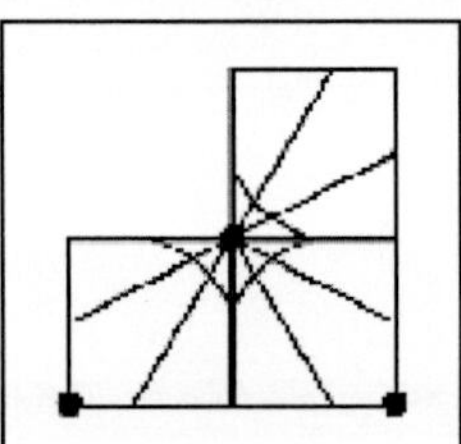

Answer Figures

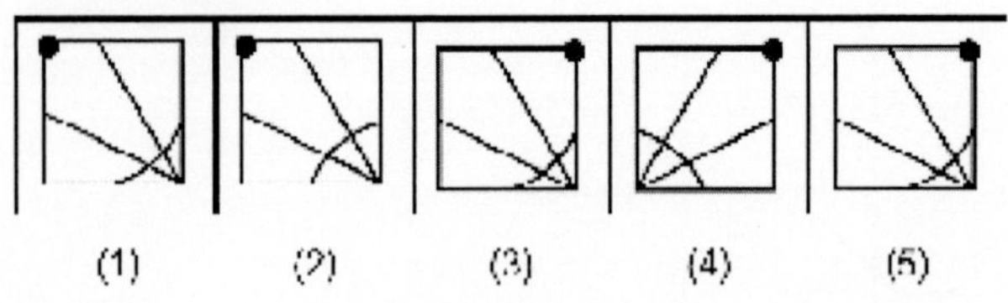

(a) 1 (b) 2
(c) 3 (d) 4
(e) 5

9. Identify the figure that completes the pattern.

[NTSE 2003 - Maharashtra second stage paper

Problem Figure

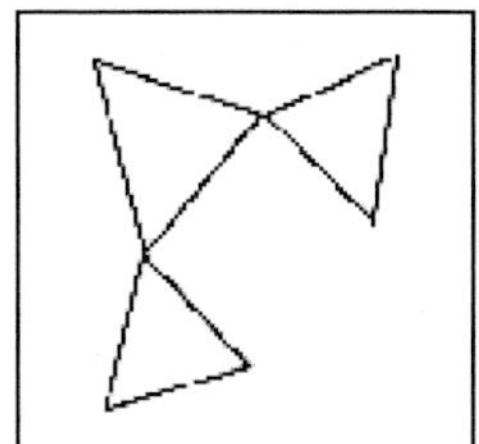

Answer Figures

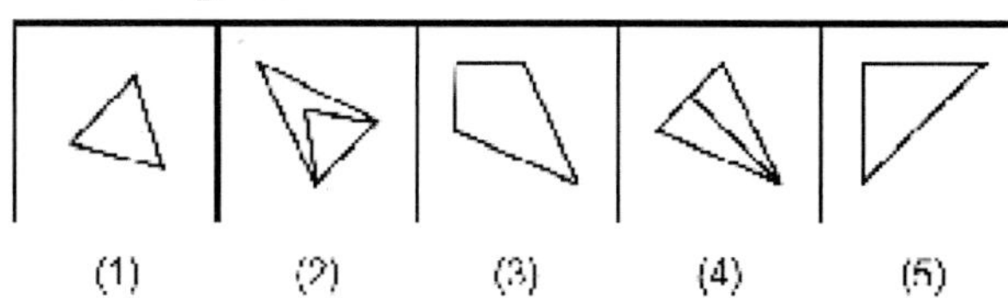

(a) 1
(b) 2
(c) 3
(d) 4
(e) 5

10. Identify the figure that completes the pattern.

[NTSE 2002 - MP second stage paper]

Problem Figure

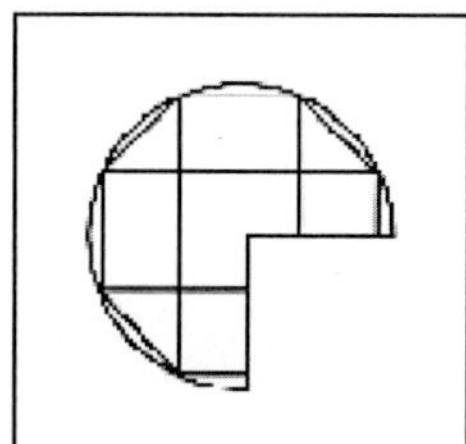

Answer Figures

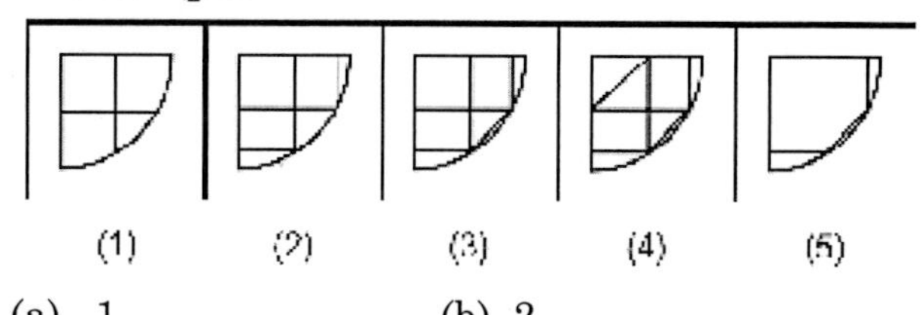

(a) 1
(b) 2
(c) 3
(d) 4
(e) 5

Answer Key

1. (e)	**2.** (e)	**3.** (d)	**4.** (b)	**5.** (a)	**6.** (b)	**7.** (c)	**8.** (a)	**9.** (a)	**10.** (c)

❐

UNIT 14

Rule Detection

In the questions based on Rule Detection, a set of figures, which obeys a particular rule and forms a series, is given. You are required to find out the set of figures that follows the particular rule.

Solved Examples

1. Choose the set of figures which follows the given rule.

Rule: Closed figure becomes more and more open.

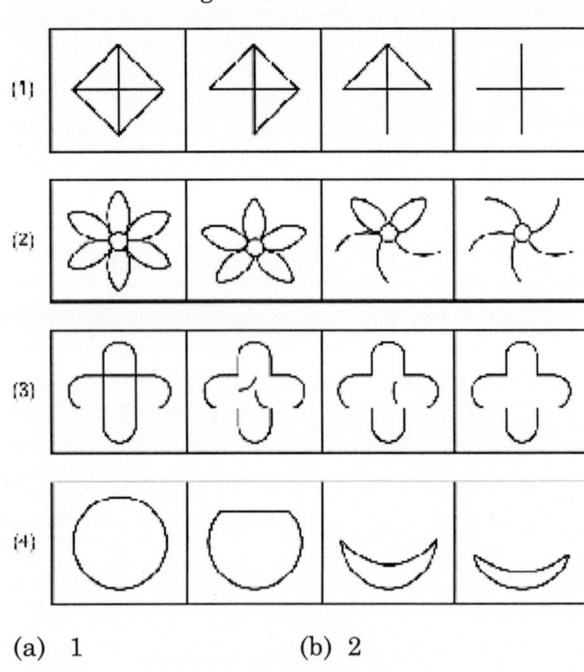

(a) 1 (b) 2
(c) 3 (d) 4

Solution: Option (a) is correct.

2. Choose the set of figures which follows the given rule.

Rule: Closed figures become more and more open and open figures become more and more close(d)

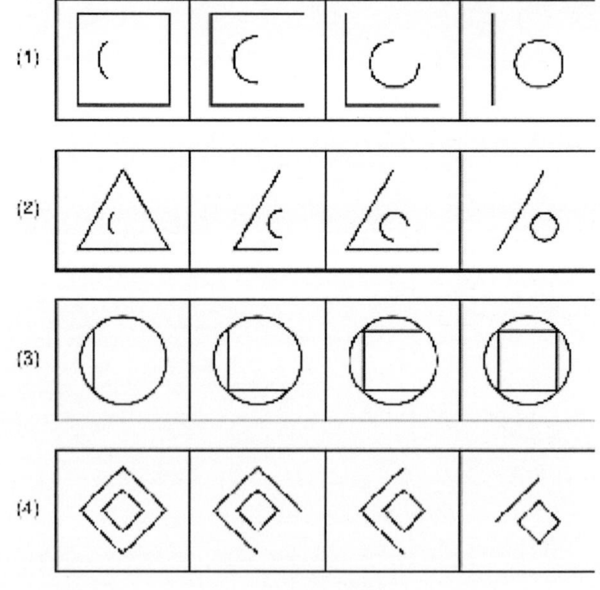

(a) 1 (b) 2
(c) 3 (d) 4

Solution: Option (a) is correct.

Multiple Choice Questions

☛ ***Direction to solve (1 to 10) :*** *In each of the following questions, choose the set of figures which follows the given rule.*

1. Choose the set of figures which follows the given rule.

   Rule: Closed figures become more and more open and open figures become more and more closed.

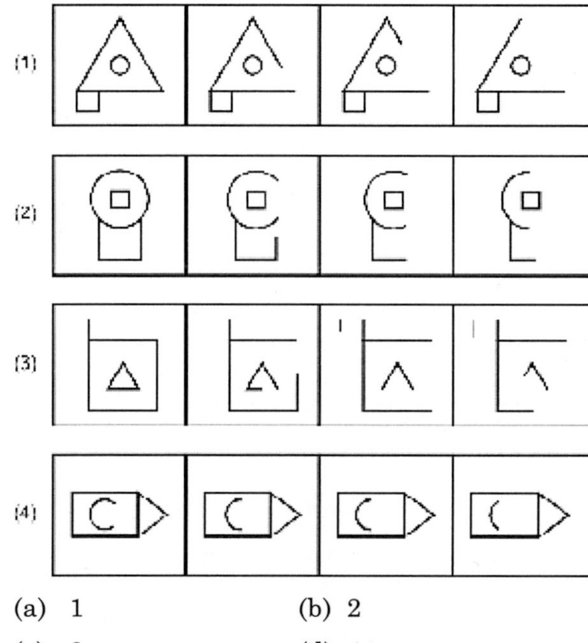

(a) 1 (b) 2
(c) 3 (d) 4

2. Choose the set of figures which follows the given rule.

   Rule: The series becomes simpler as it proceeds.

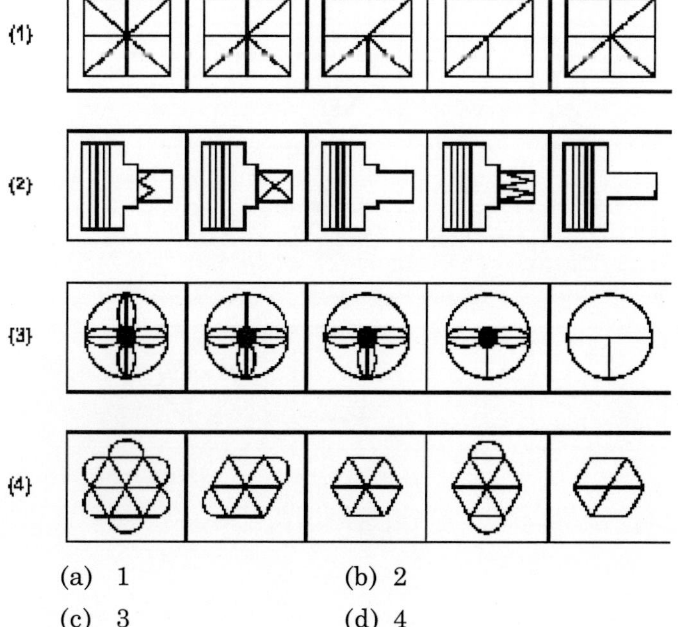

(a) 1 (b) 2
(c) 3 (d) 4

3. Choose the set of figures which follows the given rule.

   Rule: As the circle decreases in size, its sectors increase in number.

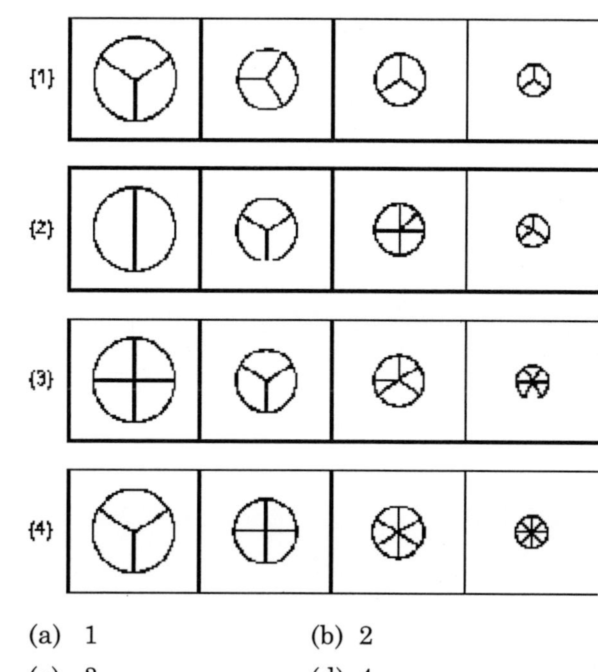

(a) 1 (b) 2
(c) 3 (d) 4

4. Choose the set of figures which follows the given rule.

   Rule: The series becomes complex as it proceeds.

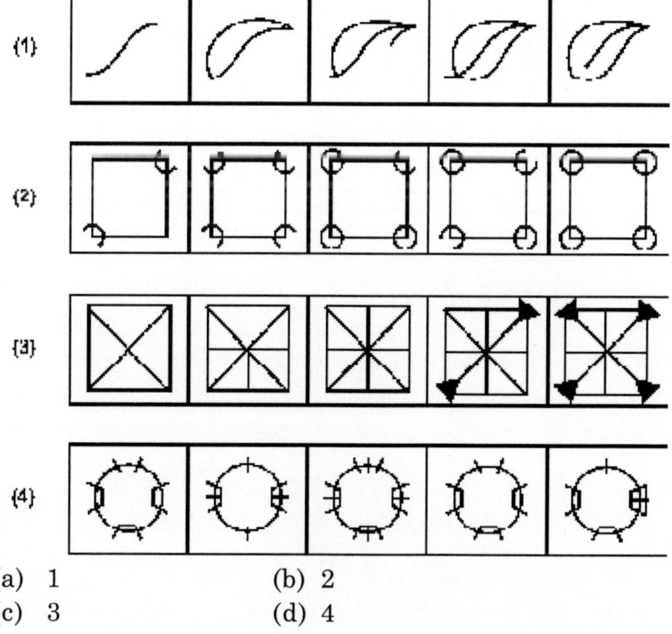

(a) 1 (b) 2
(c) 3 (d) 4

5. Choose the set of figures which follows the given rule.

Rule: Closed figures become more and more open and open figures become more and more close(d)

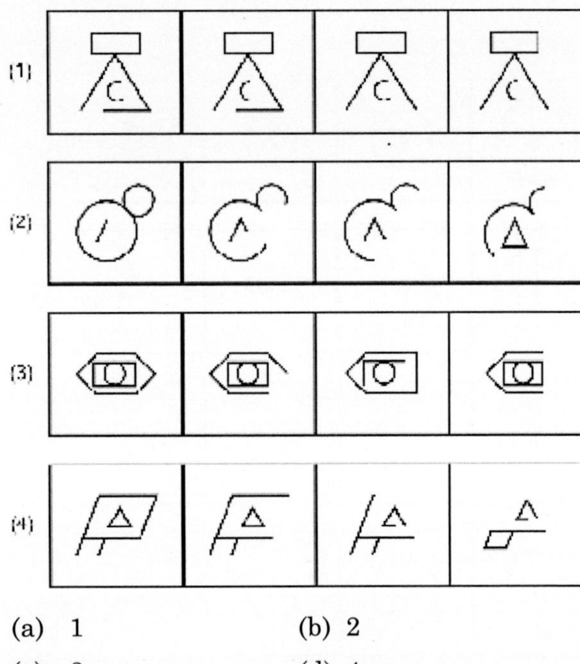

(a) 1 (b) 2

(c) 3 (d) 4

6. Choose the set of figures which follows the given rule.

Rule: Closed figures losing their sides and open figures gaining their sides.

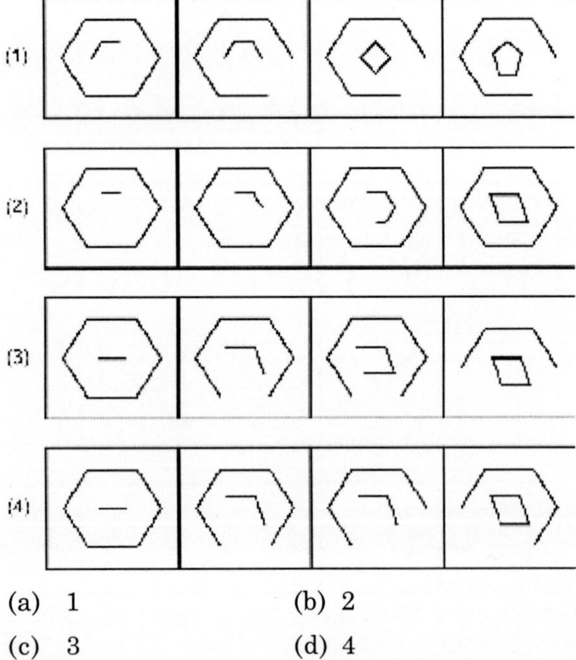

(a) 1 (b) 2

(c) 3 (d) 4

7. Choose the set of figures which follows the given rule.

Rule: Any figure can be traced by a single unbroken line without retracting.

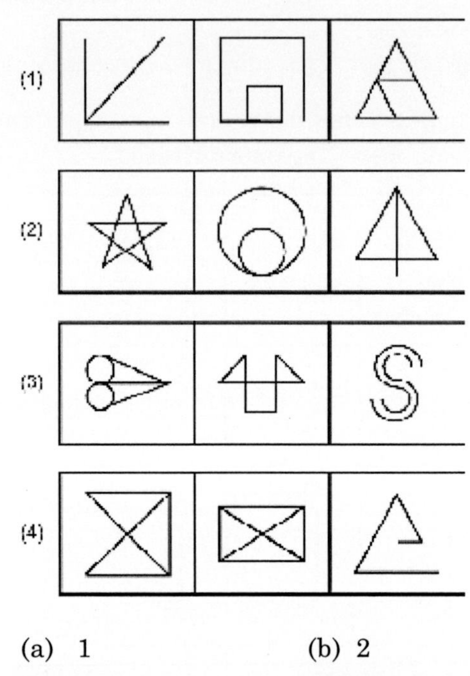

(a) 1 (b) 2

(c) 3 (d) 4

8. Choose the set of figures which follows the given rule.

Rule: Closed figures gradually become open and open figures gradually become close(d)

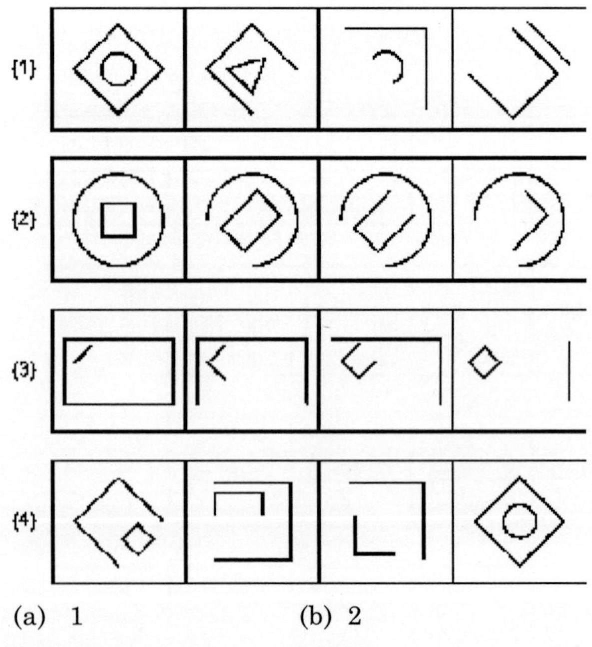

(a) 1 (b) 2

(c) 3 (d) 4

9. Choose the set of figures which follows the given rule.

Rule: Closed figures become more and more open and open figures become more and more close(d)

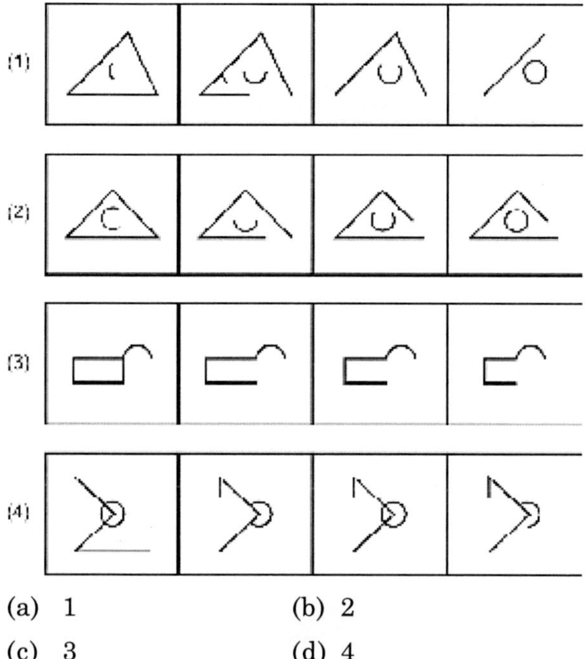

(a) 1 (b) 2

(c) 3 (d) 4

10. Choose the set of figures which follows the given rule.

Rule: The series becomes complex as it proceeds.

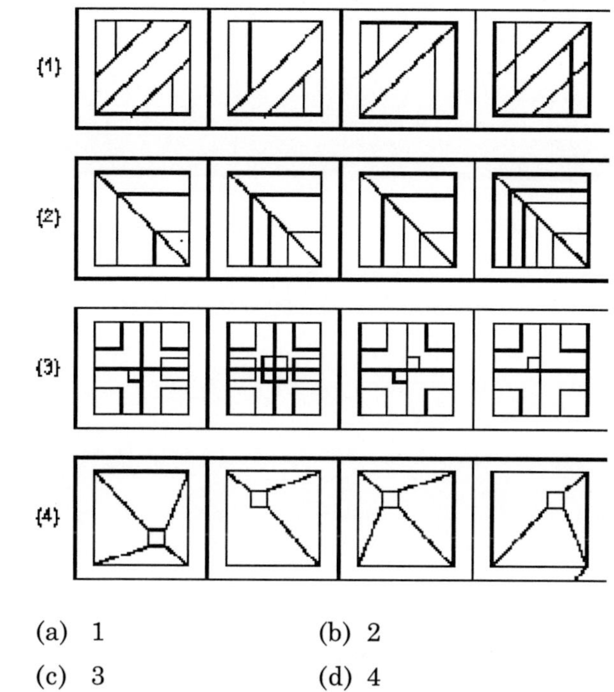

(a) 1 (b) 2

(c) 3 (d) 4

Answer Key

1. (c)	**2.** (c)	**3.** (d)	**4.** (c)	**5.** (b)	**6.** (c)	**7.** (b)	**8.** (c)	**9.** (a)	**10.** (b)

UNIT 15

Analytical Reasoning

Analytical Reasoning involves problems related to the counting of geometrical plane figures in a complex figure. The systemic method for finding the number of any particular type of elements like straight lines, triangles, squares, rectangles etc. is to start searching from smaller components to bigger components in the complex figure.

Steps for Finding A Figure

The steps involved in the analysis of the complex figure would be clear from the following examples:

Solved Examples

1. Find the number of triangles in the given figure.

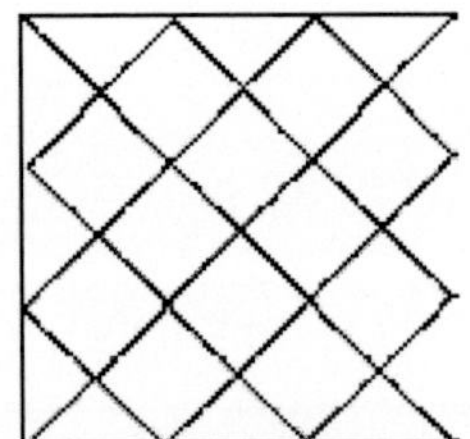

(a) 28 (b) 32
(c) 36 (d) 40

Solution: Option (c) is correct.

Explanation: The figure may be labelled as shown below.

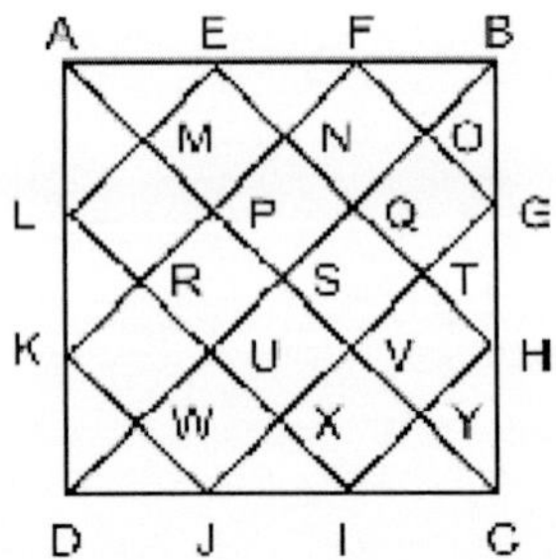

The simplest triangles are AML, LRK, KWD, DWJ, JXI, IYC, CYH, HTG, GOB, BOF, FNE and EMA i.e. 12 in number.

The triangles composed of two components each are AEL, KDJ, HIC and FBG i.e. 4 in number.

The triangles composed of three components each are APF, EQB, BQH, GVC, CVJ, IUD, DUL and KPA i.e. 8 in number.

The triangles composed of six components each are ASB, BSG, CSD, DSA, AKF, EBH, GGJ and IDL i.e. 8 in number.

The triangles composed of twelve components each are ADB, ABC, BCD and CDA i.e. 4 in number.

Total number of triangles in the figure = 12 + 4 + 8 + 8 + 4 = 36.

2. What is the number of triangles that can be formed whose vertices are the vertices of an octagon but have only one side common with that of octagon?

(a) 64 (b) 32
(c) 24 (d) 16

Solution: Option (b) is correct.

Explanation:

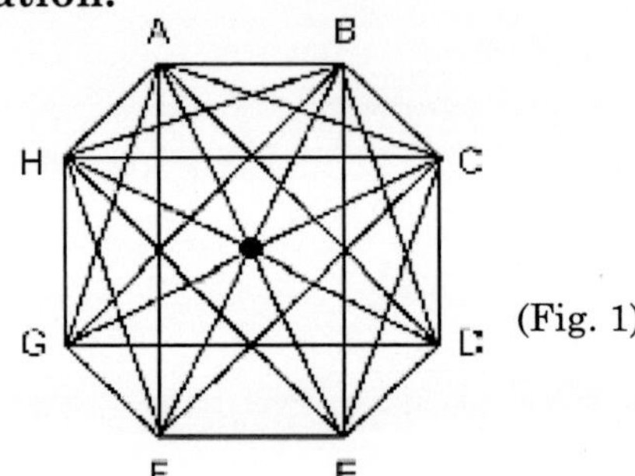

(Fig. 1)

When the triangles are drawn in an octagon with vertices same as those of the octagon and have one side common to that of the octagon, the figure will appear as shown in (Fig. 1).

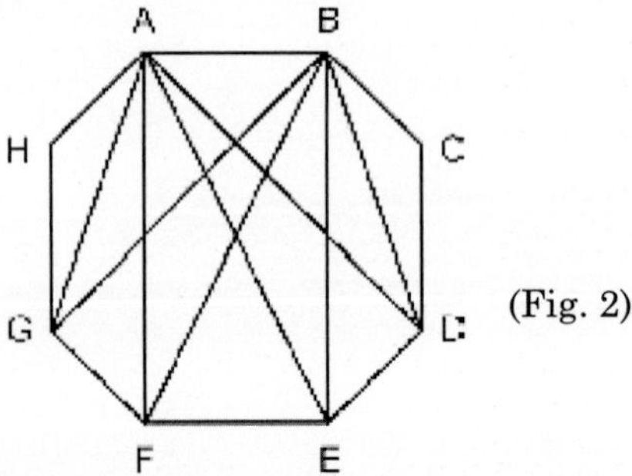

(Fig. 2)

Now, we shall first consider the triangles having only one side AB common with octagon ABCDEFGH, and having vertices common with the octagon (See Fig. 2). Such triangles are ABD, ABE, ABF and ABG i.e. 4 in number.

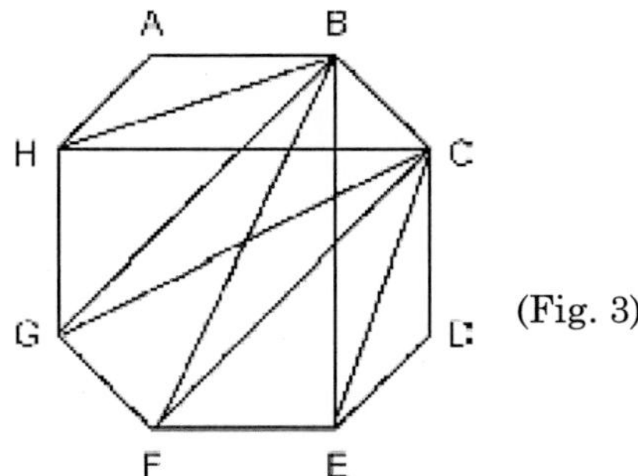

(Fig. 3)

Similarly, the triangles having only one side BC common with the octagon and also having vertices common with the octagon are BCE, BCF, BCG and BCH (as shown in Fig. 3). i.e. There are 4 such triangles.

This way, we have 4 triangles for each side of the octagon. Thus, there are 8 × 4 = 32 such triangles.

3. Find the number of triangles in the given figure.

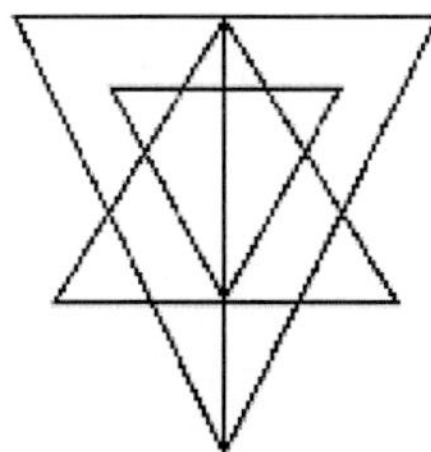

(a) 27 (b) 25
(c) 23 (d) 21

Solution: Option (a) is correct.

Explanation: The figure may be labelled as shown below.

The simplest triangles are GLK, DLJ, DJM, HMN, QRE, IRA, IPA and FPO i.e. 8 in number.

The triangles having two components each are BDO, CDQ, DLM, PRA, KFI, NEI, HJI, GJI, DKI and DNI i.e. 10 in number.

The triangles having four components each are DIE, DFI, DOA, DQA and GHI i.e. 5 in number.

The triangles having six components each are DCA and DBA i.e. 2 in number.

DEF is the only triangle having eight components.

ABC is the only triangle having twelve components.

Thus, there are 8 + 10 + 5 + 2 + 1 + 1 = 27 triangles in the figure.

4. Count the number of parallelogram in the given figure.

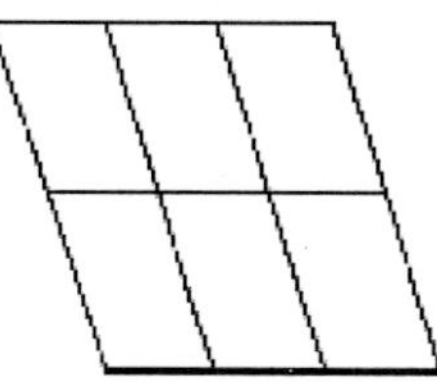

(a) 20 (b) 18
(v) 16 (d) 12

Solution: Option (b) is correct.

Explanation: The figure may be labelled as shown below.

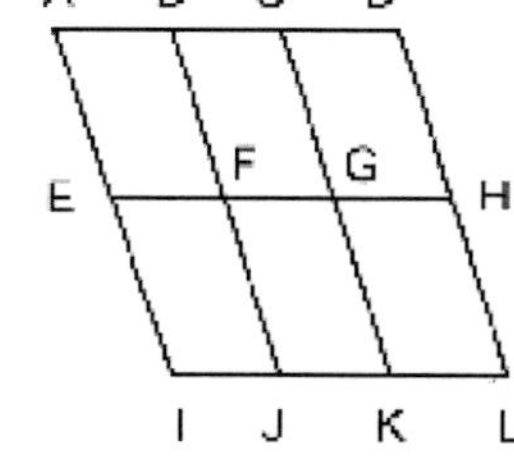

The simplest Parallelograms are ABFE, BCGF, CDHG, EFJI, FGKJ and GHLK. These are 6 in number.

The parallelograms composed of two components each are ACGE, BDHF, EGKI, FHLJ, ABJI, BCKJ and CDLK. Thus, there are 7 such parallelograms.

The parallelograms composed of three components each are ADHE and EHLI i.e. 2 in number.

The parallelograms composed of four components each are ACKI and BDLJ i.e. 2 in number

There is only one parallelogram composed of six components, namely ADLI.

Thus, there are 6 + 7 + 2 + 2 + 1 = 18 parallelograms in the figure.

5. How many triangles and parallelograms are there in the following figure?

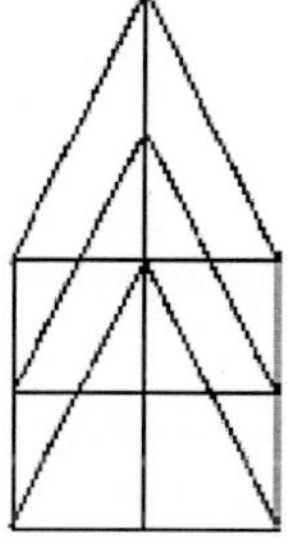

(a) 21, 17 (b) 19, 13
(c) 21, 15 (d) 19, 17

Solution: Option (a) is correct.

Explanation: The figure may be labelled as shown below.

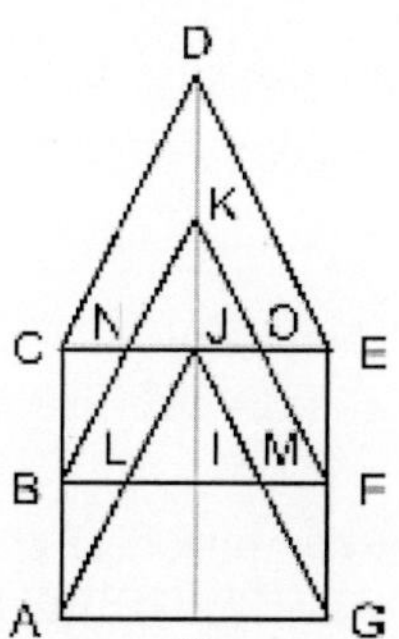

Triangles: The simplest triangles are KJN, KJO, CNB, OEF, JIL, JIM, BLA and MFG i.e. 8 in number.

The triangles composed of two components each are CDJ, EDJ, NKO, JLM, JAH and JGH i.e. 6 in number.

The triangles composed of three components each are BKI, FKI, CJA and EJG i.e. 4 in number.

The triangles composed of four components each are CDE and AJG i.e. 2 in number.

The only triangle composed of six components is BKF.

Thus, there are 8 + 6 + 4 + 2 + 1 = 21 triangles in the given figure.

Parallelograms: The simplest parallelograms are NJLB and JOFM i.e. 2 in number.

The parallelograms composed of two components each are CDKB, DEFK, BIHA and IFGH i.e. 4 in number.

The parallelograms composed of three components each are BKJA, KFGJ, CJIB and JEFI i.e.4 in number.

There is only one parallelogram i.e. BFGA composed of four components.

The parallelograms composed of five components each are CDJA, DEGJ, CJHA and JEGH i.e. 4 in number.

The only parallelogram composed of six components is CEFB.

The only parallelogram composed of ten components is CEGA.

Thus, there are 2 + 4 + 4 + 1 + 4 + 1 + 1 = 17 parallelograms in the given figure.

(Note that the squares and rectangles are also counted amongst the parallelograms).

6. Count the number of parallelograms in the given figure.

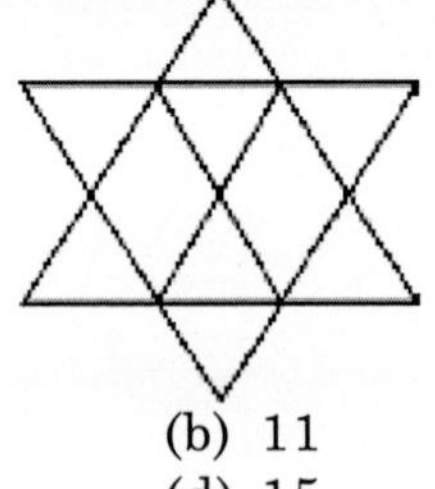

(a) 8 (b) 11
(c) 12 (d) 15

Solution: Option (d) is correct.

Explanation: The figure may be labelled as shown below.

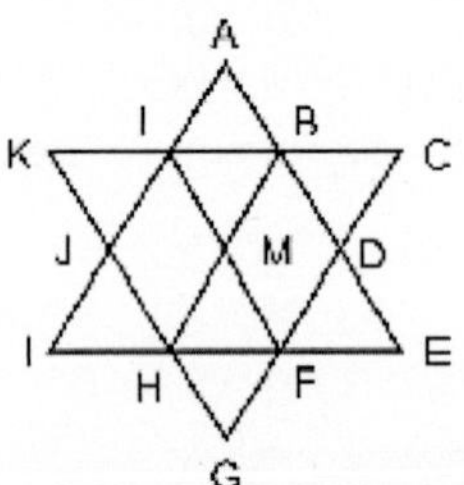

The simplest parallelograms are LMHJ and BDFM i.e. 2 in number. The parallelograms composed of two components each are ABML and MFGH i.e. 2 in number.

The parallelograms composed of three components each are LBHI, LBEF, BDGH, DFLA, BCFH, KLFH, A6HJ and LFGJ i.e. 8 in number.

The parallelograms composed of six components each are LCFI, KBEH and ADGJ i.e. 3 in number.

Total number of parallelograms in the figure
= 2 + 2 + 8 + 3 = 15

7. Count the number of pentagons in the adjoining figure.

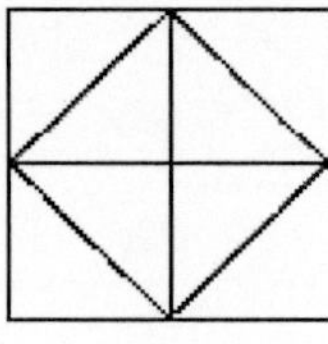

(a) 16 (b) 12
(c) 8 (d) 4

Solution: Option (b) is correct.

Explanation: The figure may be labelled as shown below.

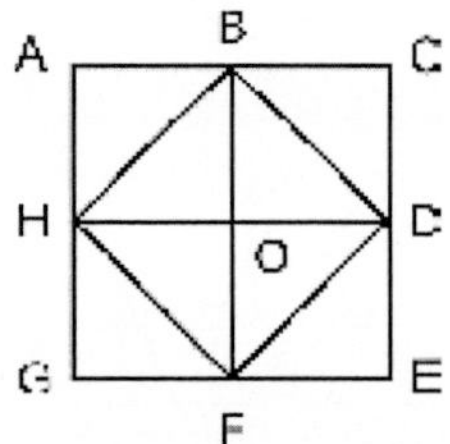

The pentagons in the figure are ABDFH, CDFHB, EFHBD, GHBDF, ACDFG, CEFHA, EGHBC, GABDE, BDEGH, DFGAB, FHACD and HBCEF. Thus, there are 12 pentagons in the figure.

8. Find the number of triangles in the given figure.

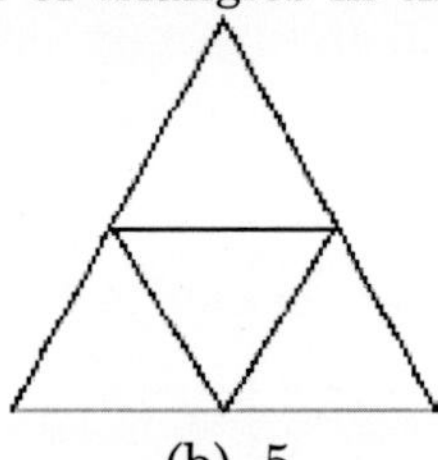

(a) 4 (b) 5
(c) 6 (d) 7

Solution: Option (b) is correct.

Explanation: The figure may be labelled as shown below.

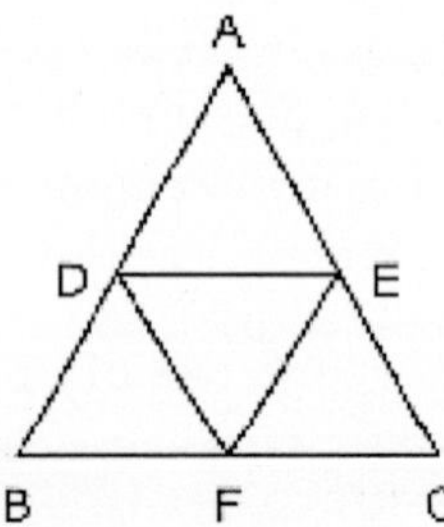

The simplest triangles are ADE, BDF, DEF and EFC i.e. 4 in number.

There is only one triangle ABC composed of four components.

Thus, there are 4 + 1 = 5 triangles in the given figure.

Multiple Choice Questions

1. Find the number of triangles in the given figure.

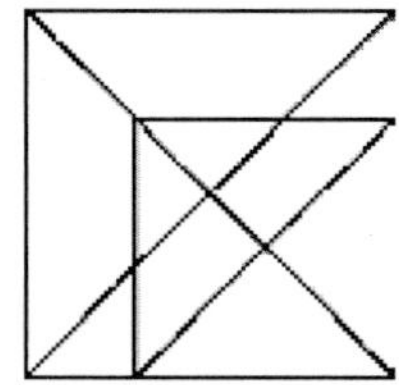

(a) 16 (b) 18
(c) 19 (d) 21

2. Find the number of triangles in the given figure.

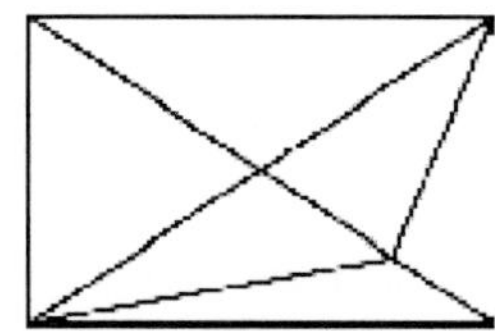

(a) 11 (b) 13
(c) 15 (d) 17

3. Find the number of triangles in the given figure.

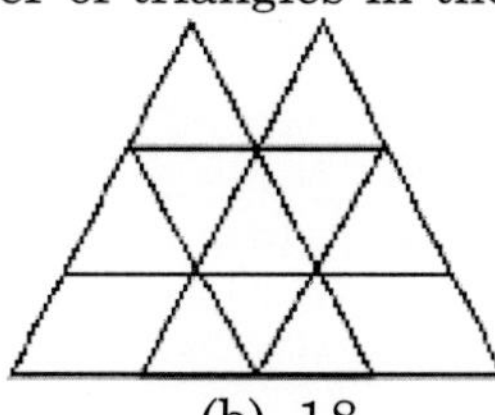

(a) 16 (b) 18
(c) 14 (d) 15

4. Find the number of triangles in the given figure.

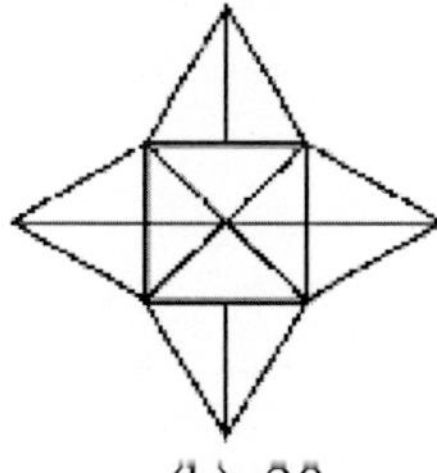

(a) 18 (b) 20
(c) 28 (d) 34

5. Find the number of triangles in the given figure.

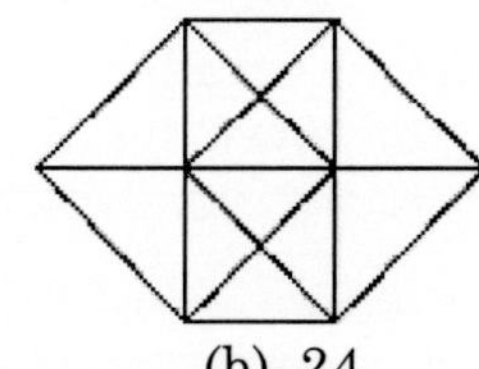

(a) 20 (b) 24
(c) 28 (d) 32

6. Find the minimum number of straight lines required to make the given figure.

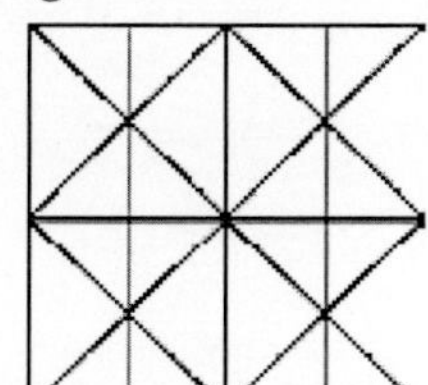

(a) 11 (b) 14
(c) 16 (d) 17

7. What is the number of straight lines and the number of triangles in the given figure?

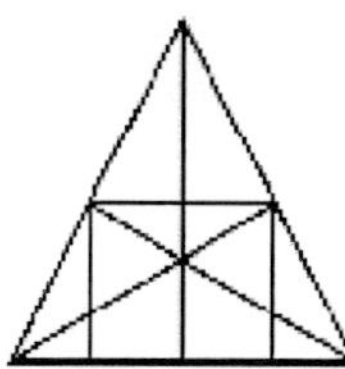

(a) 10 straight lines and 34 triangles
(b) 9 straight lines and 34 triangles
(c) 9 straight lines and 36 triangles
(d) 10 straight lines and 36 triangles

8. Find the number of triangles in the given figure.

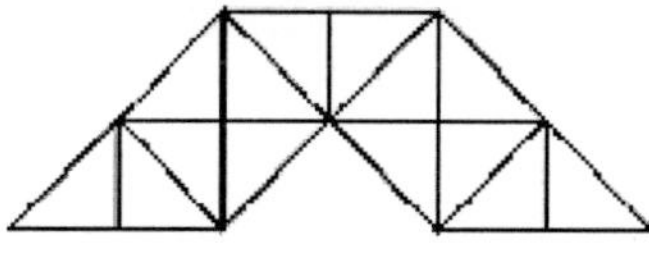

(a) 23 (b) 27
(c) 29 (d) 31

9. Find the number of triangles in the given figure.

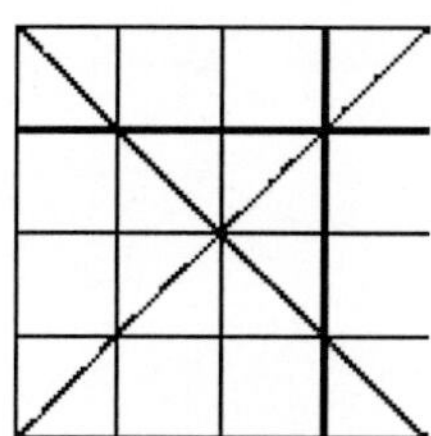

(a) 36 (b) 40
(c) 44 (d) 48

10. Find the number of triangles in the given figure.

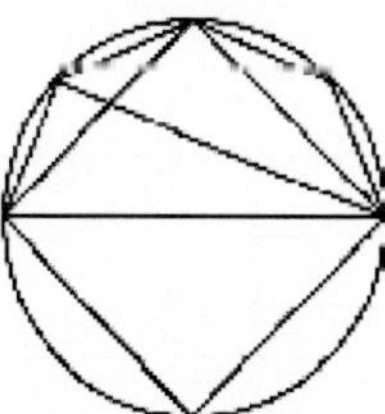

(a) 8 (b) 10
(c) 11 (d) 12

11. Find the number of triangles in the given figure.

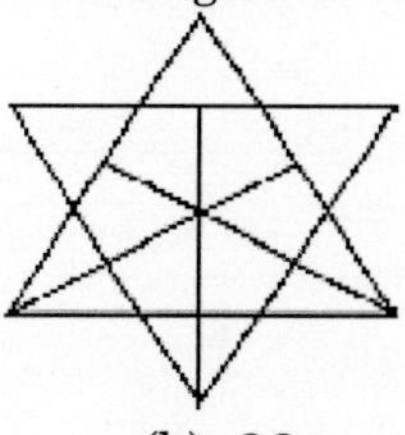

(a) 21 (b) 23
(c) 25 (d) 27

12. Find the number of triangles in the given figure.

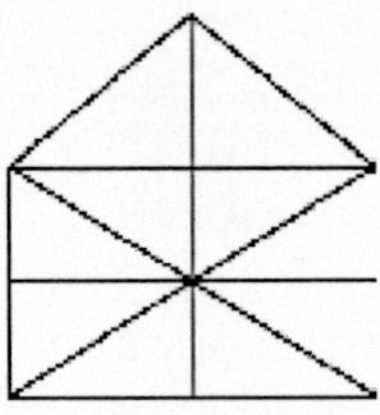

(a) 10 (b) 19
(c) 21 (d) 23

13. Find the minimum number of straight lines required to make the given figure.

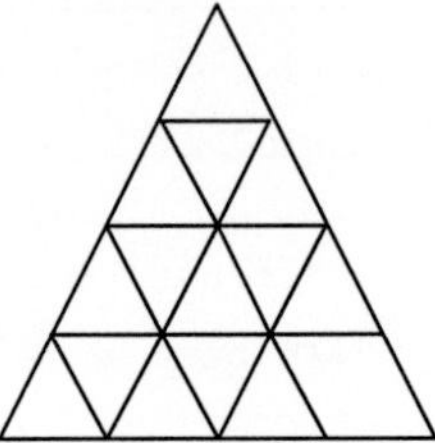

(a) 9 (b) 11
(c) 15 (d) 16

14. Find the number of triangles in the given figure.

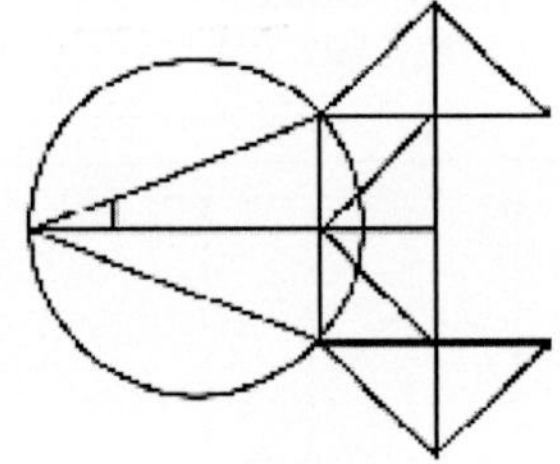

(a) 10 (b) 12
(c) 14 (d) 16

15. Find the minimum number of straight lines required to make the given figure.

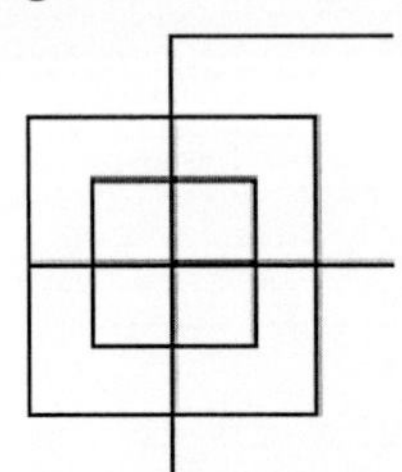

(a) 13 (b) 15
(c) 17 (d) 19

16. Find the number of triangles in the given figure.

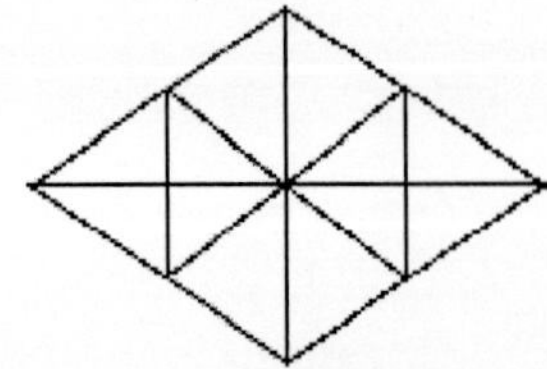

(a) 16 (b) 22
(c) 28 (d) 32

17. Find the number of triangles in the given figure.

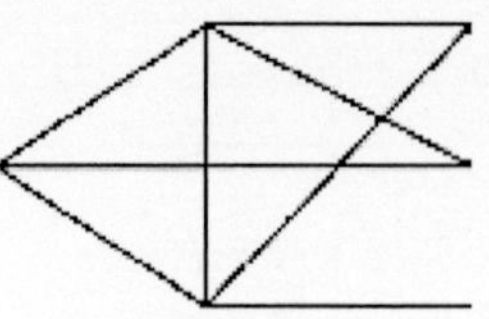

(a) 12 (b) 13
(c) 14 (d) 15

18. Find the number of quadrilaterals in the given figure.

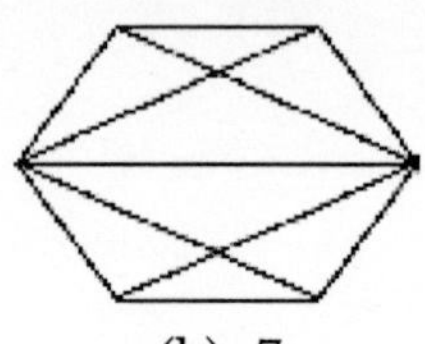

(a) 6 (b) 7
(c) 9 (d) 11

19. Count the number of squares in the given figure.

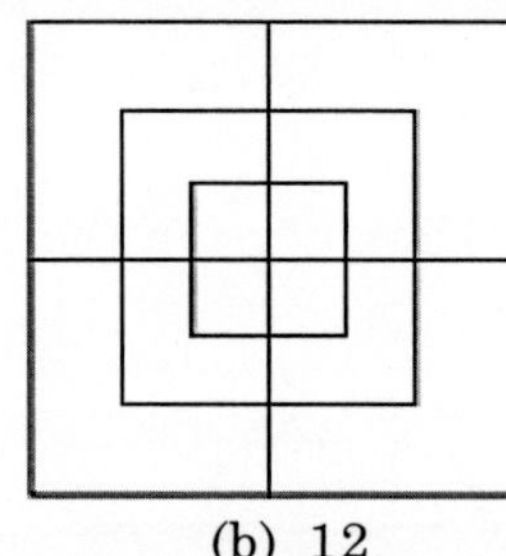

(a) 8 (b) 12
(c) 15 (d) 18

20. What is the minimum number of colours required to fill the spaces in the given diagram without any two adjacent spaces having the same colour?

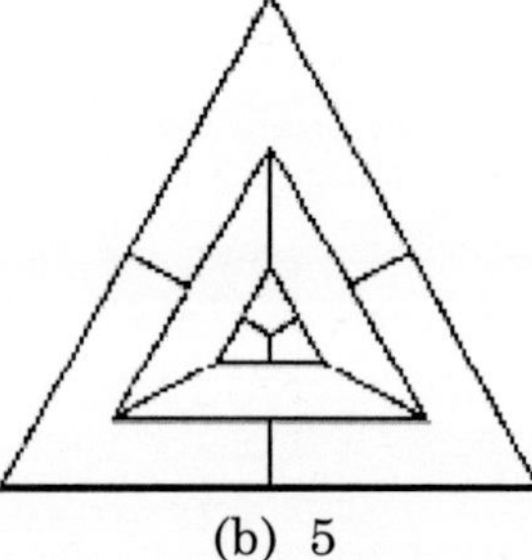

(a) 6 (b) 5
(c) 4 (d) 3

21. What is the minimum number of different colours required to paint the given figure such that no two adjacent regions have the same colour?

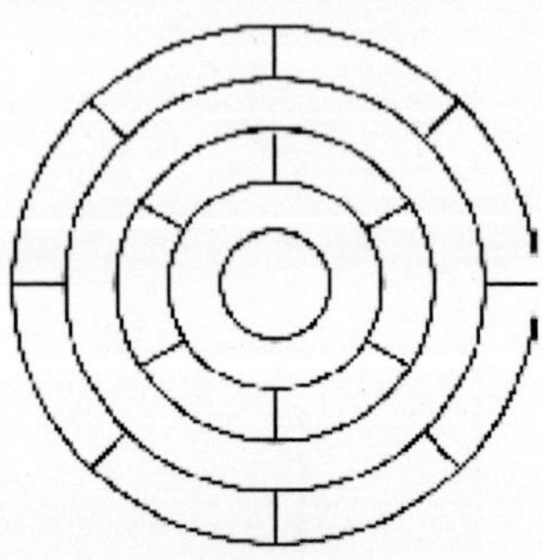

(a) 3 (b) 4
(c) 5 (d) 6

22. In the adjoining figure, if the centres of all the circles are joined by horizontal and vertical lines, then find the number of squares that can be formed.

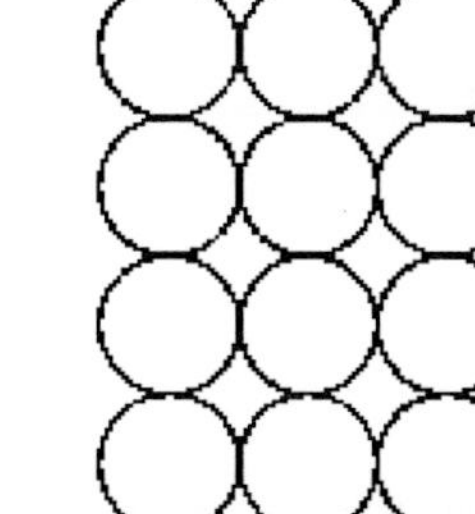

(a) 6 (b) 7
(c) 8 (d) 1

23. Count the number of triangles and squares in the given figure.

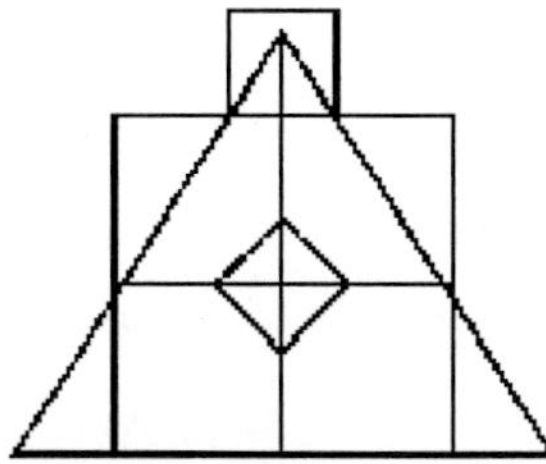

(a) 21 triangles, 7 squares
(b) 18 triangles, 8 squares
(c) 20 triangles, 8 squares
(d) 22 triangles, 7 squares

24. Count the number of squares in the given figure.

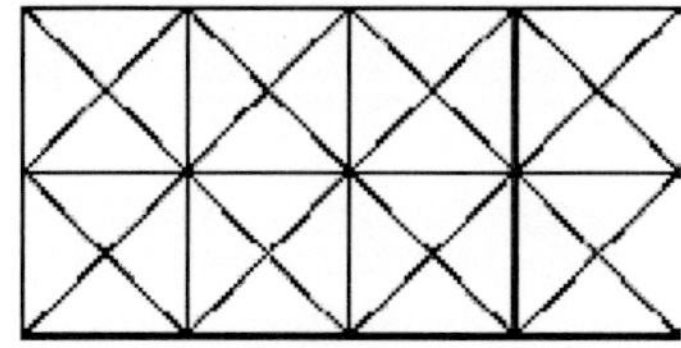

(a) 11 (b) 21
(c) 24 (d) 26

25. Count the number of squares in the given figure.

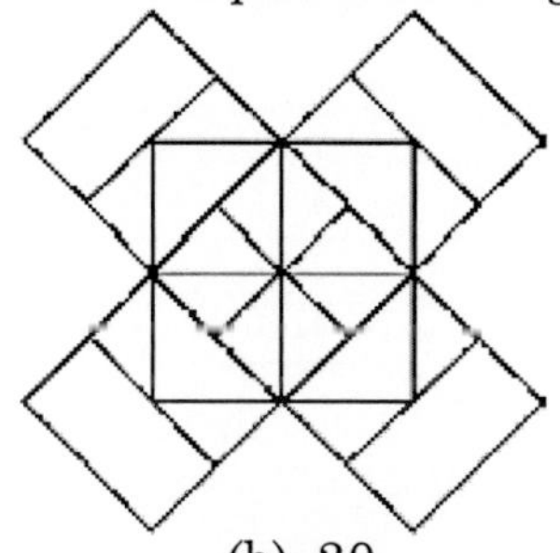

(a) 22 (b) 20
(c) 18 (d) 14

26. Count the number of rectangles in the given figure.

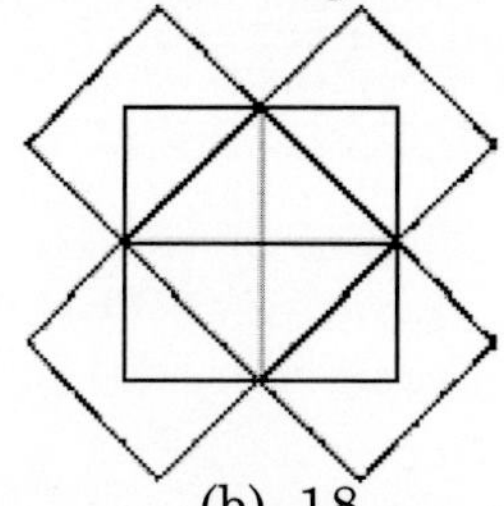

(a) 20 (b) 18
(c) 16 (d) 15

27. Count the number of parallelograms in the given figure.

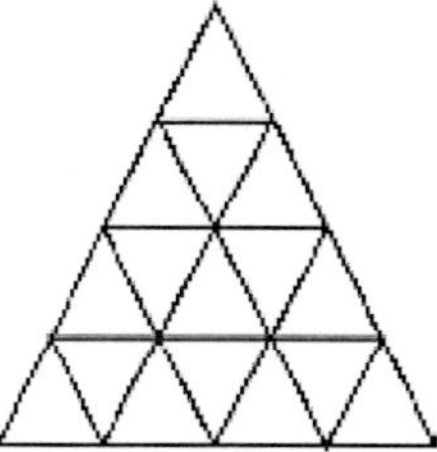

(a) 47 (b) 45
(c) 41 (d) 39

28. What is the minimum number of straight lines that is needed to construct the figure?

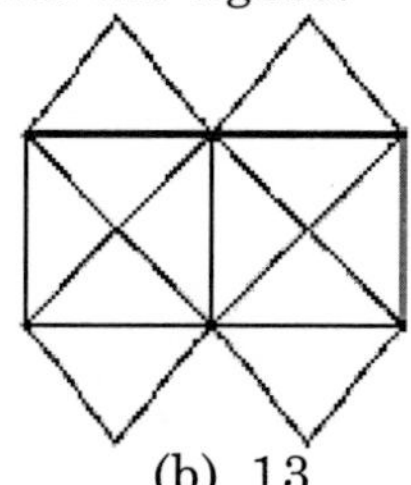

(a) 11 (b) 13
(c) 15 (d) 21

29. Determine the number of rectangles and hexagons in the given figure.

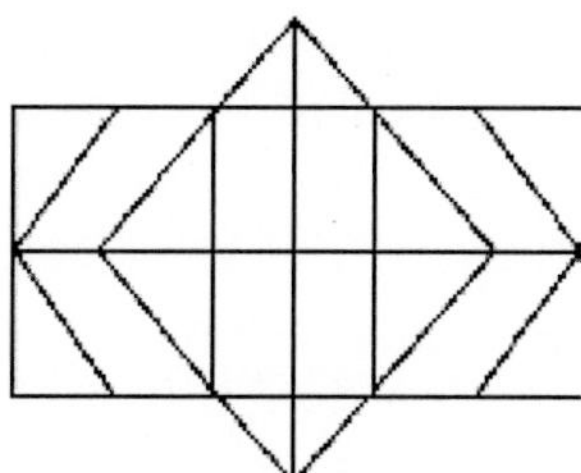

(a) 30, 5 (b) 32, 3
(c) 28, 5 (d) 30, 3

30. Count the number of triangles and squares in the given figure.

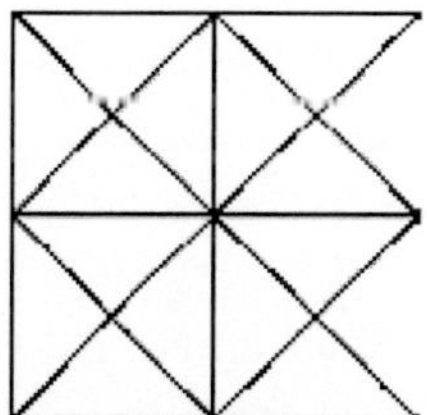

(a) 44 triangles, 10 squares
(b) 14 triangles, 16 squares
(c) 27 triangles, 6 squares
(d) 36 triangles, 9 squares

❐

Answer Key

1. (d)	2. (c)	3. (b)	4. (c)	5. (c)	6. (b)	7. (c)	8. (c)	9. (d)	10. (b)
11. (d)	12. (c)	13. (b)	14. (c)	15. (a)	16. (c)	17. (d)	18. (d)	19. (c)	20. (d)
21. (a)	22. (c)	23. (a)	24. (c)	25. (c)	26. (a)	27. (b)	28. (b)	29. (a)	30. (a)

Explanatory Notes

1. (d)
The figure may be labelled as shown below.

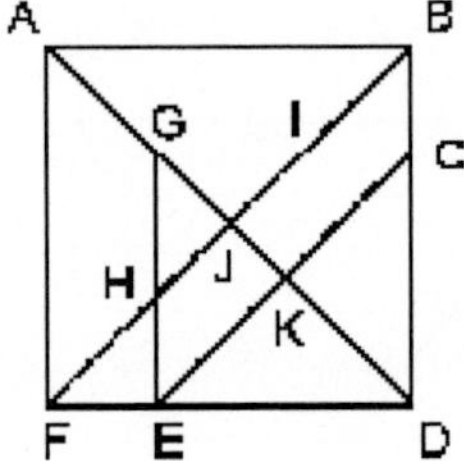

The simplest triangles are EFH, BIC, GHJ, GIJ, EKD and CKD i.e. 6 in number.

The triangles composed of two components each are ABJ, AFJ, GCK, GEK, CED arid GHI i.e. 6 in number.

The triangles composed of three components each are GCD, GED, DJB and DJF i.e. 4 in number.

The triangles composed of four components each are ABF and GCE i.e. 2 in number.

The triangles composed of five components each are ABD and AFD i.e. 2 in number.

There is only one triangle i.e. FBD composed of six components.

Total number of triangles in the figure
= 6 + 6 + 4 + 2 + 2 + 1 = 21

2. (c)
The figure may be labelled as shown below.

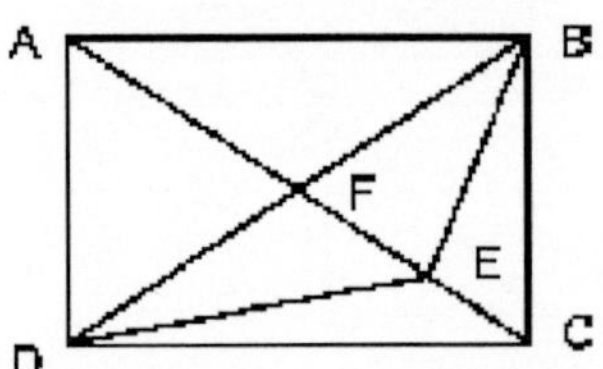

The simplest triangles are AFB, FEB, EBC, DEC, DFE and AFD i.e. 6 in number.

The triangles composed of two components each are AEB, FBC, DFC, ADE, DBE and ABD i.e. 6 in number.

The triangles composed of three components each are ADC and ABC i.e. 2 in number.

There is only one triangle i.e. DBC which is composed of four components.

Thus, there are 6 + 6 + 2 + 1 = 15 triangles in the figure.

3. (b)
The figure may be labelled as shown below.

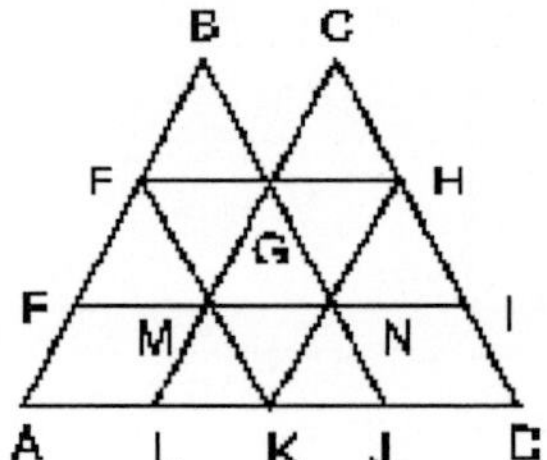

The simplest triangles are BFG, CGH, EFM, FMG, GMN, GHN, HNI, LMK, MNK and KNJ i.e. 10 in number.

The triangles composed of three components each are FAK and HKD i.e. 2 in number.

The triangles composed of four components each are BEN, CMI, GLJ and FHK i.e. 4 in number.

The triangles composed of eight components each are BAJ and OLD i.e. 2 in number.

Thus, there are 10 + 2 + 4 + 2 = 18 triangles in the given figure.

4. (c)
The figure may be labelled as shown below.

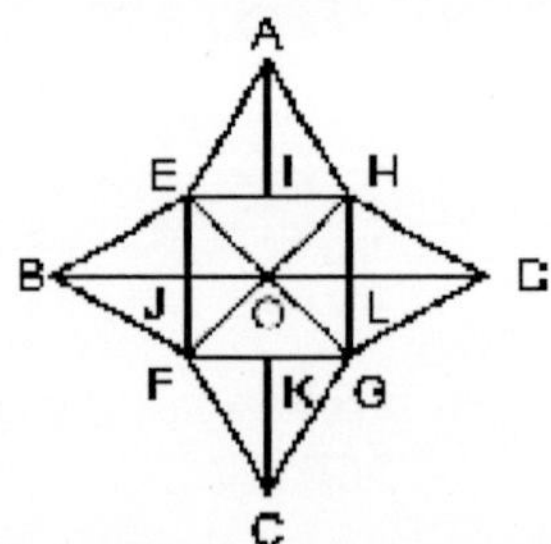

The simplest triangles are AEI, AIH, BEJ, BJF, CFK, CKG, DGL, DLH, EOJ, FOJ, FOG, LOG, HOL and HOE i.e. 14 in number.

The triangles composed of two components each are EAH, FBE, BEO, EOF, BFO, FCG, GDH, HOD, HOG and GOD i.e. 10 in number.

The triangles composed of three components each are EFH, EHG, FGH and EFG i.e. 4 in number.

Thus, there are 14 + 10 + 4 = 28 triangles in the given figure.

5. (c)
The figure may be labelled as shown below.

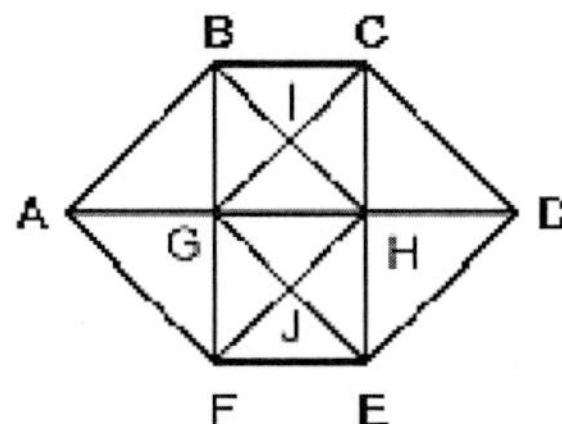

The simplest triangles are ABG, BIG, BIC, CIH, GIH, CDH, HED, GHJ, HJE, FEJ, GFJ and AGF i.e. 12 in number.

The triangles composed of two components each are ABF, CDE, GBC, BCH, GHG, BHG, GHF, GHE, HEF and GEF i.e. 10 in number.

The triangles composed of three components each are ABH, AFH, CDG and GDE i.e. 4 in number.

The triangles composed of four components each are BHF and CGE i.e. 2 in number.

Total number of triangles in the figure
= 12 + 10 + 4 + 2 = 28.

6. (b)
The figure may be labelled as shown below.

The horizontal lines are AK, BJ, CI, DH and EG i.e. 5 in number.

The vertical lines are AE, LF and KG i.e. 3 in number.

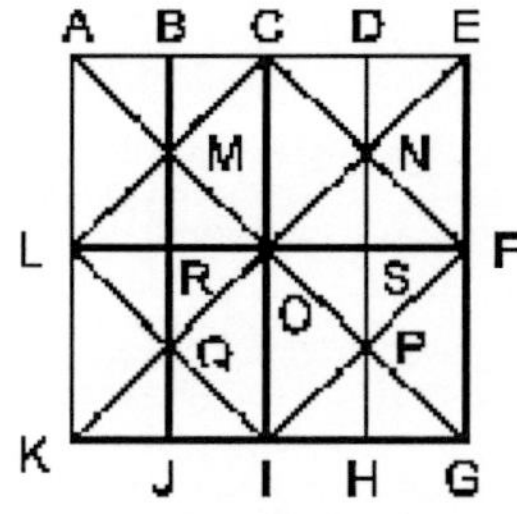

The slanting lines are LC, CF, FI, LI, EK and AG i.e. 6 in number.

Thus, there are 5 + 3 + 6 = 14 straight lines in the figure.

7. (c)
The figure may be labelled as shown below.

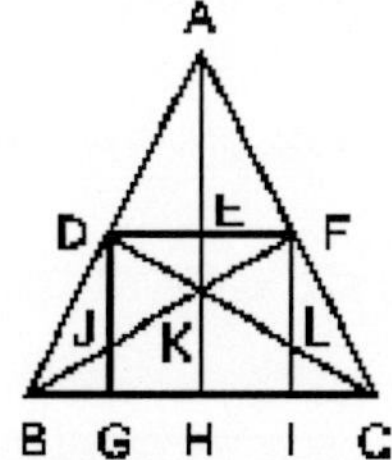

The horizontal lines are DF and BC i.e. 2 in number.

The vertical lines are DG, AH and FI i.e. 3 in number.

The slanting lines are AB, AC, BF and DC i.e. 4 in number.

Thus, there are 2 + 3 + 4 = 9 straight lines in the figure.

Now, we shall count the number of triangles in the figure.

The simplest triangles are ADE, AEF, DEK, EFK, DJK, FLK, DJB, FLC, BJG and LIC i.e. 10 in number.

The triangles composed of two components each are ADF, AFK, DFK, ADK, DKB, FCK, BKH, KHC, DGB and FIC i.e. 10 in number.

The triangles composed of three components each are DFJ and DFL i.e. 2 in number.

The triangles composed of four components each are ABK, ACK, BFI, CDG, DFB, DFC and BKC i.e. 7 in number.

The triangles composed of six components each are ABH, ACH, ABF, ACD, BFC and CDB i.e. 6 in number.

There is only one triangle i.e. ABC composed of twelve components.

There are 10 + 10 + 2 + 7 + 6+ 1 = 36 triangles in the figure.

8. (c)
The figure may be labelled as shown below.

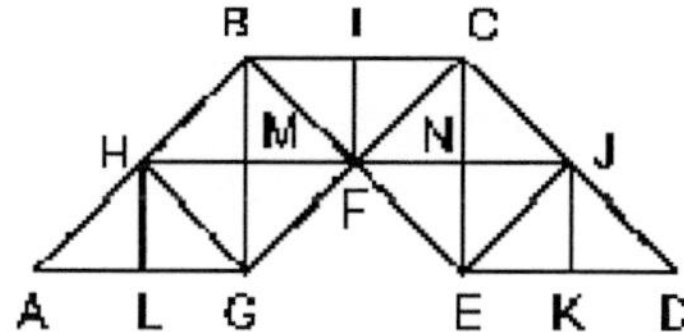

The simplest triangles are AHL, LHG, GHM, HMB, GMF, BMF, BIF, CIF, FNC, CNJ, FNE, NEJ, EKJ and JKD i.e. 14 in number.

The triangles composed of two components each are AGH, BHG, HBF, BFG, HFG, BCF, CJF, CJE, JEF, CFE and JED i.e. 11 in number.

The triangles composed of four components each are ABG, CBG, BCE and CED i.e. 4 in number.

Total number of triangles in the given figure
= 14 + 11 + 4 = 29

9. (d)
The figure may be labelled as shown below.

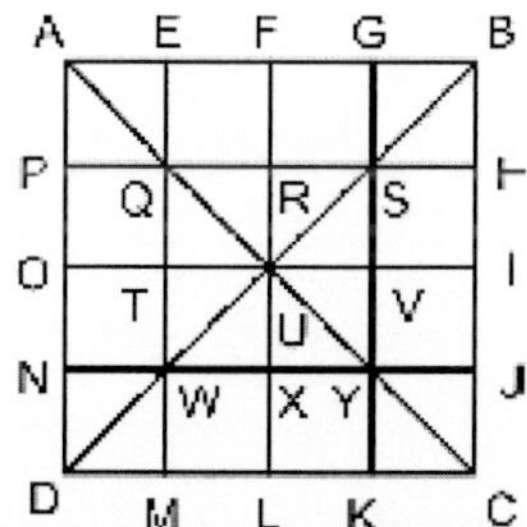

The simplest triangles are APQ, AEQ, QTU, QRU, BGS, BHS, RSU, SUV, TUW, UWX, NWD, WDM, UVY, UXY, JCY and YKC i.e. 16 in number.

The triangles composed of two components each are QUW, QSU, SYU and UWY i.e. 4 in number.

The triangles composed of three components each are AOU, AFU, FBU, BIU, UIC, ULC, ULD and OUD i.e. 8 in number.

The triangles composed of four components each are QYW, QSW, QSY and SYW i.e. 4 in number.

The triangles composed of six components each are AUD, ABU, BUC and DUC i.e. 4 in number.

The triangles composed of seven components each are QMC, ANY, EBW, PSD, CQH, AGY, DSK and BJW i.e. 8 in number.

The triangles composed of twelve components each are ABD, ABC, BCD and ACD i.e. 4 in number.

Thus, there are 16 + 4 + 8 + 4 + 4 + 8 + 4 = 48 triangles in the figure.

10. (b)

The figure may be labelled as shown below.

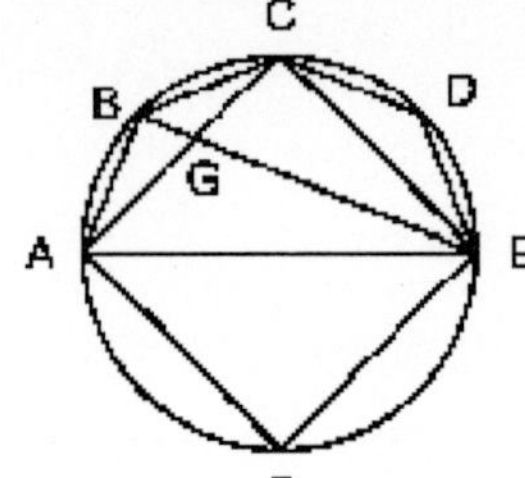

The simplest triangles are ABG, BCG, CGE, CDE, AGE and AEF i.e. 6 in number.

The triangles composed of two components each are ABE, ABC, BCE and ACE i.e. 4 in number.

There are 6 + 4 = 10 triangles in the figure.

11. (d)

The figure may be labelled as shown below.

The simplest triangles are ABL, BCD, DEF, FGP, PGH, QHI, JQI, KRJ and LRK i.e. 9 in number.

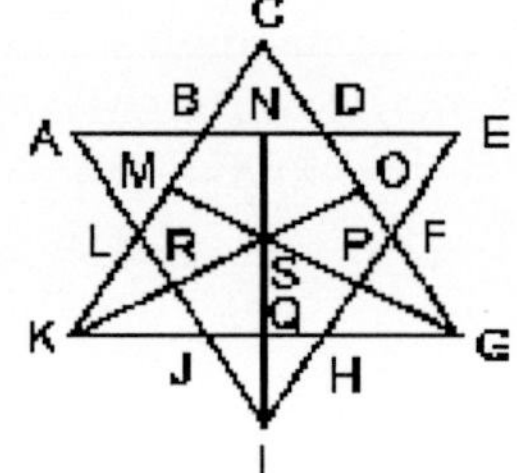

The triangles composed of two components each are OSG, SGQ, SPI, SRI, KSQ, KMS, FGH, JHI and JKL i.e. 9 in number.

There is only one triangle i.e. KSG which is composed of four components.

The triangles composed of five components each are NEI, ANI, MCG and KCO i.e. 4 in number.

The triangles composed of six components each are GMK and KOG i.e. 2 in number.

There is only one triangle i.e. AEI composed of ten components.

There is only one triangle i.e. KCG composed of eleven components.

Therefore, total number of triangles in the given figure = 9 + 9 + 1 + 4 + 2 + 1 + 1 = 27

12. (c)

The figure may be labelled as shown below.

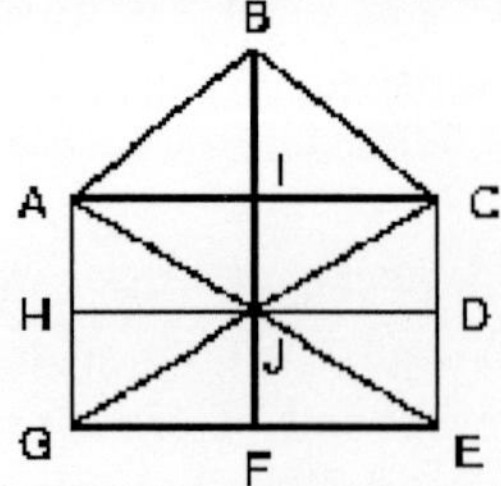

The simplest triangles are ABI, BIC, AIJ, CIJ, AHJ, CDJ, JHG, JDE, GJF and EJF i.e. 10 in number.

The triangles composed of two components each are ABC, BCJ, ACJ, BAJ, AJG, CJE and GJE i.e. 7 in number.

The triangles composed of four components each are ACG, ACE, CGE and AGE i.e. 4 in number.

Total number of triangles in the figure = 10 + 7 + 4 = 21

13. (b)

The figure may be labelled as shown below.

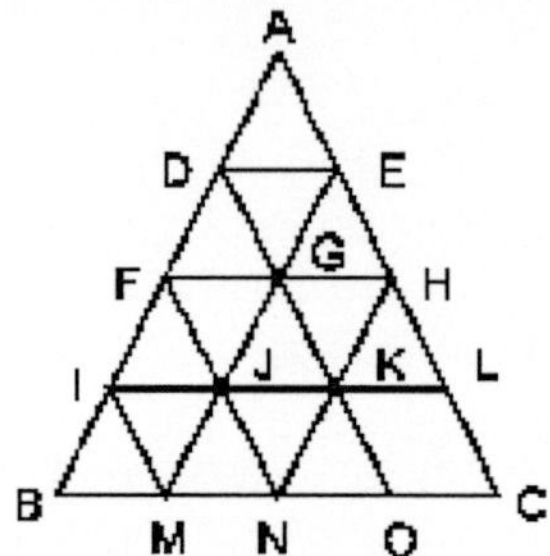

The horizontal lines are DE, FH, IL and BC i.e. 4 in number.

The slanting lines are AC, DO, FN, IM, AB, EM and HN i.e. 7 in number.

Thus, there are 4 + 7 = 11 straight lines in the figure.

14. (c)

The figure may be labelled as shown below.

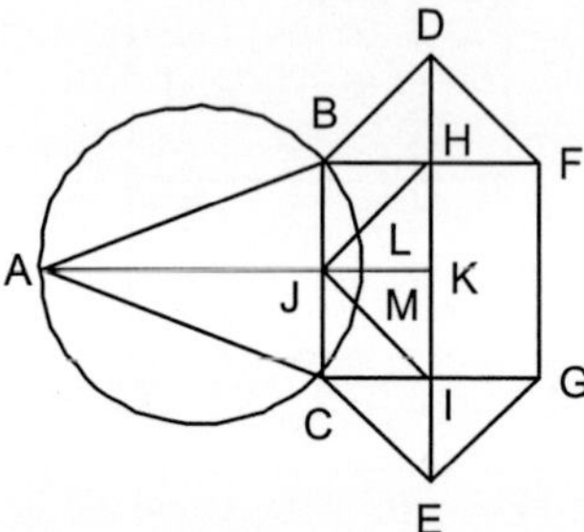

The simplest triangles are ABJ, ACJ, BDH, DHF, CIE and GIE i.e. 6 in number.

The triangles composed of two components each are ABC, BDF, CEG, BHJ, JHK, JKI and CJI i.e. 7 in number.

There is only one triangle JHI which is composed of four components.

Thus, there are 6 + 7 + 1 = 14 triangles in the given figure.

15. (a)

The figure may be labelled as shown below.

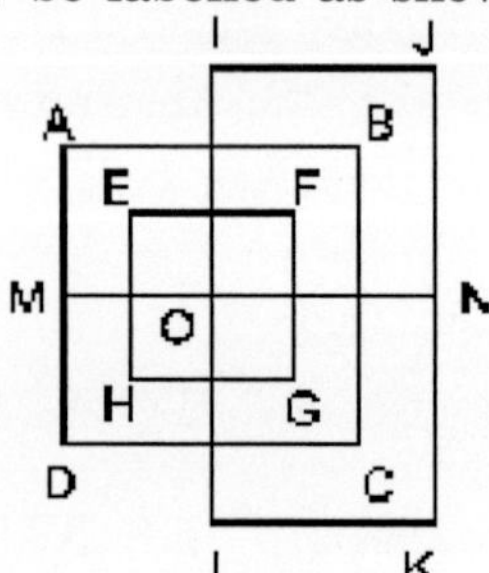

The horizontal lines are IJ, AB, EF, MN, HG, DC and LK i.e. 7 in number.

The vertical lines are AD, EH, IL, FG, BC and JK i.e. 6 in number.

Thus, there are 7 + 6 = 13 straight lines in the figure.

16. (c)

The figure may be labelled as shown below.

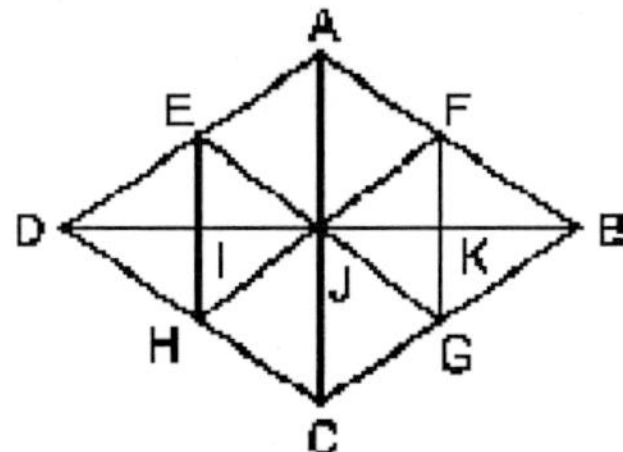

The simplest triangles are AFJ, FJK, FKB, BKG, JKG, JGC, HJC, HIJ, DIH, DEI, EIJ and AEJ i.e. 12 in number.

The triangles composed of two components each are JFB, FBG, BJG, JFG, DEJ, EJH, DJH and DEH i.e. 8 in number.

The triangles composed of three components each are AJB, JBC, DJC and ADJ i.e. 4 in number.

The triangles composed of six components each are DAB, ABC, BCD and ADC i.e. 4 in number.

Thus, there are 12 + 8 + 4 + 4 = 28 triangles in the figure.

17. (d)

The figure may be labelled as shown below.

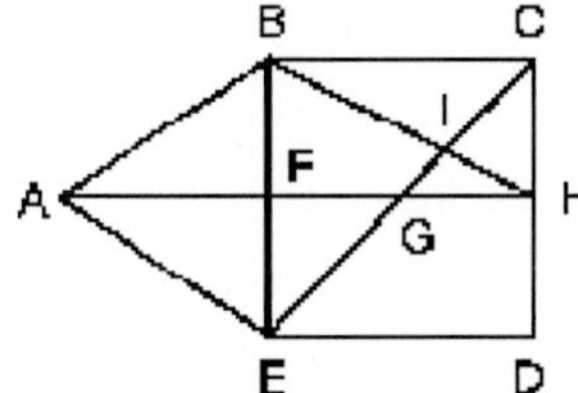

The simplest triangles are ABF, BIC, CIH, GIH, FGE and AFE i.e. 6 in number.

The triangles composed of two components each are ABE, AGE, BHF, BCH, CGH and BIE i.e. 6 in number.

The triangles composed of three components each are ABH, BCE and CDE i.e. 3 in number.

Hence, the total number of triangles in the figure = 6 + 6 + 3 = 15

18. (d)

The figure may be labelled as shown below.

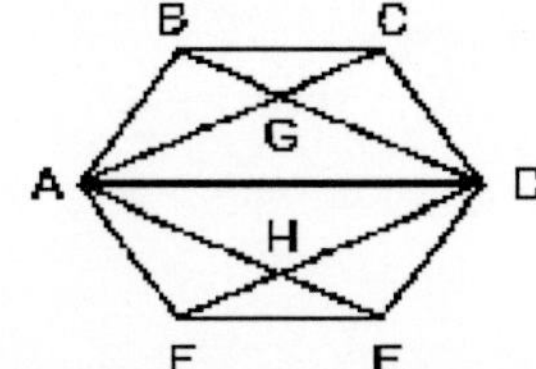

The quadrilaterals in the figure are ABCD, ABDE, ABDF, ABDH, CDHA, CDEA, CDFA, DEAG, DEFA, FAGD and AGDH.

The number of quadrilaterals in the figure is 11.

19. (c)

The figure may be labelled as shown below.

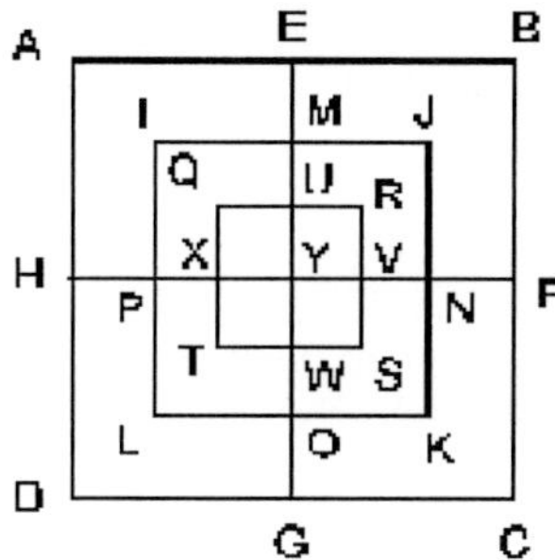

The simplest squares are QUYX, URVY, YVSW and XYWT i.e. 4 in number.

The squares composed of two components each are IMYP, MJNY, YNKO and PYOL i.e. 4 in number.

The squares composed of three components each are AEYH, EBFY, YFCG and HYGD i.e. 4 in number.

There is only one square i.e. QRST composed of four components.

There is only one square i.e. IJKL composed of eight components.

There is only one square i.e. ABCD composed of twelve components.

Total number of squares in the given figure = 4 + 4 + 4 + 1 + 1 + 1 = 15

20. (d)

The figure may be labelled as shown below.

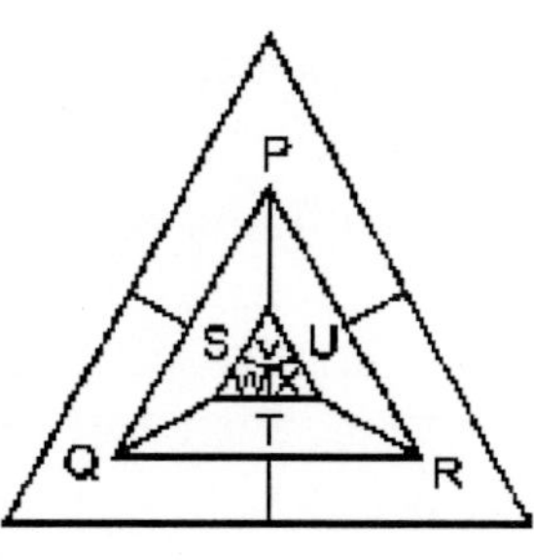

The spaces P, Q and R have to be shaded by three different colours definitely (since each of these three spaces lies adjacent to the other two).

Now, in order that no two adjacent spaces be shaded by the same colour, the spaces T, U and S must be shaded with the colours of the spaces P, Q and R respectively.

Also the spaces X, V and W must be shaded with the colours of the spaces S, T and U respectively i.e. with the colours of the spaces R, P and Q respectively. Thus, minimum three colours are required.

21. (a)

The figure may be labelled as shown below.

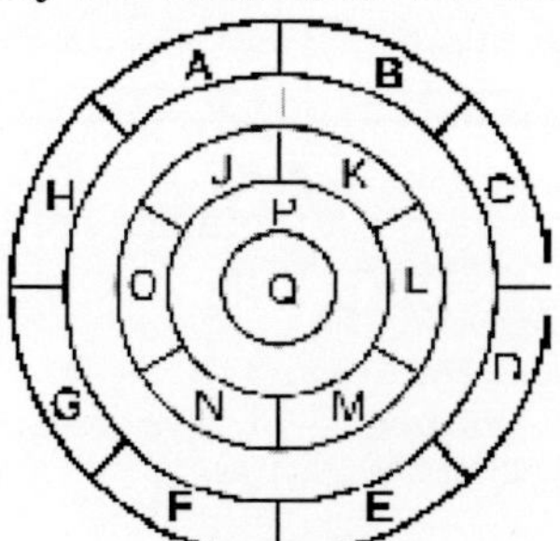

The regions A, C, E and G can have the same colour i.e. colour 1.

The regions B, D, F and H can have the same colour (but different from colour 1) i.e. colour 2.

The region 1 lies adjacent to each one of the regions A, B, C, D, E, F, G and H and therefore it should have a different colour i.e. colour 3.

The regions J, L and N can have the same colour (different from colour 3) i.e. colour 1.

The regions K, M and O can have the same colour (different from the colours 1 and 3). Thus, these regions will have colour 2.

The region P cannot have any of the colours 1 and 2 as it lies adjacent to each one of the regions J, K, L, M, N and O and so it will have colour 3.

The region Q can have any of the colours 1 or 2.

Thus the minimum number of colours required is 3.

22. (c)

The figure may be labelled as shown below.

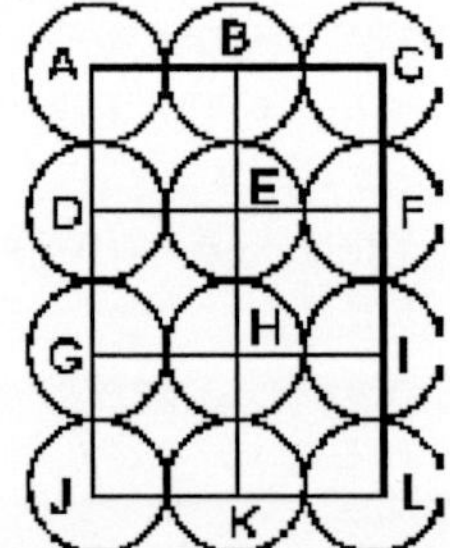

We shall join the centres of all the circles by horizontal and vertical lines and then label the resulting figure as shown below.

The simplest squares are ABED, BCFE, DEHG, EFIH, GHKJ and HILK i.e. 6 in number.

The squares composed of four simple squares are ACIG and DFLJ i.e. 2 in number.

Thus, 6 + 2 = 8 squares will be formed.

23. (a)

The figure may be labelled as shown below.

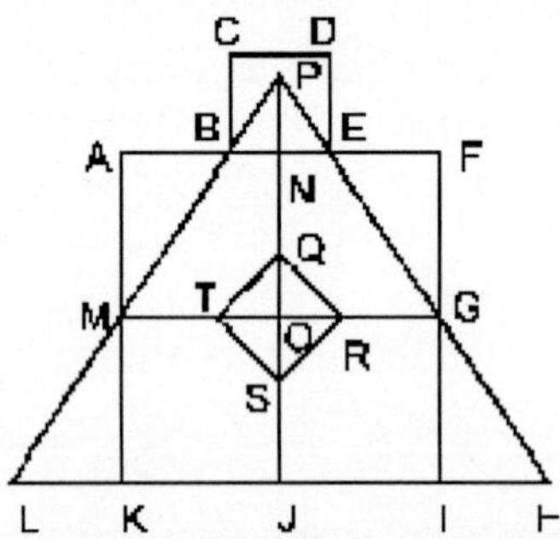

Triangles: The simplest triangles are BPN, PNE, ABM, EFG, MLK, GHI, QRO, RSO, STO and QTO i.e. 10 in number.

The triangles composed of two components each are BPE, TQR, QRS, RST and STQ i.e. 5 in number.

The triangles composed of three components each are MPO and GPO i.e. 2 in number.

The triangles composed of six components each are LPJ, HPJ and MPG i.e. 3 in number.

There is only one triangle LPH composed of twelve components.

Thus total number of triangles in the figure

= 10 + 5 – 2 + 3 + 1 = 21

Squares: The squares composed of two components each are KJOM and JIGQ i.e. 2 in number.

The squares composed of three components each are ANOM, NFGO and CDEB i.e.3 in number.

There is only one square i.e. QRST composed of four components.

There is only one square i.e. AFIK composed of ten components.

Thus total number of squares in the figure

= 2 + 3 + 1 + 1 = 7

24. (c)

The figure may be labelled as shown below.

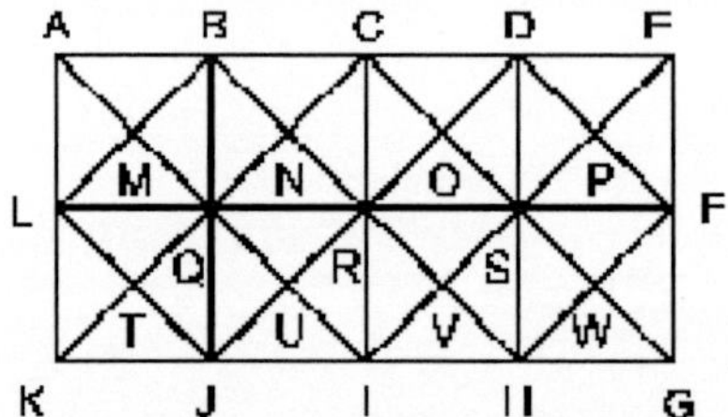

The squares composed of two components each are BNQM, CORN, DPSO, MQTL, NRUQ, OSVR, PFWS, QUJT, RVIU and SWHV i.e. 10 in number.

The squares composed of four components each are ABQL, BCRQ, CDSR, DEFS, LQJK, QRIJ, RSHI and SFGH i.e. 8 in number.

The squares composed of eight components each are BRJL, CSIQ and DFHR i.e. 3 in number.

The squares composed of sixteen components each are ACIK, BDHJ and CEGI i.e. 3 in number.

Thus, there are 10 + 8 + 3 + 3 = 24 squares in the figure.

25. (c)

The figure may be labelled as shown below.

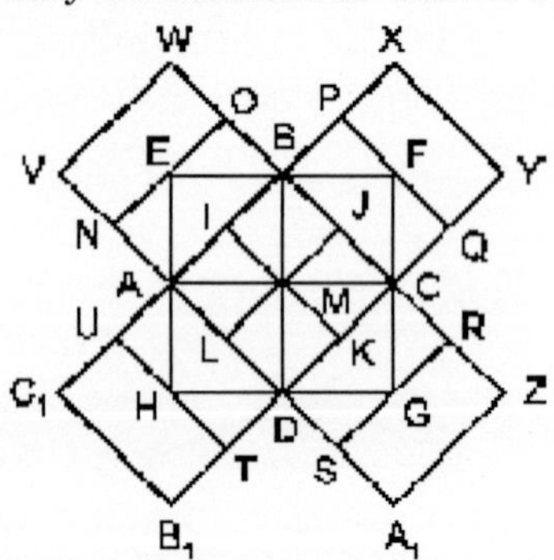

The squares composed of two components each are BJMI, CKMJ, DLMK and AIML i.e. 4 in number.

The squares composed of three components each are EBMA, BFCM, MCGD and AMDH i.e. 4 in number.

The squares composed of four components each are VWBA, XYCB, ZA_1DC and B_1C_1AD i.e. 4 in number.

The squares composed of seven components each are NOJL, PQKI, RSLJ and TUIK i.e. 4 in number.

There is only one square i.e. ABCD composed of eight components.

There is only one square i.e. EFGH composed of twelve components.

Total number of squares in the figure
= 4 + 4 + 4 + 4 + 1 + 1 = 18

26. (a)
The figure may be labelled as shown below.

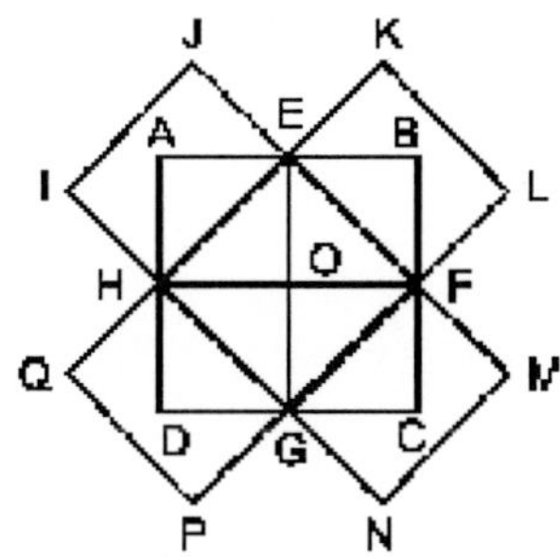

The rectangles composed of two components each are HUE, EKJF, FMNG, GPQH, AEOH, EBFO, OFCG and HOGD i.e. 8 in number.

The rectangles composed of four components each are ABFH, BCGE, CDHF, DAEG and EFGH i.e. 5 in number.

The rectangles composed of six components each are IJFG, KLGH, MNHE and PQEF i.e. 4 in number.

The rectangles composed of eight components each are IJMN, KLPQ and ABCD i.e. 3 in number.

Thus, there are 8 + 5 + 4 + 3 = 20 rectangles in the given figure.

(Note : Squares are also counted amongst rectangles)

27. (b)
The figure may be labelled as shown below.

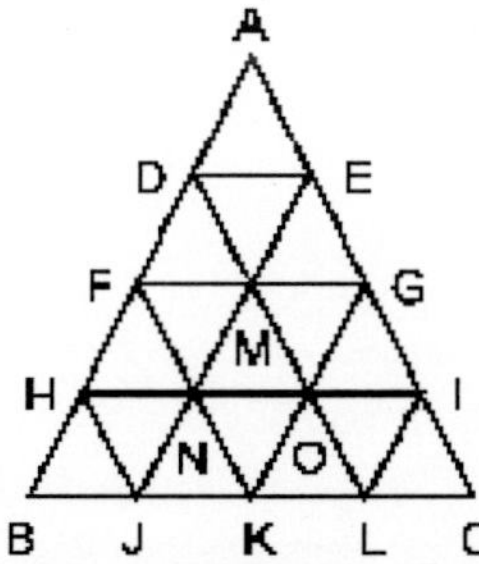

The parallelograms composed of two components each are ADME, DFNM, EMOG, FHJN, MNKO, GOLI, HBJN, NJKO, OKLI, FHNM, MNOG, DFME, HJKN, NKLO, OLCI, FNOM, MOIG and DMGE. i.e. 18 in number.

The parallelograms composed of four components each are HOKB, NILJ, FGOH, HOLJ, NICK, FGIN, FMJB, DENH, MGKJ, MGCL, DEIO, FMLK, AENF, AGOD, DMJH, DOKF, EILM and EGKN i.e. 18 in number.

The parallelograms composed of six components each are AEJH, DAIL, DECL, DEJB, HILB and HICJ i.e. 6 in number.

The parallelograms composed of eight components each are FGKB, FGCK and AGKF i.e. 3 in number.

Total number of parallelograms in the figure
= 18 + 18 + 6 + 3 = 45

28. (b)
The figure may be labelled as shown below.

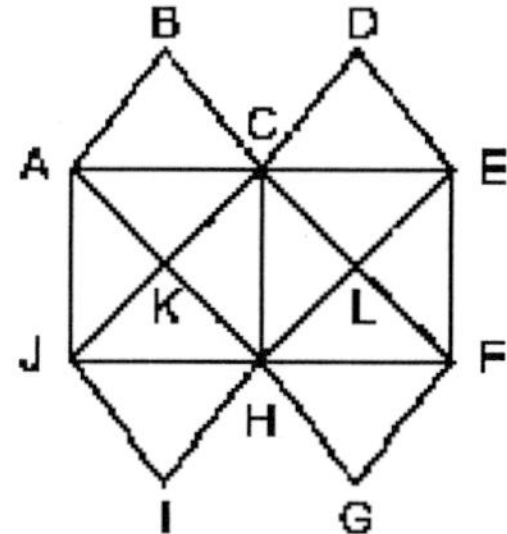

The horizontal lines are AE and JF i.e. 2 in number.
The vertical lines are AJ, CH and EF i.e. 3 in number.

The slanting lines are AG, BF, JD, IE, AB, DE, JI and FG i.e. 8 in number.

Total number of straight lines needed to construct the figure = 2 + 3 + 8 = 13

29. (a)
The figure may be labelled as shown below.

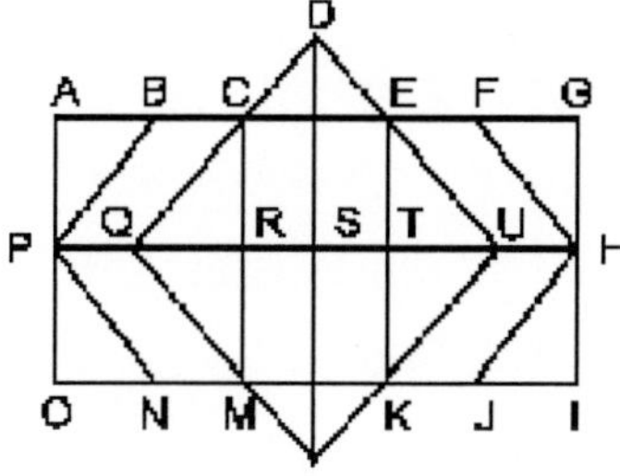

Rectangles: The simplest rectangles are CVSR, VETS, RSWM and STKW i.e. 4 in number.

The rectangles composed of two components each are CETR, VEKW, RTKM and GVWM i.e. 4 in number.

The rectangles composed of three components each are AQRP, PRMO, EGHT and THIK i.e. 4 in number.

The rectangles composed of four components each are CEKM, AVSP,TSWO, VGHS and SHIW i.e. 5 in number.

The rectangles composed of five components each are AETP, PTKO, CGHR and RHIM i.e. 4 in number.

The rectangles composed of six components each are ACMO and EGIK i.e. 2 in number.

The rectangles composed of eight components each are AGHP, PHIO, AVWO and VGIW i.e. 4 in number.

The rectangles composed of ten components each are AEKO and CGIM i.e. 2 in number.

AGIO is the only rectangle having sixteen components.
Total number of rectangles in the given figure
= 4 + 4 + 4 + 5 + 4 + 2 + 4 + 2 + 1 = 30

Hexagons: The hexagons in the given figure are CDEKLM, CEUKMQ, CFHJMQ, BEUKNP and BFHJNP.

So, there are 5 hexagons in the given figure shown below.

30. (a)

The figure may be labelled as shown.

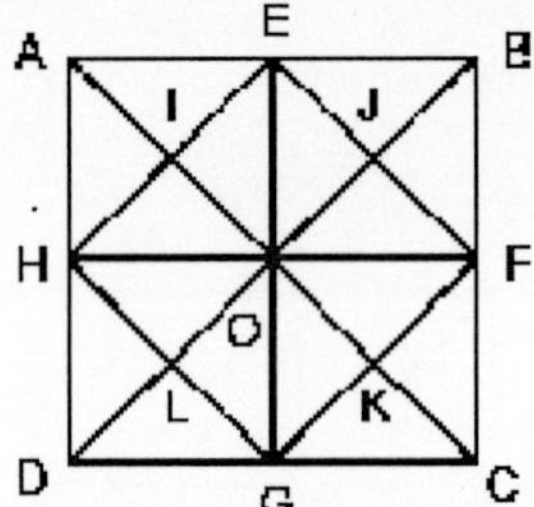

Triangles: The simplest triangles are AEI, EOI, OHI, HAI, EBJ, BFJ, FOJ, OEJ, HOL, OGL, GDL, DHL, OFK, FCK, CGK and GOK i.e. 16 in number.

The triangles composed of two components each are HAE, AEO, EOH, OHA, OEB, EBF, BFO, FOE, DHO, HOG, OGD, GDH, GOF, OFC, FCG and CGO i.e. 16 in number.

The triangles composed of four components each are HEF, EFG, FGH, GHE, ABO, BGO, CDO and DAO i.e. 8 in number.

The triangles composed of eight components each are DAB, ABC, BCD and CDA i.e. 4 in number.

Total number of triangles in the figure

= 16 + 16 + 8 + 4 = 44

Squares: The squares composed of two components are HIOL, IEJO, JFKO and KGLO i.e. 4 in number.

The squares composed of four components are AEOH, EBFO, OFGC and HOGD i.e.4 in number.

There is only one square EFGH which is composed of eight components.

There is only one square ABCD which is composed of sixteen components.

Total number of squares in the figure
= 4 + 4 + 1 + 1 = 10

❐

Previous Year Questions

1. Count the number of squares in the given figure.

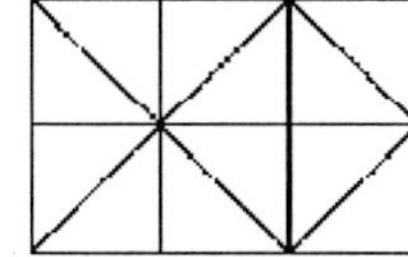

(a) 6 (b) 7
(c) 9 (d) 10

2. Count the number of squares in the given figure.
[NTSE 2004 – UP second stage paper]

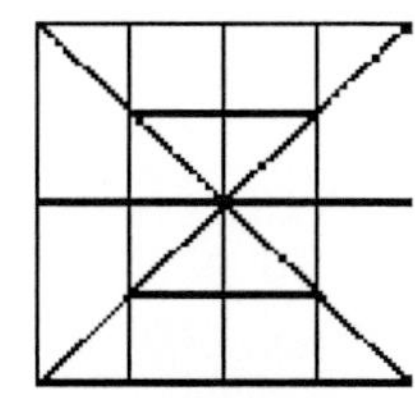

(a) 13 (b) 16
(c) 19 (d) 20

3. Find the number of triangles in the given figure.
[NTSE 2003 - Delhi first stage paper]

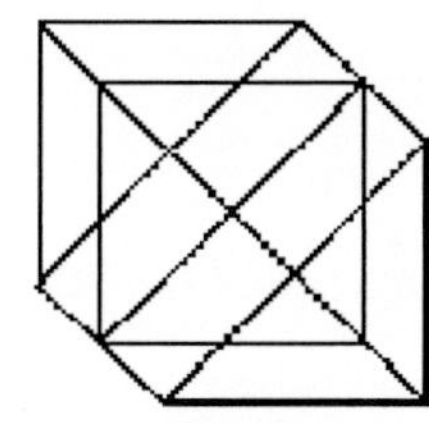

(a) 18 (b) 20
(c) 24 (d) 27

4. Find the number of triangles in the given figure.
[NTSE 1999 - Rajasthan Second stage Paper]

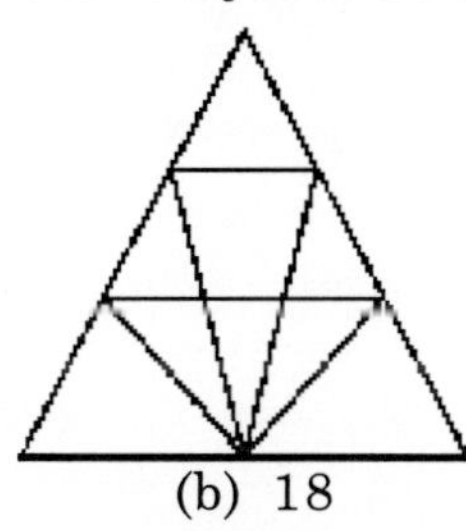

(a) 12 (b) 18
(c) 22 (d) 26

5. Find the number of triangles in the given figure.
[NTSE 2003 – Tamil Nadu first stage paper]

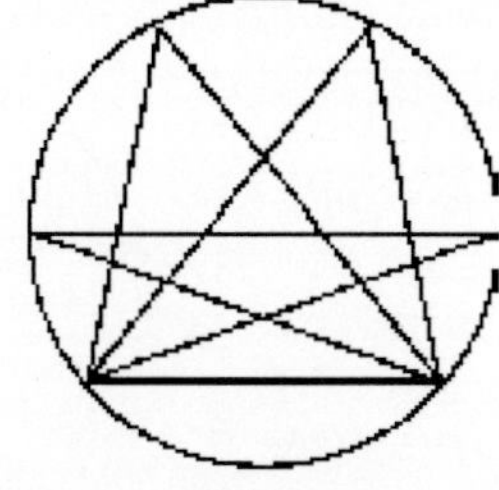

(a) 22 (b) 24
(c) 26 (d) 28

6. Find the minimum number of straight lines required to make the given figure.
[NTSE 2000 – Himachal Pradesh first stage paper]
[NTSE 2012 - Delhi first stage paper]

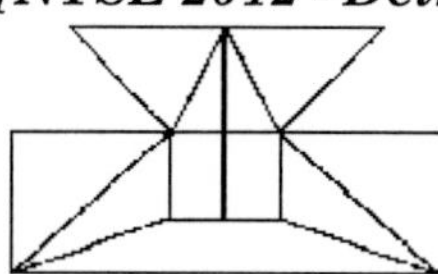

(a) 16 (b) 17
(c) 18 (d) 19

7. Count the number of rectangles in the given figure.
[NTSE 2002 Gujarat first stage paper]

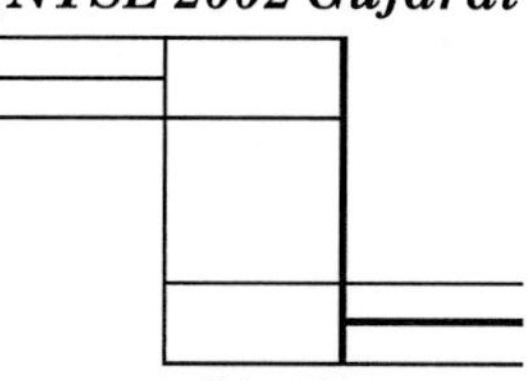

(a) 8 (b) 17
(c) 18 (d) 20

8. How many circles are there in the adjoining figure?
[NTSE 2003 - Haryana first stage paper]

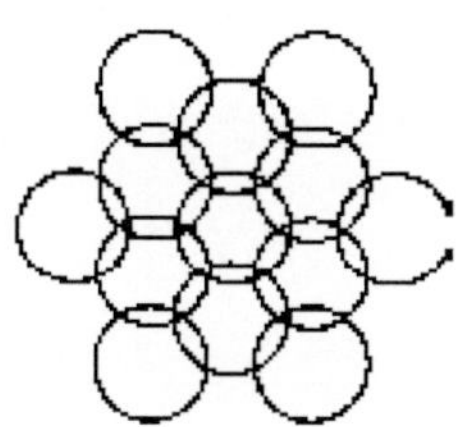

(a) 11 (b) 12
(c) 13 (d) 14

9. Count the number of squares in the given figure.
[NTSE 2005 – Jharkhand first stage paper]

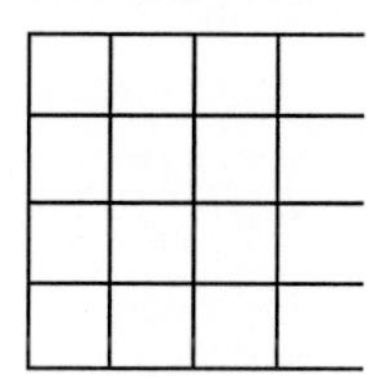

(a) 32 (b) 30
(c) 29 (d) 28

10. Count the number of triangles and squares in the given figure. ***[NTSE 2003 - Assam first stage paper]***

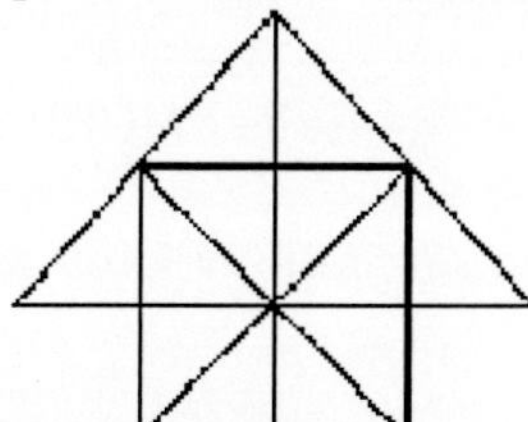

(a) 26 triangles, 5 squares
(b) 28 triangles, 5 squares
(c) 26 triangles, 6 squares
(d) 28 triangles, 6 squares

❐

Answer Key

1. (c)	2. (b)	3. (c)	4. (b)	5. (d)	6. (b)	7. (c)	8. (c)	9. (b)	10. (d)

Explanatory Notes

1. (c)
The figure may be labelled as shown below.

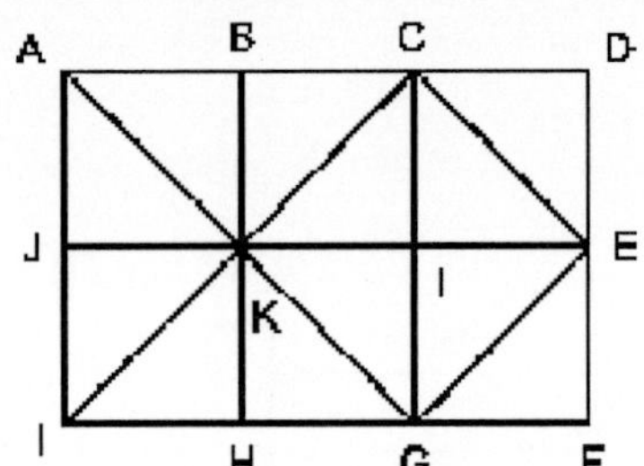

The squares composed of two components each are ABKJ, BCLK, CDEL, LEFG, KLGH and JKHI i.e. 6 in number.

There is only one square i.e. CEGK composed of four components.

The squares composed of eight components each are ACGI and BDFH i.e. 2 in number.

There are 6 + 1 + 2 = 9 squares in the figure.

2. (b)
The figure may be labelled as shown below.

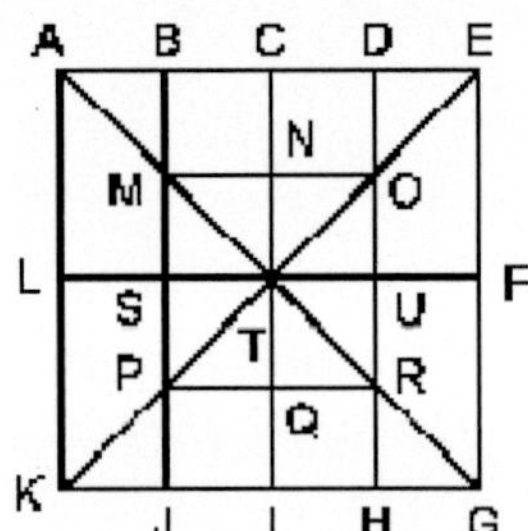

The simplest squares are BCNM, CDON, PQIJ and QRHI i.e. 4 in number.

The squares composed of two components each are MNTS, NOUT, STQP and TURQ i.e. 4 in number.

The squares composed of five components each are ACTL, CEFT, TFGI and LTIK i.e. 4 in number.

The squares composed of six components each are BDUS and SUHJ i.e. 2 in number.

There is only one square i.e. MORP composed of eight components.

There is only one square i.e. AEGK composed of twenty components.

Total number of squares in the figure
= 4 + 4 + 4 + 2 + 1 + 1 = 16

3. (c)
The figure may be labelled as shown below.

The simplest triangles are IJO, BCJ, CDK, KQL, MLQ, GFM, GHN and NIO i.e. 8 in number.

The triangles composed of two components each are ABO, AHO, NIJ, IGP, ICP, DEQ, FEQ, KLM, LCP and LGP i.e.10 in number.

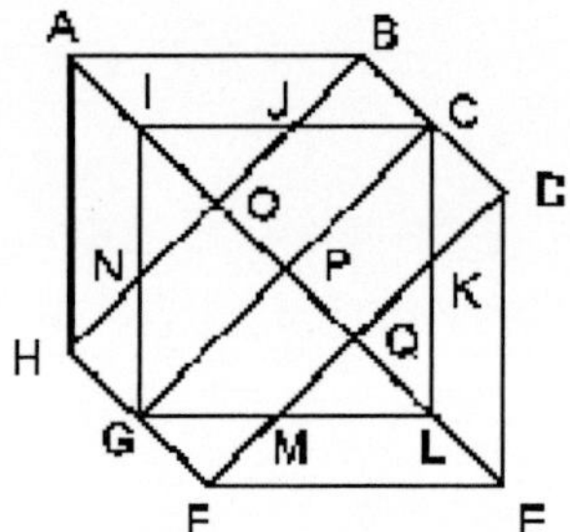

The triangles composed of four components each are HAB, DEF, LGI, GIC, ICL and GLC i.e. 6 in number.

Total number of triangles in the figure
= 8 + 10 + 6 = 24

4. (b)
The figure may be labelled as shown below.

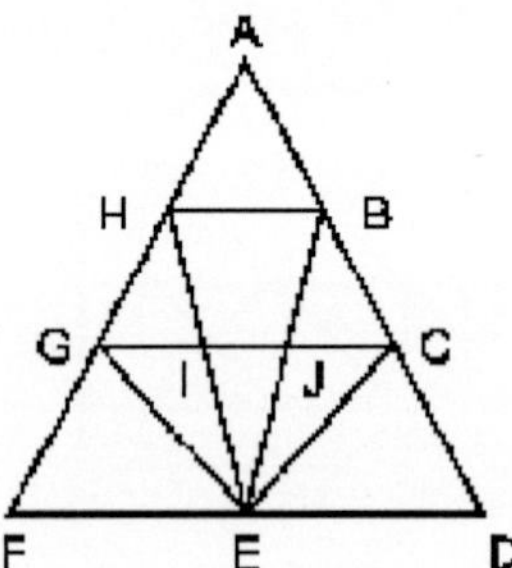

The simplest triangles are AHB, GHI, BJC, GFE, GIE, IJE, CEJ and CDE i.e. 8 in number.

The triangles composed of two components each are HEG, BEC, HBE, JGE and ICE i.e. 5 in number.

The triangles composed of three components each are FHE, GCE and BED i.e. 3 in number.

There is only one triangle i.e. AGC composed of four components.

There is only one triangle i.e. AFD composed of nine components.

Thus, there are 8 + 5 + 3 + 1 + 1 = 18 triangles in the given figure.

5. (d)
The figure may be labelled as shown below.

The simplest triangles are AGH, GFO, LFO, DJK, EKP, PEL and IMN i.e. 7 in number.

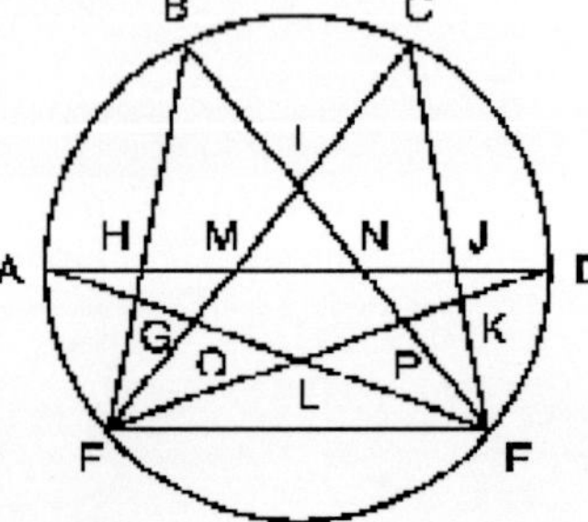

The triangles having two components each are GFL, KEL, AMO, NDP, BHN, CMJ, NEJ and HFM i.e. 8 in number.

The triangles having three components each are IOE, IFP, BIF and CEI i.e. 4 in number.

The triangles having four components each are ANE and DMF i.e. 2 in number.

The triangles having five components each are FCK, BGE and ADL i.e. 3 in number.

The triangles having six components each are BPF, COE, DHF and AJE i.e. 4 in number.

Total number of triangles in the figure

= 7 + 8 + 4 + 2 + 3 + 4 = 28

6. (b)

The figure may be labelled as shown below.

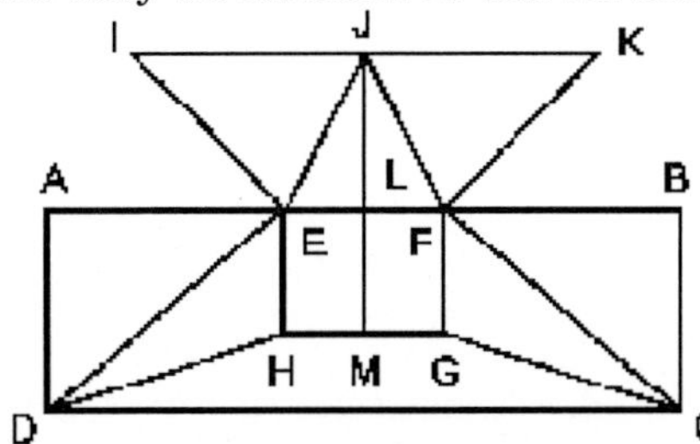

The horizontal lines are IK, AB, HG and DC i.e. 4 in number.

The vertical lines are AD, EH, JM, FG and BC i.e. 5 in number.

The slanting lines are IE, JE, JF, KF, DE, DH, FC and GC i.e. 8 is number.

Thus, there are 4 + 5 + 8 = 17 straight lines in the figure.

7. (c)

The figure may be labelled as shown below.

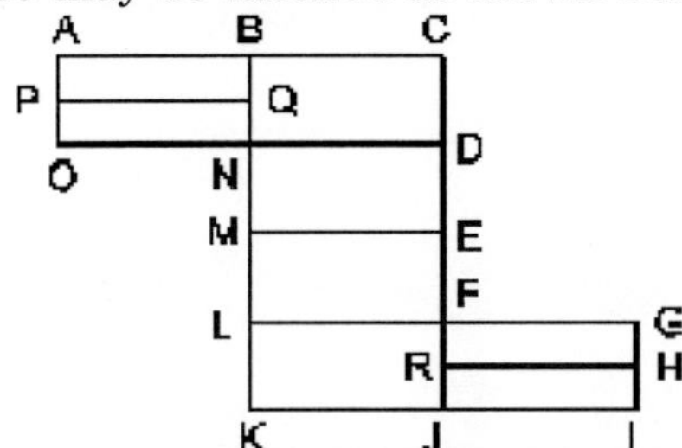

The simplest rectangles are ABQP, PQNO, BCDN, NDEM, MEFL, LFJK, FGHR and RHIJ i.e. 8 in number.

The rectangles composed of two components each are ABNO, BCEM, NDFL, MEJK and FGIJ i.e. 5 in number.

The rectangles composed of three components each are ACDO, BCFL, NDJK and LGIK i.e. 4 in number.

There is only one rectangle i.e. BCJK composed of four components.

Total number of rectangles in the figure

= 8 + 5 + 4 + 1 = 18

8. (c)

The figure may be labelled as shown below.

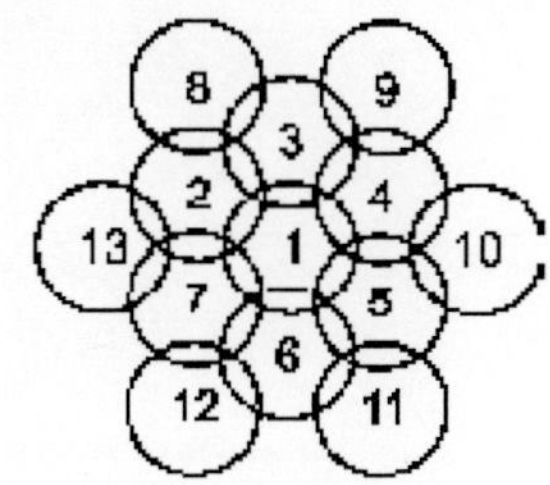

There are 13 circles in the given figure. This is clear from the adjoining figure in which the centres of all the circles have been numbered from 1 to 13.

9. (b)

The figure may be labelled as shown below.

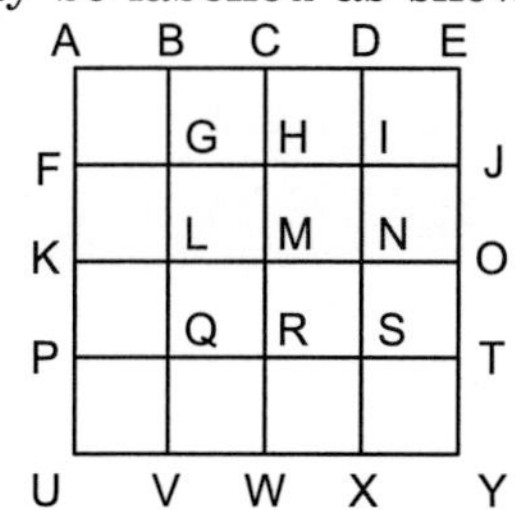

The simplest squares are ABGF, BCHG, CDIH, DEJI, FGLK, GHML, HINM, IJON, KLQP, LMRQ, MNSR, NOTS, PQVU, QRWV, RSXW and STYX i.e. 16 in number.

The squares composed of four components each are ACMK, BDNL, CEOM, FHRP, GISQ, HJTR, KMWU, LNXV and MOYW i.e. 9 in number.

The squares composed of nine components each are ADSP, BETQ, FIXU and GJYV i.e. 4 in number.

There is one square AEYU composed of sixteen components.

There are 16 + 9 + 4 + 1 = 30 squares in the given figure.

10. (d)

The figure may be labelled as shown below.

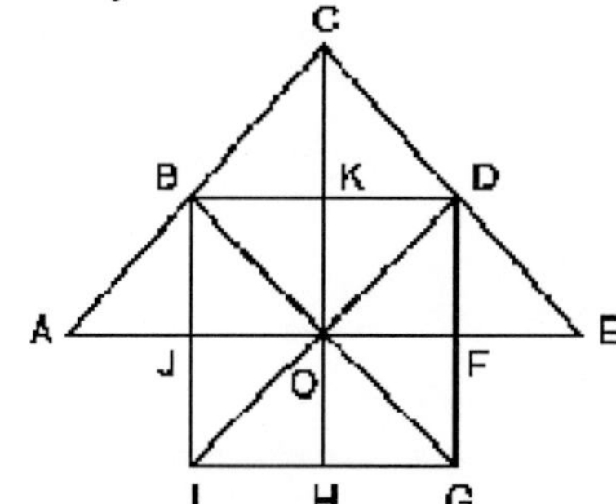

Triangles: The simplest triangles are JBO, BKO, KDO, DFO, FGO, GHO, HIO, IJO, ABJ, BCK, CKD and DEF i.e.12 in number.

The triangles composed of two components each are IBO, BDO, DGO, GIO, ABO, CDO, CBO, CBD and DEO i.e. 9 in number.

The triangles composed of four components each are IBD, BDG, DGI, GIB, ACO and COE i.e. 6 in number.

There is only one triangle i.e. ACE composed of eight components.

Thus, there are 12 + 9 + 6 + 1 = 28 triangles in the given figure.

Squares: The squares composed of two components each are BKOJ, KDFO, OFGH and JOHI i.e. 4 in number.

There is only one square i.e. CDOB composed of four components.

There is only one square i.e. BDGI composed of eight components.

Thus, there are 4 + 1 + 1 = 6 squares in the given figure.

❒